Shoghi Effendi Through the Pilgrim's Eye

This book is dedicated to

the Hands of the Cause of God

who safely captained the ship built by Shoghi Effendi, from his passing to the election of the Universal House of Justice

Shoghi Effendi Through the Pilgrim's Eye

Volume 2
The Ten Year Crusade, 1953–1963

Earl Redman

GEORGE RONALD
OXFORD

George Ronald, Publisher
Oxford
www.grbooks.com

A catalogue record for this book is available from the British Library

ISBN 978–0–85398–595–2

Cover design: Steiner Graphics

CONTENTS

PREFACE

This book is the second volume of *Shoghi Effendi Through the Pilgrim's Eye*. Volume 1 was subtitled *Building the Administrative Order, 1922–1952* and was published in February 2015. Initially, I was just writing a book about Shoghi Effendi, but it became obvious that it could not end with the passing of the Guardian because that was right in the middle of one of the most momentous and exciting times in Bahá'í history, the Ten Year Crusade. To include that amazing decade, with all of its multifarious events and happenings, though, would have resulted in a massive tome. Looking at the history of Shoghi Effendi's ministry, it appeared that everything he did before the end of 1952 was in preparation for the Ten Year Crusade. Since the Guardian's goal was to carry out the Tablets of the Divine Plan and elect the Universal House of Justice, it was decided to split the book into two parts: *Building the Administrative Order*, which covers the time from his appointment as Guardian at the beginning of 1922 until the time the international Bahá'í secretariat was firmly established in Haifa at the end of 1952; and *The Ten Year Crusade*, covering the time from the announcement of the Crusade to the election of the Universal House of Justice in 1963. A companion to this book, titled *The Knights of Bahá'u'lláh*, also by this author, will be published by George Ronald in 2016. It contains the stories of the 255 people who accepted Shoghi Effendi's challenge and became Knights of Bahá'u'lláh.

Looking back from today's vantage point, the student of Bahá'í history might wonder if Shoghi Effendi felt, in 1950, when he began to organize the first International Bahá'í Council, that the span of his earthly life might be too short to see the creation of the Universal House of Justice. He had no children and every other male descendant of Bahá'u'lláh had violated the Covenant Bahá'u'lláh Himself had established, so Shoghi Effendi must have known that there would be

no further Guardians. Was the Ten Year Crusade a dramatic effort
on Shoghi Effendi's part to push the Bahá'í world to the point where
it could establish that divinely-guided body, the Universal House of
Justice, that would safeguard the Faith into the future? The Custodians, writing to the Intercontinental Conference in Singapore in 1958,
suspected this:

> For over one hundred and fifteen years we Bahá'ís have been nursed
> and personally watched over. Now we are required to stand on our
> own feet and, in the path of service to this Holy Faith, we must our-
> selves watch over and assist our fellow-men to turn to the Supreme
> Manifestation of God for this Day, and seek their salvation through
> Bahá'u'lláh.[1]

From 1922 through 1952, Shoghi Effendi had displayed infinite
patience with the Bahá'ís in their slow development of the Bahá'í
Administrative Order and the implementation of teaching plans. As
the Ten Year Crusade got under way, those areas that responded to its
challenges with enthusiasm, such as Africa, Australia and the Pacific,
received his boundless praise and encouragement. They were held up
as examples to the rest of the Bahá'í world. He exhibited distinct impatience, however, with those countries that seemed unable to understand
his urgent call or rise to its challenges. North America had been the
driving force spreading the Faith around the world through two successive Seven Year Plans, but its response during the first years of the Ten
Year Crusade was below what Shoghi Effendi expected from the region
that had been the recipient of 'Abdu'l-Bahá's Tablets of the Divine Plan,
that had had the bounty of the Master's presence for eight months and
had been given the task of establishing the Bahá'í Administrative Order
throughout the world. The Guardian had made the station and responsibilities of the believers in the United States and Canada very clear:

> The Tablets of the Divine Plan invest your Assembly with unique
> and grave responsibilities, and confer upon it privileges which your
> sister Assemblies might well envy and admire.[2]

> The promulgation of the Divine Plan, unveiled by our departed
> Master in the darkest days of one of the severest ordeals which

humanity has ever experienced, is the key which Providence has placed in the hands of the American believers whereby to unlock the doors leading them to fulfil their unimaginably glorious Destiny.[3]

Theirs is the duty, the privilege and honor . . . for the dispatch of a handful of pioneers to some of these territories, as an evidence of the determination and capacity of a newly independent national community to assume the functions, and discharge the responsibilities with which it has been invested in those immortal Tablets by the pen of the Center of Bahá'u'lláh's Covenant.[4]

Behold the portals which Bahá'u'lláh hath opened before you! Consider how exalted and lofty is the station you are destined to attain; how unique the favors with which you have been endowed.[5]

On the members of the American Bahá'í Community, the envied custodians of a Divine Plan, the principal builders and defenders of a mighty Order and the recognized champions of an unspeakably glorious and precious Faith, a peculiar and inescapable responsibility must necessarily rest. Through their courage, their self-abnegation, their fortitude and their perseverance; through the range and quality of their achievements, the depth of their consecration, their initiative and resourcefulness, their organizing ability, their readiness and capacity to lend their assistance to less privileged sister communities struggling against heavy odds; through their generous and sustained response to the enormous and ever-increasing financial needs of a world-encompassing, decade-long and admittedly strenuous enterprise, they must, beyond the shadow of a doubt, vindicate their right to the leadership of this World Crusade.[6]

A golden opportunity, a glorious challenge, an inescapable duty, a staggering responsibility, confronts them, at this fresh turning point in the fortunes of a Crusade, for which they have so unremittingly labored, whose Cause they have so notably advanced, in the further unfoldment of which they must continue to play a leading part, and in whose closing stages, they will, I feel confident, rise to heights never before attained in the course of six decades of American Bahá'í history.[7]

And according to May Maxwell's pilgrim notes, *Haifa Talks*, in 1937 the Guardian said:

> There is a Bahá'í standard to which everyone must make sacrifices. It is not an American thing. It is God's Will that America should happen to be the first to build up this new civilization (Bahá'í), it is not that America happens to be superior. The prejudice and corruption prevailing in America is responsible for the initiation of the Bahá'í Civilization in that country first, as the Faith first dawned in the darkness of Persia. Although the Cause was born in the East its proclamation was in the West. There is a Tablet of the Master where He says the mysteries of the Cause will be made manifest in America, etc. What they are establishing is not American, it is Bahá'í, and the Americans themselves must make concessions to it. Is it American that nine people should conduct things and not be responsible to anyone? This is anything but American.[8]

Even some of the Knights who arose to answer the Guardian's call were worried about America's response in the early years of the Crusade:

> At first I had always viewed the Crusade as a group of objectives aimed at culminating at some unknown future date in the actual reality of the new world order. Though this is true, I often found myself thinking about how far off that was or how much had to be done and this left me a little dejected. Then the realization came that this great endeavor was above all a fulfillment. When evaluated in the light of the tremendous burden placed on the shoulders of the American Bahá'ís this becomes even more apparent. Everything in our past history points to this nation being prepared for some great spiritual mission. We, more than any other country, have been able to cast aside the shackles of natural law and political subjugation, thus freeing us to assume a role in the drama of coming events into which no nation has ever been cast before, that of being a prime instrument in bringing about the spiritual, physical and political unification of the entire globe. A poor and humble nation has no alternative, it must be submissive in order to survive but when a nation is blessed with greatness in practically all fields of human endeavor, it is blessed in a much greater sense; it has the right to

make a choice! It can choose the path that leads to power and vain-glory which will sow the seeds of its own eventual destruction as the past has shown us in so many instances, or it may choose the, as yet, untrodden path of humility and service. The Crusade years may well find this country making this crucial decision. Great steps have been taken in both directions but as yet the scales do not seem tipped to any definite side. In the struggle between constructive and destructive forces, which isn't really a struggle as both are necessary, the Bahá'í Crusade remains the greatest positive step taken by any group and certainly the most optimistic. Even if America should go a long way down the wrong road, it will only prove to be a stern lesson which in itself, will guide us back to fulfilling that for which we were granted such a unique birthright. This Crusade is a living example of what America, as a nation, must do and the policy she must put forth, sooner or later. Not only is it a fulfillment in that God's kingdom on earth is being built, but it is a harbinger of things to come. How we, the Bahá'ís of the world, think today, is the way tomorrow's total humanity will think. What we, the Bahá'ís of the world, do today will speed up the conscious awareness of God's will in the minds of the people. – God's Plan is the time table and Bahá'u'lláh's plan is the train that has to maintain a schedule; the Guardian is the engineer speeding us along; we must do everything in our power to make his task the easier. The pioneers must integrate themselves into their new surroundings firm in the conviction that remaining is the least of what is expected of them. An ever constant flow of funds must lubricate the new machinery we have set into motion to insure smooth operation without undue, and time con-suming, delays.[9]

During the first half of the Crusade, the Guardian told almost every Western pilgrim the same thing – that the American Bahá'í community was not living up to the station and responsibility given it by the Master in the *Tablets of the Divine Plan*. Pilgrim notes from a score of pilgrims between 1952 and 1957 carry the same warnings. Some of the Guard-ian's letters to the Americans repeat the message, though in less blunt fashion. He called them to task both for not living up to the respon-sibilities of their station as the 'chief executors' of the Tablets and also because they were not fulfilling the goals he had given them during the first half of the Crusade. Western pilgrims who had already pioneered rarely heard this message from the Guardian – but they had arisen and answered his call.

Though the Guardian's words to the pilgrims may have seemed harsh at times, they always carried the words of wisdom that could guide those communities to do what was needed to achieve their lofty stations. After the passing of the Guardian, the American Bahá'í community did arise, fulfilling all of the goals set by the Guardian and exceeding them in some cases.[10]

The Guardian lived to marshal the forces of the Faith during the first half of the Ten Year Crusade. When he did leave this earthly plane, he had set the Plan on such a firm footing that the Hands of the Cause were able, by following his detailed guidance, to shepherd the Faith to the election of the Universal House of Justice, and into its divinely protected hands.

Much of this book is based on pilgrim notes written by those who visited Shoghi Effendi, and as such, readers must be careful not to hold them up as absolute truth. The pilgrims wrote down what they remembered the Guardian saying, but they didn't always understand the point of his talks and, on occasion, they simply got things wrong. These notes, therefore, are simply recollections and not the actual words of the Guardian. None of the talks quoted from pilgrims in this book, then, can be considered to be part of his guidance to the Bahá'í World. Shoghi Effendi stressed that only his letters written over his own signature were to be considered to be infallible. Pilgrim notes should be considered to be interesting and thought-provoking highlights from the Guardian's talks, but nothing more.

> . . . the notes of pilgrims do not carry the authority resident in the Guardian's letters written over his own signature. On the other hand, each pilgrim brings back information and suggestions of a most precious character, and it is the privilege of all the friends to share in the spiritual results of these visits.[11]

Quotations by pilgrims and visitors have been used here exactly as they were written, typographical errors, grammatical stumbles, missing punctuation, apostrophes and accents included, in order not to change their meaning or emotion.

ACKNOWLEDGEMENTS

As in my previous books, a number of people were very helpful in researching and editing this one. Dr Duane Troxel, of the Heritage Project of the National Spiritual Assembly of the United States, sent me a constant stream of Bahá'í material in searchable PDF format as well as audio recordings and other interesting pieces. Lewis Walker, of the United States National Bahá'í Archives, provided me with many pages of pilgrim notes. He knew what I was searching for and commonly sent queries about whether I might be interested in some new material that had crossed his desk. Keith Munro provided me with audio CDs containing illustrative talks given by Hands of the Cause.

As he did in the first volume, Rowshan Mustapha offered his knowledge of people and events during these years. Jennifer Wiebers, who is working on a book about Alma Knobloch, shared some personal notes about Mason Remey that helped illustrate his departure from the Covenant and how others had viewed him. Ben Guhrke added a story about Mason Remey that also highlighted those issues. Mohsen Enayat graciously contributed the story of his pioneering to the Fezzan, the desert region in southwest Libya where the Sultan of the Ottoman Empire had threatened to send the Master. Marlene Make, author of the book *Take My Love to the Friends: The Story of Laura R. Davis*, graciously shared her research about Laura Davis's pilgrimage. Maurice Pickett's accounting background, with his consequent attention to detail, caught many little problems that I had missed and improved the text. Hushang Jamshidi and Paddy Vickers both provided stories about their experiences at the World Congress in 1963 and Adam Thorne generously gave me an unpublished article he had written about the Congress. I would also like to thank Suzanne Locke-Nyrenda who told me about the first native African to become a Bahá'í and who was also the first native African to pioneer to another country.

For the third time, May Hofman was my editor and for the third time, she seemed to know just what had to change, be added or be taken out to make the manuscript flow like a real book is supposed to. Her help is greatly appreciated.

My wife, Sharon O'Toole, yet again gave me immense support and encouragement. She also read many bits and pieces, catching my typos and confusing parts, resulting in a much better book. She also gave me much-needed moral support and the occasional cup of energizing coffee.

INTRODUCTION

For 30 years, from 1922 to 1952, Shoghi Effendi worked to implement the *Tablets of the Divine Plan* and to raise up the Administrative Order created by Bahá'u'lláh and defined by 'Abdu'l-Bahá, facing and overcoming a myriad challenges. These challenges began almost immediately when the Arch-breaker of the Covenant, Mírzá Muḥammad-'Alí, forcibly took the keys to the Shrine of Bahá'u'lláh, and were compounded by the seizure of the House of Bahá'u'lláh in Baghdad, along with the continual persecution of the Faith in Iran, a crisis in Egypt, the dispersal of the Bahá'í community in Azerbaijan and the confiscation of the first Mashriqu'l-Adhkár of the Bahá'í world. Well-known and respected Bahá'ís, such as Ahmad Sohrab, one of 'Abdu'l-Bahá's secretaries on His journey to the West, and 'Abdu'l-Ḥusayn Ávárih, a prominent teacher of the Faith in Persia, turned against Shoghi Effendi, thinking that his youth and inexperience left him unqualified to lead the Faith of Bahá'u'lláh into the future. Even his own family, with the exceptions of the Greatest Holy Leaf and Munírih Khánum, 'Abdu'l-Bahá's sister and wife, ultimately abandoned him for lives as Covenant-breakers.

When Shoghi Effendi became the Guardian at the very beginning of 1922, virtually every Bahá'í in the world expected him to bring about the election of the Universal House of Justice, but an intuition that he quickly learned to respect told him that the world wasn't ready for that supreme body. His heart told him that first, the divinely-inspired Bahá'í Administrative Order had to be built, that local and national Spiritual Assemblies had to be raised up and made to function, before the Universal House of Justice could be placed on a firm and universal foundation.

'Abdu'l-Bahá, in His *Will and Testament*, said that the Universal House of Justice was to be 'universally elected and established'[1] and that 'it must be elected by universal suffrage, that is, by the believers.'[2] Again,

He said that 'By this House is meant the Universal House of Justice, that is, in all countries a secondary House of Justice must be instituted, and these secondary Houses of Justice must elect the members of the Universal one', [3] and 'By this House is meant that Universal House of Justice which is to be elected from all countries, that is from those parts in the East and West where the loved ones are to be found . . .' [4] At the time Shoghi Effendi became the Guardian, there were no 'secondary Houses of Justice' (presently called National Spiritual Assemblies) and most of the Bahá'ís were in just a few countries such as Iran, India, the United States and Canada, with smaller populations in the British Isles, Germany and Malaysia. Shoghi Effendi obviously understood that those passages in the *Will and Testament* meant that secondary Houses of Justice had to be elected around the world before that divinely-inspired body could be formed.

Shoghi Effendi's charters for action were 'Abdu'l-Bahá's *Tablets of the Divine Plan* and the *Will and Testament*, and Bahá'u'lláh's *Tablet of Carmel*. The *Tablets of the Divine Plan* called for the spiritual conquest of the entire planet, and Shoghi Effendi knew that before that could happen, an administrative order was needed to systematize the work. The *Will and Testament* contained the plan for that administrative order and the *Tablet of Carmel* contained the basis for the Bahá'í World Centre in Haifa. The young Guardian began this process immediately, sending home those he had called for consultations in early 1922 to start the process for the election of National Spiritual Assemblies. Britain, Germany and India were the first to have National Spiritual Assemblies in 1923. They were followed during the next years by Egypt, the United States and Canada, Iraq, Australia and New Zealand, Iran, Turkistan, Mexico, Central America and the Antilles, Burma, South America and, in 1953, by Italy and Switzerland.

To prepare these National Assemblies, Shoghi Effendi began gently teaching them about National Conventions, how Bahá'í elections were carried out, and what the duties of the institutions of the Faith were. He began quietly implementing 'Abdu'l-Bahá's *Tablets of the Divine Plan* soon after he became the Guardian by giving the North American Bahá'í community goals within their boundaries. Then, when the National Assemblies were functioning in a rudimentary fashion, the Guardian began to implement the Divine Plan by giving them national teaching plans in order to help them develop the knowledge and resources to advance the Faith. In 1937, he began the international implementation of the Tablets by giving the North American Bahá'í community the task of spiritually conquering all of the Western Hemisphere. The next year, the National Assembly of India and Burma began their first teaching plan and in 1944, the United Kingdom initiated theirs. Nine years after North America's first teaching plan, in 1946, the Guardian expanded the American vision by refocusing them on the spiritual revitalization of Europe, as well as the rest of the world. Between 1944 and 1953, he also gave every existing National Spiritual Assembly at least one major teaching plan.

For virtually the whole of this time, Shoghi Effendi operated mostly alone, helped during short periods by the secretarial efforts of outstanding believers such as Dr John Esslemont, author of *Bahá'u'lláh and the New Era*, Marion Jack, Emogene Hoagg and Effie Baker. His most important helper was his wife, Rúḥíyyih Khánum, whom he married in 1937 and who became his primary aide and secretary. From 1922 until the end of 1950, Shoghi Effendi patiently prepared the Bahá'í world to take its place among the world's independent religions and to be ready for what was to come next.

Then suddenly, in November 1950, the Guardian appointed an International Bahá'í Council to serve in the Holy Land, followed in December 1951 and February 1952 by his appointment of 19 Hands of the Cause. In short order, Shoghi Effendi created an international secretariat and a body of spiritually aware and dedicated men and women to help him carry out his designs for the Faith on a global scale. It was the beginning of the Bahá'í World Centre as a focal point of the Bahá'í Administrative Order and a major step on the way to the election of the Universal House of Justice.

At the end of 1952, the Guardian announced a plan for the third stage in the implementation of the Divine Plan and this time gave the Bahá'í world community

a new challenge of staggering proportions . . . Impelled by historic forces that only he was in a position to appreciate, the Guardian announced the launching at the forthcoming Riḍván of a decade-long, world-embracing Plan, which he designated a 'Spiritual Crusade', engaging the energies of all the twelve National Spiritual Assemblies then in existence . . . it called for the establishment of the Faith in one hundred and thirty-one additional countries and territories, together with the formation of forty-four new National Spiritual Assemblies . . . Nothing in their collective experience had prepared the Bahá'ís of the world for so colossal an undertaking . . .

In effect, the Plan called for the Cause to make a giant leap forward over what might otherwise have been several stages in its evolution. What Shoghi Effendi saw clearly – and what only the powers of foresight inherent in the Guardianship made it possible to see – was that an historical conjunction of circumstances presented the Bahá'í community with an opportunity that would not come again and on which the success of future stages in the prosecution of the Divine Plan would entirely depend.[5]

In October 1952, Shoghi Effendi, the unerring Guardian of the Faith of Bahá'u'lláh, took the step that would lead to the establishment of the final piece in Bahá'u'lláh's Administrative Order, the Universal House of Justice. He announced the launch of the first global teaching plan, one involving every National Assembly and every Bahá'í in a 'fate-laden, soul-stirring, decade-long, world-embracing Spiritual Crusade'. That Crusade is the subject of this book.

The Ten Year Crusade was a monumentally incomprehensible leap for the world Bahá'í Community. When Shoghi Effendi announced the plan, there were just twelve National Spiritual Assemblies in the world, formed over a period of 30 years. The Plan called for at least quadrupling that number. The Faith at that time, in 1952, was represented in 129 countries and dependencies; Shoghi Effendi wanted to open an additional 131 countries to the Faith. All in just ten years.

Shoghi Effendi began the Crusade with a Holy Year and four Intercontinental Teaching Conferences. Jessie Revell, secretary of the International Bahá'í Council appointed by the Guardian, wrote to the American friends:

Our beloved Guardian tells us with regard to the Intercontinental Conferences to be held during the Bahá'í Holy Year, nothing similar has been attempted since the History of the Faith. It is a World Crusade, utilizing the agencies of a World Administrative Order which is Worldwide in character, to carry out the provisions of 'Abdu'l-Bahá's World Plan, in the service of a World Faith – a

Global Crusade in which all National Spiritual Assemblies will take part. The chief task of these Conferences will be the opening up new territories under their jurisdiction, consolidating the work, on an international scale.

One day at dinner Shoghi Effendi called for a World Map and he himself drew circles around the territories under the jurisdiction of the eleven now existing National Spiritual Assemblies, then he drew circles around eleven more territories where new National Spiritual Assemblies are to be made within the next ten years, and he called this THE WHEELS OF BAHÁ'U'LLÁH'S CHARIOT.[6]

The book *Shoghi Effendi Through the Pilgrim's Eye, Volume 1: Building the Administrative Order, 1922–1952,* by this author and published in 2015 by George Ronald, contains a narrative of this 31-year rise of the Bahá'í Administrative Order under the direction of the Guardian. This volume continues the story.

THE SIGNIFICANCE AND LAUNCHING OF THE TEN YEAR CRUSADE

The Ten Year Crusade was not just another, bigger teaching plan. According to the Guardian of the Faith of Bahá'u'lláh, the Universal House of Justice was not only the capstone of the Bahá'í Administrative Order – it was also the focus of six thousand years of spiritual evolution. In *God Passes By*, Shoghi Effendi wrote of the 'world-embracing Administrative system designed to evolve into a World Order which posterity must acclaim as the promise and crowning glory of all the Dispensations of the past.'[1] At the beginning of the Ten Year Crusade, he clearly set out the importance of the formation of the Universal House of Justice and, consequently, of the Ten Year Crusade:

Then . . . [with the establishing of the Universal House of Justice] will the vast, the majestic process, set in motion at the dawn of the Adamic cycle, attain its consummation – a process which commenced six thousand years ago, with the planting, in the soil of the divine will, of the tree of divine revelation, and which has already passed through certain stages and must needs pass through still others ere it attains its final consummation . . .

This present Crusade, on the threshold of which we now stand, will, moreover, by virtue of the dynamic forces it will release and its wide repercussions over the entire surface of the globe, contribute effactually to the acceleration of yet another process of tremendous significance which will carry the steadily evolving Faith of Baha'u'llah through its present stages of obscurity, of repression, of emancipation and of recognition – stages one or another of which Bahá'í national communities in various parts of the world now find themselves in – to the stage of establishment, the stage at which the Faith of Bahá'u'lláh will be recognized by the civil authorities as the state religion, similar to that which Christianity entered in the years following the death of the Emperor Constantine, a stage which must later be followed by the emergence of the Bahá'í state itself, functioning, in all religious and civil matters, in strict accordance with the laws and ordinances of the Kitáb-i-Aqdas, the Most Holy, the Mother-Book of the Bahá'í Revelation, a stage which, in the fullness of time, will culminate in the establishment of the World Bahá'í Commonwealth, functioning in the plenitude of its powers, and which will signalize the long-awaited advent of the Christ-promised Kingdom of God on earth – the Kingdom of Bahá'u'lláh – mirroring however faintly upon this humble handful of dust the glories of the Abhá Kingdom.

This final and crowning stage in the evolution of the plan wrought by God Himself for humanity will, in turn, prove to be the signal for the birth of a world civilization, incomparable in its range, its character and potency, in the history of mankind – a civilization which posterity will, with one voice, acclaim as the fairest fruit of the Golden Age of the Dispensation of Bahá'u'lláh, and whose rich harvest will be garnered during future dispensations destined to succeed one another in the course of the five thousand century Bahá'í Cycle.[2]

The Universal House of Justice itself, stressed the immense importance of its own formation:

It is impossible to exaggerate the significance of the achievement that brought the Universal House of Justice into existence. For some six thousand years humanity has experimented with an almost unlimited variety of methods for collective decision-making . . . the political history of the world presents a constantly shifting scene in which there was no possibility that was not seized upon by human ingenuity. Systems based on principles as different as theocracy, monarchy, aristocracy, oligarchy, republic, democracy and near anarchy have proliferated freely, along with innovations without end that have sought to combine various desirable features of these possibilities . . . The resulting series of calamitous failures . . . would seem to provide persuasive evidence that the realization of the ambition lies beyond the reach of any human agency . . .[3]

For years, Shoghi Effendi had been writing that the goal of all past Dispensations was the development of the World Order of Bahá'u'lláh. When he began to build the Bahá'í Administrative Order, he wrote that the people could not yet understand the full impact that Order would have on the world:

> All we can reasonably venture to attempt is to strive to obtain a glimpse of the first streaks of the promised Dawn that must, in the fullness of time, chase away the gloom that has encircled humanity. All we can do is to point out, in their broadest outlines, what appear to us to be the guiding principles underlying the World Order of Bahá'u'lláh.[4]

He went on, however, to state that the institutions of the Administrative Order

> are slowly crystallizing into institutions that will come to be regarded as the hall-mark and glory of the age we are called upon to establish and by our deeds immortalize. For upon our present-day efforts, and above all upon the extent to which we strive to remodel our lives after the pattern of sublime heroism associated with those gone before us, must depend the efficacy of the instruments we now fashion – instruments that must erect the structure of that blissful Commonwealth which must signalize the Golden Age of our Faith.[5]

The ten-stage majestic process

The Guardian explained the whole process of, and reason for, progressive revelation and the importance of the Ten Year Crusade within that framework in May 1953 in his ten-stage majestic process:

> The first part of this process was the slow and steady growth of this tree of divine revelation, successively putting forth its branches, shoots and offshoots, and revealing its leaves, buds and blossoms, as a direct consequence of the light and warmth imparted to it by a series of progressive dispensations associated with Moses, Zoroaster,

Buddha, Jesus, Muhammad and other Prophets, and of the vernal showers of blood shed by countless martyrs in their path. The second part of this process was the fruition of this tree, 'that belongeth neither to the East nor to the West,' when the Báb appeared as the perfect fruit and declared His mission in the Year Sixty in the city of Shíráz. The third part was the grinding of this sacred seed, of infinite preciousness and potency, in the mill of adversity, causing it to yield its oil, six years later, in the city of Tabríz. The fourth part was the ignition of this oil by the hand of Providence in the depths and amidst the darkness of the Síyáh-Chál of Ṭihrán a hundred years ago. The fifth, was the clothing of that flickering light, which had scarcely penetrated the adjoining territory of 'Iráq, in the lamp of revelation, after an eclipse lasting no less than ten years, in the city of Baghdád. The sixth, was the spread of the radiance of that light, shining with added brilliancy in its crystal globe in Adrianople, and later on in the fortress town of 'Akká, to thirteen countries in the Asiatic and African continents. The seventh was its projection, from the Most Great Prison, in the course of the ministry of the Center of the Covenant, across the seas and the shedding of its illumination upon twenty sovereign states and dependencies in the American, the European, and Australian continents. The eighth part of that process was the diffusion of that same light in the course of the first, and the opening years of the second, epoch of the Formative Age of the Faith, over ninety-four sovereign states, dependencies and islands of the planet, as a result of the prosecution of a series of national plans, initiated by eleven national spiritual assemblies throughout the Bahá'í world, utilizing the agencies of a newly emerged, divinely appointed Administrative Order. The ninth part of this process – the stage we are now entering – is the further diffusion of that same light over one hundred and thirty-one additional territories and islands in both the Eastern and Western Hemispheres, through the operation of a decade-long world spiritual crusade . . .

And finally the tenth part of this mighty process must be the penetration of that light, in the course of numerous crusades and of successive epochs of both the Formative and Golden Ages of the Faith, into all the remaining territories of the globe through the erection of the entire machinery of Bahá'u'lláh's Administrative Order in all territories, both East and West, the stage at which the light of God's triumphant Faith shining in all its power and glory will have suffused and enveloped the entire planet . . .[6]

The Guardian had spent 31 years bringing the world through the eighth stage in order to prepare them for the ninth, the Ten Year Crusade. During that time, he had built the divinely-ordained Bahá'í Administrative Order and trained it through a series of national teaching plans. The world, he explained, needed to complete the ninth stage and elect the Universal House of Justice, which would open the tenth, and final, stage of God's majestic process. The culmination of that stage will fulfil the goal of the progressive revelation of God's purpose by His series of Messengers.

Of the Ten Year Crusade, the House of Justice has written:

> In effect, the Plan called for the Cause to make a giant leap forward over what might otherwise have been several stages in its evolution. What Shoghi Effendi saw clearly – and what only the powers of foresight inherent in the Guardianship made it possible to see – was that an historical conjunction of circumstances presented the Bahá'í community with an opportunity that would not come again and on which the success of future stages in the prosecution of the Divine Plan would entirely depend.[7]

The Ten Year Crusade, therefore, was a big deal.

Launching the Ten Year Crusade

The Guardian had first hinted at the Ten Year Crusade on 25 February 1951 when he gave the British National Spiritual Assembly, working with four other National Assemblies, the task of opening up Africa. That Two Year Plan was, he said, 'a prelude to the launching of worldwide enterprises destined to be embarked upon, in future epochs of that same age [the Formative Age], by the Universal House of Justice . . .' The message both suggests the Ten Year Crusade and the possibility that there would not be a Guardian in the future:

> On the success of this enterprise, unprecedented in its scope, unique in its character and immense in its spiritual potentialities, must

depend the initiation, at a later period in the Formative Age of the Faith, of undertakings embracing within their range all National Assemblies functioning throughout the Bahá'í World, undertakings constituting in themselves a prelude to the launching of world-wide enterprises destined to be embarked upon, in future epochs of that same Age, by the Universal House of Justice, that will symbolise the unity and coordinate and unify the activities of these National Assemblies.[8]

This reference to plans operating under the direction of the Universal House of Justice caused some to wonder why he hadn't said that they would operate under the direction of the Guardian.[9]

Shoghi Effendi first specifically mentioned what became the Ten Year Crusade at Riḍván 1952 when he wrote that he would be giving the 12 National Spiritual Assemblies a plan 'to promote in the course of the ten years separating the second [stage of the Formative Age] from the Most Great Jubilee the Global Crusade designed to hoist the standard of Bahá'u'lláh in the remaining dependencies and islands of the whole planet'.[10]

On 30 June 1952, Shoghi Effendi wrote a message that hinted that significant events and serious difficulties lay ahead:

No matter how long the period that separates them from ultimate victory; however arduous the task; however formidable the exertions demanded of them; however dark the days which mankind, perplexed and sorely-tried, must, in its hour of travail, traverse; however severe the tests with which they who are to redeem its fortunes will be confronted; however afflictive the darts which their present enemies, as well as those whom Providence, will, through His mysterious dispensations raise up from within or from without, may rain upon them, however grievous the ordeal of temporary separation from the heart and nerve-center of their Faith which future unforeseeable disturbances may impose upon them, I adjure them, by the precious blood that flowed in such great profusion, by the lives of the unnumbered saints and heroes who were immolated, by the supreme, the glorious sacrifice of the Prophet-Herald of our Faith, by the tribulations which its Founder, Himself, willingly underwent, so that His Cause might live, His Order might redeem a shattered world and its glory might suffuse the entire planet – I adjure them, as this solemn hour draws nigh, to resolve never to flinch, never to hesitate, never to relax, until each and every objective in the Plans to be proclaimed, at a later date, has been fully consummated.[11]

'Alí Nakhjavání remembered 'the deep emotion of those days . . . when these messages were received':

> The messages had an electrifying impact on the minds and hearts of the friends. Indeed, a few of us even thought that the Plan Shoghi Effendi had in store might be considered as part of his Will and Testament, for he refers to the grievous 'ordeal of temporary separation from the heart and nerve-center' of the Faith.[12]

On 8 October 1952, Shoghi Effendi announced two big events, the first ever Bahá'í Holy Year and the Ten Year Crusade. The Holy Year was to mark the Year Nine – a reference to the Báb's statement that nine years after His Declaration a new Revelation was to begin, making the Holy Year also the centenary of the Revelation received by Bahá'u'lláh in the Síyáh-Chál in Tehran.[13] Shoghi Effendi wrote that the Revelation of Bahá'u'lláh marked the 'consummation of the six thousand year cycle ushered in by Adam, glorified by all past prophets and sealed with the blood of the Author of the Bábí Dispensation.'[14] Of the Holy Year, he cabled to all National Spiritual Assemblies that the

> Centennial festivities of Year Nine continuing throughout Holy Year commencing October 1952 must include, apart from consummation plans initiated by various National Assemblies both hemispheres, the formal dedication for public worship of Mother Temple of West in heart North American continent, and possible termination superstructure of Báb's Sepulcher in Holy Land, the convocation of four intercontinental Bahá'í Teaching Conferences to be held successively in course historic Year on continents of Africa, America, Europe, Asia.[15]

He then set the stage for the other announcement by recalling the sacrificial history of the first century of that Revelation, saying that he would

Evoke on this auspicious occasion the glorious memory and acclaim the immortal exploits of the Dawn-Breakers of the Apostolic Age of the Bahá'í Dispensation in the cradle of the Faith and the mighty feats of the champion builders of its rising World Order in the Western Hemisphere as well as the multitude of valorous achievements of the past and present generations of their brethren in the European, Asiatic, African and Australian continents, whose combined accomplishments during the one hundred and nine years of its existence contributed to the survival of God's struggling Faith, the reinforcement of its infant strength, the safeguarding of the unity of its supporters, the preservation of the integrity of its teachings, the enrichment of the lives of its followers, the rise of the institutions of its administrative order, the fashioning of the agencies for the systematic diffusion of its light and the broadening and the consolidation of its foundations.[16]

The Guardian then went on to announce a mind-boggling plan, ten years in length, starting at Riḍván 1953 and ending at Riḍván 1963, that was designed to expand the Faith more in that single decade than it had accomplished in the previous 109 years:

Feel hour propitious to proclaim to the entire Bahá'í world the projected launching on the occasion of the convocation of the approaching Intercontinental Conferences on the four continents of the globe the fate-laden, soul-stirring, decade-long, world-embracing Spiritual Crusade involving the simultaneous initiation of twelve national Ten Year Plans and the concerted participation of all National Spiritual Assemblies of the Bahá'í world aiming at the immediate extension of Bahá'u'lláh's spiritual dominion as well as the eventual establishment of the structure of His administrative order in all remaining Sovereign States, Principal Dependencies comprising Principalities, Sultanates, Emirates, Shaykhdoms, Protectorates, Trust Territories, and Crown Colonies scattered over the surface of the entire planet. The entire body of the avowed supporters of Bahá'u'lláh's all-conquering Faith are now summoned to achieve in a single decade feats eclipsing in totality the achievements which in the course of the eleven preceding decades illuminated the annals of Bahá'í pioneering.[17]

Some of the goals the Guardian set for this critical decade included:

> First, development of the institutions at the World Center of the
> Faith in the Holy Land. Second, consolidation, through carefully
> devised measures on the home front of the twelve territories des-
> tined to serve as administrative bases for the operations of the twelve
> National Plans. Third, consolidation of all territories already opened
> to the Faith. Fourth, the opening of the remaining chief virgin ter-
> ritories on the planet through specific allotments to each National
> Assembly functioning in the Bahá'í world.[18]

To achieve these goals meant opening 131 new countries to the Faith,
thus doubling the number that existed at that time, and more than
quadrupling the number of National Spiritual Assemblies. The plan
also included the construction of the International Bahá'í Archives
building and the acquisition of Temple land on Mount Carmel. But
before any new building could be started, the work on the Shrine of the
Báb had to be completed.

On 4 May 1953, just after the Plan officially began, the Guardian
defined what it was and who would accomplish it:

> Let there be no mistake. The avowed, the primary aim of this Spir-
> itual Crusade is none other than the conquest of the citadels of men's
> hearts. The theater of its operations is the entire planet. Its duration a
> whole decade. Its commencement synchronizes with the centenary of
> the birth of Bahá'u'lláh's Mission. Its culmination will coincide with
> the centenary of the declaration of that same Mission. The agencies
> assisting in its conduct are the nascent administrative institutions of
> a steadily evolving divinely appointed order. Its driving force is the
> energizing influence generated by the Revelation heralded by the Báb
> and proclaimed by Bahá'u'lláh. Its Marshal is none other than the
> Author of the Divine Plan. Its standard-bearers are the Hands of the
> Cause of God appointed in every continent of the globe. Its generals
> are the twelve national spiritual assemblies participating in the execu-
> tion of its design. Its vanguard is the chief executors of 'Abdu'l-Bahá's
> master plan, their allies and associates. Its legions are the rank and
> file of believers standing behind these same twelve national assem-
> blies and sharing in the global task embracing the American, the

European, the African, the Asiatic and Australian fronts. The charter directing its course is the immortal Tablets that have flowed from the pen of the Center of the Covenant Himself. The armor with which its onrushing hosts have been invested is the glad tidings of God's own message in this day, the principles underlying the order proclaimed by His Messenger, and the laws and ordinances governing His Dispensation. The battle cry animating its heroes and heroines is the cry of Yá-Bahá'u'l-Abhá, Yá 'Alíyyu'l-A'lá.

So vast, so momentous and challenging a crusade that will, God willing, illuminate the annals of the second epoch of the Formative Age of the Faith of Bahá'u'lláh, and immortalize the second decade of the second Bahá'í century, and the termination of which will mark the closing of the first epoch in the evolution of 'Abdu'l-Bahá's Divine Plan, will, in itself, pave the way for, and constitute the prelude to, the initiation of the laborious and tremendously long process of establishing in the course of subsequent crusades in all the newly opened sovereign states, dependencies and islands of the planet, as well as in all the remaining territories of the globe, the framework of the Administrative Order of the Faith, with all its attendant agencies, and of eventually erecting in these territories still more pillars to share in sustaining the weight and in broadening the foundation of the Universal House of Justice.[19]

Leroy Ioas, Shoghi Effendi's closest helper, a member of the International Bahá'í Council and one of the first group of Hands of the Cause, was one of the first to learn of the plan. When Shoghi Effendi returned to Haifa in the autumn of 1952 after his summer away, Leroy collected him and Rúhíyyih Khánum at the airport. He noticed that there was something different about the Guardian – he was 'speaking in a different vein'. That night after dinner, Shoghi Effendi laid out the Ten Year Crusade and asked those present what they thought. Leroy and the others were 'staggered' and didn't know what to think. The Guardian then turned to Leroy and asked what would be the easiest part to accomplish. Leroy replied that it would probably be the opening up all of the new countries and territories. The Guardian then asked what would be more difficult and Leroy said it would be raising the funds. Finally, Shoghi Effendi asked what would be the hardest part. Leroy again answered, saying, 'the consolidation work you have outlined,

Shoghi Effendi, because that is drudgery, just plain drudgery, right on the home front where there's no glory associated with it'. Shoghi Effendi agreed with him.[20]

One day, when Leroy spoke of the Guardian's achievement in developing the Administrative Order, Shoghi Effendi replied:

> Leroy, did you think I had a blueprint to follow when I did this? Did you think that God had shown me a picture of how this was to evolve? No. When God guided me to do something, I did it, and then when He guided me to do something else, I did that, so that every step which has been taken has been taken under the direct and unfailing guidance of Bahá'u'lláh. As Guardian of the Bahá'í Faith, I have supreme confidence that God will inspire me to do whatever is necessary for the good of the Cause at the time it must be done.[21]

Leroy wrote about the development of the Ten Year Crusade:

> The ten year global crusade was developed fully by the Guardian long before it was given to the friends. In the summer of 1952 while away from Haifa he formulated the ten year plan. Then he drew it in detail on the world map, with his own hands. Then he decided how it should be presented to the Bahá'ís. It was unfolded to them through cables which he sent to the national communities at the opening of the Holy Year (1952–53) and at special events held during that year, then through Riḍván cables to all the National Conventions, and finally through the release of a statistical book which included his map and outlined the details of the crusade. The Guardian prepared his messages well in advance of their release to assure that they would reach all parts of the world in proper time. He worked over these carefully, changing and revising as necessary.
>
> Thus the focal point of the creative work of the Faith was the Guardian. The spirit operated through him, and he disseminated it. Never in speaking of the teaching plans did he refer to them as 'my' plans, even speaking of them as if he personally had nothing to do with them, which indicates to what an extent he was the vehicle of the spirit. The ten year crusade can thus be seen as the Will of God for that period. It came to us through the nerve center, the heart of the Faith.[22]

At Riḍván 1953, the final National Spiritual Assembly assigned to carry out the monumental plan was elected, for Italy and Switzerland.

Goals of the Ten Year Crusade

Shoghi Effendi laid out a daunting list of 27 goals, some of which involved the Baháʾí World Centre, others requiring action on the part of national communities, and still others that necessitated the rising up of individual believers. Those involving the Baháʾí World Centre included:

1. The adoption of preliminary measures for the construction of Baháʾuʾlláhʾs Sepulchre

2. The acquisition of land for a Mashriquʾl-Adhkár on Mount Carmel

3. The development of the Institution of the Hands of the Cause

4. The establishment of a Baháʾí Court in the Holy Land

5. The codification of the Laws and Ordinances of the *Kitáb-i-Aqdas*

6. The extension of the International Baháʾí Endowments on Mount Carmel and the plain of ʿAkká

7. The construction of the International Baháʾí Archives

8. The reinforcement of the ties between the Baháʾí World Community and the United Nations

9. The convocation of a World Baháʾí Congress in Baghdad on the Centenary of Baháʾuʾlláhʾs declaration in the Garden of Riḍván

The goals for national communities were:

1. To the American, British, Indian and Australian Baháʾí commu-

nities: more than doubling the number of languages into which the Writings of the Faith have been translated (91 more)

2. To America: Erection of the first dependency of the Mashriqu'l-Adhkár in Wilmette

3. The construction of a Mashriqu'l-Adhkár on both the Asian and the European continents

4. The purchase of land for eleven future Temples

5. The establishment of National Bahá'í Courts in Tehran, Cairo, New Delhi, Baghdad, Karachi and Kabul.

6. To Iran: Construction of the tomb of the Wife of the Báb in Shiraz

7. To Iran: Identification of the resting places of Bahá'u'lláh's Father and of the Mother and Cousin of the Báb and their reburial in a Bahá'í cemetery near the Most Great House in Baghdad

8. To Iran: Participation of women in the membership of the National and Local Spiritual Assemblies

9. To Iran: Establishment of a National Bahá'í printing press

10. To Iran and Iraq: Acquisition of the Síyáh-Chál in Tehran, the sites of the Báb's incarceration at Chihríq, the site of the Báb's Martyrdom in Tabríz, and the Garden of Riḍván in Baghdad

11. A sevenfold increase in the number of National Ḥaẓíratu'l-Quds (National Centres, 49 new)

12. More than quadrupling the number of National Spiritual Assemblies

13. The framing of national Bahá'í constitutions and establishment of national Bahá'í endowments in capital cities

14. More than quintupling the number of incorporated National Spiritual Assemblies

15. The establishment of six national Bahá'í Publishing Trusts

16. The establishment of seven Israeli branches of National Spiritual Assemblies

The goals for individual believers included:

1. The doubling of the number of countries open to the Faith (131 new countries)

2. The inclusion in the Administrative Order of the Faith of 11 republics in the Soviet-dominated region[23]

The Knights of Bahá'u'lláh

On 28 May 1953, Shoghi Effendi announced that those who took up the challenge of opening the new territories would have their names inscribed on a scroll that would be placed under the entrance to the inner Sanctuary of the Shrine of Bahá'u'lláh.[24]

A flood of pioneers streamed out across the world to fill Shoghi Effendi's goals for the Ten Year Crusade during 1953 (see the forthcoming book by this writer, *The Knights of Bahá'u'lláh*, for the stories of the Knights). The first to reach his post (and later to be named as a Knight of Bahá'u'lláh) was Suhayl Samandarí who arrived in Mogadishu, then part of Italian Somaliland, on 19 March. During the first year of the Ten Year Crusade, from Riḍván 1953 to Riḍván 1954, 90 of Shoghi Effendi's goal areas were opened by 189 Knights of Bahá'u'lláh.

Shoghi Effendi didn't immediately give the pioneers who filled his goals the title 'Knight of Bahá'u'lláh'. On 28 May, he wrote that he would be 'making periodic announcements of the names of the valiant knights upon their arrival at their posts'.[25] On 8 June, a letter written on behalf of the Guardian to the National Spiritual Assembly of India stated that 'an illuminated 'Roll of Honor' on which will be inscribed the names of the 'Knights of Baha'u'llah' who first enter these 131 virgin areas' would be placed 'inside the entrance door of The Inner Sanctuary of the Tomb of Baha'u'llah.'[26] This was the first time the title 'Knight of Bahá'u'lláh' was used.

Rúḥíyyih Khánum explained where the term 'Knight' of Bahá'u'lláh came from:

> Shoghi Effendi said that posterity would be proud of these souls who were the spiritual conquerors, his own term, of the entire globe. And on whom he conferred the unique title of Knights of Bahá'u'lláh. I remember when he devised this title, how astonished I was that he should go back to the middle ages . . . (When) you received your knighthood, you had certain oaths of allegiance and service to take. It's not a light term, knighthood. Shoghi Effendi attached tremendous importance to the Knights of Bahá'u'lláh.[27]

The Knights of Bahá'u'lláh are listed in Appendix I by goal area and Appendix II by name.

1953

PROJECTS AT THE WORLD CENTRE

In 1953 Shoghi Effendi asked for a survey of all lands that were needed for the development of the properties in the Holy Land. Leroy Ioas was his 'land man' and over the next few years he was able to buy more than a million dollars' worth of property on Mount Carmel. To safeguard this land, he had Israeli Branches established for various National Spiritual Assemblies, starting with those of the United States and Canada, then expanding to include the British Isles, Alaska, Australia, New Zealand, and Iran.[1] Once these were formally recognized as 'Religious Societies' by the Israeli Civil Authorities, they were able to own land on behalf of their parent bodies.

Shoghi Effendi had set an extraordinarily short timespan for the completion of major construction projects on Mount Carmel during the Plan, among them the construction of the International Bahá'í Archives, the extension of international Bahá'í endowments, and the acquisition of a site for the future Bahá'í temple on Mount Carmel. And first, the superstructure of the Shrine of the Báb needed to be completed.

Completing the Shrine of the Báb

Five years previously, on 3 July 1948, Shoghi Effendi had announced to Sutherland Maxwell: 'Well, the historic decision to commence work on the Shrine has been taken at 10:15 (p.m.) today!' Between 1948 and 1953, the work proceeded and is described in detail in the first volume of this book. In summary, on 16 November 1948, the first shipment of stone was sent by Ugo Giachery from Italy. Ugo had had to find the right stone, which had been a challenge, then have it converted from mountain bedrock to carved panels and columns. Each block of rock cut from a quarry had to be

> cut to a size prescribed by the plans made by the architect, then carved, finished to a smooth surface, and placed with its neighboring stones in the actual part of the building erected in the marble works, in sections held together by plaster of Paris. Specialized workers then went over every single stone to eliminate any imperfection to the fraction of a line. The stones were then numbered, the temporary part of the building dismantled, and every piece placed in a strong wooden box made especially for it, to be shipped to Haifa.
>
> A detailed list would give the number of the case and the number of each stone contained in it, while a master key-plan indicated the location of each stone in the building. A fascinating gigantic puzzle.[2]

The work on the superstructure of the Shrine of the Báb was under way, but there were always problems: a contractor wanted too much money; heavy rains delayed the delivery of over eighty cases of stone that were sitting on the Haifa dock;[3] a lighter sank carrying a large load of stones (luckily, the water was not too deep and a salvage company rescued every case of stones undamaged); a drought in Italy restricted the availability of electricity needed to cut and work the stones; a strong earthquake near the shipping port of Leghorn, Italy, sent the populace, including those loading the ships, fleeing into the countryside; and the captain of a ship being unloaded at Haifa panicked when a plane flew over and immediately set sail, returning to Italy with most of his cargo still aboard. Finally, another ship caught fire, but none of the stone was damaged.[4]

Shoghi Effendi spent almost every day at the Shrine directing the work. On 14 March 1949, the first of the foundation stones, weighing half a ton, was set into place. There were 140 foundation stones in all and base stones for each of the corners followed rapidly. On 8 May 1950, the last shipment of stone left Italy and arrived in Haifa twelve days later.[5] Then, at 3:30 on the afternoon of 29 May 1950, the last piece of stone, a small piece only a foot long, was fitted and the Arcade and Parapet were finished.[6]

On 1 September 1950, Shoghi Effendi announced the initiation of work on the 'octagon', an eight-pointed star-shaped structure that would support the dome. This was a critical part of the design because the dome, which would weigh about a thousand tons, could not be built on the roof of the original building constructed by 'Abdu'l-Bahá. Professor H. Neumann of the Haifa Institute of Technology solved the problem by designing a

> very ingenious system to support the entire superstructure by planning to sink eight mighty piers . . . all the way through the original Shrine to reach the bedrock lying under its foundation. It was a truly gigantic and delicate task to break through the masonry of the Shrine without damaging its structure or impairing in any manner the sacred entirety of the Holy Tombs.[7]

The octagon required eight huge pipes, called Manesmann pipes, and 100,000 pounds of cement. At first, no Manesmann pipes could be found in Italy, England or Germany, but then some were found in a neglected collection of building materials in Milan. Shoghi Effendi needed eight and there were exactly eight.[8] The cement was in short supply in Italy and could be exported only with a special government licence. Twice cement was found only to have its shipment blocked by ever-changing laws. A second cement shipment had similar problems and an official who finally signed the export license said that 'This is an exceptional measure, as no such permit has been granted for months, even to large corporations with world-wide trade.'[9]

By January 1952, the cylinder, or clerestory, above the Arcade was well under way. The clerestory contained 18 tall windows which represented the 18 Letters of the Living. When the windows were installed, in September 1952, Andrea Rocca, the chief architect in Italy, was there to watch. Even the masons were in awe of what they were doing and took great pride in their efforts. The clerestory was finished at the end of 1952, leaving only the crown and the dome to be completed.[10]

Between the cylindrical clerestory and the dome were a wide, downward angled brim and the crown. The brim was tricky because solid slabs of marble were too heavy. This was solved by using two thinner slabs anchored together. The crown, immediately above the brim, consisted of 36 carved points up to two meters high.[11]

The dome itself was a great challenge because it could bear no heavy stone. Professor Neumann, from the Technion in Haifa, came up with the idea of spraying a mixture of cement, sand and water on a mould to create the structure on which the gold tiles would be fixed. Everything at this point was theoretical and it wasn't certain that this method was sufficiently strong to carry the load of tiles. Ugo Giachery went off in search of tiles, but he quickly discovered that every company he found either said that it could not be done or that they couldn't do it. Then he attended the Fourth European Bahá'í Teaching Conference in the Netherlands in September 1951 and made an effort to look for a company capable of the work there. At first, it was the same story as elsewhere – until he found a small, struggling company in Utrecht run by Junker Robert de Brauw. De Brauw had never done what Ugo wanted, but was willing to try; he was a chemist, which proved invaluable because the problems were chemical: tile composition, the gold coating and the glazing. Robert de Brauw spent six months, at no expense to the Faith, trying to see if he could do the needed work. He sent a stream of samples to Professor Neumann to test. Finally, he built a one eighteenth-scale replica of the dome at Ugo's request and they were able to test Neumann's idea for the dome. Everything worked, so in September 1952, a contract was signed with de Brauw for the 12,000 tiles needed to cover the dome. But even that wasn't simple because since the dome was a combination of a cylinder (at the bottom), a sphere (at the top) and a cone (in the middle), it required 50 different sizes of tile. And then there was the gold which, only because de Brauw had connections in high governmental places, he was able to acquire.[12]

Finally, in May 1953, a wooden form 14 meters in diameter was constructed with reinforcing steel woven into it. This was sprayed with the concrete and, after drying for eight days, was ready for the tiles. But first, Shoghi Effendi had something important to do. A few tiles were placed in the bottom-most row for the celebration of the Ninth Day of Riḍván. On that morning, Shoghi Effendi called Leroy Ioas into his office and showed him a small silver box. Inside the box was a fragment of plaster from the cell of the Báb in Máků. Just that morning, Leroy had told the workmen to remove the scaffolding below those first tiles and now he rushed to have it put back up. Once it was up, Leroy wanted to test it to ensure the Guardian's safety, but Shoghi Effendi said, 'You forget, I am a mountaineer.' Then Shoghi Effendi, followed by Leroy and Lotfullah Hakím, climbed up to the tiles and, before the pilgrims and resident believers gathered below, carefully placed the silver box beneath a tile and sealed it. Shoghi Effendi then kissed the tile and circumambulated the dome on the scaffolding before descending.[13]

During the next two months, 18 marble ribs and floral ornamentation were placed on the concrete dome and the lantern at the very top of the dome was completed. Those tasks done, the rest of the tiles were laid. On 19 August, Shoghi Effendi announced that all the structural work on the dome had been completed. A month later, the Shrine of the Báb was finished.[14]

After the completion of the Shrine, Shoghi Effendi came to dinner one night in an extremely happy state and he explained why:

> Last month I received a letter from Mr. Bushrui [Badí Bushruí], one of 'Abdu'l-Bahá's secretaries. He said he had found among his papers a diary kept during the days when he served 'Abdu'l-Bahá. He wrote to ask if I'd like to read the diary and I said, of course I want to read it. He sent it to me, and what do you think I found today? I found a talk that 'Abdu'l-Bahá had given, recorded in this diary, in which 'Abdu'l-Bahá explained how the Shrine should be embellished and beautified. And there it is on Mt. Carmel, just as the Master had described it.[15]

On 25 May, Leroy's mother had passed away and the Guardian expressed his sympathies. Then Shoghi Effendi gave him a surprise:

> You remember on the 29th of April, after the placing of the plaster from the ceiling of Máh-Kú under the golden tile of the dome of His Shrine here, I expressed my appreciation of what you had done? I had a gift and reward for you, which I thought of telling you then. But I thought I would wait until the Shrine was completed.
>
> Now I am going to give you that gift and reward now, with the hope that it will lessen your sadness.
>
> The one remaining door of the Shrine of the Báb will be named after you. You owe this door to Sutherland, who has designed the Shrine in such a way as to have nine doors. There are eight doors on the ground floor and one door, the ninth, in the octagon. It is the door that gives access to the dome of the Shrine, to the portion

of the Shrine with which you have been associated. That door will be named after you, because of your services on that section of the Shrine.[16]

'Abdu'l-Bahá had named five of the doors of the Shrine. The western door leading to the Shrine of the Báb was named after Hand of the Cause Ḥájí Amín, while the one on the east was named for Ustád Áqá Bálá, a Bahá'í mason who worked on the Shrine. The western door entering the Shrine of 'Abdu'l-Bahá was named for Mírzá Abu'l-Faḍl, the famous Bahá'í scholar, and the eastern one was named for Ustád 'Abdu'l-Karím, who was also a mason who worked on the construction. The door facing the terraces was named for another mason, Ustád 'Alí-Ashraf. When Shoghi Effendi added the three rooms at the back of the Shrine, he named the one on the west for Ugo Giachery, who had helped find the stone required and organized its delivery from Italy to Haifa. The one on the east, he named for Ḥájí Maḥmúd Qassábchí, who had provided the funding for the additional rooms in 1929. The door to the room at the back, Shoghi Effendi named for Sutherland Maxwell, who designed the superstructure.[17]

One day, Leroy met with Levi Eshkol, the Israeli Minister of Finance who closely controlled foreign exchange and gold. They got along well, so Leroy

> remarked that he had heard the Minister didn't like the Shrine being built in Haifa. Astonished, the Minister said he found it very beautiful, an asset to the State of Israel. I'm glad to hear it, Leroy said, but the word is that you particularly don't like the dome. More astonished, the Minister said, but why shouldn't I like it . . . what do you mean? Leroy said, they tell me because it's the only gold in Israel that you don't control. Laughing, Eshkol said, now don't give me any ideas![18]

The temple site on Mount Carmel

In October 1953, Shoghi Effendi announced that preliminary steps had been taken to acquire the area on top of Mount Carmel near the Carmelite monastery for a Mashriqu'l-Adhkár. This was made possible by a $100,000 donation by Milly Collins. It would, however, take two years of frustrating and complex negotiations before the acquisition was completed.[19] A member of the International Bahá'í Council, after the deed was done, said, 'When the full account of its acquisition is written, it will read like a mystery story.'[20]

The donation from Milly Collins came about because she saw the Guardian's light on very late one night. The next morning she asked him why he had been up. Praying, he said. Milly insisted that he share his burden and, after some reluctance, he said that he needed a piece of land for the temple site, but the land had to be purchased within the next few days and he did not have the funds. Milly immediately went to the telegraph office and ordered the sale of mining shares she had in Argentina. Her agent was only able to get half of the value, but the money was promptly sent, arriving just the day before the deadline. Shoghi Effendi was 'exceedingly happy' to be able to buy the land.[21]

One day, Shoghi Effendi took Leroy to the top of Mount Carmel and they walked over the site he wanted for the temple. The Guardian pointed out the exact spot for the centre of the temple, which Leroy marked with a stone (now replaced by a marble obelisk). The Guardian said that this was the spot from which Bahá'u'lláh revealed the Tablet of Carmel in a voice with such 'supreme majesty and power' that 'even the monks, within the walls of the monastery, heard every word uttered by Him. Such was the commotion created on that historical occasion, the earth seemed to shake, while all those present were overpowered by His majesty and wondrous spirit.' Then he told Leroy to 'get busy and buy that land.'[22]

Leroy worked on that task for the next two, very frustrating, years. Ownership was very convoluted. The land had been owned for 900 years by the Carmelites. During the British Mandate, the British bought the land with the understanding that the Carmelites could buy it back in the future. When the British left in 1948, they agreed to sell it back to the Carmelites, but the Carmelites did not have the money to pay for it. Then Israel claimed ownership because of a law stating that all British lands would be transferred to the new government. On top of this mess, the Israeli Defence Ministry requisitioned the land for its strategic value. That was where Leroy started.[23]

Leroy was able to gain the backing of the Israelis for the Bahá'ís, but this resulted in the Carmelites becoming extremely upset. The dispute was resolved when a high Israeli official said that the Carmelites had done nothing to develop the land in nine hundred years and it was now in a highly deteriorated condition. If we give it to the Baháʼís . . . in two or three years we will have beautiful gardens there, it will be an asset to us . . . Ask the Order what they do with their hard currency, do they bring it into Israel? What do the Baháʼís do? They carry on their work with hard currency; they bring us what we need. Who is bringing pilgrims here from everywhere in the world? Whose world center is here?[24]

The next obstacle was the Defence Department. It finally came down to a single obstinate official who demanded to know why the Baháʼís didn't just move their temple. Why did it have to go exactly there? Leroy countered by asking why the Jews didn't move their Wailing Wall or pick another place? The Wailing Wall was a holy place very important to the Jews and couldn't be moved. For the same reason, neither could the future Baháʼí temple.[25]

The next major problem turned out to be the Vatican. The Carmelites had finally agreed to a reasonable purchase price, so their representative went to Rome to have the sale authorized. He came back two months later saying that the property could not be sold to the Baháʼís. Leroy was crushed, but he could not tell the Guardian that he had failed. He went back to the Carmelites and ultimately negotiated a way around this last problem. The land was sold to a third party, Shoghi Effendi's lawyer, Mr Weinshall, and then transferred to the Baháʼís. This roundabout purchase, however, threatened the Baháʼís with a high tax. The Israelis charged a 7 per cent tax on every property sale – and the temple land, which was registered as owned by the British War Office, would technically have to be sold to the Carmelites, then to Mr Weinshall and finally to the Baháʼís. Luckily, the Government agreed to circumvent this by transferring the property directly from the British War Office to Shoghi Effendi.[26]

Shoghi Effendi hadn't waited for the land to be purchased before planning the House of Worship. He considered the Shrines of Baháʼuʼlláh and the Báb and the Mashriqu'l-Adhkár to be a spiritual trinity, and that the Mashriqu'l-Adhkár would be 'as a silent teacher' and 'proclaim the One Faith of Baháʼuʼlláh'.[27] In 1947, Shoghi Effendi had asked Mason Remey to design a Temple and over the next several years he did so, with constant input from the Guardian.[28] At the end of

May 1952, the design was finished and approved by Shoghi Effendi. A wooden model, made in Florence, Italy, from the plans, was unveiled at the Intercontinental Teaching Conference in Chicago in 1953. So, the Guardian had the design completed before he had even begun to acquire the land.[29]

Shoghi Effendi knew that the actual construction of the Mashriqu'l-Adhkár was something for the future, so he decided to place a monument to mark the site. He asked Ugo Giachery what he thought would be appropriate. Ugo responded that the Romans had used columns or obelisks to celebrate important people or events. Shoghi Effendi decided to place an obelisk and Ugo collected designs and costs. Ultimately, a design by Professor Ugo Mazzei, of the company of Enrico Pandolfini, was selected on 29 April 1954. It consisted of

a quadrangular base surmounted by a pyramidal pillar tapering to a point, made of solid blocks of travertine, with a mosaic on one side of the pillar – facing south – bearing the symbol of the 'Greatest Name'; the base is hollow and made of large slates of marble. The total height of the obelisk, from the lower plinth of the base to the tip of the needle, is eleven metres (thirty-six feet).[30]

Though all the pieces of the obelisk were in Haifa by the end of 1954, the monument could not be raised because 'the Israeli Government, for security reasons, would not allow the raising of such a visible structure during the years of the unsettled relations with neighbouring countries'.[31] They were afraid it could be used as an target for artillery. When permission was finally granted in 1971, the obelisk was taken by truck one night to the temple site. On the way, the big flatbed truck was blocked on the narrow road (now called Hatzionut) by two parked cars. The cars were carefully lifted by hand and moved out of the way. Once at the temple site, a crane began hoisting the long pillar when it

suddenly snapped, dropping the obelisk and breaking it into two pieces.

Everyone was stunned and motionless and quite concerned. A Hand of the Cause suggested that they get closer to examine what had happened. Closer examination revealed that the obelisk had a very clean break as if cut by a knife and each piece fell to one side.

29

Looking closer they noticed an inscription: 'Amelia Collins' just at the break point. They realized that the obelisk had been originally made from two pieces joined together with the inscription hidden inside the joint.[32]

No one had known that the inscription was there, so the next day they asked Rúḥíyyih Khánum about it and she shared the story that Shoghi Effendi had had Milly's name put in the obelisk in recognition of her sincere and loving service to the Faith. Shoghi Effendi, however, had revealed the secret to some pilgrims in February 1954. He said the obelisk would have the names of Mason Remey, the architect of the temple, and Milly Collins, the donor of the land, on a scroll buried below it. It is not known whether Mason's name is, indeed, on a scroll beneath the obelisk, but the workers discovered where Shoghi Effendi had placed the name of his first living Hand of the Cause.[33]

Another land acquisition in 1953 was one that bisected the Bahá'í properties and was owned by Covenant-breakers. They had been offered $60,000 for the ground, but wanted more. Unfortunately for them, the government decided that it wanted a large area of Mount Carmel to remain open and green, so it reclassified it as permanently open ground where no one could build. This decimated the commercial value of the property in question and the owners then became eager to sell it at any cost. Leroy negotiated a price of $15,000, a quarter of what they had originally been offered.[34]

1953

FOUR INTERCONTINENTAL TEACHING CONFERENCES

To celebrate the Holy Year and to give impetus to the Ten Year Crusade, Shoghi Effendi called for Intercontinental Teaching Conferences to be held on four continents. The first was to be convened in Africa, by the British National Spiritual Assembly, in Kampala, Uganda, in early spring. This was to be followed by another convened by the United States National Spiritual Assembly in Wilmette during the Riḍván period. The third conference, in Stockholm, Sweden, was held in the summer, convened by the American European Teaching Committee. The final conference was to be convened in New Delhi, India, in the autumn by the National Spiritual Assembly of India.

African Intercontinental Teaching Conference

The first Teaching Conference was held in Kampala, Uganda, from 12 to 18 February. Two hundred and thirty-two Baháʾís attended, of whom about half were Africans representing 30 ethnic groups from 19 countries. The Guardian had specifically invited every African believer to the Conference. Some of them were tempted to stay home for the harvest and others were warned that the whites would sell them for slaves. But ʿAlí Nakhjavání went around telling them that they were being invited by the Guardian himself and would be his guests.[1]

Leroy Ioas represented the Guardian. When he arrived, he was met by Isobel Sabri, an American married to an Egyptian, Hassan Sabri, and pioneering in Dar es Salaam. The Guardian had asked Leroy to greet every African believer at the Conference, embracing every man and shaking the hand of every woman. Shoghi Effendi knew that many would not understand English and greeting every single African believer would show the love he had for each one. Since many women cut their hair very short like the men, Leroy took Isobel as he went down the line to make sure he embraced only the men. The Hands of the Cause who attended were, in addition to Leroy, Horace Holley, Dorothy Baker, 'Alí-Akbar Furútan, Músá Banání, Ṭarázu'lláh Samandarí, Valíyu'lláh Varqá, Shu'á'u'lláh 'Alá'í, Mason Remey and Dhikru'lláh Khádem.[2]

Mildred Mottahedeh wrote:

> From the very moment that the African Baháʼís began to arrive in Kampala and to meet the Baháʼís of other countries, new and dazzling facets of the unity of the human race appeared to all the participants with brilliant clarity. Racial and cultural differences disappeared into a pattern of unity. For all the world to see, here was the example of an emerging world commonwealth . . .
>
> The Conference . . . was also the first time that large groups of Baháʼís from different continents had gathered to work together . . . Midway in the Conference it would have been difficult for an outside observer to guess that the participants had, for the most part, never met until the Conference opened.[3]

As the representative of the Guardian, Leroy brought a picture of the Báb to share with the participants at the Conference. Dorothy Baker was there and Leroy's daughter, Farrukh, asked her if Leroy still used strong language, something he was apparently known for at one time. Dorothy told her that

> I believe we have to revamp our definition of saints. Your father was the Guardian's representative . . . and it was his job to see that the Guardian's gift – a photograph of the portrait of the Báb – was shown at that conference. Leroy met with those in charge and asked what was the appointed time on the agenda. They told him not to worry, that it would be taken care of. The next day nothing was mentioned so Leroy asked them again to make a decision as to when it would be shown. They assured him that it would be taken care of – but it wasn't. Leroy called them together then and told them that the Guardian's gift would be displayed that day at 2 or 3 p.m. and

that if it wasn't he would tell the Guardian they didn't give a damn.[4]

When the Africans finally did see the portrait of the Báb, they displayed great reverence. 'Alí Na<u>kh</u>javání said:

> Africans have a sense of reverence for the sacred that maybe most of us in the West, and in some parts of the East even which have been affected by materialism, we have forgotten . . . But the Africans had this sense of reverence, respect for something which was sacred. So, when they would be passing by the portrait of the Báb, they were not only viewing the face of the beloved, Blessed Báb, but they would bow. Some of them would kneel down. Even one or two of them would prostrate themselves before that portrait. This was something that touched everybody to see the degree to which they had this love, this great reverence for the Báb.[5]

The Guardian dearly loved the native African Bahá'ís, describing them as 'pure-hearted'. This was clearly demonstrated when one of the African Bahá'ís addressed the Conference:

> 'We have received the fire of the love of God. We will take this fire back with us and set the jungles ablaze.' When asked to identify himself, the man refused, saying, 'My name is not important. It is the message of Baha'u'llah that is important.' He was asked again to please state his name for the sake of the conference participants. Again he refused, saying, 'It doesn't matter who I am. There are many of us dedicated to this Cause. I am only acting as a representative.' This kind of purity and selflessness touched our hearts.[6]

Javidukht Khadem, wife of Hand of the Cause <u>Dh</u>ikru'lláh <u>Kh</u>ádem, wrote that both she and her husband were deeply affected by the Conference:

> The palpable love and appreciation conveyed to participants at the Kampala conference through the Guardian's message, combined with Mr. Ioas' acts of tenderness, released a potent spirit that permeated the conference, transformed it, and gave rise to a new level of unity and dedication that welded a diverse representation of races,

nations, and backgrounds into one entity. To see such unity among the races in Africa in 1953 was not only unique. It was miraculous! Words cannot adequately describe our experience, but it seemed as though God, in His great generosity, had permitted us a glimpse of the true meaning of the unity of mankind. For years afterward Mr. Khadem often spoke of that historic conference in Kampala.[7]

Nine Americans attended the Conference, but Shoghi Effendi was disappointed that there were so few.[8] Marguerite Sears did attend and was so inspired that she and her husband, Bill, were soon pioneers to the continent.

Translation was a problem because people came from so many places. The meeting was held in a large tent and the organizers placed chairs in five widely-spaced groups: one for the largest group, the English-speakers, one for the largest African language group, Ateso, one for Persian, and one for Swahili and Luganda speakers. Philip Hainsworth said it was quite an experience listening to the multiple translations:

> when the speaker was using English, immediately he or she paused the translation was loudly made in the four other languages; if it was in Ateso, it then had to be repeated in English and then simultaneously translated into Persian, Luganda and Swahili. Some likened it to bedlam, others to Babel, and Horace Holley opened one of his talks by saying that he had spoken in great halls each with a difficult echo to contend with, but that this was the first time he had experienced the echo coming back to him in four different languages! [9]

A local newspaper reporter covered the conference, but in his article, every time Dorothy Baker had said 'Revelation of God', the reporter wrote 'Revolution of God'. Leroy and 'Alí Nakhjavání went to talk with the editor and clearly explained the fundamentals of the Faith, but the editor wasn't interested and wouldn't change the story. With a final rejection, the editor stood up and extended his hand in obvious dismissal. Leroy, however, did not get up, but said, 'I refuse to accept your hand, and we will not go from here until we are satisfied that you understand our position.' After again explaining the Faith and being rejected one more time, Leroy got up to leave, but demanded that the editor print a letter rebutting the story. The editor agreed. As they left,

Leroy told 'Alí to watch the paper and its editor. He said that 'no individual or institution which deliberately strove to misrepresent the Faith and its growth had ever met with good fortune. This man and his paper would be disgraced.' The original article came out as written and the editor did publish Leroy's rebuttal, but he had added his own offensive remarks to the letter. A few years later, 'Alí again met the editor, but at that time the 'once powerful editor' had a broom and was sweeping the post office.[10]

One African in particular arose to pioneer after the conference. This was 27-year-old Enoch Olinga. Not only did he become a Knight of Bahá'u'lláh when he reached his pioneering post in Cameroon, but five of those he brought into the Faith – Dr Benedict Eballa, Martin Manga, Samuel Njiki, Edward Tabe and David Tanyi – ended up pioneering to goal areas, thus becoming Knights of Bahá'u'lláh themselves.[11]

All-American Intercontinental Teaching Conference

The All-American Intercontinental Teaching Conference was held in Chicago between 2 and 6 May, preceded by the dedication of the Mashriqu'l-Adhkár on 1 and 2 May, exactly 41 years after 'Abdu'l-Bahá laid the foundation stone. On the first day of the dedication, there was a simple consecration service for Bahá'ís only, after which the Bahá'ís enjoyed their great achievement. Valíyu'lláh Varqá, who had been present with 'Abdu'l-Bahá in 1912, chanted the Tablet of Visitation on this occasion. The next day was the public dedication. Over 2,500 people attended, a crowd so large that they had to hold three services. The Psalms and words of the Qur'án were read at the direction of Shoghi Effendi.[12]

For the Teaching Conference, Rúḥíyyih Khánum represented the Guardian and read his message to the Conference, which called it 'the second and, without a doubt, most distinguished of the four Intercontinental Teaching Conferences . . .' There were a dozen Hands of the Cause, including Mason Remey, Músá Banání, Fred Schopflocher, Dorothy Baker, Horace Holley, Milly Collins, 'Alí-Akbar Furútan, Leroy Ioas, Ṭarázu'lláh Samandarí, Valíyu'lláh Varqá, Shu'á'u'lláh 'Alá'í and Dhikru'lláh Khádem along with three members of the Bahá'í International Council. A total of 2,344 Bahá'ís from 33 countries attended.[13]

Shoghi Effendi was greatly concerned with the slow progress of the Faith in America. Leroy Ioas, who had arrived in the Holy Land just a year before, offered to write a letter to the American National Convention that was to be held immediately before the All-American Teaching Conference, to share the Guardian's concerns. The letter was read at the Convention and 'caused quite a stir'. He wrote:

> The reason we are not achieving our goals on the home front is because the friends are concentrating on so many other things that there is little time for teaching. This must be reversed. The friends must be consecrated to teaching so that things of lesser importance fall into their proper place. Consecration is the motive power of the individual in the teaching field. The Guardian said if the friends attain this ideal condition and arise and act and teach, their actions will become a magnet attracting the confirmations of Bahá'u'lláh. Every Bahá'í must teach at all times; it is the source of spiritual life for the giver as well as for the recipient . . . Such teaching work includes living the life of service as well as talking, because one real and genuine act of love and kindness may confirm a soul as readily as his listening or studying the books. The Guardian feels we have more than sufficient materials. What we need is not more materials, not different methods of doing this or that – but doing.[14]

The Guardian's message to the Conference emphasized the importance of what lay ahead and tried to light a fire under the American believers:

> This infinitely precious Faith, despite eleven decades of uninterrupted persecution, on the part of governments and ecclesiastics, involving the martyrdom of its Prophet-Herald, the four banishments and forty-year-long exile suffered by its Founder, the forty years of incarceration inflicted upon its Exemplar, and the sacrifice of no less than twenty thousand of its followers, has succeeded in firmly establishing itself in all the continents of the globe, and is irresistibly forging ahead, with accelerating momentum, bidding fair to envelop, at the close of the coming decade, the whole planet with the radiance of its splendour . . .
>
> So vast, so momentous and challenging a crusade that will, God willing, illuminate the annals of the second epoch of the Formative

Age of the Faith of Bahá'u'lláh, and immortalize the second decade of the second Baha'i century, and the termination of which will mark the closing of the first epoch in the evolution of 'Abdu'l-Bahá's Divine Plan, will, in itself, pave the way for, and constitute the prelude to, the initiation of the laborious and tremendously long process of establishing in the course of subsequent crusades in all the newly opened sovereign states, dependencies and islands of the planet, as well as in all the remaining territories of the globe, the framework of the Administrative Order of the Faith, with all its attendant agencies, and of eventually erecting in these territories still more pillars to share in sustaining the weight and in broadening the foundation of the Universal House of Justice . . .[15]

All Bahá'ís wanted to do what the Guardian asked, but according to delegate John Allen who would became a Knight of Bahá'u'lláh to Swaziland, they 'are trying to make the job too difficult . . . they haven't gotten themselves to the point where they are willing to devote their time to their neighbors and friends but are thinking of grandiose plans for the multitudes, and from such plans few Bahá'ís result.'[16]

In an effort to promote pioneering, Dorothy Baker repeated a story Shoghi Effendi had told her when she was on pilgrimage, about 'Alí Nakhjavání. Shoghi Effendi

spoke of the fact that this intrepid youth had gone into the jungles of Africa . . . and, assisted by Philip Hainsworth of Britain, they lived with the Teso people; they ate the food of the Teso people; they slept on straw mats or leaves, or whatever it is that you sleep on among the Teso people. The rain falls on your head and salamanders drop in your tea, if there is tea. And they stayed! And they did not say, 'Conditions do not warrant it because these people eat herbs and things that would kill us.' They stayed! Is there an 'Alí Nakhjavání, then, in America? At the present, no. I mean, up to the present. Is there a Philip Hainsworth! Up to the present, no. . . .[17]

Dorothy then talked about the 'dark skinned people' who would have an 'upsurge that is both spiritual and social'; that 'all the world's prejudiced forces will not hold it back'. She passed on the Guardian's words that the dark skinned people are really rising to the top – a cream that has latent gifts only to be brought out by Divine bounties. Where do the Bahá'ís stand on this? Again and again he pointed out that the Bahá'ís must be in the vanguard of finding them and giving them the base . . .

. . . My sights were lifted immeasurably and I saw the vistas of these social repercussions coming because of our spiritual negligence through the years, and I saw the Indian tribes dotted about this continent unredeemed, waiting – waiting for an 'Alí Nakhjavání. Are the African friends going to have to come and awaken us for the dark skinned races in our midst?[18]

There were four pioneering tables set up and they were crowded with people. Since North America was the recipient of 'Abdu'l-Bahá's *Tablets of the Divine Plan* and held so highly by Shoghi Effendi as the country which would establish the Bahá'í Administrative Order, he expected great things from them. By the time the Conference was over, 495 people had volunteered to pioneer. But the enthusiasm of the Conference struggled afterwards in the face of the difficulties of daily life. To Shoghi Effendi's later dismay, only 200 of those who pledged to pioneer finally fulfilled their pledge and actually pioneered. He had hoped 3,000 would arise and move.[19] It was something that he raised with almost all American pilgrims until his death.

Some people arose immediately. Five members of the American National Spiritual Assembly set the example by resigning from the Assembly and pioneering to goal areas. Elsie Austin went to Morocco, Kenneth Christian moved to Southern Rhodesia, Mamie Seto pioneered to Hong Kong, and Matthew Bullock went to the Dutch West Indies. Dorothy Baker, the Hand of the Cause, also arose and was returning from a lengthy teaching trip in India en route to pioneer in Grenada when her plane exploded over the Mediterranean.[20] Cora Oliver, a member of the National Assembly for Central America, Mexico and the Antilles, resigned and pioneered to British Honduras while Katharine Meyer, serving on the National Assembly for the Leeward, Windward and Virgin Islands, resigned her post to pioneer to the Margarita Islands.

Two young new Bahá'ís, Ben Guhrke and Les Marcus, were asked to assist Hand of the Cause Mason Remey in setting up his model of the proposed Mashriqu'l-Adhkár for Mount Carmel. Initially overjoyed at the prospect, afterwards they 'came away with grave misgivings as to the appointment of such a personality as a Hand of the Cause . . . we discussed, analysed and soul-searched the issue to finally conclude that the Guardian had his reasons . . .' It was an early indication of the path the future breaker of the Covenant was treading.[21]

In June, after attending the All-American Conference, Hand of the Cause Fred Schopflocher went to visit and inspire the Bahá'ís in western Canada. The next month he fell ill and passed away on 27 July. Jalál Kházeh was elevated to the rank of Hand of the Cause in December to replace him.[22] The telegram naming Mr Kházeh as a Hand arrived in Tehran while he was in a remote village looking for a certain Bahá'í's address, but had

> no luck finding it and it would be 24 hours before another bus would come along. Exhausted, he sat on his suitcase and said a silent prayer to the Guardian saying, 'If you want me to see him, you find him.' A stranger came upon him and asked what he was doing. He explained who he was looking for and the man said that was his neighbor, and led him right to the door. When he returned to Tehran, there was a cable awaiting him from the Guardian, appointing him a Hand of the Cause. He noted the time the message was sent and calculated it was sent at the same time he had given up on finding the person he was looking for, and mentally turned the search over to the Guardian.[23]

European Intercontinental Teaching Conference

Three hundred and seventy-seven Bahá'ís from 30 countries gathered in Stockholm, Sweden, from 21 to 26 July. Those attending as Bahá'ís included a descendant of Násiri'd-Dín Sháh and a descendant of Imám Jum'ih, whose father's uncle was the Son of the Wolf, the recipient of a powerfully denunciatory epistle from Bahá'u'lláh. Fourteen Hands of the Cause, including Ugo Giachery, Músá Banání, Horace Holley, Shu'á 'u'lláh 'Alá'í, George Townshend, Dhikru'lláh Khádem, Tarázu'lláh Samandarí, 'Alí-Akbar Furútan, Hermann Grossmann, Amelia Collins, Dorothy Baker, Mason Remey, Adelbert Mühlschlegel and Valíyu'lláh Varqá, were also there. Seven hundred people attended a public meeting held on the first night of the Conference.[24]

The Guardian had asked Hand of the Cause Ugo Giachery to present his greetings to the friends. Dr Giachery unveiled a portrait of the Báb for the participants to view and also appealed to the Bahá'ís to support the Funds to buy land for the proposed House of Worship in Frankfurt.[25] When he unveiled the portrait of the Báb, one of the Afnán recited the Tablet of Aḥmad, then the believers passed by. It took two and a half hours for the Bahá'ís to reverently experience seeing the Báb's visage.[26]

Most of the Conference was in English, but Hand of the Cause Hermann Grossmann surprised everyone:

> The dominant language of that conference was English. Several of the Hands of the Cause addressed the friends. I remember Dr Grossmann walking to the podium; his very walk, his bearing reflected his personality, his humility and love for every one of us. And then Dr Grossmann addressed the friends. He did not speak in English. Dr Grossmann spoke in Spanish. He addressed the minority among us, touching the hearts of the Spanish friends and every heart in the gathering, as his voice rang through the auditorium. Although I did not speak Spanish, I understood the language of his heart. Dr Grossmann's loving heart knew the needs and longings of every soul he encountered.[27]

On the Friday afternoon of the Conference, a film was shown of the superstructure of the Shrine of the Báb, which was nearing completion. Ugo Giachery wrote to Leroy Ioas: 'We saw the beautiful motion pictures of Haifa and 'Akká, and I cannot believe my eyes.'[28]

When the goals of the Ten Year Crusade were presented to the Conference, the response was powerful. Sixty-three people declared themselves ready to pioneer. By the end of the conference, every one of the pioneering goals had been filled. At one point, when Dorothy Baker reported that all goals assigned to the United States had been filled except for Andorra, a believer immediately volunteered to go. Ugo Giachery then announced that the Italo-Swiss National Spiritual Assembly had filled all its goals with the exception of Liechtenstein and San Marino, but, again, volunteers immediately stepped forward. John Ferraby said that there were pioneers for all the goal areas of the National Spiritual Assembly of the British Isles, but that funds were lacking. A believer quickly offered the funds for pioneers to the Channel, Hebrides and Orkney Islands, and Sweden offered to send a pioneer to the Faroe Islands. The German National Assembly announced that all of its goals were filled.[29]

After the Conference, Shoghi Effendi requested that the Persian Hands travel through Europe encouraging the friends. Mr Faizi went to Germany, Spain, France, Portugal and Egypt.[30] Dorothy Baker went to Finland.[31]

Asian Intercontinental Teaching Conference

The last of the great Intercontinental Teaching Conferences was held in New Delhi, India, from 7 to 15 October and was attended by 489 Bahá'ís from 31 countries. Twelve Hands of the Cause also attended: Mason Remey, Horace Holley, Ugo Giachery, Dorothy Baker, Amelia Collins, 'Alí-Akbar Furútan, Clara Dunn, Músá Banání, Dhikru'lláh Khádem, Tarázu'lláh Samandarí, Shu'á'u'lláh 'Alá'í and Valíyu'lláh Varqá.[32] The organizers of the Conference were invited by India's President, Rajendra Prasad, the Prime Minister, Jawaharlal Nehru, and members of his Cabinet, to meet with them. The President told the group that he admired the Bahá'í Faith and assured them of his support for their aims.[33]

The Guardian stressed the importance of this Conference in a letter to the National Assembly of India dated 30 June 1952:

> The Guardian attaches the greatest possible importance to the forth-coming Inter-continental Conference to be held during the Holy Year in New Delhi; as the National Assemblies of Persia, United States, Canada, Central and South America, Iraq, Australia and New Zealand, as well as your own body, are to send representatives to it, it will, through having eight N.S.A.s pooling their thoughts and suggestions, be, no doubt, the most important of the four Inter-continental Conferences to be held. Also, aside from the numerical importance of the participating bodies, the vast field their plans must embrace is truly awe-inspiring. In view of this he feels that the members of your Assembly have very heavy responsibilities to discharge during the coming months, and that all petty details and misunderstandings must be put aside, once and for all, in order to

ensure a brilliant success – a success, whose repercussions must be felt during ten years of Baha'i history between this coming great Jubilee and the Most Great Jubilee which will take place in 1963.[34]

A number of youth were given the task of meeting speakers from foreign countries. One of the youth was to collect a speaker coming from Bahrain, and thinking he would not speak English very well, spoke to him in very simple English when he arrived. To her embarrassment, she later saw the same person 'skillfully translating the Persian talks into English'.[35]

This was Hand of the Cause Mr Faizi, who was the chief translator at the Conference and after the sessions was surrounded by people, including those who were not Bahá'ís, wanting to ask questions. He was sometimes so engaged until midnight. This left him so exhausted that on the last day of the Conference, he fainted when he stood up to chant a prayer.[36]

One of the participants at the Conference described Dorothy Baker when Dorothy gave her presentation:

> . . . we faced the speaker's stand in that makeshift auditorium with its folding chairs, whirring fans, dampened India prints draped to cool the large circus-sized tent that held us. She [Dorothy] was . . . almost motionless, her gaze directed to her left, slightly past the speakers, with no flicker of emotion to show she was listening. I wondered at the time if she was trying to avoid showing any evidence of pain, since her fingers were folded under, as though clenched, so much of the time, or because her face was so serene, if she were just communing with the Abhá Kingdom. But the moment she rose to address us she showed complete awareness of all that had been said during the preceding consultation, and her poise, her encompassing love, her vivid speech, radiated vitality to us.[37]

To showcase Indian culture, there was a programme one evening of Indian dancing and music. On another day, ten forty-seater buses took participants on a sightseeing trip to historical places in the area.[38]

During the course of the Conference, 74 people offered to fill the pioneering goals. Twenty-five of those left immediately after the Conference.[39] Members of National Spiritual Assemblies set an example of arising to serve by pioneering. From the National Assembly of Australia and New Zealand, six members resigned and set out to fill Shoghi Effendi's goal areas. These included Gertrude and Alvin Blum (Solomon Islands), Stanley Bolton (Tonga), Dulcie Dive (Cook Islands), Gretta Lamprill (Society Islands) and Lilian Wyss (Samoa). Kamil 'Abbás, from the National Assembly of Iraq, and 'Abdu'l Rahman Zarqani, from the National Assembly of India, both pioneered to the Seychelles.[40]

In addition, US$45,000 was contributed for the purchase of Temple sites in New Delhi, Baghdad and Sydney, and a US$10,000 pioneering fund was raised. As in the other Conferences, the Bahá'ís had the opportunity to view the portrait of the Báb. Hand of the Cause 'Alí-Akbar Furútan wrote that 'no one could resist the flood of emotions which overcame him. The scene was enough to transport anyone to the realms of the spirit'. There were also events for those who were not Bahá'ís, including one at the Hotel Imperial which was attended by about a thousand interested people.[41]

After the Conference, Hand of the Cause Mr Furútan, along with Clara Dunn and Abu'l-Qásim Faizi, made a 51-day teaching trip through Ceylon, Australia and New Zealand[42] while Dorothy Baker, Mason Remey and Horace Holley visited many parts of India to teach and encourage the Bahá'ís. Dorothy ended up spending three months travel teaching in the country. The Guardian also asked Ugo Giachery to go to Persia, Valíyu'lláh Varqá and Shu'á'u'lláh 'Alá'í to go to Iraq, Dhikru'lláh Khádem to Malaya and Japan and Tarázu'lláh Samandarí and Músá Banání to the Arabian Peninsula.[43] The Hands were busy people.

1953

PILGRIMS, VISITORS AND PIONEERS

Visitors had been coming to Haifa to meet Shoghi Effendi since the inception of the Guardianship and, just because the Bahá'í world was on the cusp of a momentous decade, that didn't change.

Dorothy Baker, Elsie Austin and Matthew Bullock

In February 1953, a group of pilgrims arrived, each destined for great things in the future. The group included Dorothy Baker, Elsie Austin and Matthew Bullock, and all were on their way to the Intercontinental Teaching Conference in Kampala.

Hand of the Cause Dorothy Baker had been trying to go on pilgrimage for ten years, but something had always seemed to get in the way. Finally, on 2 February, she reached Haifa. Dorothy took few notes while on pilgrimage, but was obviously taken with a talk the Guardian gave on the connection between the material and spiritual worlds:

> There is a very close connection between the souls beyond and souls here. This connection depends upon certain difficult conditions – concentration, purity of heart, purity of motive. It will be possible to communicate, but do not attempt to experiment now.
>
> One can even smell the presence of these souls. The Master said, 'I can smell the spirit and the fragrance of the writer from this letter, when I opened it.'
>
> The Supreme Concourse are beings of whom we have no conception, but it includes souls of people who have been very devoted and other beings as well of whom we are not aware. The higher the

position, the greater the influence. They rush to the assistance of the sincere servants who arise now.

We need to develop greater concentration and purity in prayer. Prayer and action attract the assistance.

God assures each one that every act is a magnet for the Supreme Concourse.

The Master said . . . 'As to the question that the holy and spiritual souls influence, help and guide the creatures after they have cast off their elemental mold, this is an established truth of the Bahá'ís.'[1]

Rúḥíyyih Khánum remembered Dorothy's last night:

> I remember going up to her bedroom the night before she was to leave and telling her how distressed I was that after waiting so many years to come on the pilgrimage, she only had seven nights (due to airplane connections) . . . She said that she felt that when people came here they were like a dry sponge and that when they had the experience of the pilgrimage – the Shrines, the Guardian – in an instant they were filled like a sponge being plunged into water and that very little more could be added . . .[2]

After leaving Haifa, Dorothy attended the Intercontinental Teaching Conferences in Kampala, Stockholm, Chicago and New Delhi, as well as the US National Convention at which she was elected to the National Spiritual Assembly. Despite her election, by August she and her husband, Frank, had decided to pioneer to Grenada to answer the Guardian's call.[3] But first, she went as a Hand of the Cause to the New Delhi conference in October. At its conclusion, Shoghi Effendi asked the Hands of the Cause present at the Conference to 'disperse . . . to teach for one or two months in Asia, Africa and Australia, in order to establish close contact with the respective National Assemblies, and assist the local assemblies to attain the goals of the Ten Year Plan.'[4] Dorothy, Horace Holley and Mason Remey were given the task of helping with teaching activities in India and Pakistan.[5] After that month, Dorothy was asked by the Guardian to stay for yet another month.[6] In early January 1954, her suitcase with everything she owned was stolen, then, on 9 January, she gave her last talk where she called for pioneers. Twenty people answered her call and, having nothing else, she told them that 'I have nothing to give you as a gift. All I can offer you is my life.'[7] That night she boarded a BOAC flight for Rome on her favourite plane, the new Comet, and flew to Beirut and Rome. Shortly after leaving Rome for London, the plane exploded. A few days later, a purse was found containing a Bahá'í pamphlet. Dorothy had taught the Faith to the end.[8] Twenty years earlier, Dorothy had told her family that 'If I could really have my choice, I would be buried at sea. And if I could choose the sea, then it would be the Mediterranean whose waves will lap eternally on the shores of 'Akká.' Her wish had been granted.[9]

Elsie Austin, an African-American and a future Knight of Bahá'u'lláh, was greatly impressed by Shoghi Effendi. Of their first meeting, she wrote:

> I think we were all in awe because the beloved Guardian was very warm and gracious. I remember that he stood at the entrance of the dining room . . . and shook each one of us by the hand and bid us welcome. Then he embraced the men and we were all just too filled with awe and with love and devotion to say anything. The Guardian had a tremendous atmosphere of majesty and love about him and a very wonderful eye full of light . . .[10]

All the pilgrims wanted to remember every word uttered by Shoghi Effendi and Elsie noted that they would 'busily scribble in our note-books all the wonderful things that he said. Then we would each read each other's diaries because some of the friends took shorthand and we wanted to make sure that we hadn't missed a precious word of what he said to us.'

Matthew Bullock, another African-American member of the US National Assembly and also a future Knight of Bahá'u'lláh, found that Shoghi Effendi had a profound impact on him: 'The Guardian has cleared up many things for me. My visit to him and to the Holy Shrines are experiences beyond words. I don't think I will ever be able to express what it meant to me; nor do I think that any Bahá'í is the same after being with the Guardian. I wish every Bahá'í could have the bounty which has been mine.'[11] One night, Matthew, who was from a 'very politically-oriented background', asked Shoghi Effendi why a Bahá'í could not be involved with a political party and 'help it achieve idealism' from inside. The Guardian 'emphatically said no and he went on to say that the political machine was so corrupt and so fastened to its current of corruption that the presence of one or two enlightened and good-hearted souls would have no effect upon it'.[12]

Marcus Bach

Another of the first visitors of that portentous year was Marcus Bach, who came seeking spiritual illumination. He came to Haifa on Friday the 13th, in either February or March, specifically to meet Shoghi Effendi. Marcus was on a spiritual search which began when he realized that Christianity had been broken into many sects. He had concluded that 'When these religious varieties were sifted down, it was apparent that an interpretation of Him [Christ] or an opinion about Him was often the sole reason for schism and strife. One group insisted that He was this and another claimed He was that.'[13] So he went to interview a number of people, including Helen Keller, Pope Pius XII, Albert Schweitzer and Shoghi Effendi.

Marcus crossed from Jordan into Israel and went to Akka where he first visited the Most Great Prison and wondered about Bahá'u'lláh and 'His successor', the Guardian. Marcus had met a number of Bahá'ís in various countries and they had all said very complimentary things about the leader of Bahá'u'lláh's Faith, Shoghi Effendi. After visiting the prison, he went to Bahjí, asking to see the Mansion. A young Bahá'í took him in to Bahá'u'lláh's room where the Bahá'ís prayed and Marcus wondered that in

every country, no matter how torn by war, or how divided by man hating man, voices were being raised to heaven by way of prophets and messiahs. In caves and cathedrals, in tombs and temples, these everlasting chants were going on and just how or when this cacophony concerning the Fatherhood of God could ever be transposed into the harmony of the Brotherhood of Man was a mystery. It was a mystery for me, but not for the Baha'is.[14]

His guide was surprised to learn that Marcus had an upcoming interview with Shoghi Effendi, but he sent him back to Akka saying of the Guardian that 'He writes as Baha'u'llah writes, to draw men to God. He plans as Abdul Baha planned, for world citizenship. He works so that God's Kingdom should come on earth as it is in heaven.'[15] With that preparation, Marcus went to Haifa to meet this much talked-about man.

Marcus was welcomed at the Pilgrim House by Jessie Revell who told him, 'After you have seen the Guardian you will never be the same.' Marcus was impressed by the great variety of Bahá'ís he had met:

> Whatever kind of man he was, he had drawn together into one procession many races, creeds, and minds. Great people and little people were marching with him toward the citadel of a united world. Rich and poor were finding a common ground, in senti-ment, at least. Strong and weak were joining hands and hearts in an idea. His Eminence was leading them onward to what he called a 'world-girding mission' and they knew what he meant.[16]

While he talked with Jessie, 'a trim, attractive woman entered, sud-denly and unannounced. She had a dog on a leash, a fur stole around her neck, and she walked like a Persian queen.' The woman sat down near Marcus and most directly asked, 'So. Tell me about yourself. You are interested in religions. What have you found in all this searching?' Marcus was quite surprised to be asked for his views, having expected to be a listener. After explaining his search, the woman told him that 'Each faith draws upon the inner well of experience. In each there is something beautiful and disciplined and prophetic. The great religions are the leaves of the same tree. The thinking person can and must find harmony among all true prophets and unity in all true scriptures.' As they talked, Marcus kept expecting to be told about the Bahá'í Faith, but the woman continued to talk about universal themes saying, 'You know, a believer in the Unity of God must recognize in every created thing the evidence of the revelation of God.' Finally, Marcus asked, 'I hope I'm not being too inquisitive, but with whom do I have the honor of visiting?' The woman replied simply that 'my people were Baha'is and a few years ago it was my great privilege to become the wife of the Guardian'. It was in this way that Marcus Bach met Rúḥíyyih Khánum.[17]

That evening, Marcus dined with Rúḥíyyih Khánum and Lotful-lah Hakím. During their conversation about the Bahá'í Faith, Marcus realized that though 'Most of my Protestant and Catholic friends considered it a glorified fraternal order with a utopian dream about making the whole world one native land, here in the heart of Haifa, at this pleasant table, I came to realize that the religion of Baha'u'llah is interested in an inner personal development as well as in a global plan, and I concluded that the latter would be unrealizable unless the former were first attained.' At 9 p.m., Rúhíyyih Khánum took Marcus to the House of the Master to meet the Guardian. Sitting and waiting, questions flooded his mind: 'Why . . . accept a new prophet when we have not yet lived the principles and teachings of the old? . . . Would not every organized religious movement see in Baha'u'llah a threat [to] its own messiah, rather than a blessing to all mankind?' [18] Then a man entered the room:

> I saw coming through the adjoining room a small, dark-com-plexioned man, dressed in Western attire but wearing a fez. His clean-shaven face and slender figure registered indomitable strength. He walked with head up as though an entourage of the faithful might be following him. He strode in, bowed to me with an almost imperceptible nod, and held out his hand . . .
>
> The expression of his dark eyes . . . gave a hint of inner judge-ment based not on what was said but, rather, on what was sensed. He was self-possessed, self-sufficient, purposeful. I had been told he was a man of fifty-seven, but, judging from his unlined, youth-ful face, he might have been only forty. And though I stood head and shoulders above him, I felt diminutive. I envied him the sense of security and holy mission in life that filled his whole soul with confidence, beyond doubt and beyond question.
>
> He looked at me steadily for a moment as if to determine whether I was truly a pilgrim or whether I had dropped around for sensational information about what I might consider the rise and romance of another sect . . .
>
> Quietly he took me at once into the heart of the Baha'i Cause and though I had heard much of this before from members of the faith, it was a new experience for me to meet a religious leader who was not defending one Book, but, rather, Books; who had no argu-ment for one Messiah, but for Messiahs; who was not pointing out one way, but ways to God . . .
>
> This, then was the man I had come to see, a beardless prophet,

one who might have been a successful businessman, artist, or teacher; an intense and vital man, whose all-seeing eyes always read my thoughts in advance, whose sharp mind had a ready answer the moment my questions were asked . . .

He spoke . . . in words tinged with poetry and power. He spoke in melodious, faultless English, with a firm and staunch authority as if what he had to say was said by divine right. He blended the vast run of world events for the past century into the hub of the 1863 proclamation that Baha'u'llah had come to do God's work and will . . .

. . . He had no other purpose than to see his mission accomplished. Build the faith! Resist the enemies of the Cause! Trust in God! The divan on which he sat might have been a throne; his words, the words of a king.

But the thing that struck me most as our meeting progressed was his unquestioned devotion to the Galilean. He was fully as faithful to Jesus as he was to Baha'u'llah. Any basis for understanding the Baha'i concept would have to start with the premise that Shoghi Effendi was a thorough-going Christian in the philosophical, if not the theological sense . . .

To the Guardian the relationship between Jesus and Baha'u'llah was consistently unvarying. The world, he recalled, had rejected Christ. It was again seeking to reject the Splendor of God. But as the Prophet of Nazareth seized and conquered the minds of men, so the Prophet of Teheran was conquering, too . . .[19]

As Marcus walked away that night, he realized that his notebook had stayed in his pocket during the whole interview: 'It might have helped me to remember his words, but not his faith. That was something to be felt and cherished. His awareness of God was paramount. With him all is God's will and the Prophets have revealed it'.[20]

Marguerite Sears

With the initiation of the Ten Year Crusade, Shoghi Effendi's relationship with pilgrims took on a notable change. Where he had previously been full of encouragement, praise and gentle guidance, some Western pilgrims began experiencing something different. For 30 years, the

Guardian had been carefully preparing the Bahá'í world for this massive Crusade. He had nurtured immature institutions and individuals to maturity. Now, he began to expect them to act like mature assemblies and grown-up Bahá'ís. Those who responded to his historic call received abundant praise and encouragement. Those who didn't were told in no uncertain terms what lay ahead and what he, the Guardian, expected of them.

Marguerite Sears (the wife of future Hand of the Cause William Sears), Ben Levy, a German who was in Haifa between 9 and 16 March, Ludmila von Sombeck and Amelia Bowman had their pilgrimages as the Teaching Conferences began. Marguerite came away from the African Teaching Conference in Kampala greatly affected by her experience.[21] It was Marguerite, the American, who returned home with notes about America's failure to arise. To them all, Shoghi Effendi praised the example of Marion Jack, the efforts of the German Bahá'ís, and the Bahá'ís in the Pacific. He said that if there were more than fifteen Bahá'ís in a community, some must disperse. He cautioned the pilgrims about trying to teach officials or outstanding people because they tended to keep their old ties and Bahá'ís 'must not sacrifice the principles of the Cause for popularity'. Instead, the Bahá'ís should teach people with spiritual capacity. Bahá'ís, he emphasized, must avoid all involvement with politics – anything that affects the policy of a nation.[22]

The Guardian said:

There are two plans operating in the world. 1. The Major plan or God's plan. It is mysterious and we have nothing to do with it. 2. The Minor plan or the World Crusade of the next ten years, about which we have everything to do. God's plan involves disturbances. People must be shaken, aroused, their eyes opened in order to acquire the capacity to accept the Faith.

America was given the privilege of being the Chief executors of the Divine plan. America now stands 5th in rank in service to the Faith. The English are the best organizers in the Bahá'í World, the Americans, the best administrators . . .

The Americans and the Persians are too emotional. They are both alike in this respect. They are not impersonal enough, not objective in their thinking. They think of themselves or people first and the Cause second or last. The Cause must come first . . . Americans spend too much money on luxuries, the Persians spend too much money on hospitality. . .²³

Americans are too concerned with their homes, trivialities, business. These things keep them back like a dead weight, they put these things first and Africa and the Faith last. Africa should have been the first concern of every American believer. The distinguished American Bahá'ís should have immediately arisen – regardless of anything else – spontaneously. America didn't arise at all so God inspired the Persians and the British . . .²⁴

Marion Jack typifies the true spirit the pioneer should have. We must follow her example. Marion Jack went from Canada to Bulgaria . . . When the war broke out I wrote her urging her to go to Switzerland or to come to Haifa. She begged to stay where she was . . . The Canadians must be very proud of her. Even the Oriental believers have not risen to this height of detachment. She stayed in Bulgaria during the war. The Americans took the first boat home . . .

New York and Chicago are the most dangerous places in the world. The skyscrapers of which Americans are so proud will fall like houses of cards . . .

. . . 'Abdu'l-Bahá was very disappointed in America. He wrote and spoke there of the dangers of materialism and He went unheeded, and they are still unheeding.²⁵

Finishing this powerful and sobering talk, the Guardian walked to the door where he stopped and turned, saying 'Don't discourage them.' When he had gone, Rúḥíyyih Khánum turned to the pilgrims and said of the Americans, 'They have to face facts, they have to grow up. The Guardian is trying to talk to them as adults now, they can't be coddled as children.'²⁶

America took great pride in 'Abdu'l-Bahá's journey through its cities in 1912, but the Universal House of Justice comments on the lack of response in Western countries to His message:

However much one may rejoice in the praise poured on the Master from every quarter, the immediate results of His efforts represented yet another immense moral failure on the part of a considerable portion of humankind and of its leadership. The message that had been suppressed in the East was essentially ignored by a Western world . . .[27]

Future Hand of the Cause Bill Sears and his wife, Marguerite, pioneered to Africa within months of the Conferences. Not everyone who pioneered during the Ten Year Crusade became Knights of Bahá'u'lláh. For some, service was more important than a title. Bill and Marguerite listened to Rúḥíyyih Khánum tell the participants at the All-American Intercontinental Teaching Conference to 'Go to Africa' and felt that she was speaking to them. They immediately sent a cable to Shoghi Effendi offering their services and asking where to go. The reply read, simply, 'Johannesburg'. So, less than two months after the Conference, Bill, Marguerite and their 16-year-old son, Michael, boarded a ship bound for Africa.[28]

The first step toward pioneering was for Bill to tell his boss. Bill had a popular sports radio show called *In the Park*, and the station manager told him that 56 people depended on the show for their jobs, plus a company had a contract to sponsor the show that could not be broken. Surprised at this immediate roadblock, Bill and Marguerite did the only thing they could think of – they turned to prayer. They decided to say the Tablet of Aḥmad and other prayers for 19 days. If things hadn't changed by then, they wouldn't go. Near the end of the 19 days, Bill's boss called and said that the sponsor for Bill's show was suffering from a debilitating labour strike and had been forced to cancel its contract. The Sears were free to go.[29]

Only a few days after arriving in Johannesburg, South Africa, Bill suffered a heart attack which forced them to stay in one of the most expensive hotels in the city, and the Sears watched their funds, which they had hoped would last for two years, rapidly shrink. While waiting for Bill to recuperate, they examined their new home and were aghast. With apartheid, they found that a white could not even teach his cook to be a better cook because it might encourage blacks to try to improve themselves. How could they teach the Africans? They soon discovered that the restrictions were greatly reduced on farms, so they decided to look for a farm to buy.[30]

To get their permanent visas for South Africa, the Sears first had to go to Kenya. On their way, they stopped in Uganda and conducted the first Bahá'í school programme held below the Sahara, in the village of Tilling, the home of future Hand of the Cause Enoch Olinga. A local family moved in with a neighbour so that the Sears could stay in their home. Since these were Americans and used to luxury, the host family decided to fill in the one-hole outhouse and make a proper toilet. The new one consisted of a single shed which had three holes, one for each of the visitors. Water came from the river about a mile away and one day Michael decided to help bring up water. Michael imitated the women who usually did the work, but unlike the women, he ended up soaked from water splashing out of the container on his head.[31]

When they finally went to Kenya for their visas, it took just 19 days, the quickest visas the local people had ever known about. The family returned to Johannesburg and found a farm on the outskirts of the city. Most of their money had gone to the hotel during Bill's illness, so they could not afford it. But another miracle happened. Bill Smits, a Hawaiian Bahá'í, had saved $2,500 to go pioneering, but found himself drafted into the army so could not go. Smits contacted Larry Hautz, who was on pilgrimage at that time, requesting that he ask Shoghi Effendi what to do with the money. The Guardian said, 'Give it to Bill Sears.' With that money, the Sears bought the farm which became known simply as 'The Farm'.[32]

Bahá'í classes with the native Africans were held in their house, though that could have gotten them into a lot of trouble. To avoid that trouble, the African students always came wearing work clothes, and rakes, hoes and dusters were placed by every door in the house. The idea was that if anyone unexpected arrived, the students would grab a tool and look busy. The Faith grew rapidly.[33]

In October 1957, Bill was appointed a Hand of the Cause by Shoghi Effendi.

Ella Bailey

Another pioneer who, though she did not win the accolade of Knight of Bahá'u'lláh, yet received the highest praise from Shoghi Effendi, was Ella Bailey. When she heard of the Ten Year Crusade, she had a tremendous desire to arise and serve – her 88 years and frail health notwithstanding. Ella had met 'Abdu'l-Bahá when He was in America and had always striven to serve the Cause to the best of her ability, even though restricted by a variety of ailments and the crippling pain from having had polio as a child. Ella knew that she would be a great liability if she pioneered, but that didn't stop her hoping. When Bahia and Robert Gulick decided to pioneer to Tripoli, they asked Ella to go with them. Ella travelled from California to New York in July 1953. While in New York, Ella had a fall and was confined to bed for a time, under strict orders not to be bothered. A Hand of the Cause, though, was an exception and Dhikru'lláh Khádem paid her a visit. When he asked about her health, she replied, 'I will be all right. I just pray that God will give me enough time to reach Africa. Did you hear the comment that the old people can take their bones and bury them in the goal areas? This is my most cherished desire.'[34]

Ella managed to reach Tripoli on 20 July, travelling with an oxygen mask. On 26 August, she passed on to the Abhá Kingdom and achieved her desire. Shoghi Effendi confirmed Ella's high station:

> The irresistibly unfolding Crusade has been sanctified by the death of heroic, eighty-eight year old Ella Bailey, elevating her to the rank of the martyrs of the Faith, shedding further luster on the American Bahá'í Community and consecrating the soil of the fast-awakening African continent.[35]

William Foster and the Collins Gate

The large gate which forms the entrance to the Shrine of Bahá'u'lláh is called the Collins Gate, after Hand of the Cause Amelia (Milly) Collins. It had its origins in Milly's childhood love of gates and her open-hearted financial contributions to the Faith. As a child, Milly had built little gates for her dollhouses. When she and her husband, Thomas, built a house in New England, he asked her about a gate, but at that time she didn't want to spend the money. After Thomas's death, Milly was appointed to the first International Bahá'í Council and moved to Haifa, where she was constantly making financial contributions. Many times when making a contribution, she would ask Shoghi Effendi to use it for something he himself desired. He always replied that his wants were very few. Then one day, Milly received a letter from Shoghi Effendi with a photograph of a 'gigantic and very beautiful gate', along with a note asking how she liked it. It had been purchased, he added, with funds she had contributed. Milly replied that it was 'Exceedingly beautiful'.[36]

When William (Bill) Foster, a pioneer in Africa, came on pilgrimage following the Kampala Conference, he had planned only on staying for the usual nine days. One night at the Western Pilgrim House, however, Bill asked Shoghi Effendi if he could do some service for him. Since Bill was a building contractor, the Guardian gave him the special task of erecting Milly's gate.[37] In a letter to his wife, Bill wrote:

> Been using [William Sutherland] Maxwell's office to make drawings and sketches, one pertaining to the dome of the Shrine of the Báb. My main work here is to erect two gates at Bahjí, one 12 x 18 ft. and the Collins main gate 36 x 16 ft., also four sets of marble steps adjoining the Holy Precincts of the Shrine at Bahjí.[38]

For the next two months, Bill delighted in serving Shoghi Effendi and Milly got her gate.

Bill Foster was one of only two black American Bahá'ís who arose and pioneered to Africa when the Guardian called for the black Bahá'ís to arise and go there. The first was a young woman from Cleveland, Ethel Stevens, who went to Kumasi in the Gold Coast (now part of Ghana) and taught school. After a year, she was forced to return home 'because her husband was not a Bahá'í and was at that time not entirely hospitable to the demands which the Faith made of her'. Bill Foster pioneered to Liberia in January 1952 and had a very difficult time, but, even so, by the following November, there were 26 believers there.[39] Two years later, he was allowed to resettle in Casablanca, Morocco. Bill was elected to the Regional Spiritual Assembly of North and West Africa in 1956. He and his family remained in Morocco until 1963 when the family returned to Liberia. The Foster family returned to America in 1967.[40]

First native African Bahá'í pioneers

The first native African to accept the Faith of Bahá'u'lláh became a Bahá'í before the Ten Year Crusade. This was Denis Dudley Smith Kutendele, who was working as a clerk. Músá Banání and Jalál Nakhjavání, along with their families, arrived in Dar es Salaam, Tanganyika, in June 1951. Soon afterwards, Jalál introduced the Faith to Denis Dudley Smith, and, when he accepted the Faith in July, he became the first native African believer.[41] The next native African believers, Chrispin Kajubi and Fred Bigabwa, became Bahá'ís in December 1951, followed by Enoch Olinga in February 1952. In September 1952, Denis Dudley Smith, who was originally from Nyasaland (now Malawi), arose with his family and returned to what was then the capital of their native country, Zomba, to spread the message of Bahá'u'lláh. This act made him the first native African pioneer.[42] He was joined in early 1954 by Iranian Enayat Sohaili, the first pioneer during the Crusade.[43]

On 1 May 1953, Dunduzu Chisiza went to Ruanda-Urundi (now the countries of Rwanda and Burundi) with Rex and Mary Collison to fulfil one of the Guardian's goals, thus becoming Knights of Bahá'u'lláh.[44] This made Dunduzu the first native African Knight.

Artemus Lamb, Gertrude and Alvin Blum, Curtis and Harriet Kelsey and other pilgrims

Sometime during the latter half of 1953, Artemus Lamb, a pioneer in Costa Rica, went on pilgrimage. One day, he was sitting opposite the Guardian at the dinner table and the Guardian began speaking about the cables he had sent to the Regional Spiritual Assembly of Central America, on which Artemus was serving. Shoghi Effendi quoted from cable after cable which he had sent to the Assembly. Then he asked Artemus, 'You remember, don't you?' Artemus later recalled: 'Of course, I did not remember all those cables.' But when he returned home, he took the lesson to heart and carefully studied every cable the Guardian had sent. Just before Artemus left, the Guardian suddenly asked him what his plans were. Artemus wrote that

> From Haifa, I was going to Los Angeles, California, to treat a serious family problem which, seemingly, would force me to leave my pioneering activities indefinitely, to my deep sadness. As we were taking leave of the Guardian, he turned to me and unexpectedly asked me about my plans. Completely surprised by the question, as he had not asked the other pilgrims about their plans, and I had not informed him of my problem, I found myself answering that I was returning to Costa Rica. The Guardian rubbed his hands with evident pleasure and said: 'Splendid. Magnificent. Splendid. Magnificent.'

On arrival two days later at the airport in Los Angeles, the problem was resolved in a completely unforeseen manner, and a week later I returned to Costa Rica. As the beloved Hand of the Cause, Mr Khadem, used to say: 'The Guardian knows everything!'[45]

Americans Gertrude and Alvin Blum, living at that time in New Zealand, had attended the Intercontinental Teaching Conference in New Delhi, where Alvin was on the organizing committee. Since they were due to go on pilgrimage in late November, and not wishing to return home before pilgrimage, they asked Shoghi Effendi what they could do. The Guardian simply replied, 'Teach India', so the couple spent the next three weeks travelling almost 4,000 kilometres all across the country. When they finally arrived in Haifa, Shoghi Effendi welcomed them, saying that it was their home. They had the bounty of spending two days as the only pilgrims in the Mansion at Bahjí and greatly enjoyed the opportunity to pray whenever the feeling came to them. Back in Haifa, the Blums met Rúḥíyyih Khánum. Gertrude had first met her (as Mary Maxwell before her marriage) in 1931 at Green Acre and remembered her as the 'freest spirit' she had ever encountered.[46]

Gertrude asked about how to run a Bahá'í summer school. Shoghi Effendi's reply was:

> The summer schools will evolve until they become institutions; then they will study the books of Abul Fadl. First they will become institutes, then colleges, and then universities. In the American summer schools there is too much relaxation and recreation, especially for the youth. The German Bahá'ís do too much rationalizing. In Persia the friends like to drink tea and pray. Australia, New Zealand and England have more balance. They do not go to extremes.[47]

Alvin told Shoghi Effendi that he would love to stay and teach in Israel, but the Guardian said that it was not yet the time. Shoghi Effendi said that the million Jews who had come to Israel since it became a nation were not attached to religion, but to race. He told Alvin that the Israelis would develop the country and over time would slowly begin to understand the teachings of Bahá'u'lláh. After world leaders began acknowledging the Faith, their eyes would be opened.[48]

The Guardian also talked about kings. He said that they would 'become the chief support of the Faith' and that kings 'will assume great power and influence. The Bahá'í state will be headed by kings.' He also noted that governments of the future would not be like those of America, France, or England, 'with its antiquated ceremonials. Not drab or colorless like Germany or Russia. It will be quite distinguished. It will retain the good elements and reject those that are defective.'[49]

When the Blums went to the Intercontinental Teaching Conference in New Delhi, Alvin had cabled the Guardian asking where they could pioneer. Shoghi Effendi had responded by cabling, 'Advise any virgin island Pacific.' One night in Haifa, Shoghi Effendi brought out his original map that displayed all his goals, pointing specifically to the Solomon Islands. Then he brought out a beautiful parchment he had acquired in Florence, Italy. It was, he said, 'designed to perpetuate the memory of the exploits of the spiritual conquerors', those who arose and opened the territories shown on his map. Then he told them 'It will be used for a Roll of Honour and include the names of the pioneers. I would like your names to be on it.' Less than three months later, their names were.[50]

Curtis Kelsey, who had last been in Haifa when he installed electrics in the Shrines of the Báb and Bahá'u'lláh in 1921–22, returned in early December, this time with his wife Harriet. Curtis was amazed at the difference that 30 years had made. This trip to the Holy Land had been just a few airplane flights compared with the 20 days of ships and trains the first time.[51] On that first visit, Haifa had been a quiet town, but was now a bustling city with a busy port. Shoghi Effendi was also very different from the young man he'd met in 1922. Curtis noticed that the Guardian's shoulders were like his grandfather's and he felt the same spiritual power in Shoghi Effendi that he had felt in the Master. One difference Curtis noticed between Shoghi Effendi and 'Abdu'l-Bahá was that the Guardian was much more focused on the expansion of the Faith and the Administrative Order. He thought of Shoghi Effendi as a 'Divine General commenting on the unfoldment of a grand global campaign'. The Master had been more concerned with individual spiritual development.[52]

Curtis and Harriet had left America just a day before their first grandson was born. They learned of the birth by phone. The new parents, Richard and Mary Suhm, requested them to ask Shoghi Effendi where he would like them to pioneer. A month later, the younger couple received a postcard from Haifa saying that they could go to Tangier, Morocco, which they did less than four months later.[53]

Part way through their pilgrimage, Shoghi Effendi asked the Kelseys to stay for three more weeks so that Curtis could help with the installation of a water pump at Bahjí. Curtis delightedly doffed his good clothes, donned work clothes and got busy. Finally, after 26 days, Curtis and Harriet returned home.[54]

Alan McCormick arrived on pilgrimage in December just as another pilgrim, Leslie Boles, was about to leave. Alan's first impression of the Guardian was that he was a 'tiny person, but it is not something you would notice about him. You notice only the tremendous vitality about the man – strength beyond description. It seemed to come out of every pore.' Most of Shoghi Effendi's conversation was directed at Leslie since he was leaving the next day, but he finally turned to Alan and stated that Alan was from Chicago. Alan was a member of the Chicago Local Assembly. The Guardian then proceeded to say what he thought about America – and it wasn't pleasant:

> What the Guardian had to say was extremely unpleasant as far as I was concerned. He is extremely frank and vivid. I was not prepared for this. I was prepared to have the Supreme Concourse itself floating around the dining room table, I guess.
>
> The Guardian is a very hard working and driven person. I felt that if the Supreme Concourse were there, they had been sent out on a specific task and that was why I had not seen them.
>
> I was unable to take down any notes, because all I was doing was sinking down deeper and deeper in the chair. Fortunately, the Guardian was very busy, and could only spend an hour and fifteen minutes. If he had been there another fifteen minutes I am sure I would not have been on the chair at all.[55]

The next night, Alan was sufficiently recovered to begin taking notes. He thought it quite interesting that pilgrims at different times heard different things. Most of Shoghi Effendi's talks during pilgrimages were about what was to be done. When Horace Holley had been there, the talk was about spiritual aspects. For Alan, Shoghi Effendi talked of the big, materialistic cities in America and said that the Bahá'ís should get out of them because they would suffer like London had suffered during the last war. The Guardian said he was very disappointed with 'the greatest centers of materialism', New York, Chicago and San Francisco:

> He felt they were losing their great opportunities. They have done such magnificent service in the past – he felt they are not performing the service of which they are capable. He went on to talk of the materialism of the day which is all about them.[56]

Having said these things, Shoghi Effendi turned to Ethel Dawe, a pilgrim from Australia, and expressed many compliments about her country. There were only 400 Bahá'ís in Australia at that time, but Shoghi Effendi was very happy that they had leapt ahead with the Plan before he had even given them their goals. His only complaint about Australia was racism. They had to overcome this because they had to work closely with Japan and be the leaders in the Pacific. Returning to the topic of America, Shoghi Effendi said that the American Bahá'ís were too prone to attack Communism. He agreed that Communism was evil, but he stated that 'you in America have a great evil in common with them, this is materialism. Capitalism and Communism have many evils, but they both have materialism.'[57]

But Shoghi Effendi showed his lighter side, as well. He said that Chicago should pick the difficult places for pioneering, like South Africa, Spitzbergen, the Falklands or Tibet. But then he laid out the problem: in the sight of God, there was no excuse for inaction: 'he was not talking about the community as a whole, he spoke on the love of the individuals. This is a movement of individuals. This is something each and every one of us must answer for ourselves.'[58] Shoghi Effendi went on to say that Chicago and New York were modern day Babylons and that their

> material civilization we have today is the curse of our age . . . the friends ought to leave Chicago and New York before they are trapped. He also added as an afterthought that London and Paris are equally materialistic. And then he ended this evening by saying that these people who would arise to go out to teach would not find it easy. They should not feel that the mere fact that they are going out to teach would be the 'open sesame', but rather it would be very difficult to teach, and we must not compromise.[59]

Raḥmatu'lláh and Írán Muhájir, and Violette Nakhjavani

In 1953, the pilgrimage ban for Bahá'ís in Iran was finally lifted and one of first to go was Raḥmatu'lláh Muhájir, who went with his wife, Írán, his mother and other ladies. Being the only man in the group, Dr Muhájir had the bounty of the Guardian's company most days in the gardens of the Shrine. The Guardian's talks were focused on the Ten Year Crusade and its pioneering needs, particularly in the Pacific, Southeast Asia, and, more specifically, Indonesia. Dr Muhájir was infected by both the presence of the Guardian and his enthusiasm. On his return home to Tehran, he began to fervently pray that he be made worthy enough to be one of the pioneers.[60] A year later, Raḥmatu'lláh and Írán Muhájir became Knights of Bahá'u'lláh to the Mentawai Islands of Indonesia.

Violette Nakhjavani was also on pilgrimage in 1953, coming from her pioneering post in Kampala, Uganda, but without her husband, 'Alí. During their two years in Uganda, 'Alí had gone out into the villages on teaching trips, but Violette stayed home.

When we first went to Uganda, I was by nature very fussy. I remember that I hated travelling because I didn't like sleeping on beds that were not my beds and pillows that were not my pillows. So, when 'Alí started going into the villages, I wasn't keen at all to go out of Kampala. I was very frightened so he would go and come back, usually, sick. And I asked him, 'Alí, what did you eat? What was the food in the village?' 'It was alright.' 'Where did you sleep? How was the tea? How was the cup? . . .' So, he knew what I was thinking. He never encouraged me to go. He said, 'You do plenty of service in the town. You can do a lot of work here. You don't need to come to the villages.' And he used to tell me, people, the Africans, particularly in the villages, they are sensitive and if you are going to be frightened of cleanliness or lack of hygiene, you'd better stay home. Don't come and offend people, don't insult people. So, I was perfectly happy and comfortable that I didn't need to go.

Then I came here in 1953 on pilgrimage and the last day when we were leaving, the beloved Guardian looked at me and said, 'Now, when you go back to Uganda, you will take my greetings to every one of the believers.' You know at that moment, I didn't get the significance of this message of Shoghi Effendi. I remember I was in the aeroplane and it suddenly hit me that he said 'every believer in Uganda'. There are ten in Kampala. The rest are mostly in villages. So, I came home with the message to 'Alí, I said, "Alí, you should go and tell them that Shoghi Effendi has sent his love and his greetings.' 'Alí said, 'No, he didn't say I should give it, he said you should give it. You should do it.' 'I have never been to the villages!' 'It is high time to go.'

So, he did something which was a good training for me. My parents were away at that time so he said, 'I'll stay and take care of Bahíyyih and you go.' The only pioneer couple at that time in Kampala were Mr and Mrs Nelson. They said, 'Alright, we will take you.' I suddenly was launched with complete strangers into the villages of Africa, of Uganda. Enoch Olinga took one week leave, bless his heart, and he came as my interpreter. We were twelve days away. And I tell you, every night I wept for regret for what I had missed for two years.[61]

She made up for those missed years when, starting in 1969, she spent two years travelling throughout Africa visiting countless villages with Rúḥíyyih Khánum.

Mohsen Enayat, pioneer to the Fezzan

Shoghi Effendi told a number of pilgrims that he had encouraged the Americans to pioneer to Cyprus and Fezzan (one of the three provinces, a large desert area in the south west of Libya), because Mírzá Yaḥyá had been sent to the former and 'Abdu'l-Bahá had been threatened with exile in the latter in 1905 and 1907. The threats of exile to Tripoli were not exaggerated. In 1914, the former Governor of Tripoli visited 'Abdu'l-Bahá and said that in 1907 he had received a telegram from Sultan 'Abdu'l-Hamíd informing him that 'Abdu'l-Bahá would be arriving in just a few days on His way to exile in Fezzan, deep in the Sahara desert. The Sultan told him to be ready to take Him to Fezzan with a large escort of horsemen. The Governor waited, but 'Abdu'l-Bahá never arrived.[62]

The Guardian told pilgrims Maud and Albert Reimholz in 1954 that the people of New York had been especially privileged by Abdu'l-Baha because He had singled out this community for the City of the Covenant and proclaimed His Covenant there. To go to Cyprus and Fezzan now would be an act of fidelity, and this they must prove by their actions. Yet, neither New York with its privileges, nor Chicago, the oldest Baha'i community had done anything to set an example . . .

He said the Americans were too soft and lacked the spirit of adventure. They are too busy thinking 'What shall I do when I get there? What comforts can I take with me? Shall I have a refrigerator? Will there be television? Which of my possessions can I take with me?' . . . They should learn from the British who led the world in pioneering. 60% of all the British Baha'is had become pioneers either at home or abroad.[63]

Since the Americans did not go, the Guardian sent word to the Representative of the Egyptian National Spiritual Assembly at the United Nations Non-Governmental Organizations Regional Conference for the Middle East held in Istanbul, Turkey, in April 1951, asking for pioneers from Egypt to open Libya and Algeria. In the summer of 1953, the Guardian specifically asked the Local Assembly in Benghazi (capital city of the province of Cyrenaica, Libya) to send a pioneer to Fezzan. Mohsen Enayat, who was 21 years old and a member of the Benghazi Assembly, volunteered to go. Mohsen was attending the Stockholm Intercontinental Teaching Conference when the Guardian announced in His cabled message to that Conference that 'A pioneer is en route to Fezzan, Libya, the chosen scene of 'Abdu'l-Bahá's banishment by 'Abdu'l-Hamíd'. Mohsen hastily left the Conference and went to Tripoli to find a way to reach his goal and to gather more information about it. Europe was being rebuilt at that time through, among others, the Marshall Plan and the European Recovery Plan, and unexpectedly some of the funds were being sent in technical assistance to Sebha, the provincial capital of Fezzan. Mohsen was promised a job as a teacher. The description he heard from a resident of the area, however,

was not of the nature to make him rush to go and he had thought to await the signing of the expected contract before embarking. Then the Guardian's instructions were received requesting that as soon as the pioneer arrives on Fezzan the World Centre should be informed immediately. This instruction did not leave any room for delay. A little suitcase got closed and a one way ticket on Air France was acquired, and on the fixed day he flew to this place without knowing where he would spend the night; he already knew Sebha had no hotels or hospices. After a few hours the aeroplane landed and the passenger started to descend.

First shock: there was no airport or any kind of buildings around, just a vast space of endless sand. A few private cars came to pick up those who had arrived on the plane – friends or relatives, and quickly left. Nobody paid any attention to him except a police officer who got out of his jeep and walked towards him. 'Who are you?' he asked. 'I have been sent by the office of ERP [European Recovery Plan] in Tripoli to expedite the process of signing the agreement with it so that they can proceed with appointments of teachers for the schools here.' He put the suitcase at the back of his jeep, and we drove for about ten minutes.

On our way I remembered the name of a cousin of one of our contacts in Cyrenaica who told me he may be helpful as he holds a high position in the administration of Fezzan. So I asked about him. The answer was: 'Yes, he is now in prison, what is your relation with him?' 'Nothing, just his cousin asked me to convey his greetings.' But that was enough to give me a second shock with no break in between.[64]

The officer took the newly arrived pioneer to a square white building with many arches that was to be the government resthouse. At that point, it had just been finished, but was empty and Mohsen was its first guest. His room had a bed with a mattress filled with palm leaves and a chair. Being alone gave him plenty of time for prayer and reading the Writings. His isolation and worries about teaching vanished when the Governor-General of the province called the first meeting of the provincial Parliament:

Invitations went to the heads and notables of different tribes scattered over Fezzan to come to Sebha where they would be roomed in the government guesthouse. All of a sudden this abandoned building became like a beehive: so crowded, full of movement and the sound of various tribal languages: Bedouin Arabic, Amazigh, Tuareg, as well as the local dialect. The previously silent building became overnight a Babel-like city.

There was no need for means of transportation or giving a good reason for mixing with the population, their leaders are all there at my door step, so eager to talk to me and find out new stories to tell their people when they go back. The younger ones wanted to seize the occasion to learn mathematics, which was not taught in the traditional Qur'ánic schools. Others wanted to deepen their knowledge in the meaning of passages of the Qur'án. It was a relatively busy time.

During these simple gatherings strong ties of friendship were developed and many of the individuals present heard of the Bahá'í religion for the first time, with a big shock of course, but they got over it through the signs of true love and friendship. A few began reading Bahá'í literature, especially the book of Bahá'í Proofs by Abu'l-Fadl.[65]

Mohsen was able to teach the Faith to two provincial ministers, including the Minister of Finance. When he was forced by the government to leave after ten months, this helped him to get another young Bahá'í from Egypt, Foad Rushdy, recruited by the Minister to 'hold the fort' after he left. Mohsen's efforts proved the truth of the Writings which say that those who arise and put their faith in God will be assisted.[66]

1954

HELPING PILGRIMS UNDERSTAND THE GOALS OF THE TEN YEAR CRUSADE

Many things happened in 1954. There were important land acquisitions, and the first results of the Ten Year Crusade began to appear. A high point for Shoghi Effendi was the first official visit to the Bahá'í World Centre of a Head of State.

Many of Shoghi Effendi's international pioneering goals had been filled during 1953, but the home-front goals of various nations were proving to be more difficult. On 2 January 1954, Leroy Ioas wrote to the Canadian National Spiritual Assembly about internal and external goals:

> The Ten Year Crusade is dual in nature. Teaching in foreign fields, and teaching on the home front. Now that the work is going ahead nicely abroad, the Guardian is hoping the friends at home will arise with the same spirit of sacrifice and determination as the pioneers abroad have evinced. The reservoirs at home must be kept filled to overflowing, if the work abroad is to prosper. More Bahá'ís, more groups, more Assemblies, is the immediate goal before the friends.
>
> The Guardian feels sure all the friends will arise as never before, and filled with gifts of the Holy Spirit, quicken the seeking souls, and lead many to the bourne of Immortality.[1]

Land acquisitions

Shoghi Effendi was constantly examining the map to find the properties he needed to develop the Bahá'í World Centre. Three parcels of land stood out in 1954: one that directly overlooked the Shrine of the Báb and the gardens, another just above the Tombs of the Greatest Holy Leaf, Navváb and Mírzá Mihdí, and a third just above the apex of the Arc. The first parcel required Leroy Ioas to negotiate with the Israeli authorities, but was finally consummated when Shoghi Effendi agreed that the land should only be used for gardens.[2] The second parcel belonged to the wife of Sydney Sprague, who was also the sister of Ameen Faríd, 'Abdu'l-Bahá's secretary during His travels in the West who defied the Master in 1914 and had become a Covenant-breaker. When Sydney's wife supported Faríd, Sydney had initially remained loyal to her and was expelled from the Faith. Ultimately, he left her and came back to the Faith. His wife, however, remained in opposition to the Faith and refused to sell the land. The issue was finally resolved when the State of Israel took possession of the land, as it did with the holdings of many Arabs and some others who fled the country during the War of Independence. Israel then sold the land to the Bahá'ís.[3] The third piece was more difficult because there were already plans afoot to build a hotel on it overlooking the gardens. Shoghi Effendi announced the construction of the Arc and the buildings on it. The Guardian then said to Leroy, 'Now you had better buy that land!' Which he did.[4]

Marion Hofman

Marion Hofman (originally Marion Holley, an American Bahá'í who had moved to England and was serving as a member of the National Spiritual Assembly) was on pilgrimage between 9 and 18 February. Shoghi Effendi spoke of many things while Marion was there. On her first day, he talked about kings:

> Bahá'u'lláh does not wish countries to be deprived of Kingship; so when there are Bahá'í States, they will follow the wish of Bahá'u'lláh. America will have a king . . . It is a secondary detail as to whether the office will be hereditary or elective . . . Kingship will continue to be punished (referring to the seizure of power from two ranks, kings

and clergy), but there will come an end to this process . . . and kings
will then be re-established . . . Kings will not have political power,
but will be honorary, and represent the majesty of God; and kings
will have an honorary position in relation to the Houses of Justice
. . . The ceremonial connected with kingship, as in England, will be
much moderated.[5]

Shoghi Effendi also stated that all of Ireland, both Eire and Northern
Ireland, would ultimately have a single National Assembly, though he
wasn't sure about what would happen politically.[6]

On the 11th, he told Marion that it was important to purchase
a Ḥaẓíratu'l-Quds in London as soon as possible, suggesting that
Knightsbridge was ideal, but that Chelsea, Earl's Court and Paddington
were too far out and the West End was too expensive. Shoghi Effendi
said that the British were 'persistent, wide-awake, alert'. He went on to
describe them as 'slow but sure. They warm up late, but they remain
warm, and don't have to be told to keep warm. (American Bahá'ís have
to be told to keep warm. They flare up and die down again).' He also
said that the British, unlike the Americans, were very law-abiding,
which was reflected in their attitude toward the Administrative Order.
He also talked about pilgrimage in the future, when pilgrims would
first visit the Qiblih, the Shrine of Bahá'u'lláh, followed by the Shrine
of the Báb and then, at dawn, the Mashriqu'l-Adhkár. Marion listened
as Shoghi Effendi and Leroy Ioas discussed the possibility of building
something over the Síyáh-Chál in Tehran. There were land problems
because a bank building was planned adjacent to the site.[7]

Shoghi Effendi explained the 'ten-stage Majestic Process' to Marion.
He began by explaining three processes: 1) the evolution of World
Order; 2) the evolution of humanity; and 3) the evolution of Divine
Revelation. The evolution of the World Order came about as the
'result of the union of the Law of Bahá'u'lláh . . . and the Covenant of
Bahá'u'lláh, the Mind of 'Abdu'l-Bahá.' The first assemblies and institu-
tions in the time of the Master were the 'germ' of the World Order. The
Administrative Order that Shoghi Effendi himself was building was the
'embryo' which would result in the 'child', the World Order. The evolution of humanity he compared to the development of a human being
from an infant through childhood and the coming of age to maturity.
Humanity was in the stage of infancy and childhood from the time of

Adam to the Báb, and today was in adolescence. The establishment of the Lesser Peace would mark the coming of age of humanity.[8]

On 13 February, the Guardian said Russia would be conquered spiritually from Alaska on the east, Germany on the west and Iraq and Persia from the south, and that the Cause would be established in all Soviet Republics. Siberia would have Local Spiritual Assemblies and a Mashriqu'l-Adhkár.

Shoghi Effendi talked about 'national characteristics' of the Bahá'ís of that time:

> British NSA reports are precise, concise, not diffused. They think clearly, express themselves concisely . . . They always distinguish between the essential and the non-essential. Their minutes are just what they should be, neither too detailed nor too (abridged). The U.S. still have too many details. The Persians mix theirs with anecdotes; they forget what the original subject was.[9]

> I have been singing the praises of the British Bahá'ís, but they require more audacity. They have sound judgment, are persistent, tenacious, loyal, efficient, but they must demonstrate greater audacity. Courage is different from audacity. They have courage; but they must have more audacity. They must take a certain amount of risks. Here the Americans are very different; they go ahead and take risks . . .[10]

> The Germans are very thorough; they do much research. (Laughing) 'I'm impatient by nature, so I can't be too patient when they start research work.' Americans are the reverse, too hasty; impulsive decision. The British are a happy medium, not so much research as the Germans, not so hasty as the Americans.[11]

> The Germans have a great destiny in Europe, and the British not only in the British Isles but throughout the Empire; and the American believers all over the world.[12]

On Marion's last day, Shoghi Effendi talked about one of the greatest problems the British faced: class differences.

Pilgrims from four continents: Maud and Albert Reimholz, Irene Bennett, Loyce Lawrence, Hiroyasu Takano

Maud and Albert Reimholz, from Wauwatose, Wisconsin, also went on pilgrimage in February. Shoghi Effendi had specifically asked them to visit as many Bahá'ís as possible as they travelled to the Holy Land, so they stopped in New York, Amsterdam, Frankfurt, Munich, Zurich, Geneva and Rome, meeting many Bahá'ís. When they arrived at the airport near Tel Aviv, they encountered Loyce Lawrence, Knight of Bahá'u'lláh from Lofoten, Norway, so they all shared a taxi to Haifa.[13]

When the new pilgrims attained the presence of the Guardian, he immediately put their apprehensions to rest. Maud and Albert wrote that he held them all spell-bound: 'When he speaks, you feel his eagerness and firm determination. His vision of the Cause is beyond our imagination and when you see what he has accomplished in a few short years, you realize as never before that he is indeed divinely inspired and guided.'[14]

One thing that surprised them was how Shoghi Effendi treated them:

> The Guardian puts us on a pedestal and treats us like the mature individuals we should be. He takes for granted that we are 'seeking the Kingdom of God first', that we are not concerned with the security of a home or our health or our investments. We are supposed to have attained the maturity of faith in God that He will protect and take care of us if we arise to serve Him. Words to this effect we had read many times but the true impact of the meaning was not brought home to us until after we had listened to the Guardian.[15]

Loulie Albie Matthews spent two days in Haifa. The author of *Not Every Sea Hath Pearls*, she was very old and frail at that time and was on a cruise through the Mediterranean. Shoghi Effendi told her that she would have to change the title of her book, because now every sea had pearls and that a new one was lying at the bottom of the Mediterranean, a reference to Hand of the Cause Dorothy Baker.[16]

On 18 February, Irene Bennett joined the pilgrims. Irene was a new Bahá'í, having become a Bahá'í in Nairobi, Kenya, just the year before, but she was intensely active and was serving as the secretary of the

Nairobi Local Assembly. She had evidently delayed going on pilgrimage until she received a telegram from the Guardian which read, 'Not too late, Shoghi'. Upon her arrival, she was immediately sent to Bahjí to join Maud and Albert Reimholz and Loyce Lawrence. Since it was winter, Irene was told to take warm clothes, but having come from Africa, she had none. Sylvia Ioas promptly outfitted her with woollen jumpers, knee-length socks and warm pyjamas. Just before Irene left Haifa for Bahjí, Jessie took her out onto the balcony where she had her first glimpse of Shoghi Effendi as he left to meet with the Eastern pilgrims at the Shrine of the Báb.[17]

Shoghi Effendi's chauffeur, Muhammad Bahá'í, drove Irene and Leroy and Sylvia Ioas to Bahjí, where they arrived just as darkness was falling:

Just as we arrived, Saleh the caretaker of the Mansion and the Shrine, switched on all the lights. These hung in groups of four lamps, spaced so lavishly that when lit they formed what the Guardian called a sea of light and brilliantly illumined every little corner of the gardens with breath-taking loveliness.

The gardens so far developed, stretched in just a quarter of the present circle, around the north and north-west of the Shrine, from which they radiated in long vistas, symbolic as Dorothy Baker had described them to us in Nairobi a year previously, of the way the Guardian's vision works – in long vistas. Leading to the door of the Shrine from the lovely Collins Gate is a broad pathway of Jordan Valley pebbles like sugared almonds, which Rúḥíyyih Khánum said would be kept constantly free of weeds if every pilgrim plucked out nine on walking over them. All the Guardian's paths both at Bahji and on Mount Carmel were made either of these pebbles or of broken pieces of red tiles so that, viewed from a distance, they made attractive patterns of red and white among the greens of the gardens. As well as peacocks (birds of paradise and symbols of immortality), Italian urns and vases, each pathway had marble steps leading to it and on pedestals two snow-white marble eagles, each feather carved to perfection. Growing in the gardens were baby cypress trees, a few artistically spaced off the original olive trees, and beds of flowers, of which the latest planted contained in circles nine rose-bushes. In the still undeveloped three quarters of the grounds stood five hundred and fifty olive trees.[18]

Leroy and Sylvia led Irene into the Shrine of Bahá'u'lláh, after which they went to the pilgrim house. There Irene met Loyce, who was to become her closest pilgrim friend, and Albert and Maud. Initially, Irene and Maud had simply shaken hands, but Lotfullah Hakím insisted that they embrace, a moment he caught with his little Brownie camera. That night, Irene slept in the room decorated with pictures of popes and kings. The next day, the pilgrims visited the Most Great Prison and the House of 'Abbúd, then returned to Haifa.[19]

The day after, Rúḥíyyih Khánum was ill so Irene didn't expect her to hold her usual afternoon tea for all the pilgrim women. Thinking she had a couple hours of free time, Irene took a bath and washed her hair. But she had just barely finished, and with her hair still very wet, when she was told that the Guardian's wife was meeting the pilgrim women at that moment. Jessie Revell quickly wrapped Irene's wet hair in a towel, turban-fashion, then they dashed across the road to the House of the Master. All the other women were already there when she arrived, and when Rúḥíyyih Khánum quickly identified her and noted that she was a 'baby Bahá'í', it was an embarrassed Irene who stood there in her turban. A few days later, almost the same thing happened. Irene had again washed her hair and, while it was still wet, she was called to meet with Rúḥíyyih Khánum and the pilgrim women. That was not how she had expected to meet the wife of Shoghi Effendi.[20]

The night after returning from Bahjí, Irene had her chance to meet the Guardian and she was worried that she wasn't spiritual enough and prayed for help with the moment. As was normal, being the most recent pilgrim, Irene had to go in first – but Shoghi Effendi quickly put her at ease:

> Shoghi Effendi moved forward to greet me. While shaking my hand he assured me that I was welcome, indeed I was very welcome, for I had come from Africa. Every feeling of unworthiness and anxiety that I had been earlier entertaining was immediately dispelled, for looking at me with shining eyes and a smiling face, he astonished me by adding that I was a fine Bahá'í, I was active, I was determined and even that I was consecrated! He recalled that I was the secretary of the first Spiritual Assembly of Nairobi and said that that was a great bounty and privilege for me. Then he said I was to take the chair facing him at the table, and leaving me overwhelmed with

such loving attention, he next proceeded to shake hands with each and everyone behind me and ask how they were before they moved to their places at table . . . When all had been individually greeted and taken their seats he sat down in his own place at the table, an end seat on the long side facing down the hall. At the head, i.e. between himself and me was the 'seat of honour' occupied by Joyce [Loyce], she being the Knight of Bahá'u'lláh. The chair at the opposite end, facing Joyce, was the place of Mason Remey . . .

That night the Guardian addressed the majority of his remarks and questions to me. Pilgrims seemed to become to the beloved Guardian more than representatives from the country in which they served the Cause, indeed their very personification. He addressed any remarks about a particular area to the person associated with it and in so doing it seemed as if he concentrated himself entirely on that person. So vividly could I experience this feeling that on one particular occasion all assembled at dinner seemed to have melted away leaving just the Guardian leading me heavenwards. He had the most wonderful fascinating countenance constantly changing and radiating light, so that when sitting opposite to him I never wanted to take my eyes from his face. Furthermore, I was in the distinguished position of having a double identity. I was both Africa and Britain. While I was there he recalled outstanding services of British Bahá'ís, such as their record of sixty per cent who left their homes to pioneer during the Teaching Plan requested by the National Spiritual Assembly of the British Isles immediately upon the conclusion of the Second World War.[21]

During his evening talks, Shoghi Effendi talked of many things, but brought up one subject that was being heard by almost all Western pilgrims during this time. He told the pilgrims that the Bahá'ís should leave the large cities before they were trapped by materialism. 'There was a time for consolidation', he said, 'but now is the time to scatter. No community should have more than 15 members. Move to a new place, stay until the membership reaches 15, then move again, thereby establishing the Faith in many places. It is better to have three groups than one assembly except in places where we are trying to establish N.S.A.s.' Shoghi Effendi also told them that the Bahá'ís must not hide their plans, because that created suspicion. One pilgrim asked if future

Mashriqu'l-Adhkárs would be as beautiful as the one in Wilmette and he responded saying that 'each new Temple will be more beautiful because we will be developing Bahá'í architecture'. As he did on occasion, the Guardian compared national characteristics, saying that 'the Germans are too thorough, the Americans too hasty, and the English a happy medium. He wonders if the Americans even take the time to read his messages.'[22]

One night, there was a social dinner party for a group of Israeli government officials. Since Shoghi Effendi did not attend these types of events, Rúḥíyyih Khánum served as the host. Though she had been ill, the Guardian's wife took on the challenge. She even prepared the salads:

> On the dinner table was a fine evidence of her originality, for with fruit cans and fresh produce all around her bed she had created an individual side salad for each of us, a 'girl' salad set beside the places for the gentlemen and a 'boy' salad beside those allocated to the ladies. Dresses for the former were arrangements of lettuce with frills of pineapple, shirts for the latter were also of lettuce, with trousers of peach slices. The faces of the girls were cut from peaches and of the boys from pears, each having shredded carrot for hair, raisins for eyes, clove for a nose, cherry for lips, and the cheeks were made rosy with a touch of something resembling rouge. Legs and arms were made from small pieces of pineapple, and shoes from cherries.[23]

At the end of February Hiroyasu Takano arrived unexpectedly early for his pilgrimage. He was returning home to Japan after a year studying in America. While in America, Hiroyasu had discovered the Faith and become a Bahá'í. Irene had to move out of her room into Loyce's room in haste since Hiroyasu, whom they called 'Hero', was to have her room and he was on his way there.[24] That night at dinner, Irene noted that the pilgrims represented the 'four compass points of the globe': Hiroyasu from Japan, Albert and Maud from America, Loyce pioneering in Norway and Irene in Africa.

When Hiroyasu was settled in, Shoghi Effendi's message to him was that Japan must work with Australia and be like the two poles of a magnet so that they could magnetize the Pacific. Japan was the only North Pacific country with the goal of forming a National Spiritual

Assembly during the Ten Year Crusade. The Guardian emphasized that isolated centres must first be established. These would in turn become Local Assemblies. He concluded by saying that 'Japan is the only country that has experienced the atom bombing. That was their sacrifice. It is wonderful what the Japanese Baha'is have accomplished these past two years . . .'[25]

With Hiroyasu's arrival, Irene was again able to visit the Shrine of Bahá'u'lláh along with her Japanese companion and the Revell sisters. This time, as she walked that long path to the Shrine, she 'plucked about ninety-nine weeds from among the smooth pebbles' in atonement for not having picked her nine, as Rúḥíyyih Khánum suggested, on her first visit.[26]

Just before Irene was to depart, Rúḥíyyih Khánum called her over to say goodbye. In striking contrast to her previous encounters with the Guardian's wife, this time Irene sat next to her and began chatting as if she was a 'close old-time friend in whom it was natural to confide'. Their previous meetings had been 'official' audiences, but this one was heart to heart:

> I felt so natural and so much at home perched beside her on the wall, and was no longer tongue-tied, as we laughed and talked together. I realised that she had been holding audience in her sitting-room, getting up for weeks when she should have been in bed, because she could not bear to miss the pilgrims who had come so far, and especially the Persian ladies who met her only at those times. Her adorable soul that I had so eagerly hoped to recognise on this special pilgrimage was fully revealed to me. I felt her love and loved her in return. She told me how pleased she was that I had been able to come and continued by adding. 'When we heard here in Haifa that you had become a Bahá'í I said to myself that this new Bahá'í must be a little old lady and that was how I imagined you until you came here. I am so glad to find how wrong I was and to know now that you are so young with many years ahead for service to the Cause.'[27]

William Sears

William (Bill) Sears came to Haifa on 1 April, staying until the 10th. His first meeting with the Guardian was powerful:

He held out his arms and embraced me.

'We have been expecting you for a long time', he said, as he kissed me on the right cheek, then the left, then the right. I clung to him ever so tightly. My predominate [sic] feeling was, 'I have come home.' My chest hurt, it felt so big. My throat was stopped up. My eyes tried to shed tears that were pouring from every part of my being, but the task was too great for them. They stored up and blinded me.

'We have heard much about you', he said. I held him tightly hoping I need never let go. 'Now we are happy that you are with us at last.'

I turned back to the table to find my seat. It was directly opposite him, so close I could have reached over and touched his hand. When my vision cleared, I could see that every other eye was also misty. When the next pilgrim arrived, I would know why. Every Bahá'í heart is knitted to the other here and shares this ecstasy when the Guardian greets the new pilgrim for the first time. When I saw the next pilgrim come, I too, wept with joy for them. I thought of the words of the obligatory prayer, 'burn away the veils that have shut me out from Thy beauty and (be) a light that will lead unto the ocean of Thy Presence.'

My fears had all vanished now, and I felt only a transcendent happiness. I watched the Guardian with wrapt attention and ever increasing devotion. This was as close, in our day, as man could come to the direct source of the power of God, His Majesty, His Justice, His Mercy, His Love. I felt them all flowing from the Guardian.

When he asked me about my journey I answered him and my words shamed me. I had made my living by words, but could think of nothing to say in his presence. My words were feeble, clumsy and uncertain. It was as though a glib tongue had been made fearful that it might try to say something witty or clever. This Guardian could be impressed by only one thing, service to the Faith. Nothing would ever influence his judgement; not wealth, position, power, or friendship. The only gift that could be given him was a gift of service.[28]

Like many other pilgrims, Bill tried to describe Shoghi Effendi:

Now I know why there have been no adequate descriptions of him by the Pilgrims. It is completely unimportant. It is describing a mirror when you can't behold the sun that shines in it. It is describing a symphony by saying it has four movements, when you can't express the exhilaration and joy that its music stirs in you. This is more true of the Guardian. His is a music unique to the planet. It is a spiritual language which transcends even a musical language. 'Abdu'l-Bahá said there was a spiritual language as different from our language as ours is from the cries of animals. This is the language of the presence of the Guardian. It cannot be expressed, it must be experienced. What is written here is but the shadow of the reality. Only a pilgrimage of your own will clothe it in flesh. If you have seen him, you will understand this.

The Guardian, as I remember him, is short in stature. His hair is dark, greying on the sides. He is of medium to dark complexion. He has dark eyes that seem to become a shade lighter when they are most animated, as though they burned with some inner fire. His features are regular. He is smooth shaven except for a dark moustache. There is an energetic quality about his person, even when at rest. He is very sturdy. I judge this by the firmness I felt when he embraced me. He has very small, slender hands which are shapely and expressive. All of his gestures are extremely graceful. He wore a rust colored topcoat over his inner clothes all during the time I was there. His tie was always brown. He wears a slender gold Bahá'í ring on the second finger of his right hand. He wears a black fez with a black button in the center of the top. Almost every evening he brought some new cable, drawing, or document with him to the table. Frequently he discusses the work of the Faith with the Hands and the members of the International Council. The dinner table is long and narrow. It seats ten comfortably. The latest pilgrim used to sit at the head of the table. Now Mason Remey sits there. The Guardian sits on his right, and the latest pilgrim on Mason's left, opposite Shoghi Effendi. Ruhiyyih Khanum sits on the Guardian's immediate right. The pilgrim is only three feet away, yet a world away from him.[29]

On his first night with the Guardian, Shoghi Effendi spoke of Africa and the Africans:

We have been thinking too much about the white race and not enough about mankind in general . . . Now is our chance to contribute our share to the conversion of these races.

We must work in order to have the majority of believers belong to these races. Only love can do this. Complete elimination of our own wishes and supplanting them with service to the African. This is the keynote to be sounded . . .

This complete lack of prejudice will attract the African. We must prefer them to ourselves. Wherever possible, whenever possible, we must accept them into our homes. Not accept them on the platform or at public functions, but privately in our homes on a social basis, and on a basis of absolute equality . . .

When we approach the negroes in Africa for the first time, they are openminded. Nothing must be done to discourage them or disillusion them. It will be very difficult to establish confidence if it is once lost. We must meet all situations and suspicions with pure motives and love, otherwise they will see no difference, and we will be classified with the missionaries . . . We must teach them thoroughly. We must make them eager to serve the Faith and then when our task is finished we must leave. We should say to them 'We have come for one purpose only; we have come from America to serve you.' This is the message in a nutshell.[30]

Shoghi Effendi also emphasized that the Bahá'ís should teach the native people, 'not waste time on the political leaders' or whites:

We teach the Africans because they are the native inhabitants of that continent. We do not teach the Africans in the Pacific, we teach the brown-skinned people there. We must reach the people who are in the majority in each area. This is why we teach the Africans in Africa. Do not waste time on the European. Teach the American in America, the Hindu in India, the British in England, but teach the African in Africa. We don't want a colony of American believers in South Africa. We want a majority of African believers. After all, he said with a smile, the American whites there are an undesirable element.

Do not waste time on the European. It is not worth the energy and the results will be negligible. Teach the Africans. This is your single mission, your purpose for being in Africa. The European will not respond and might involve the Faith in difficulties and public-ity. This is to be avoided at all times. It is dangerous to teach the Europeans.

Do not waste time on the political leaders, he said. (Leroy Ioas told us that the Guardian had said to an earlier pilgrim, "Abdu'l-Bahá said that the leaders were ashes, and that's what they are, ashes, nothing more.') The leaders . . . can do nothing about the world problems now. They are helpless, useless, they cannot prevent the coming crisis. We are not concerned with this. This is God's plan, which is the ten-year crusade. We have a clear-cut, well-prepared plan. We must execute it. The outside world we leave to God.[31]

And Shoghi Effendi returned to the problem of the Bahá'ís in Ameri-can cities. 'New York and Chicago are very dangerous places,' he said. He continued saying that the Bahá'ís should leave the cities, but 'not to go to the suburbs. This is not the time to open suburbs. This is the time to open territories.' Bill was overwhelmed by the Guardian's words:

'America', he said, 'is no longer even actively quarreling. They are passively stagnant.' This is why, he said, that he asked them to dis-perse; so that they may become alive again and not wither . . .

You are in the Guardian's presence but a short time when you wish to saddle your horse, buckle on your sword, and casting aside the joy of the rest of your pilgrimage, cry out: 'Mount your steeds, O heroes of God!' Ruhíyyih Khánum, herself, said one night, 'Shoghi Effendi, if you keep on speaking so movingly, I'll have to leave and pioneer.'

You have the desire to be commanded in order that you may obey. Here you lose forever that feeling, so common in the west, of rebellion at commands. You see that obedience in a new light; a light of protection, service, accomplishment and joy.

When Shoghi Effendi leaves the room after the evening meal, the room becomes quite silent for some time. All eyes are watching the door through which he has gone. Part of our hearts have gone with him. It is a good thing because the part he has left with us is too much for us to carry. We must share it with each other or burst. Eyes slowly, unwillingly, turn from the door of his departure. We look at each other as though we remember for the first time who we are. Deep sighs are heard on every side as we breathe out the last of that air of his presence. These sighs are more eloquent than words. They say, 'Isn't he wonderful! Oh, if only we could be worthy of him!' [32]

Shoghi Effendi commonly contrasted the Americans and the Persians as being opposite in the ways they did things. One day he said that

reverence is a quality in which the Americans are lacking. Their over-accentuation of democracy and personal independence is the cause of this. The Persians . . . carry it to the other extreme. The Americans have too little reverence while the Persians are overly demonstrative. It needs a balance. Reverence and self-respect go together . . . The American think so much of their self-respect that they are lacking in reverence. The Persians, on the other hand, go to such extremes in trying to express their reverence that they forget their self-respect. It is necessary that we have both reverence and self-respect. [33]

Bill and the other pilgrims went to Akka one day, stopping first at the House of Abbúd. With the literary style that made him a well-known Baháʼí author, Bill described the visit:

This was once the sanctuary of the Supreme Pen. Its walls had resounded to the words of the Most Great Book, the Mighty Aqdas! Here were formed the laws which would stand inviolate and unaltered for a thousand years. Here were fashioned the provisions which would lay the foundation for the greatest structure in the social history of mankind . . .

What a plain, unimposing structure. Two stories in height with a small balcony around the second floor, drab grey in color, bleak in appearance – beautiful to the believer!

We were staring silently up at the balcony which surrounds the bedroom of Bahaʼuʼllah. Many long hours He had paced this balcony, looking out over the sea and down upon the very earth where we were standing. This small balcony, which can be crossed in less than ten paces, furnished almost the only outside exercise for Bahaʼuʼllah in seven long years of imprisonment within the walls of this house.

There was a long quiet pause as the Pilgrims looked up in thanks-giving to the Almighty for this humble house. Once these stories had been but words caught between two covers, but now during the Pilgrimage they were all coming alive with reality.

Finally one of the Pilgrims coughed. The spell was broken. Cameras appeared on all sides. We had come back from that other sweet reality to this plane to laugh and talk and walk. This expe-rience is repeated time after time throughout the Pilgrimage, as the poor pilgrim with his weak human body flies back and forth between these two worlds so unlike, one of God and one of man. The transfer is shattering, and by the end of one's stay it has com-pletely exhausted these untrained spirits.[34]

First official visits

Several members of the International Bahá'í Council had gone to Jeru-salem on 1 February to pay an official visit to the President of Israel, Itzhak Ben-Zvi. During the visit, the President said he would like to meet the Guardian, so a date was set for 26 April. When the day arrived, Leroy Ioas and Mason Remey went to the President's hotel and found him and his wife still at breakfast. Not standing on ceremony, the President invited them to sit down and join him and his wife for coffee. At 9 o'clock, they all drove to the House of the Master, where they were met by Shoghi Effendi and Rúḥíyyih Khánum. This was the first official visit by the Head of an independent country to the Bahá'í World Centre.

During the conversation, the President mentioned that he had met 'Abdu'l-Bahá at Bahjí in 1909 or 1910, shortly after he and his wife were married. They had set out on foot to explore their country and had one day passed by Bahjí and met the Master. He had been very kind and had served them tea. After Shoghi Effendi had explained the basic aims and objectives of the Faith, the group went to the Shrine of the Báb. The Guardian walked the President and his wife through the gardens and to the Shrine where Leroy suddenly wondered how to tell the President that he would have to remove his shoes before entering. When he did, the President turned to him and said: 'I quote to you what God said to Moses when He approached the Burning Bush: Put thy shoes from off thy feet, for the place whereon thou standest is holy ground. Of *course* I will take off my shoes. This custom originated with us, when God spoke to Moses.'[35]

As the President was leaving, he remarked how impressed he was with the spirit of the Shrine and the beauty of the gardens and spoke of his pride that the Bahá'í World Centre was in his country. He also wished the Bahá'ís well in their work throughout the world. Leroy was walking with one of the President's aides as they left and suggested that a press release be made. The aide thought it was a very good idea, but said he was so busy he didn't think he could write it. Would Leroy write it? So Leroy did. On 26 May, Shoghi Effendi and Rúḥíyyih Khánum went to Jerusalem to return the visit.[36]

Creation of the Auxiliary Board, and Crusade results at Riḍván

To aid in raising up the Bahá'í Administrative Order during the Ten Year Crusade, Shoghi Effendi on 6 April announced the creation of five Auxiliary Boards to assist the Hands of the Cause in their work. The American, European and African Auxiliary Boards were to have nine members each, while the Asiatic and Australian continents would have seven and two, respectively. To further help the Hands and their Auxiliary Boards, the Guardian strongly urged that five Continental Bahá'í Funds be created.[37] The Auxiliary Boards were needed because of the rapid advances being made by the Faith in many parts of the world.

At Riḍván, five Local Spiritual Assemblies were elected in new areas, the first successes of the Knights of Bahá'u'lláh. Four of the Assemblies were in Africa (Tanganyika, British Cameroon, Ruanda-Urundi and Morocco) and one was in the Malay Peninsula.[38] A small beginning but a significant one. Shoghi Effendi was elated by the success in Africa, writing in his Riḍván message:

> The African Campaign, outshining the brilliant success of the enter-
> prise launched in Latin America, throwing into shade the splendor
> of the victories won in recent years on the European continent,
> eclipsing all previous collective pioneer undertakings embarked
> upon in the Asiatic and Australian continents, has almost doubled,
> in the course of a single year, the number of territories opened since
> the introduction of the Faith in that continent over eighty years ago
> . . .

83

A single territory out of the forty-five territories already opened to the Faith in the African continent, situated in its very heart and which, a little over two years ago did not possess a single Baha'i, now boasts of over five hundred colored converts, who are settled in over eighty localities, are drawn from thirty tribes . . .[39]

The Guardian then outlined the results of the World Crusade and the new tasks that lay ahead:

The spiritual conquest of one hundred territories of the globe, the steady rise of the embryonic World Order of the Faith, and the multiplication and consolidation of its institutions have, in the course of the opening year of this World Spiritual Crusade, been paralleled by a no less startling decline in the fortunes of the enemies of the Faith, as evidenced by the removal, by the Hand of Providence, of its arch-enemy in Persia who, for thirty years, savagely attacked its Founders and its chief Promoter, and tirelessly schemed to extinguish its light, dishonor its name and wreck its institutions, as well as by the death of two others, who, in varying degrees, demonstrated their ingratitude and infidelity to the Center of Bahá'u'lláh's Covenant.

The opening phase of this gigantic, divinely propelled, world-encircling Crusade has been triumphantly concluded. The success crowning the initial stage in its unfoldment has exceeded our fondest expectations. The most vital and spectacular objective of the Ten Year Plan has been virtually attained ere the termination of the first year of this decade-long stupendous enterprise. The second phase, now auspiciously ushered in, must witness, in all the territories of the planet, whether newly opened or not, an upsurge of activity which, in its range and intensity, will excel the exploits which have so greatly enlarged the limits, and noised abroad the fame, of the Cause of God.[40]

With a full year of the Crusade completed, the Faith was established in 228 countries, an increase of 97, and 2,900 localities. In addition, the Writings of the Faith had been translated into 39 new languages during the year.[41]

1954

PILGRIMS AND PILGRIM KNIGHTS

The gardens were very important to Shoghi Effendi, but some didn't always see things as he did. One day he was walking with Ugo Giachery through what is now known as the Monument Gardens. Some of the paths were quite steep and, with the crushed roofing tiles underfoot, sometimes a little difficult to walk. Ugo asked why they were so steep. He remembered that Shoghi Effendi 'looked at me with a mild expression of surprise on his face, as if I should have known the answer, that the beauty of the gardens surpassed in importance the convenience of the ever-increasing number of visitors'.[1]

More on American materialism: Ramona Brown and Clara Edge

Ramona Brown, who had met 'Abdu'l-Bahá in California, was in Haifa on 11 May and Shoghi Effendi told her what he told all Americans: America was too materialistic, the most politically disturbed nation on earth, and that its cities were doomed. He said that it was time

> for a new pattern starting with villages, etc. Material civilization is becoming like the ancient city of Babylon and it must be destroyed . . . The Americans need shock medicine. They do not obey . . . They have fallen down on their job. They are inactive – over administered. Their home front is an absolute failure. They were given the Divine Plan first. The Administration was given to the American Bahá'ís. The whole world depends upon America . . .
>
> . . . Sell your property and pioneer. Buy property in Central Africa. Those with independent means must pack up and go, and

not wait for the committees to move them. Those with 'spirit' must pack and go! I can warn them, I can urge them, but I cannot make them go. Those who will not arise to serve, create unhappiness for me and danger for the believers.[2]

Shoghi Effendi asked Ramona to visit the Bahá'ís on the Mediterranean islands on her way home, so she stopped in Cyprus, Rhodes, Greece, Crete, Sardinia, Malta, Sicily, Palma de Mallorca and Corsica.[3]

On 16 May, Clara Edge arrived at the Western Pilgrim House and rang the bell. 'That precious little package of humanity – Jessie Revell, came to the door . . .' Lillian Richards, a pioneer in Turkey, and Allen and Mary Elston, pioneers in Uganda, were also there. That night at dinner there were two people who were not Bahá'ís in addition to the pilgrims and staff. One asked about elections and Shoghi Effendi responded:

> In America, the power is now in the hands of the masses. This is not good for they can be and are swayed by the press. It is far better to elect, as the Baha'is do, in a three way election, Local Spiritual Assembly, State Convention, National Convention. The masses voting for a majority do not pick for the best qualities for office, but from the influence [of the press]. The Baha'is is a three-way election. They pick the best for their spiritual and practical qualities . . .[4]

Shoghi Effendi noted that at the All-American International Teaching Conference of the previous year, 495 people had volunteered to fulfil its goals as pioneers, but only 200 actually left. Shoghi Effendi said, 'People say, "I have read the Iqan like a tourist who says: 'I have done Paris, I have done London in 2 hours and know all about it.'" They have too many material preoccupations, they read so many magazines, which are absolutely trivial; they should throw them away into the wastebasket. This is what is called materialistic civilization.'[5] To another pilgrim, Shoghi Effendi is reported to have said, 'What do they want me to write? Magazine articles that they can read in ten minutes. I want them to think.'[6]

Edith McLaren

Edith McLaren was on pilgrimage between 2 and 10 May. She arrived on the anniversary of the Martyrdom of the Báb according to the lunar calendar and was able to join Rúḥíyyih <u>Kh</u>ánum with all the Baháʼí women from Akka and the International Baháʼí Council for a luncheon. Edith was the only Western pilgrim. Later in the afternoon, she wrote,

> we were all taken to the Shrine of the Bab where we waited in the little portico outside the Eastern Pilgrim house until the beloved Guardian finished his conversation with the men pilgrims from Persia. Just at twilight when the stars were beginning to come out I had my first glimpse of the beloved as he came out of the house, slowly walked up the path to the Shrine followed by the men. The lights went on at the Shrine and the women followed going into the side reserved for them. There in that matchless room, that sacred spot, I suddenly heard the voice of the Guardian chanting the Tablet of Visitation of Baháʼuʼlláh as the fragrance of attar of roses permeated the evening air. Next we entered the room to the left where Abdul-Baha is situated and heard the Guardian chant again. To have had this tremendous experience during the first hours of the first day was like being lifted into another world. It was nearly nine o'clock when we went in to the dining room for dinner. The overwhelming feeling of unworthiness that comes over one as he walks across the dimly lighted room for the first time and sees Shoghi Effendi rise from the table in the dining room and come forward to greet him is felt to a great degree by every pilgrim. One can scarcely eat seeing his eyes for the first time and hearing him speak.[7]

The next evening, 3 May,

> we found the Guardian very happy and healthy. His eyes were sparkling and his cheeks were pink. He had many cables and letters which had come that day. They all had good news. He could scarcely eat for he wanted to read so many of them to us. Several new pioneers had arrived at their posts, the NSAs had sent cables . . . from Canada, Australia, India, Persia, Sweden. He was displeased with Sweden because the NSA has spent $21,500 for land for the Temple, 20 miles from their capital when they had only 3000 in their fund. He was very pleased with Africa especially and Canada and Australia. He spoke of several youth who had gone to pioneer in different places. He also read to us the very cordial and friendly

letter which had just come that day from the president Ben Svi [Zvi] of Israel who expressed great pleasure and appreciation of his recent visit with the Guardian and Ruhiyyih Khanum. He spoke warmly of the unity and friendly relations which exist between the Bahá'í Faith and the State of Israel and that both were working for the welding of the nations . . . Leroy Ioas was to speak at the Rotary Club in Jerusalem the following day. The Guardian said that he wished to send some Bahá'í books to the president, since he had asked for literature. (I remember so well that he spoke of the books then – Prayers and Meditations, Gleanings, Dawnbreakers and the Appreciations of the Bahá'í Faith.) He also said that he would send some plants to Mrs. Ben Svi for her garden. The reason the Guardian was so happy over this visit was because this was the first time a president or high official had called on him. The minister of religions had been invited to come but had refused . . . Finally he read to us his cable to the U.S. in which he said that the Honor Roll was now being closed and giving us the latest information on the growth of the Faith. At the end of the dinner time there [were] maps of the property of the Siyah Chal prison which the Guardian brought out and talked about with the members of the Council. He mentioned that the individual who bought the property should now work with the NSA of Persia and decide with Bahá'í consultation how the building should be developed and financed.[8]

The Síyáh-Chál had been purchased at a cost of $400,000.[9] Unfortunately, the property was confiscated by the Iranian Government before the end of the Ten Year Crusade.[10]

Ruth Moffett

Ruth Moffett was in Haifa on 20 May for her second pilgrimage, 27 years after her first. Even though she had met the Guardian before, she described him again:

It is impossible to describe the Guardian in words, any more than one can describe a symphony by saying it has four movements. The Guardian is like a symphony himself. He is unique to this planet. It is a spiritual language above description which he seems to emanate;

when you speak to him you begin to understand. He is like heavenly music speaking in the language of the spirit. He is not tall, but seems to grow taller the longer you are with him. His hair is dark and graying at the sides. He has dark eyes that seem to become darker and burn with an inner fire. He has strong, firm, regular, sensitive features, and is smooth-shaven with a small dark mustache. He is sturdy and full of energy. He has very expressive hands and I was told they were much like Baha'u'llah's.

All of his gestures are very graceful and exceedingly expressive. He wore a rust-colored top coat with a matching tie, usually, though sometimes, he wore a black coat with a black tie. He wears a slender gold Baha'i ring on the second finger of his right hand, and he wears a black fez with a black button in the center of the top.

Almost every evening he brought a cable or a drawing or some kind of document which he laid on the tablecloth and explained.

The dinner talks are long and the table usually seats ten people. The incoming pilgrim is seated at the head of the table the first night and the second directly across from the Guardian. Madame Khanum sits at his right and the other pilgrims are sitting around him at the table.[11]

The Guardian yet again brought up the problems of American materialism, Bahá'í over-administration and a lack of commitment to the Faith. He also pointed out the dangers of living in the cities and of what would happen to them at some point. Then he noted that he

had been told that some of the friends are disturbed over reports brought back by the pilgrims concerning the dangers facing America in the future whenever another world conflagration breaks out. He said that he does not feel that the Baha'is should waste time dwelling on the dark side of things. Any intelligent person can understand from the experiences of the last world war, and keeping abreast of what modern science has developed in the way of weapons for any future war that big cities all over the world are going to be in tremendous danger.

He has urged the Baha'is, for the sake of serving the Faith, to go out from these centers of materialism.[12]

Shoghi Effendi said the same thing 'officially' to the Americans on 28 July:

> The mighty and laudable effort exerted, by a considerable number of pioneers, in the course of the opening phase of this world-encircling Crusade, in the virgin territories of the globe, must, if this primacy is to remain unimpaired, be increased, doubled, nay trebled, and must manifest itself not only in foreign fields where the prizes so laboriously won during the last twelve months must, at whatever sacrifice, be meticulously preserved, but throughout the entire length and breadth of the American Union, and particularly in the goal cities, where hitherto the work has stagnated, and which must, in the year now entered, become the scene of the finest exploits which the home front has yet seen. A veritable exodus from the large cities where a considerable number of believers have, over a period of years, congregated, both on the Atlantic and Pacific coasts, as well as in the heart of the country, and where, owing to the tempo and the distractions of city life, the progress of the Faith has been retarded, must signalize the inauguration of this most intensive and challenging phase of the Crusade on the home front. Most certainly and emphatically must the lead be given by the two focal centers of Baha'i activity which rank among the oldest of and occupy the most honored position among the cities throughout the American Union, the one as the mother city of the North American continent, the other named by 'Abdu'l-Bahá the City of the Covenant. Indeed, so grave are the exigencies of the present hour, and so critical the political position of the country, that were a bare fifteen adult Bahá'ís to be left in each of these cities, over which unsuspected dangers are hanging, it would still be regarded as adequate for the maintenance of their local spiritual assemblies.[13]

But, after they have suffered and been purified, he said, America would lead the world spiritually. Shoghi Effendi greatly praised Ruth for her non-stop teaching efforts and that she should continue as she had been doing, telling her only to move out of the city.

Violet and Hugh McKinley

Violet and Hugh McKinley, mother and son and Knights of Bahá'u'lláh to Cyprus, arrived on their pilgrimage by ship on 28 November. It was a powerful experience for both. Violet wrote that 'it was a quite indescribable event without precedent'. Hugh described the Guardian:

> The Beloved Guardian is so far from what human experience has hitherto encountered that the intellect registers only a blank on first meeting him.
>
> We know, to some extent, or have heard from other Bahá'ís more or less the impressions made upon them, as well as having read or left unread those references to him and to the Institution of Guardianship in the Writings, most especially the closing passages of the Will and Testament of 'Abdu'l-Bahá.
>
> This is the Guardianship in theory. Meeting Shoghi Effendi is the Guardianship in practise: something beyond words to convey – the power, the authority the ENERGY, THE NEVER CEASING ENERGY AND DRIVE that carries the Bahá'ís forward with it like the crest of a mighty wave to heights they would not even dream existed. Alas, if we were only one eighth as obedient IN THE LITERAL SENSE OF THE TERM and as willing, how much more would have been achieved. Those who speak of the Master and those who speak of Bahá'u'lláh speak of the crescendo of love and of justice. Meeting Shoghi Effendi one just begins to see how completely unapproachable They were.
>
> One night at dinner he was speaking of the deeds of the Covenant-breakers; his voice ran out, and his eyes flashed fire, and one could feel a tangible majesty and the authority of divine justice as an unquestionable reality. It struck us dumb.
>
> Yet such tender love and care after the happiness of the friends and the pilgrims, those known and unknown, and above all such joy when letters bring news of the progress of the Cause and any victory newly won. If we could see that smile and hear the joy and exultation in that voice how we should speed to achievement.[14]

Ugo and Angeline Giachery

Ugo and Angeline Giachery were able to have their pilgrimage starting on 11 December. Meeting the Guardian that night was the fulfilment one of Angeline's greatest desires. As their pilgrimage neared its end, Shoghi Effendi surprised them by extending it. When they finally did leave on 24 December, he told Angeline, 'I would very much like to keep you and Ugo here indefinitely, but Ugo must return to Italy and start immediately to work on the International Archives.'[15]

John and Valera Allen and family

John and Valera Allen, Knights of Bahá'u'lláh in Swaziland, along with their sons, Dale and Kenton, and Valera's mother, Maude Fisher, arrived in Haifa after dark on 15 December. Their taxi driver took them to a dark, unlighted gate, where he honked his horn to no avail. The Allens said that it did not look like the right place, but the driver insisted that this was where he always took people, particularly one doctor (who turned out to be Lotfullah Hakím). The driver finally found a young Persian who directed them to the Western Pilgrim House where they arrived to find Lotfullah himself. They soon found themselves passing through a room to meet the Guardian, whom they could see in the dining room ahead, seated at the table. Valera wrote:

> On his head was a black 'taz' and he wore a tan coat. He looked so far away and I felt even more as though I were walking in a dream. As I made my way through the room leading to the dining room, I was vaguely aware of large dark objects on each side in the semi-darkness. Later I found they were monuments and ornaments for the Gardens at Haifa and Bahji that the Guardian had purchased while he was away. We were told that he gets many things for the Gardens from old estates which are being sold. Upon reaching the dining room the beloved Guardian rose to greet us most cordially saying we were most welcome and kissing John on both cheeks. His eyes shone and one feels an encompassing love as if returning home after a long journey.
>
> He asked about our trip and then launched into the subject of Africa. How many believers were there now? How was the work progressing? We stumbled around a little bit saying we were not

too up-to-date on statistics as we had been to America and were just now returning to Africa . . . He smiled and said, 'Then I shall tell you.' And we sat absolutely amazed as he told of the progress of the Faith in Africa without the least hesitation or uncertainty. We thought that surely he must have had a letter just that day to have it so absolutely at his finger-tips. And our amazement grew as we would hear him speak with equal knowledge and understanding of any and all places connected with the world-wide Crusade. He knew exactly who was where and what was happening. He paid great tribute to Mr. Banani, Hand of the Cause for Africa, saying his great love and sacrifice were responsible for the rapid progress of the Faith in Africa.[16]

After dinner, the Guardian left and the Allens, Rúḥíyyih Khánum and Leroy Ioas talked about what he had said. They were surprised at the great difference in opinion they had about what exactly Shoghi Effendi had told them: 'It made us acutely aware of why Pilgrim's notes must always remain on the basis of personal understanding and cannot have any official standing.' They talked about this until late. When the Allens went to their room, they found hot water bottles tucked in at the foot of their beds, placed there by Homa and Shayda, two Persian girls who attended the pilgrims.[17]

The next day the Allens were taken for their first visit to the Shrine of the Báb by Jessie and Ethel Revell. Valera wrote:

To try to explain the experience of entering the Shrine of the Blessed Youthful Martyr-Prophet is not possible. It is only something that one can experience. However, to me it was like entering into a sanctuary that completely shut out the world and one felt absolute peace, except for the anguish of one's own heart while meditating upon the tribulations and eventual martyrdom He had suffered for our sakes. We said prayers for all our friends, relatives (living and dead), for the progress of the Faith in America, Africa and all the world. One had the feeling of being really in contact with the 'Prayer-Hearing, Prayer-Answering God'.[18]

When the Shrine and Gardens were open to the public on certain afternoons, people would 'flock there from far and near'; there would be several hundred people each day. Valera was able to serve as a guide, holding peoples' cameras and instructing them to remove their shoes.

> Some rebelled at removing their shoes but would walk around trying to peer into the Shrine without actually going in, but in practically every instance their curiosity overcame them and finally they would remove their shoes and go in. Many stayed a long time in the Shrine and when they came out, there was reverence and respect written on their faces, and one could see they were deeply moved. Many stayed to ask questions or wanted literature, but the Guardian prefers to let the Shrine and the Gardens speak for themselves and we give answers as briefly as possible – now is not the time to give the Message to the people of Israel, but rather we show friendship and cooperation to the new Government. Two young girls dressed in the Israeli army uniform (girls must give two years compulsory military service along with the men) stayed for a long time watching the crowd and waiting to ask a question. Finally they approached and asked why I, an American, was serving at the Shrine of a Persian religion. The act itself had been a teacher, so all I answered was, 'This is not a Persian religion, it is a World Religion and you will find coming here Baha'is from every country of the world.' I told them also that I thought they were very privileged to have in their country the World Center of a World Religion. They asked to know more but I gave them only some of the Principles and the barest outline of the Faith.[19]

John and Valera had brought Shoghi Effendi a new car and John spent so much time chauffeuring Leroy around in it that Shoghi Effendi had to stop him, so that he would more acquire spiritual value from his pilgrimage.[20]

During the afternoon of 16 December, Valera helped Rúḥíyyih <u>Kh</u>ánum prepare for the visit of Josephine Baker, the famous black American jazz singer, actress, resistance fighter and racial equality activist who spent most of her life in Paris. She had begun her career by dancing on stage nearly naked, but during the Second World War worked with the Red Cross in France and ultimately joined the French Resistance. Her fame allowed her access to many areas and she smuggled out information mixed in with her sheet music or in her underwear.

For her efforts, she was awarded the Croix de Guerre and the Rosette de la Resistance and was made a Chevalier of the Legion d'Honneur by General Charles de Gaulle. When she visited the United States in the 1950s and experienced its rampant racism, she became an activist for racial equality, refusing to play in clubs unless they integrated their audiences. In 1963, she spoke alongside Martin Luther King when he gave his famous 'I have a dream' speech.[21]

Valera remembered that she helped 'polish silver, wash dishes, arrange flowers, set tables, clean house and do the 'million and one' things that need to be done for such an event'. On receiving Rúḥíyyih Khánum's invitation, Josephine had said 'We will be very glad to accept.' So, Valera noted, 'Rúḥíyyih Khánum did not know whether "we" meant two or twenty.' In the event, Josephine Baker arrived with a party of about 22, including the American and Italian Consuls and their wives as well as various Haifa dignitaries. The next day, Rúḥíyyih Khánum gave Josephine a tour of the Shrine and the Gardens.[22]

Early on 18 December, there was 'a great deal of hurrying around' as 'food was packed in baskets and the station wagon was loaded with various and sundry things. One had the feeling a picnic was in the offing.' Actually, they were going to Bahjí and were told to take their warmest clothes, wool socks and a hot water bottle. Two cars went carrying John and Valera, Rúḥíyyih Khánum, Milly Collins, Leroy Ioas, Ugo and Angeline Giachery, Jessie and Ethel Revell, Lotfullah and Iraj Hakím, Mr and Mrs Esfandiar Bakhtiari (he was a National Spiritual Assembly member from Pakistan) and Shayda, a Persian girl who came along to cook. They were met at Bahjí by Salah Jarráh, the caretaker, who first took them to the Shrine of Bahá'u'lláh. Afterwards, Salah showed them the miracle of gardening wrought by the Guardian in just a few days in April 1952.[23] This was well described by a later pilgrim, Alice Dudley, in 1957:

> To give an idea of how fast the Guardian works – when the Israeli court awarded the house at Bahjí which had been occupied by Covenant Breakers, to the Baha'is – that very same day the decree was awarded, the Guardian had the house demolished . . . and every portion of it carried away and inside of 4½ days had created a formal garden 12½ meters wide and 80 meters long. In the process of making the garden he had a row of large trees uprooted by

bulldozers, raised the garden by 1 meter, built roads, paths, installed lighting, made terraces, placed statuary and planted trees, flowers and shrubbery according to a design. All this monumental work was accomplished in 4½ days.[24]

Over the weekend, the pilgrims visited the Mansion, where they stayed overnight, then Mazra'ih, the House of Abbúd, the Most Great Prison and the Riḍván Garden.[25]

Returning from Bahjí, John and Valera joined Rúḥíyyih Khánum, Milly, Leroy and the Giacherys to visit two of Shoghi Effendi's cousins in Nazareth to celebrate the transfer of land at Bahjí from them to the Faith. The Allens wrote that

> It is one of those strange events that convinces one that 'God works in mysterious ways His wonders to perform'. It seems that the land had once been owned by a staunch Christian who used to observe Baha'u'llah and Abdu'l-Baha and was impressed enough to recognize that these men were not molded of ordinary clay yet he was antagonistic in the extreme. So much so that he made his son promise that the land would never be sold to the Baha'is. The son was very friendly to Abdu'l-Baha and in order to cover up his friendship he would tell his father that he was associating with Abdu'l-Baha in an effort to convert him to Christianity. However, he did promise his father not to sell the land to them. Time went on and the old man died and the son needed money so he sold the land to some Arabs. When the war between the Arabs and the Jews broke out the owners of the land fled from the country and the Government took it over. Now the cousins of Shoghi Effendi lived in Jordan and their farm land was appropriated by the Government because it was in the war zone. The cousins made application for an exchange of their farm for the land adjoining Bahji and it was granted to them. They immediately gave it to the Guardian and this was the event we were going to Nazareth to help celebrate. And what a celebration! The luncheon had been prepared for Ruhiyyih Khanum, Milly Collins, Leroy Ioas and the Giacherys and John and I were invited because we happened to be on pilgrimage so were included. Ruhiyyih Khanum came down with a very bad cold at the last minute and could not go and I could see well why one with a cold would not, or could

not eat the terrifically rich food that was served to us. There were courses and courses of all kinds of delicacies we had never heard of or tasted. We ate from 1 o'clock until 3 and then had to go over to the other cousin's house and had sweets which lasted for another hour. We really had difficulty rising from the table when it was over! They were really two of the loveliest families one could ever want to know, and with them was living a little old lady who was a relative of Baha'u'llah and looking very much as if the least breeze would blow her away yet her eyes shone with an inner brilliance as if she might have 1000 watt lights concealed behind them.[26]

They ate so much that they were still full when they met Shoghi Effendi that night at dinner. The Guardian was very 'happy and jovial' that night as he piled the pilau onto their plates in spite of their objections, joking about John having a good appetite.

Shoghi Effendi talked about marriage that evening and said that in America, husbands were slaves to their wives. They worked all day, but when they came home to relax, their wives would drag them off to cocktail parties or to the theatre. He said that Germans and Americans should intermarry because German wives are slaves to their husbands and intermarriage would bring about balance.[27]

When the Allens left Israel for Africa, they learned first hand the appreciation of the Jewish people for the Bahá'ís. Bahá'í pilgrims rarely had their luggage checked when they entered the country. Leroy Ioas and Ugo and Angeline Giachery took them to the airport where they met the airport manager. Leroy invited him to a personally guided tour of the Gardens as his guest, and the man was very pleased. When it came time to board the plane, the manager personally took them on ahead of the other passengers and asked the hostess to show them 'every consideration'.[28]

Bernard Leach

Bernard Leach, the famous potter, was also in the Holy Land in December. He, too, was struck by Shoghi Effendi's

strange intuitive faculties and directness of perception with such frankness, sincerity and humor, and at the same time deep reverence.

He seems to be constantly guided by an inward propulsion of which he is the willing servant. [Rúḥíyyih Khánum] said that after 15 years with him, day and night, she does not know a Shoghi Effendi separate from the Guardian. The most remarkable features of his mild face are his brown soft eyes which wander, taking in things and people, looking through rather than at. At other times he looks straight at one with a penetrating and compelling glance but not from the eye. Ruhiyyih Khanum is delightful and full of fun and sunlight, no stuffy religiousity with her.[29]

Olivia Kelsey and Laura Davis

Olivia Kelsey, a Knight of Bahá'u'lláh to Monaco, and Laura Davis from Toronto arrived independently at the same time at the Western Pilgrim House on 23 December 1954. Olivia had been in America at the beginning of the Ten Year Plan and when Nellie French, who had become a Knight of Bahá'u'lláh by pioneering to Monaco, passed away while at her post, Olivia was asked to replace her. She arrived for her pilgrimage by ship and, as they came into the port at Haifa, the upper deck was crowded with people, including an Australian Christian minister. The minister pointed the Shrine out to his fellow passengers and said, 'Now, that is Baha'i. I don't know much about it. But they're for peace.'[30]

When Olivia reached the Western Pilgrim House, she knocked on the big brass knocker. The door was opened by a girl and Olivia said that she 'told her my story and she understood not a word. Then she spoke and I understood not a word. My heart sank.' But then Milly Collins came, saying that they hadn't expected anyone that day, but that she had come over because she had thought she should. Twenty minutes later, Laura arrived, having flown to Tel Aviv. Olivia wrote:

You step from the porch . . . right into the large room; it is long, not square. To the left end was the living quarters of Mr. and Mrs. Ioas. It was probably a sleeping and sitting room combined; he had a small reception room; there was a desk; and a stove he had just brought from the United States. You see there was no such thing as central heating. They told us – Ruhiyyih Khanum and Jessie and Ethel Revell, how they suffered for lack of heat when they first went there . . .

Going to the left there was another room used as a business office but also I think a bedroom; then Jessie's room; then the two large doors; and the room occupied by Laura and me was next. Then you looked to your right and saw another large room at the end of the beautiful central room; It had a great glass window and window seats; there was a stove and a large, round table in the center and it was there that the pilgrims gathered and waited for the call to go down to dinner with the Beloved Guardian. On that side was a bathroom, the descending stairs . . . The large central room that you entered from the porch was beautifully furnished; there were pillars and an alcove.

The dining room was not square but long; there was a long table, with a beautiful linen cloth, exquisite china and silver. (Ruhiyyih Khanum told us there were many sets of dishes; the Holy Family, her mother's and more).[31]

Like many pilgrims, when Olivia first met the Guardian, she tried to describe him, but she remembered what Dr Katharine True had written in her pilgrim notes, about a man who met Shoghi Effendi 14 times. When he first met the Guardian, the man said, 'He is short,' but the last time he saw the Guardian, he said, 'He is a giant.'

In stature, the Guardian resembled Baha'u'llah; 'Abdu'l-Baha was taller than they were. His face was oval, olive skin, a closely clipped black mustache; he wore a black fez, a soft white collar and black tie. He wore a long tan robe; loosely woven with a bright figure in it.

His voice was melodious and his speech not English, as I had been told, but rather a Harvard accent. Just pure English . . . His eyes; Ruhiyyih Khanum has said they were hazel. To me they looked dark. An extraordinary thing happened one evening. I do not remember what subject we were on; suddenly his eyes became two immense orbs; protruding; they seemed to me to be ruby red with shafts of fire or light. It lasted . . . perhaps 30 seconds. There was silence – no one moved. Then he continued as usual.[32]

One night, Shoghi Effendi talked about the buildings that would be erected on the Arc:

He took his pen and drew a semi-circle, marked in the corner . . .
where the archives building would be; it was just the beginning. . .
Often he would refer to the drawing on an easel in the corner of
the drawing room; one could see his joy and pride in it. Then there
would be the Universal House of Justice and a building resembling
the Pentagon – offices and assembly rooms. There would be offices
for the Hands, for NSA branch offices; every National Assembly
will have a branch office at the World Center . . .

Mr. Ioas interposed a question . . . Will there be a home for the
Guardian? There was silence. He did not reply. Afterwards, when he
passed away, I recalled that strange silence; He knew then that he
would not live in that house.[33]

Roy Mottahedeh was also on pilgrimage at the same time. One day,
he spent part of the afternoon with Shoghi Effendi in the gardens. The
Guardian had heard that Mr Mottahedeh had been afraid to meet him
and Laura Davis noted that he told his guest:

what strange things the returning pilgrims must be saying about
him, that any pilgrim should fear to meet him. He said this with a
twinkle. Then he said 'How strange, it is a wonder that Mr. Mottehedeh is from New York, a business man and a Jew, and still he is
spiritually minded!' Also there was a twinkle when he said this.

Mr. Mottehedeh came in later, so filled with joy that it spilled
over him, he flung out his arms and hugged himself, and said, over
and over again, 'O, what a Guardian! What a Guardian!' and tears
of happiness glistened in his eyes.[34]

Of her first meeting with Shoghi Effendi, Laura wrote that

He stood at the head of the table waiting to welcome his friends.
With a quivering heart I waited that welcome, as I stood at the end
of the line which is always led by the newly arrived pilgrim. How
often through the passing years I had tried to imagine being here,
where I now stood. In a dream once I had found myself here. Now,
at long last that dear dream had come true . . .

Who is this man for whose 'welcome' I have waited so long? This
man who holds himself like a king, for king he is yet there is such

profound humility, the humility of the truly great.

He wears a black coat over his suit, a black fez or taj which shows dark hair slightly greying at the temples. He is not tall, yet stately, slight yet breathing strength. Eyes of hazel brown that can glow with hidden fire, with flashing light, with rich enthusiasm – or lower in deep thought.

The face is heart-shaped, delicately moulded, the nose straight, the mouth beautiful, as though made more beautiful than is usual by the beautiful words that have flowed from it through the years, the small mustache not hiding any of that beauty.[35]

It is difficult to describe our Guardian . . . Delicacy, utmost refinement, spiritual qualities beyond our thinking. He is a small man in stature, with very fine hands, the hands of an artist. His eyes are filled with power and spirit, joy or pathos, for he reflects the feeling of the whole world in its wonder, having also the realization of its sorrow in his heart.

He changes continually, depending upon the subject he is speaking upon. All his gestures are graceful, his hands most expressive, so finely made . . . He points out to you how to use to the utmost that capacity which God has given you . . .

Another quality of our beloved Guardian is his extreme humility. He is so humble, as a man, that one might think he does not exist as an entity or an individual. [For] instance this – he never refers to the Ten Year Plan as 'his' plan. He refers to it as 'the Bahá'í World Plan'. He never says 'my' my plan my work . . .

One night at dinner the Guardian was very upset by a letter from a prominent believer who had written a bitter complaint about another Bahá'í. The Guardian said, 'This man is lying because he is the cause of the trouble.' He showed the letter to LeRoy and said, 'I have written to tell him he will be put out of the Cause, for he is lying to me. Who does he think he is that he can lie to me? Who does he think I am?'

The pulse of the whole world is in his hand. So you can see the character of the instrument of the Cause. He reflects success and failure. When news is good he is very happy, when it is bad he is very sad . . .[36]

Laura Davis noted that at dinner on 29 December, there were thirty-one ladies and that they ate pilau, 'green onion Turkish bread, tea, cha served in the most beautiful glasses and little plates. Ruhiyyih Khanum talked of American luxuries to the Persian ladies, told them of our wonderful gadgets and then, what we would do if we had no electricity.'[37]

Laura's visit to the Mansion of Bahjí was a powerful experience:

After one enters that lovely wrought iron gate and walks along the pathway to the north of the Mansion, and arrives at the leather-covered door with its metal studs, there is a flight of about 32 steps of wide white marble leading to the upper floor, where the living rooms are . . .

The main . . . room has lovely rugs in the center with four tables scattered around the room. On these are models of the Temple in Wilmette, the Shrine of the Báb on Mount Carmel, and the Temple that is to be built on Mount Carmel in the future. The fourth table has many of the Incorporations of Assemblies, National and Local, and framed so that one may realize the growth of the Cause.

The room at the north-east corner [sic] is that in which Baha'u'llah ascended. It has a lovely rug, and though not a bed-stead, it has a large cushion bed on the floor as it was when He slept there. Beside the bed a little white table with an oil lamp on it. At the east of the room a divan running the entire length of the room. It was here that He sat when interviewing Professor Browne and others. At the spot where He sat His taj has been placed. It is a high hat of brocade material, as seen in pictures . . .

In the corridor is hung a very large picture by Marion Jack. It is one of the scenes from the balcony showing the olive orchard with Akka in the distance, and the sea. It is beautifully painted.

One night Dr Lotfullah told me that, after all others had retired I might go to the room of Baha'u'llah by myself. That night I did not sleep. The Mansion was so quiet, so still. Quietly I arose, went to that door with the curtain embroidered with His Name, gently pushed it aside and entered. The room will always remain my most wonderful memory. The moonlight glowed. There was a little light burning. On the floor a glorious rug of soft colors and in the Center of that rug the little white bed which had His slippers at the bottom. I prostrated myself with my forehead on those slippers. At that hour the old world ceased to be for me, and a new world opened. I begged for His protection that I might, however humbly, serve Him. For a long time I lay there and knew that now, at long last, I had reached heaven.[38]

One day Laura Davis saw an old man sitting in the window of an old, almost derelict house beside the Mansion at Bahjí. This was Mírzá Majdi'd-Dín, the man who had conspired with the Arch-breaker of the Covenant Mírzá Muhammad-'Alí, 'Abdu'l-Bahá's half-brother. Because of his arrogance and his attempts to destroy the Master, 'Abdu'l-Bahá told him that he would be given long life – but a life wracked by misery, one which he would pray to be released from.[39] Laura wrote that

he is paralysed, even his tongue, so he cannot speak. Years ago . . . 'Abdu'l-Bahá went to him, and told him that, for his enmity toward the Faith he would be compelled to live to see its victory . . .

At that time this man may have thought that long life would be a blessing . . . He became ill, then paralysed, and still he could not die. He prayed for death but death passed him by, taking all that he had loved from him.

Now he sits, and looking out of his window he sees lovely gardens rise, sees the great care taken of the home of Baha'u'llah, the stately mansion of Bahji. He sees the success of the Faith.[40]

Mírzá Majdi'd-Din died the next year and the Guardian immediately had the house removed and replaced by a beautiful garden.

Ahmad Sohrab's continued rebellion

Ahmad Sohrab, one of 'Abdu'l-Bahá's secretaries on His travels to the West and in Haifa, who had rejected Shoghi Effendi, was enraged at the success of the Ten Year Crusade. In 1954, desperate to slow the rapidly growing influence and prestige of the Faith and the Guardian, Sohrab went to the Holy Land and contacted the few remaining Covenant-breakers still living. Laura Davis recorded the story of his visit to Haifa and Akka during that summer. Leroy Ioas, hearing of his arrival, had told the Bahá'ís that Sohrab was not to be allowed to visit the Holy Places in Haifa, but the Guardian said

'Let him go.' So Sorab visited all the Holy Places [on Mt Carmel] in about 15 minutes. He did not chant one prayer. Leaving, he was asked, 'Do you not wish to see the Shrine of the Master?' He said, 'Well, yes.' He entered, stayed one minute, then left . . .

He made the statement that he had attended the University of Beirut with Dr L Hakim, but this was not true as the Doctor had never attended the University . . .

Sorab stayed only a few minutes in the Shrines [at Bahjí] and in the room of Bahá'u'lláh. He said that the gardens were spoiled by the ornamentation which was done by the Guardian. He wanted the books that were written by the Guardian, but Salah [Jarrah] told him that he had better buy them in America . . .[41]

While in the Holy Land, he publicly denounced 'Abdu'l-Bahá, saying that He had violated the Will of Bahá'u'lláh by appointing Shoghi Effendi as the head of the Faith instead of Mírzá Muḥammad-'Alí. His conflicting statements simply confused his listeners. In a press conference in Haifa, Sohrab said that 'Abdu'l-Bahá was a Muslim, but at another in Tel Aviv, he called himself 'the secretary of 'Abdu'l-Bahá and His leading disciple'. When the Tel Aviv interviewer asked him about the Will of the Master appointing Shoghi Effendi as the Guardian, Sohrab said that while he had hoped that Shoghi Effendi would be a good Guardian, that had not proved to be the case and that the problem he was trying to solve was 'how to get rid of Shoghi Effendi'.[42]

A couple of years later, when Sohrab's activities were mentioned to the Guardian, He said that Sohrab was trying to copy the Bahá'í administration:

At first he attacked organization, now he sees it is more effective. We have Assemblies, he has chapters. We have a fund, he established a fund. We have conferences, he has conferences . . . When you meet up with members of this group (New History Society or Caravan), ignore them. Do not try to convert them; it is of no use now. When he dies, they will all become Baha'is. Our enemy is doing us a favor. Ignore them and be confident. Do not be afraid.[43]

Sohrab's organization did not survive his death in 1958.

Knights of Bahá'u'lláh

During 1954, 16 more of Shoghi Effendi's virgin territories were settled and 45 more people gained the title of Knight of Bahá'u'lláh. Shoghi Effendi closed the Roll of Honour on 4 May, writing 'The Roll of Honor, after the lapse of one year since the launch of the World Crusade, is now closed, with the exception of pioneers who have already left for their destination, as well as those first arriving in the few remaining virgin territories . . .'[44]

Before this date, anyone pioneering to one of the Guardian's goals during the first year of the Plan had won the title, even if there were other pioneers there. It meant that the new pioneers going to a goal area that already had pioneers after that date could no long acquire the title. The first pioneers going to virgin goal areas after that date still earned the title of Knight of Bahá'u'lláh, but others who followed them did not.

1955

The International Archives Building

One of the major projects of the Ten Year Crusade was the construction of the International Archives Building. When Ugo Giachery had been in Haifa a few years before, Shoghi Effendi had one night brought out a mysterious bundle wrapped in a colourful silk handkerchief, typical of Persia, that had arrived that day from Tehran. When everyone was seated at the table, he carefully opened the bundle and revealed a handwritten manuscript. It was two Tablets, the *Kitáb-i-Íqán* and another, in the beautiful calligraphy of 'Abdu'l-Bahá when He was about eighteen years old. In the margins were notes written by Bahá'u'lláh. Shoghi Effendi said that he had never before seen an original of the *Kitáb-i-Íqán*. He was amazed to discover that the passage he had used on the title page of *The Dawn-Breakers* was one of Bahá'u'lláh's additions. Everyone there was in awe of the obvious spiritual link between Bahá'u'lláh and Shoghi Effendi. Shoghi Effendi told also about the discovery of the 20 original Tablets from the Báb to the Letters of the Living and to Bahá'u'lláh – after 'Abdu'l-Bahá's ascension, the Tablets were found with the Master's papers. No one had known that they existed.[1]

Because of these priceless Tablets, the Guardian was determined to build a suitable repository, the International Archives. Earlier, in the winter of 1952, he had asked Mason Remey to make preliminary drawings based on the design of the Parthenon in Athens and the size of the Madeleine Church in Paris, which was a copy of the Parthenon. Each night at dinner, Shoghi Effendi would hang up the drawings for inspection and make whatever modification his uniquely focused eye thought necessary. When he was finally satisfied, he sent the pen and ink drawing to Ugo to present at the International Teaching Conference in New Delhi in October 1953.[2] When Shoghi Effendi was asked why he had chosen a Greek style, he replied that it was beautiful and had withstood the test of time.[3]

Shoghi Effendi didn't use a surveyor to lay out the Archives Building. The building was set on what was then a steep hillside, but the Guardian laid it out himself using white string and stakes. Rúḥíyyih Khánum wrote that to build the Archives, he used 'untrained "gardeners", an Italian chauffeur who carried out the instructions of his employer standing directing him, an ex-railway executive [Leroy Ioas], a doctor of chemistry [Ugo Giachery] and an old man who, though an architect, had had little experience in such undertakings [Mason Remey].'[4]

Previously, at Riḍván 1954, Shoghi Effendi sent the following message to the worldwide Bahá'í community:

> The design of the International Bahá'í Archives, the first stately Edifice destined to usher in the establishment of the World Administrative Centre of the Faith on Mt. Carmel – the Ark referred to by Bahá'u'lláh in the closing passages of His Tablet of Carmel – has been completed, and plans and drawings forwarded to Italy for the purpose of securing bids for its construction immediately after the conclusion of the necessary preliminary steps taken in the Holy Land for its forthcoming erection.[5]

When Ugo Giachery returned to Italy in December, he arranged for Architect Rocca to prepare more drawings and an estimated cost. The building was to be made of the same Chiampo marble used in the Shrine of the Báb. The contract for the work was accepted by Shoghi Effendi on 3 January 1955. The building was to be 100 feet long, 46 feet wide, and 36 feet high with 46 columns. The columns were composed of three stacked parts, all of which were fluted with grooves running from top to bottom, a task requiring great care and precision. When the first column was completed in Italy, all the workers gathered around to see Ugo's reaction – and they weren't disappointed: 'I could not believe my eyes; its beauty and perfection were beyond any possible imagination!' He congratulated each worker.[6] The first of seventeen shiploads of marble left Italy for Haifa on 10 August 1955 and the first column was raised in Haifa in December.[7]

Ugo's next challenge was to find someone to make the stained glass for the high window at the back of the building. Professor B.

Gregoriette, of Palermo, won the task and did the whole job of making the glass to the exact colours wanted by the Guardian and soldering hundreds of yards of lead alloy binding. The double front doors were another problem Ugo had to solve. He ended up going back to the same carpenter who had created the door at the Shrine of Bahá'u'lláh, Saiello Saielli. Like the door of the Shrine, these had two rows of large rosettes, but unlike the Shrine, they were to be laminated with brass. The doors took six months to complete and then, since they weighed almost two tons, special ball-bearing hinges had to be made.[8] Inside the building, Shoghi Effendi had two balconies for additional display space and he wanted special balustrades for them. Looking through architectural books, he found those at the Villa La Rotonda in Vicenza to be what he wanted, so off Ugo went to make drawings and measurements. Saiello Saielli skilfully completed the final balustrades.[9]

The last pieces were large chandeliers, for lighting, and the tiles for the roof. Shoghi Effendi had Ugo send him catalogues of crystal chandeliers from which he chose one with 60 lights and many prisms and pendants. Ugo ordered six from a Bohemian glass company in Czechoslovakia. The roofing tiles were a bigger problem. Shoghi Effendi wanted the cobalt-green colour of weathered copper because it sometimes blended with the sky. He didn't want to use copper because it could stain the marble, so the company that had made the gold tiles for the Shrine of the Báb, Utrecht of Holland, was contacted and they developed fired clay tablets glazed to match the colour. Sheila Banani remembered a discussion at the dinner table in May 1956 when Shoghi Effendi asked

> Mason's (Remey) and Leroy's (Ioas) opinions of the Archives' roof tile selections – much earlier discussion had been held while I was on pilgrimage about the African and German Temple designs and the building of the Archives, 'business' decisions at table being interspersed with other conversations. He asked Leroy to order the green, non-shiny tile from Holland (earlier he had asked me to go up on Mt. Carmel and look at the various tiles to see the differences of shading as they were slanted on boards at the angle they would be when placed on the roof).[10]

The contract for 7,892 tiles was signed on 6 June of the following year, 1956.[11]

Violence in Iran

Early in 1955, Shoghi Effendi announced that a design by Mason Remey for the Mashriqu'l-Adhkár in Tehran had been accepted. A model was placed on display in May.[12] This announcement, unfortunately happened at a time of violent attacks on the Faith in Iran.

This wave of violence wracked the country during much of 1955. It began on 18 January when five Bahá'ís in Hisar, Khurasan, were arrested and beaten, with four of them being dragged through the town. In addition, Bahá'í homes were attacked, looted and set afire. Then on 23 April, during Ramadan, Shaykh Muḥammad-Taqí Falsafí preached an incendiary sermon against the Bahá'ís in the Fhu'ís Mosque in Tehran which was broadcast on national radio. By 2 May, during the Bahá'í National Convention, feeling against the Bahá'ís had exploded. The National Bahá'í Centre in Tehran was locked, preventing the conclusion of the Convention, then five days later it was taken over by the Army. Ten days after that, the Ministry of the Interior announced in the National Parliament that the Bahá'ís were to be suppressed and Bahá'í Centres 'liquidated'. On 22 May, a great mass of people, supervised by Army officers and Shaykh Muḥammad-Taqí Falsafí, attacked the National Bahá'í Centre in Tehran and destroyed the dome. Photographs of the destruction ignited an outburst of fanatic activity across the country that resulted in many Bahá'ís being beaten, local centres and Bahá'í homes being destroyed or burned and Bahá'í shops looted and set afire. Even Bahá'í children and women didn't escape the mob's wrath, being beaten as well. Some women were publically stripped or raped and some young women were abducted and forced to marry Muslims. The House of the Báb was destroyed and the House of Bahá'u'lláh in Mazindaran was taken over. On 28 July, seven Bahá'ís in Yazd were beaten to death. Many Bahá'ís who had government jobs lost them.[13]

The mobs ran virtually without restriction and a massacre was 'openly promised in the press and in public meetings'. Shoghi Effendi asked Bahá'í communities around the world to protest directly to the Shah of Iran, the Prime Minister and the Majlis (Parliament) and thousands of cables inundated their offices. In July, Shoghi Effendi told the Bahá'í International Community to lodge an appeal for assistance to the Economic and Social Council of the United Nations.[14]

The Iranians were not worried about world opinion or the United

Nations. A newspaper stated that 'the United Nations cannot interfere in the internal affairs of a nation. If they put an appeal, we shall
declare that the Bahá'í Faith is not a religion.' But then the newspapers
of the world splashed stories of the violence across their pages. One
paper bluntly told Iran: 'The Persian Government will harm itself in the
world's eyes if it allows the persecution of the Baha'is to continue.' The
Iranian Government issued a statement claiming that the Bahá'ís were
a political organization and not a religion. It also said that the Bahá'ís
were a very small minority who were not being bothered at all. When
confronted by an English journalist, an Iranian minister was forced to
admit that the statement was not true and that it should never have
been written.[15] World opinion definitely gave Iran something to worry
about.

At the United Nations, the Economic and Social Council had thousands of appeals to consider and it appeared that it would be impossible
for the Bahá'í petition to be reviewed before the Council adjourned.
Therefore, a Committee, composed of Ugo Giachery, Hermann Grossmann, John Ferraby, 'Azíz Navidí and Mildred Mottahedeh, went to
Geneva and appealed directly to the members of the Council. The
Committee tried to contact everyone, but they faced failure. A few
days before the massacre was scheduled to begin, the Secretary-General
Dag Hammarskjöld gave in to the pressure and sent the High Com-
missioner for Refugees, Dr G. J. van Hueven Goedhart, to meet with
the chief Iranian delegate to the United Nations and his brother, the
Minister of Foreign Affairs of Iran. The Iranian Government had not
expected any reaction from the United Nations and the world and were
'astounded'.[16]

Shoghi Effendi asked the National and Local Spiritual Assemblies
around the world to write directly to the Shah and this led to some
interesting teaching opportunities. Sabri Elias in Djibouti, had the following conversation:

> 'This cable is addressed to the Sháh. How can you correspond with
> kings?'
> 'Yes, we are Baha'is and we are sending this cable to the king of
> Persia because of the tyranny that our brothers there are now facing.
> The Baha'is all over the world have sent similar cables because we are
> all as one family and have loving and sympathetic feelings for each

other. I suppose you have heard about the attacks on the Baha'is of Iran?

'Yes, we have read about them.'

Then the clerk went in the office and came out later saying: 'We have to get permission from the director before sending this. Few minutes later, the director of the telegraph office came and said: 'Must we send this cable today?' 'Yes, if possible!?'

'Is there a Baha'i community here?'

'Yes!'

'We must inform the Governor about this cable.'

'I brought this cable knowing very well that the Governor shall know about it, we are people of peace and do not interfere in political matters; moreover, we have no secrets.'

The following day: 'Do you still insist on sending this cable? It is going to cost you a lot.'

'Yes, with pleasure.'

Here all the employees gathered and read the cable and were repeating the words with wonder: Baha'is! Sháh!

'Then wait a moment until I get the permission.'

Few minutes later– 'The permission has been granted.'

Two hours later the representative of the Assembly received a summons to call at the Mayor's office immediately.

I went with one of the friends who acted as interpreter. After preliminary talks asking me whether I understood French, he said: 'Is the Baha'i Faith a branch of Islam?'

'No, the Baha'i Faith is an independent religion and is not a sect any other religion.'

'What are the teachings of the Baha'i Faith?'

'The Baha'i Faith is a new religion advocating world peace and love between the people of the world. It also teaches the equality between men and women, universal language, the ending of wars and the suppression of prejudices. It believes in all the religions including the Brahman and Buddhist, believing they are from divine origin.'

'Do you believe in reincarnation?'

'We believe in life after death but not reincarnation.'

'Are there Baha'is here?'

'Yes, my family and probably others.'

'Why is Islam against you?'

'They say Muhammad is the last of the Prophets and there should be no religions after Islam, We say, God's Revelation has not and will never stop.'

'The Baha'i Faith started in Persia and spread all over the world, because it is a world religion and not a national one. I belong to this world religion.'

'I can see that your religion is clean.'

'May I present you with some books?'

'Please send me books. Thanks for coming and excuse the inconvenience.'[17]

Condemnations came from every quarter, including Prime Minister Nehru of India, Eleanor Roosevelt and Professor Arnold Toynbee. Iran was again and again reminded that it had signed the United Nations Declaration of Human Rights that guaranteed freedom of religion. 'I hope that the government of Iran will have sufficient moral and religious responsibility and just common sense to stop this sort of persecution,' wrote a professor at Harvard University. The flood of protesting cables and bad publicity forced one newspaper in Tehran to write, 'This has created an international problem for the government.' The world-wide denunciation didn't stop the persecution, but it did bring to an abrupt end to the overt violence against the Bahá'ís. And, in the face of such a hostile environment, the Persian Bahá'í community continued to advance. In 1953, there were 260 Local Spiritual Assemblies in Iran. Six years later there were over 500.[18]

Zebby Whitehead

O. Z. (Zebby) Whitehead arrived for his pilgrimage in the second week of January. John Ferraby was there at the same time. The first night Zebby walked into the dining room and saw Shoghi Effendi's face, he said that it was

filled with deep thoughts, with feeling and sensitivity of the finest kind. And as he stood up and greeted us and asked us to come near to him . . . I could sense he was not just a spiritual person, that he represented the entire universe since the passing of his Grandfather.

I felt as if I was in the presence of the Manifestation of God, which he was not, but he was the Sign of God on earth, but the power that exuded from him was overwhelming, and yet at the same time, it made you completely happy to be in his presence . . .

And he looked at you with those wonderful eyes that seemed to penetrate into your heart . . .[19]

Zebby noted that the Guardian was very informal and spoke with a 'clipped Oxford accent'. Shoghi Effendi's talks, as usual, ranged over a variety of subjects, but always related to the Faith. Zebby learned that the Writings in *Gleanings from the Writings of Bahá'u'lláh* came from a dozen volumes and that the two things that make a Covenant-breaker are 'ambition and arrogance'. One night, Zebby asked Shoghi Effendi what he thought of Winston Churchill. Rúḥíyyih Khánum immediately interjected: 'Oh Zebby, don't get the Guardian going on Churchill!' The Guardian replied simply that 'Churchill is very capable, but lacking in principle. More capable than Eisenhower or Roosevelt.' Then he added that President Woodrow Wilson was 'very pure-hearted'. At another time, they were talking about the book *The Dawn-Breakers*. Zebby said that he preferred Shoghi Effendi's own books, to which the Guardian replied with a smile, '*The Promised Day Is Come* won't be at all popular with the clergy because it is very hard on them.' Zebby also asked if it was okay to teach morally bankrupt people, such as gangsters. With a twinkle in his eye, Shoghi Effendi replied that it was okay, 'If you don't get robbed'.[20]

The Ten Year Crusade was the main topic. Shoghi Effendi said that Africa had 'outstripped his expectations' and that the Bahá'ís in the cities should disperse and move into rural areas. He specifically mentioned that the Bahá'ís in New York, where Zebby was living at that time, should disperse. Shoghi Effendi said that he had asked the Persians to disperse, but that only 3 per cent had responded. He added, 'Americans should disperse in great numbers. If they would do so, it would have an enormous effect on the Cause.' But when he learned that Zebby was taking care of his 83-year-old mother, he immediately said, 'Oh, then you cannot possibly pioneer.'[21]

On his last day, Zebby and Rúḥíyyih Khánum were talking about marriage and he asked her if she had had any intimation, as a young girl, that she would marry the Guardian. In response, Rúḥíyyih Khánum told of a dream she had when she was sixteen and on pilgrimage:

> I dreamt that I had rescued the Guardian from a burning house.
> I took this dream very seriously and when I came downstairs that
> night for dinner, I looked at Shoghi Effendi and I thought of what
> I had seen in my dream. He looked at me very stirringly and I dis-
> missed the thought. And then he turned towards me and smiled.

When he did ask her to marry him in 1937, she initially thought that
this union of East and West would be good for the Faith. But then she
thought, 'I love him anyway. Of course I want to marry him.'[22]

John, Audrey, Patrick and Nina Robarts

Also in January, John and Audrey Robarts, with their son Patrick and
daughter Nina, arrived for pilgrimage. They were Canadians pioneering
in Africa, and Knights of Bahá'u'lláh. At dinner on the first night, there
was one other pilgrim who asked a question on behalf of someone else.
Shoghi Effendi replied with 'patient exasperation':

> 'Why don't they read my book [God Passes By]?' In that moment
> my heart was touched to think how much he had done, how much
> he had suffered, writing, translating, planting magnificent gardens
> to beautify the holy places, at the same time carrying on a worldwide
> correspondence and keeping watch over the Bahá'í Faith in the new
> State of Israel. Pilgrims came and went much of the time. How tire-
> less was his deep devotion to Bahá'u'lláh, to 'Abdu'l-Bahá, how great
> was his integrity, and how modern his style. Yet, he showed only the
> slightest wondering impatience with bothersome questions.[23]

Various members of the Robarts family found things they could help
with. Audrey and Nina jumped right in and, while Milly Collins made
bran muffins for lunch, Nina made a dark chocolate cake with white
icing that Shoghi Effendi really liked, and Audrey sewed curtains.
Patrick pruned shrubs in the garden.

Shoghi Effendi said that the pioneers should remain in the background and the Africans should be in front. He illustrated this concept
by saying that the pioneers should be like a reference library. He further

explained what he meant by saying that when the Robarts family had first crossed into Bechuanaland, the young and inexperienced Patrick was driving the car, but his older, wiser father was in the back seat. The pioneers should similarly let the young, inexperienced African believers drive the car of the Faith. The pioneers should be in the back seat ready to offer guidance whenever it was needed.[24]

One day, Rúḥíyyih Khánum told the Robarts that Shoghi Effendi had received word that three pioneers were leaving their posts. The Guardian wrote the name of every pioneer in a little black notebook, but would cross off the name of any pioneer who left. That day he only crossed off the names of two of those pioneers because it upset him too much to cross off all three at the same time.[25]

At one point, the Guardian showed them the Scroll of Honour, which contained the names of John, Audrey and Patrick, but not Nina. This bothered Patrick, so Shoghi Effendi explained that Nina was not yet 15 when they arrived at their post, therefore she wasn't of age. For that reason, she was not given the title of Knight of Bahá'u'lláh.[26]

One night, John had the privilege of walking after dinner with Shoghi Effendi to the House of the Master. Arriving at his door, the Guardian told John that 'I hope you will serve on the national assembly to be formed in Africa next year (1956).' John responded that that was 'an honor I had hoped to be spared'. When Shoghi Effendi concluded the evening by saying, 'I hope you will be on that assembly. My prayers will always be offered on your behalf . . .', John knew that he would indeed be on that Assembly.[27]

The Robarts had brought Shoghi Effendi a present of a kaross, a mat made from the skin of a springbok, inlaid with designs made of other animal skins. The Guardian said that he would put it in the Mansion. After Shoghi Effendi's death, when John, then a Hand of the Cause, attended the First Conclave of the Hands that met in the Mansion, he looked for the kaross, but didn't see it. He thought that the Guardian hadn't completed his promise. The next year at the Second Conclave, he again looked, but again did not find it. Then he asked Rúḥíyyih Khánum if Shoghi Effendi had put it in the Mansion. She replied, 'Yes, indeed he did. Come to my room and see it.' Shoghi Effendi had put the kaross in his own room and used it as his personal prayer mat.[28]

Claire Gung, the Mother of Africa

Claire Gung, pioneering in Southern Rhodesia, arrived for her pilgrimage on 17 January, a few days after the Robarts. She had almost cancelled her pilgrimage after flying from Salisbury, Rhodesia to Nairobi, Kenya. The flight in a small plane had been extremely rough and had thoroughly shaken her up. Claire only continued because of the persuasiveness of Aziz Yazdi, a pioneer in Nairobi. The rest of her trip, fortunately, was smooth. When she arrived at the Pilgrim House, she met the other pilgrims, including John Ferraby, and learned that they would all be going to Bahjí that same afternoon. At that point, Claire had not been assigned a room, so to prepare for her stay in Bahjí she began to repack. Kneeling down on the floor surrounded by her luggage, she suddenly saw Rúḥíyyih Khánum approaching and leaped to her feet to meet the Guardian's wife. Rúḥíyyih Khánum told her that Shoghi Effendi sent his regrets that he couldn't see her before she left for Bahjí, about which the relieved Claire wrote that she was 'jolly glad, because I was too scared and nervous to meet the Guardian'.[29]

The pilgrims arrived to see the Shrine of Bahá'u'lláh illuminated, then went into the Mansion. Claire was so strongly affected by the spiritual power emanating from Bahá'u'lláh's room that she was not able to enter it. She was up at 5 a.m. the next morning and went to the Shrine to pray. For an hour, she had the Shrine to herself and she wrote that 'I was all alone with my Lord. Never have I prayed from the bottom of my heart as I prayed then.' During the day, the pilgrims visited Akka, guided by Lotfullah Hakím and Mason Remey, and then went to the Riḍván Garden. That night, Claire was in the room with the pictures of the popes and the kings and got very little sleep.[30]

The next day, back in Haifa, Claire learned that she would meet the Guardian that evening at dinner:

> Claire tried to rehearse mentally how she would conduct herself, but by the time dinner was announced, she was still unprepared for the meeting. 'Gosh, my knees would hardly hold me.' She stood aside, as they all approached the dining room, waiting for others to go in so she could enter last, 'but Milly [Collins] pushed me forward. "None of your nonsense," she said. "The new pilgrim goes in first."' So go in first she did, and was introduced to Shoghi

Effendi as the first pioneer to Africa.[31]

Claire had not been the first pioneer to arrive in Africa following the Guardian's call in 1950, but she was the first to leave for her post, going by ship. Jalál Nakhjavání had actually arrived in Africa first, flying from Iran, but he left Iran after Claire had departed from England.

Claire's introduction to Shoghi Effendi was not what she had hoped for. She was seated opposite him. At one point,

> She lifted her arm and became entangled in the sleeve of Marguerite Sears' fur coat, then in an effort to extricate herself, her chair became stuck in the carpet. She rose slightly, lost her balance somewhat and nearly fell over backward. While trying to set the chair and herself upright, her handbag, which was on the chair, slipped to the floor. As she reached down to retrieve it, the serviette dropped from her lap. Clutching at it frantically, Claire was finally able to settle herself amid much fluster and confusion. Needless to say, it was not the most desirable first impression she would have liked to make.[32]

As many other pilgrims learned to their embarrassment, Shoghi Effendi knew much more about their country's activities then they did. Claire discovered this as well when the Guardian asked how many African believers and tribes there were. Claire didn't know, but he did.[33]

Pilgrim activities at that time depended on the availability of staff guides, who were commonly the Hands of the Cause or members of the International Bahá'í Council, who had many other duties. Consequently, the pilgrims were left to themselves at times, but were encouraged to visit other parts of the Holy Land. Claire and two other pilgrims joined a tour to Tiberias and Nazareth. Returning from the excursion, Claire's back ached, a problem that had afflicted her for a long time. Rúḥíyyih Khánum sent a doctor to examine her. Claire wrote that 'he twisted and bashed me about. I thought he was breaking every bone. How I screamed and yelled.' The chronic back pain that she had suffered, however, completely disappeared.[34]

Claire was granted three extra days for her pilgrimage, but they passed all too fast. On her last night, Shoghi Effendi, after asking her about her pioneering to Southern Rhodesia, said, 'I am so glad you could come. I am very proud of you. You have rendered historic service. Your name

will go down in Bahá'í history. I will pray for you and your success.'
When she arrived back in Salisbury, she learned that the Guardian had
designated her a Knight of Bahá'u'lláh.[35]

Ethna Archibald

Ethna Archibald was a New Zealand Bahá'í who had moved to London
in 1952. In New Zealand she had been an isolated pioneer in Tauranga
before serving on the Local Spiritual Assembly of Auckland, then a
small community, but in London she had the bounty of listening to
an almost endless stream of amazing speakers: Hasan Balyuzi and John
Ferraby, both of whom would become Hands of the Cause; Ian Semple,
who would serve on the Universal House of Justice; and Mrs Mehrangiz Munsiff. In December 1954, Ethna had received her invitation for
pilgrimage. Because it had been sent to New Zealand and forwarded
to London, she only had three weeks to prepare.[36] After arriving at the
airport in January, she hopped on a bus 'packed with people, goats (on
top) and bicycles' and had 'a most unusual and leisurely trip to Haifa'.
She arrived at 11 o'clock and wrote that

> the Revell sisters took me in and immediately said 'There is just
> time for you to go to the Shrine of the Báb, the beloved Guardian
> will be glad you have had your first visit there before you meet him
> this evening.' So Ethel literally ran me up the slopes of Mt. Carmel
> and I had the great bounty of being alone with her for that first
> magical experience. I remember I tried to read a prayer for forgive-
> ness through the tightest throat I had ever experienced. We strolled
> back down to the Pilgrim House, Ethel filling me in with badly
> needed advice, and I told her my Bahá'í life story.
>
> Back at the Pilgrim House I met Amatu'l-Bahá Rúhíyyih
> Khánum and Hand of the Cause Mason Remey and the two other
> Western Pilgrims, one an older woman from the United States the
> other from Canada who had just returned from a brief visit, at
> Shoghi Effendi's direction, to Nazareth which, in those days was
> very much like the pictures Dorothy had seen in the back of her
> childhood Bible, camels in the street, children everywhere, and the
> flies. Our lunch was hilarious as she described in shocked accents
> the things she had seen . . .[37]

Then came the moment she had been waiting for:

> We had assembled in the breezeway ready when Rúḥíyyih Khánum
> came to tell us that Shoghi Effendi had arrived . . . and led us down
> the stairs to the dining room. At the entrance stood the beloved
> Guardian to whom we were in turn presented . . . He greeted me
> with a smile that would melt any heart . . .
>
> This was the start of nine blissful days. Each evening we would
> listen as the Guardian told of the progress of the Faith – stirring
> messages were coming in of victories in Africa, and these and other
> news he shared with us. At the time he was busy with plans for
> the possible building of a Mashriqu'l-Adhkár in Tihran and we all
> examined the various parts of the entries that had been sent in by
> architects world-wide . . . One night Shoghi Effendi spoke about
> deep and stirring matters and we were all alert to its importance
> and after the Guardian left to return to his home we went upstairs
> . . . Amatu'l-Bahá, Mr. Ioas, Jessie, Ethel, Amy, Dorothy and I, and
> discussed what had been said. Each of us had heard something dif-
> ferent. Rúḥíyyih Khánum undertook to ask the beloved Guardian
> and the next day we found that not one of us had grasped the salient
> point!! So much for instantaneous pilgrim notes![38]

It was another good example of why pilgrim notes carry no authority.

One night, it was announced that they were going to have pomegranate stew for dinner. To their surprise, the purple meal was so good
that everyone had seconds. An article by Abu'l-Qásim Faizí later related
the story of the source of those pomegranates. He had visited a small
village in Persia and had spent an evening listening to the stories of the
villagers, many of whom had visited Bahá'u'lláh in Akka. At the time
of Bahá'u'lláh, disease had killed almost all of the pomegranate trees in
the area of Akka. Knowing that Bahá'u'lláh loved the fruit, and having
the best pomegranates in Persia, they set out with a large watermelon in
which they had implanted 144 pomegranate seeds. They walked for six
months, carrying the watermelon on their shoulders and taking turns
with the burden, until they reached Akka. About two dozen pomegranate shoots were still in good shape when they reached Bahá'u'lláh. All
the pomegranates in the Holy Land were supposed to be derived from
these.[39]

The women who came on pilgrimage commonly helped in the kitchen by making something. Ethna made dessert one night for 30 people out of a packet with no instructions. She was so surprised to find that it came out well that she offered to make a cake for the visit of a United Nations dignitary. She had to pull the recipe out of her memory and then find some rather uncommon ingredients. When she went to a local store, she

> had a most hilarious time trying to make myself understood. But one man realized what I wanted and I ran back in great glee and the cake was duly made and came out just the right degree of pinkness and light as a feather. There must have been a cordon bleu among the Concourse on duty that day![40]

Ethna had wondered whether she should pioneer to Africa, but was unsure. Rúḥíyyih Khánum said to her, 'Well, the decision is yours. All I can tell you is that if you don't want to go to Africa, don't let Shoghi Effendi hear you mention it.' That night, Leroy and Sylvia Ioas had just returned from the dedication of the new Ḥaẓíratu'l-Quds in London and there was a lot of excited talk. Ethna tried to vanish behind the conversation, but Shoghi Effendi caught her eye and asked, 'And what are YOU going to do?' 'I wonder if I should go to Africa,' Ethna squeaked. Shoghi Effendi then proceeded to tell her how to get to Africa, stating only that she should not go to Kenya, Uganda or Tanganyika, which already had enough pioneers. Nine months later, Ethna was a pioneer in Northern Rhodesia (now Zambia).[41]

Dorothy Ferraby

Dorothy Ferraby, a member of the British National Spiritual Assembly, and wife of future Hand of the Cause John Ferraby, arrived in Haifa for her pilgrimage in February. There were few other pilgrims at that time and she had the Guardian to herself on two evenings. She later wrote that it was

> awfully hard to give memories of Shoghi Effendi. You were sort of overwhelmed. I remember my first evening on pilgrimage. There were little customs attached to meeting Shoghi Effendi. Every

evening he would come over for dinner to the Western Pilgrim House with Rúḥíyyih Khánum. We would wait until one of the maids came to tell us that the Guardian had arrived. Then we would go downstairs to the dining room to meet him and always the last-to-arrive pilgrim had to go in first. I was very scared as I didn't know what I was going to say to him. But he just shook hands and said: 'You are welcome, very welcome. I am very glad you have come.' Another thing I noticed was that he never greeted people with Alláh'u'Abhá, like the Baháís do to each other. He never used it. It was always: 'I am pleased to see you – How do you do?' – just general politeness. I wasn't very conscious of what he looked like. I know that he wasn't very tall. He had very impressive eyes and he spoke extremely good English and – well, you just listened and he talked. Sometimes you asked a question and sometimes he addressed you specifically and said: 'What do you think?' or 'What are you doing in your country?' or something like that, and you would answer him. Every evening after he had gone I used to hur-riedly write down what he had been saying before I forgot it. I was in a sort of general daze of being tremendously impressed without registering details. It was interesting because if you wanted to ask him something, you could tell it to Rúḥíyyih Khánum in advance and she would slip it in somewhere during the conversation . . . Mrs so and so wanted to know about this . . . but in general he chose his own subjects and they were very varied.

One evening, when the beginning of the digging of the founda-tions of the Archives Building had just begun, the Guardian showed us a drawing of how it was going to be and he discussed the possibil-ity of the different kinds of Grecian pillars that might be used – the Corinthian, the Ionic or the Doric. Then another night he had an architect's drawing on the wall and it was for something that hadn't yet been built. It was the Mashriqu'l-Adhkár for Tehran in Persia, and it had been designed by one of the Baháí architects according to five or six ideas. He talked about architecture and said you could mix the different periods if you did it carefully – a bit of Gothic and a bit of Renaissance and a bit of so on – it could look very good. It was better than using the modern architecture because that is the product of a decadent period and it wouldn't turn out to be very good and wouldn't last, whereas the others had already lasted for hundreds of years and would continue to do so. He looked at me and said: 'Do you recognise those pinnacles on there?' I looked at them and they looked Gothic and he said: 'I have had those copied from the Palace of Westminster. They are from your Houses of Parliament and I have put them on the Persian Mashriqu'l-Adhkár.' And there they still are, and one of these days it will be built. I was secretary of the Africa Committee at the time and he talked to me about Africa quite a lot.[42]

Riḍván 1955

The Faith expanded into eight new countries during the year, for a total of 108. There were now Bahá'ís in 3,200 different localities across the globe from 40 different races. Language translations of the Writings had increased to 167. A total of 140 Local Spiritual Assemblies had been incorporated. Africa's advance was conspicuous with 58 territories opened to the Faith and 50 Local Assemblies functioning. Ninety tribes were represented in the Faith.[43]

Roberta and Kenneth Christian, Nureddin Momtazi, Fujita and Fred Schechter

At the end of the year, on 25 December, Roberta and Kenneth Christian, Knights of Bahá'u'lláh for Southern Rhodesia (now Zimbabwe) arrived in Haifa. When they asked their taxi driver to take them to 10 Persian Street, he replied, 'Oh, yes, the house of 'Abbas.' They arrived at 11 o'clock and a maid took them to their rooms, but Jessie Revell gave them no chance to unpack, hustling them up to the Shrine before it opened to the general public at noon. First, they went to the Shrine of the Báb: 'The inner room, beneath the floor of which lies the body of the Báb, seems like a sea of light. Beauty and peace surround you . . . Everything drops away here. This is a place for the certain and lasting realities.' Afterwards, they walked back down to the Pilgrim House and met Rúḥíyyih Khánum, Milly Collins and Ethel Revell. That evening, the Christians nervously met Shoghi Effendi for the first time:

> The Guardian rose to greet us, and his warmth seemed to reach out. He shook Roberta's hand and told her that she was welcome. And as

he welcomed me, he embraced me in the Persian fashion and kissed me on both cheeks. My concern dropped away and I felt at home. He placed Roberta at the head of the table next to him and seated me opposite him . . .

The Guardian is difficult to describe. He wears a simple, black Persian hat (a kulan). His long jacket coat this first evening was brown. Otherwise his clothes are western. His face is handsome and expressive. His eyes seem to be those of the Master; they look into you. His voice is strong and clear, and he speaks at times with rapid fluency. His short stature I noticed only at first. After that I was aware only of Shoghi Effendi himself, a man with unlimited reservoirs of strength and power ready for instant use . . .

The Guardian showered us with kindness. He was loving and appreciative. He emphasized that we are in the valley of Search and must be patient. It is difficult to adjust to the flow of his ideas; the scope and range is staggering. I found at times that I was not clearly aware of the sentence he was then speaking because I was still reaching out with my mind to grasp the last thought.[44]

Shoghi Effendi did bring up America's increasing corruption, but only once and then briefly. After all, these were people who had answered his call and had done what he wished.

One day, they walked up to where the new Archives Building was under construction. The front row of columns was being erected, with two capitals completed. The Christians were impressed with Shoghi Effendi's planning. Though the building was hardly more than started, the flower urns had already been placed on the lower steps and the gardens immediately in front of the steps had been planted – quite the reverse of normal construction. As they walked along the wide, arcuate path above the Monument Gardens, the Christians noticed that above their path, one garden was finished and another, higher up, had been laid out. Above that swept the Bahá'í properties to the top of Mount Carmel.[45]

Fujita, 'Abdu'l-Bahá's and Shoghi Effendi's Japanese servant before the war, returned to Haifa on 27 December, after an absence of 17 years. Fujita arrived with Nureddin Momtazi, who was a Persian pioneer in Japan and would be elected to the first Regional Assembly of North East Asia. When Fujita and Momtazi came into the presence of the Guardian, they both threw themselves at his feet. Momtazi wrote that

Fugita and I had lost our minds and all we knew was that we were on his holy feet. He tried to lift us up but Alas; our hands were tightly bound to his holy feet. Fugita and I had each of us, one of his holy feet in our hands. Fugita was told to leave his holy feet and to stand up; but since he was told so in English I took it as addressed only to him and not to me: and when the same was addressed to me; and I was told to stand up Fugita took advantage of the situation: and thus each of us was holding one of his holy feet in his arms . . .

Here was my reward after 35 years of depression and sufferings . . .

This was our situation for a few minutes until Fugita and I were somehow unconsciously and with the help of our beloved Guardian lifted up and stood humbly at his presence. . .

It was at this moment that my wife arrived too and ignorant of our presence threw herself on his holy feet; and since she was alone she had his two feet in her arms.[46]

Once having recovered from this display of affection, Fugita quickly moved back into his room and went straight to work.[47] Momtazi, at one point, wanted to tell Shoghi Effendi that he had met 'Abdu'l-Bahá in 1920, but before he could say anything, Shoghi Effendi reminded him that he had been on pilgrimage in 1920 and had met the Master.[48] Shoghi Effendi had high praise for the Momtazis and their efforts in Japan. He said that, because of Hiroshima, the Japanese people had suffered much and therefore were prepared to accept the Faith. He reminded them that Japan was to have a National Spiritual Assembly in 1957; at that point, Japan had only two Local Assemblies. The US National Assembly was to help the Japanese form their National Assembly. Until that happened, the Tokyo Local Spiritual Assembly would be the intermediary between Japan and the United States. The Guardian also emphasized that five National Spiritual Assemblies, Japan in the north, Australia and New Zealand in the south, Fiji in the east and Indonesia in the west, would form the foundation of the Administrative Order for the Pacific.[49]

That evening, Shoghi Effendi talked about the Ten Year Crusade, calling it the first World Plan. He pointed out that Africa was the only continent with all of its territories open. Over 2,000 native Africans had already come into the Faith in only two years. When Kenneth noted that they would soon overtake the number of American Bahá'ís, the Guardian said that was as it should be, since there were far more dark-skinned people in the world than white-skinned ones. The master of statistics, Shoghi Effendi told them that in the last two years, the number of languages into which the Writings were translated had leaped from 90 to over 180.[50]

Knight of Bahá'u'lláh Fred Schechter arrived on Wednesday 28 December from Addis Ababa, Ethiopia. He had originally pioneered to Kenya in May 1953 and then filled the Guardian's goal of French Somaliland in August of that year. When the French Somaliland authorities expelled him after just three months, he had moved to Addis Ababa. The next day, the three Western pilgrims went to see the dawn from the steps of the Archives Building, and then visited the Shrine of the Báb. Later, the Guardian pointed out the flat panels around the arcade, saying that they would be inscribed with the words of the Báb from the Qayyúmu'l-Asmá' about the 'Remnant of God'. The words would be carved in an artistic Arabic script similar to that used on the tombs in Egypt, rather like Gothic lettering in English.[51]

On Friday, they all went up to the Temple land on the top of Mount Carmel with Lotfullah Hakím. On the way back, they drove by the upper Cave of Elijah, the one Bahá'u'lláh had visited and which was now inside a large and ornate church. To enter the cave, they went into the church and then down into a natural depression in the rock about 15 feet deep. The cave, which had electric lights and a marble floor, was dominated by a marble altar that took up half of the space. Their French guide told them that the cave had been left 'just as discovered'. Kenneth noted that this was the first time that he had realized that Elijah 'had lived in such luxury'.[52]

The next day, Kenneth and Fred went up to the Shrine of the Báb and offered to help since it was the Sabbath and there was a constant stream of visitors. Jessie Revell told Kenneth to watch for an American couple, whom he should conduct to the Shrine. Shortly, the couple arrived. As they were preparing to enter the Shrine and were taking off their shoes, the man said that he was from Lansing, Michigan. A speechless Kenneth had to wait until they returned before he could tell them that he, too, was from Lansing and had worked at Michigan State University. The man also taught at the university, but was spending a year in Israel on a teacher exchange. They had come to the Shrine because they had seen an advertisement about the Faith in the *Lansing State Journal.*[53]

Knights of Bahá'u'lláh

In 1955, four more of the Guardian's goals were filled and several more people earned the title of Knight of Bahá'u'lláh. Mírzá Áqá Kamálí Sarvístání reached the Socotra Islands near the Horn of Africa, and Frank Wyss was able to spend 17 days on the Cocos Islands in the Indian Ocean. Udai Narain Singh pioneered to Tibet and Daniel Haumont moved to the Marquesa Islands in the Pacific.

1956

The Roll of Honour

On 1 January 1956, Fred Schechter, Kenneth and Roberta Christian, Ethel Revell and Fujita went to Bahjí and the Shrine of Bahá'u'lláh, also visiting the Most Great Prison, the House of Abbúd and the Riḍván Garden. At Bahjí, Salah, the caretaker, took them around the circular path to the Collins Gate. They were impressed by the rapid development of the Gardens. That night, Roberta was given the stunning, for her, privilege of sleeping in the room in the Mansion that was used by the Guardian when he visited there. When they returned to Haifa, Shoghi Effendi told them that the initial Gardens had been started by 'Abdu'l-Bahá, Who sometimes brought in soil in His cloak on foot from the Riḍván Garden. Then He would bring jugs of water for the plants. At that time, the Covenant-breakers controlled the Mansion and as the Master did these sacred tasks, they would jeer at Him from the balcony, saying He was doing the work of a servant.[1]

Then came the last night for Kenneth and Roberta. That was when Shoghi Effendi brought out the great scroll that contained the names of all the Knights of Bahá'u'lláh:

> The scroll was spread out and it took almost the length of the table. It is beautifully inscribed, each country on the list of 131 countries and territories and islands have a space to itself. These are listed alphabetically in four columns. The Guardian explained that some of the blank spaces had been filled and the proper names would be inscribed. He asked us to find our own names.
>
> When the Roll was first being placed on the table, Ruhiyyih Khanum said to Roberta, 'now don't cry, it will spot the parchment'. And the Guardian smiled and said, 'You came happy your first night. You must be happy tonight – your last night of the pilgrimage.'

After we had found our names on the list and talked a bit more, the Guardian brought out from his pocket two vials of attar of roses and gave one to Roberta and one to me, telling us why he was doing so. He was so loving. And then he rose to bid us good-bye.

. . . As he left the room, he flashed us another wonderful smile.[2]

Marjorie Stee

Canadian Marjorie Stee came on pilgrimage on 15 January. At one of the evening meals, the Guardian said that the Revelation of Bahá'u'lláh was 'the seed; the Administrative Order is the growing plant; the World Order is the flowering of that plant, and the World Civilization is the fruit of that plant! We were told that the world civilization will come under succeeding Manifestations . . .' He also said that the Bahá'ís should pray and meditate as the Persians did, study as the Germans did and act as the Americans did. The Bahá'ís needed all three for balance. Perseverance was also very important.[3]

One afternoon following lunch, Rúḥíyyih Khánum told a humorous story to illustrate why other religions were broken into so many sects:

Three ministers could not agree on anything. Finally one said: 'Surely there is one statement we can agree on in the Bible (regarding its meaning), what about this one: "Noah danced before the Ark."' One said, 'Of course, that means that Noah danced before the Ark was built.' The second said, 'Oh, no, it means that Noah danced in front of the Ark.' The third said that they were both wrong. It meant that first Noah danced and then the Ark danced![4]

Gayle Woolson

Gayle Woolson, Knight of Bahá'u'lláh for the Galapagos Islands, was on pilgrimage from 16 to 25 February, coming as a pioneer from South America. Some of the things that Shoghi Effendi talked about with Gayle were common to other pilgrims, such as non-involvement in politics, but other topics were more focused on her part of the world, like spiritualism, Freemasonry and secrecy. He also spoke about the Administrative Order:

The A R K (he spelled this out) will be built around the Arc. We are building the seat of the Ark of Safety. The only Ark of Safety is the Administrative Order. Noah's Ark was built and the deluge came. This Ark is being built and the deluge will come . . .

The Tower of Babel of today are the sky-scrapers. These will be destroyed. The people of the Tower of Babel were haughty, proud, filled with vain-glory; they had turned away from God and were arrogant, so God punished them. This will happen again for the same reason. The world is in the same condition today. The protection for the Bahá'ís is in dispersing. This is good for the Cause and good for themselves. (Then he repeated): Protection for the Bahá'ís is in dispersal.[5]

Milly Collins told Gayle and the other pilgrims that one day the Guardian showed her a copy of the *Bahá'í News* in which his answer to a particular question was printed. Then he told her that he had just received a letter from a prominent Bahá'í asking that exact question. Shoghi Effendi emphasized that 'They don't study the Messages. They are not just to be read; they are to be studied. They are to be read at a 19-day Feast.' Milly said the Guardian expends days writing his messages, making sure each word says precisely what he wants it to say. One reason they do not read, he said, is that they like to have pioneers and travel teachers come and give talks.[6]

Ben Schreibman

Just before Riḍván, Ben Schreibman came on pilgrimage. On his first trip to the Shrine of the Báb, with Leroy and Sylvia Ioas, no sooner had they entered the Shrine and bowed down at the Threshold than tears began streaming down Ben's face. He was totally surprised at his own reaction:

> I don't know what happened to me. Perhaps my soul was so overjoyed that my body though unaware of the bounty just cried for joy. So much of my tears ran over my tie and collar I looked like I was caught in the rain. At the Bab's Shrine I prayed for all the friends I could remember. Then all the Baha'is near Phila[delphia]. Then all the Baha'is in West Chester and all friends in the surrounding

territory. I found that only when I prayed for others did I feel something warm in me. As soon as I started praying for myself – that
something left me.[7]

At the Shrine of Bahá'u'lláh, he was again affected, though without the
tears. He went to the flower-covered Holy Threshold to pray and when
he arose, he had petals stuck all over his forehead. With six Persian pilgrims, they each took turns saying prayers.

Nahid Aschari and the Reyhani family

At Riḍván, Nahid Aschari was on pilgrimage along with her parents,
Naim and Sabete Reyhani, and her brother. The family wanted to
pioneer and asked the Guardian where he would suggest. He mentioned Austria. Within about six months the family had moved from
Iran to Graz and at Riḍván 1957, Nahid and her parents were elected
to the Local Spiritual Assembly of that city. Unfortunately, Sabete died
just a few days later. Sabete's mother, Javahir Madzjoub, happened to be
on pilgrimage just at that time and Shoghi Effendi told her the news.
Javahir later said: 'The beloved Guardian spoke about the passing of my
daughter in such a way that I felt no grief. He carried me to the heavenly
realm of God and showed me Sabete in the presence of Bahá'u'lláh.'[8]
Shoghi Effendi also paid for the headstone.[9]

Brigitte Hasselblatt

Brigitte Hasselblatt (later Lindstrom), the Knight of Bahá'u'lláh for the
Shetland Islands, arrived on pilgrimage in the spring. With the help of
Marion Hofman, Brigitte had found a book on English gardens to give
to the Guardian. The Revell sisters welcomed her to the Western Pilgrim
House and gave her the room formerly used by Milly Collins, who had
moved into the House of the Master. That evening, she met Shoghi Effendi
and he spoke about the Shetland Islands with so much knowledge that it
seemed as if he had been there. One afternoon, Rúḥíyyih Khánum had
various materials out trying to choose the best for the display cabinets
for the Archives Building, and asked Brigitte and the other two pilgrims
for their opinions. Brigitte was very quiet and Rúḥíyyih Khánum, at one
point, looked at her and said, 'Say something!'[10]

Brigitte greatly enjoyed her one night in the Mansion at Bahjí. For a time, she was allowed to be the only person in the Shrine of Bahá'u'lláh and she said that she was 'close to paradise. Especially in 'Akká, I felt that the oneness of mankind was a reality. There, I felt, as never before or after, a deep love for humanity as a whole.' During her last evening with Shoghi Effendi, he told her that she should pioneer to her home country of Estonia when the Faith was established in Shetland. Brigitte tried to fulfil his wish, but was prevented by the fact that the country was closed by Communism, so she pioneered to Finland, the closest she could reach, returning only later to Estonia.[11]

Sheila Banani

Sheila Banani, Knight of Bahá'u'lláh for Greece along with her husband Amin, arrived for her pilgrimage on 27 April. Shoghi Effendi spoke much about Greece and the difficulties the pioneers faced. When Sheila returned from her visit to Bahjí, where she saw shelves full of copies of *Bahá'u'lláh and the New Era* in Greek, she asked if it would be possible to have a few for their teaching efforts since they only had one copy in Greek in the country. The Guardian gave her six copies of Esslemont's book, including one in Turkish.

As usual, Shoghi Effendi spoke on many topics during her pilgrimage. One day, he talked about the spiritual conquest of Russia:

> He said it will be approached and settled by America from the north through Alaska, Greece from the south-west through the Balkans, Persia from the south, and Germany through Poland, Latvia, Lithuania and Estonia. He said they are all Slavs through the Balkans, they will be easy to teach. We must find a Greek Olinga (!).[12]

He also contrasted the maturity of national communities. He

> was disturbed because he hadn't heard from the U.S. NSA – he said Horace used to answer his messages by cable. He said when Greece has its Assembly to pattern it after the British, not the American. Australian and Canadian Assemblies are good too. British are very loyal – they are mature, in fact, old! America is young. They will mature, but by hardship. He said Greece is very difficult – the more

difficult the place the more meritorious the service of the pioneers –
Greece is not like Africa – it is very difficult (his emphasis).[13]

Riḍván 1956

Riḍván was exciting for the Bahá'ís of Africa because, due to the tremendous success of the pioneers, they were able to elect four Regional
Spiritual Assemblies that covered the whole of the continent. These
Assemblies were formed for South and West Africa in Johannesburg,
for Central and East Africa in Kampala, for North West Africa in Tunis,
and for North East Africa in Cairo.[14]

The North East African Assembly comprised an expansion of the
National Spiritual Assembly of Egypt and Sudan, with its centre in
Cairo. The first Regional Convention was held on the site of Egypt's
temple land on the banks of the Nile. The site had been purchased on
18 February 1956 and had a view of the great pyramids of Giza.[15]

In February 1952, there were but two native Bahá'ís in Kampala
and a few pioneers. But those pioneers included Músá Banání and his
wife, Samíḥíḥ. By Riḍván 1956, Uganda and Kenya had 1,400 Bahá'ís
and 61 Local Spiritual Assemblies.[16] As a consequence, on 23 April
1956, the first Regional National Spiritual Assembly of Central and
East Africa was formed. It included four Ugandans: Sylvester Okunat,
Max Kanyerezi, Oloro Epyeru and Tito Wanatsusi; the other members
were 'Alí Nakhjavání, Aziz Yazdi, Philip Hainsworth, Hassan Sabri and
Jalál Nakhjavání .

The North West Africa Regional Convention, called for by the
National Spiritual Assembly of Egypt, was held in Tunis from 30 April
to 2 May. The Regional Assembly formed was composed of: Musta-
pha Bouchoucha (Tunis), 'Abdu'l-Ḥamid Khemiri (Tunis), Elsie Austin
(Morocco International Zone), Shoghi Ghadimi (Tunis), Valerie
Wilson (Liberia), William Foster (French Morocco), Enoch Olinga
(British Cameroon), Riaz Rouhani (Canary Islands), and Rowshan
Mustapha (Tunis). The newly elected Assembly met with Hand of
the Cause Músá Banání, 'Alí Nakhjavání and Muhammad Mustapha,
Auxiliary Board members, and 'Abdu'l-Rahim Yazdi, representing the
National Assembly of Egypt.

Initially, this new Assembly was supposed to have four meetings per
year, but this proved difficult because of the expense of gathering all

the members together. During the first year, the Assembly was able to meet three times and the consultation required translation between English and Arabic. However, in subsequent years of its eight-year existence, some members who spoke only Persian were elected, requiring translation into that language as well. In its correspondence with the community, the new Assembly did so in the three languages, and a few times in Spanish.

The main problem was the cost of holding the meetings, and in February 1957 when Enoch Olinga was on pilgrimage, the Guardian told him that he had written to the Regional Assembly that they should economize on expenses and that money should be spent on teaching; the delegates to the Convention could vote by mail. Shoghi Effendi had already sensed the problem and dealt with it. The Assembly therefore started a consultation system by correspondence that went on all through the remaining years of its existence, with two or three quorum meetings whenever and wherever it was possible.[17] In another letter, Shoghi Effendi told them to take heart because what they were doing was building a model that was being spread around the world and they should see their efforts in that perspective.[18]

The Administrative Order was growing rapidly. At the beginning of the Ten Year Crusade, there were 681 Local Spiritual Assemblies across the world.[19] By 1956, there were 900 and the Faith had spread to 3,700 different localities in 247 countries or territories. The Writings were being translated into more and more languages and were available in 190 tongues.[20]

More pilgrims

Charlotte Stirratt was on pilgrimage in April. She noted that Shoghi Effendi stressed the importance for the believers of morality. She wrote:

> Everything he speaks about, he repeats at least three times so that there can be no misunderstanding as to what he meant. He says that any act which affects the community or harms it in any way, should be investigated by the Assembly – even though it is a personal matter. In the West, the Baha'is do not like to submit personal matters to the Assembly. In Persia, they go to the opposite extreme. In America, they are too individualistic. The youth especially must exercise the

greatest vigilance in regard to morality – they must have the highest moral standards in order to be an example to the world, in this day moral standards are so low. 'But when any moral issue affects the community, the Assembly must interfere.' The youth must be disciplined and disciplined in their moral conduct and attitudes. If for example a believer drinks, he must be warned and warned again. If he does not heed the warnings, then his votes are taken away. Any act that harms the Community must not be tolerated.

As the Guardian spoke, one realized that this Faith is far from being just a religious organization, as we have known them in the past, but a completely new and wonderful order with the highest standards of morality, the highest standards of discipline, courtesy, and behavior, and the purest motives and thoughts. Otherwise, how can there be a new race of men?[21]

Mr Mohtadi, a pioneer in Japan, arrived for his pilgrimage on 23 November. His pilgrim notes are full of the details and statistics of the Ten Year Plan, but few personal feelings. On 3 December, Bill Carr joined him. Bill was a Canadian pioneering in Greenland. Shoghi Effendi was delighted to have a pioneer so far north.[22]

Reginald Turvey was also on pilgrimage in 1956. He had become a Bahá'í in Johannesburg, South Africa, in 1936 and for many years was the only Bahá'í there. By the time he made his pilgrimage, however, he was able to live with Bill and Marguerite Sears and thus enjoy close Bahá'í companionship. When Reg met Shoghi Effendi, he wrote that he was 'a wonderful person; he has a great sense of humor, a great kindness in his eyes'. In talking about South Africa, the Guardian explained that the main reason the Faith had not become strongly established was that the Administrative Order was not yet firmly established.[23]

Infallibility of the Guardian

Leroy Ioas was always mystified about how the Guardian's infallibility worked. Leroy said that he didn't know where Shoghi Effendi ended and where the Guardian began. One day he asked Shoghi Effendi about this. The Guardian replied, 'Leroy, have you not read the Will and Testament of the Master?' Leroy answered that he had, many times. 'What does it say?' Shoghi Effendi countered. Leroy fumbled for an answer

until the Guardian said: 'In the Will and Testament, there are no limi-
tations placed on the infallibility of the Guardian.' Leroy still didn't
understand, but he constantly saw the evidence of that infallibility.
Shoghi Effendi once was speaking about how the Universal House of
Justice and the National Assemblies would work together. While he was
speaking, it occurred to Leroy that under certain circumstances, what
Shoghi Effendi was describing would not work, so he made a mental
note to ask for clarification later. When Shoghi Effendi finished what
he was saying, he sipped his coffee then turned to Leroy and said, 'You
wouldn't think this would work under certain circumstances, but I will
explain to you how it does.'[24]

Knights of Bahá'u'lláh

During 1956, only one of Shoghi Effendi's remaining goals for the
opening of new territories was filled. Mary Zabolotny was able to enter
North America's most difficult goal, Anticosti Island. The difficulty lay
in that the island was privately owned and the only way to get onto the
island was as an employee of the company. Mary managed to acquire
the job that gave her the title Knight of Bahá'u'lláh.

1957

THE CRUSADE SURGES AHEAD

Bill Washington and Habib Sabet

Bill Washington, from Adelaide, Australia, and Habib Sabet from Tehran arrived in early January. Habib, who had made many visits to Haifa, said that the Guardian was happier than he had ever seen him, always smiling, laughing and even joking with the pilgrims. The main reason he was so cheerful was that the Ten Year Crusade was going very well. Four years into the Crusade, most of the goals had already been achieved. Shoghi Effendi told them that there were 4,000 Bahá'í centres in 250 countries, territories and islands. One hundred and two island groups had been opened to the Faith since 1953 and over 110 of the 131 countries listed to be opened to the Faith had been opened. The Writings had been translated into 220 languages. Shoghi Effendi was delighted to add that there were now 3,000 black Bahá'ís in Africa and 2,000 brown Bahá'ís in the Pacific.[1]

When Bill went to the Shrine of the Báb, he felt that it was filled with a feeling of sorrow and an atmosphere of the Heroic Age. The Shrine of 'Abdu'l-Bahá, in contrast, 'held an air of happiness, as before your mind is the picture of Abdu'l-Baha's smiling compassionate face and his constant exhortation to the souls sheltering under his spiritual wing, "be happy".' The Shrine of Bahá'u'lláh was

> pervaded with the mightiest atmosphere, far beyond the compass of any mortal word or expression, – an air that overwhelms the pilgrims, dispels all thought of the outside world and seems to fill the heart well beyond capacity. It can only be described – and then in failing words – as an air of deep joy, beyond the confines of this

world and a very deep spiritual peace.[2]

Bill ended his pilgrimage notes with the reflections of a pioneer in the Pacific, published in the *New Zealand Newsletter*:

There are certain words and phrases in constant use among Baha'is which should be forever eliminated from our vocabulary. This is not hair-splitting over phraseology. Words clothe a thought, express an attitude or an emotion. These words and phrases, borrowed from the high-pressure salesmanship of the business world, are: – 'contacts'; 'handling contacts'; 'making contacts'; 'technique of . . .'; etc.

Ponder over these for a while and I think you will recognise the picture they conjure up.

Then contrast this with the words of the beloved Exemplar, One Whose ways of teaching stand the test of passing years faultlessly. What does He say?

'Walk a little way with the friend until he has learned to love you; then will he turn and walk with you.'

'Hast thou love? Hast thou sympathy? Then all the stars will sing thy praises.'

'Look into the eyes of every soul as if he were a letter from God.'

'Consider the candle, how it weeps its life away that it may shed its light.'

'The Divine Teachings should be offered as you would offer a cup to a king.'

How different! How very, very different . . .[3]

Charles Dunning

Charles Dunning, the Knight of Bahá'u'lláh for the Orkney Islands, came on pilgrimage in January. Leroy Ioas later noted, 'Shoghi Effendi was interested in the service a Bahá'í rendered the Faith and the degree of his devotion, not in exterior traits'. Then he recounted the story of his first meeting with Charles:

One day a person came to the Western Pilgrim House sick and looking like a refugee, poorly dressed. I asked what I could do for him and he said he was on pilgrimage. I took him to his room.

When it came time to meet the Guardian I suggested he change his clothes. I didn't realize the only clothes he had were on his back. We went down to meet the Guardian. The Guardian said that this guest of honor must sit at the head of the table; this man was a Knight of Bahá'u'lláh. When this man left he kissed him likewise on both cheeks and said that this man is one of God's heroes.[4]

Shoghi Effendi wasn't interested in clothes or outward appearances. He saw a man who had pioneered to a 'cold, bleak place'.[5] After dinner, Charles took a cigarette butt out of his pocket, stuck it on a needle and proceeded to smoke it, to the horror of the others at the table. When Shoghi Effendi asked him why he smoked such a short cigarette, Charles answered: 'I am a poor man and have to use everything to the very last in order to get by.' The next night, Charles found a pack of American cigarettes at his place, a gift from the Guardian.[6]

Enoch Olinga and Ursula Samandari

On 3 February, Ursula Samandari and Enoch Olinga arrived in Haifa on pilgrimage. Enoch, in the five years since he had become a Bahá'í in Uganda, had raised up the first Local Spiritual Assembly of Kampala, become a Knight of Bahá'u'lláh, raised up five others who went out and became Knights of Bahá'u'lláh, and been elected chairman of the Regional Assembly of North-West Africa.[7]

Ursula had seen a 'large, dignified African' at the airport in Athens, but didn't realize that he was Enoch until their flight landed in Israel. At the airport, Ursula met Dr Farhoumand who asked 'Where is Olinga?' Enoch was impatient to reach Haifa so he and Ursula went on a 'long, dark wet taxi ride'. They arrived at the Eastern Pilgrim House at 2:30 in the morning and woke up Lotfullah Hakím, who, in spite of the hour, gave them a 'warm and wonderful welcome'. Enoch was supposed to stay at the Pilgrim House, but since it was so late and Ursula didn't want to disturb anyone else, she also stayed there that night.[8]

Once Enoch had received permission to come, he went to Tunis and then Rome, where he met Ugo Giachery. Enoch's English passport was several years out of date so Ugo took him to the British Consulate where 'the wax-moustached Consul, for a solid twenty minutes, denied the possibility to renew' it. Ugo told Enoch not to speak, but just to say the 'Remover of Difficulties' prayer. Finally, Ugo told the Consul that the Guardian of the Bahá'í Faith in Haifa had called for Enoch to come. That enabled the Consul to find a way and a new passport was issued. Ugo then took Enoch to the Israeli Embassy for his visa, after which he got him a meal since he had not eaten since the day before. (Enoch used the 'Remover of Difficulties' constantly on his travels. On one trip, his baggage was overweight and the woman at the counter said that he must either pay the cost or leave his baggage. Since he had no money, Enoch pulled out his prayer book and began to pray. When the woman asked what he was doing, Enoch said, 'I am praying, what else can I do?' The woman waved him through.[9])

Shoghi Effendi had accommodated Enoch in the Eastern Pilgrim House and spent considerable time walking in the Gardens of the Shrine of the Báb with him. Later, Enoch said that the Guardian 'taught me all things'.[10] Enoch was thrilled to meet the Guardian, saying that 'he walked like a lion'. He later told his children that Shoghi Effendi 'was like a lion, but at the same time very gentle' and that he answered his questions before Enoch could ask them. In letters written after his pilgrimage, Enoch wrote that 'having visited and prayed in the Blessed Shrines, gazed on the holy face of our Guardian and heard his melodious voice, I am sure a new day has dawned upon me!'[11]

On their second day of pilgrimage, Leroy Ioas took Ursula and Enoch to the Shrine of Bahá'u'lláh. Back in Haifa that night for supper, Enoch was extremely happy. Leroy was telling funny stories and Olinga laughed so hard that his ribs hurt. Everyone else was weak with laughing at it all. At one point, Leroy asked Enoch for the secret of his success in teaching. Enoch modestly replied that his secret was prayer.[12]

Ursula Samandari wrote that barely an evening passed when the Guardian didn't say 'Mr Olinga is very pure-hearted,' or 'Mr Olinga has a luminous face,' or 'Mr Olinga is very modest. I said to him, "Mr Olinga, you are the first Bahá'í of Uganda," and he replied, "One of the first, beloved Guardian."' At one point, the Guardian asked Enoch how many languages he spoke. Enoch at that time was trying to learn Arabic, so answered: 'I spoke Swahili, Teso, English, etc, and I thought but did not say, "and I am learning Arabic". The Guardian stopped, turned around and said, But Persian is easier.'[13]

Patrick Robarts, Knight of Bahá'u'lláh and son of future Hand of the Cause John Robarts, recounted a story about Enoch's eyesight:

Enoch Olinga was born with very bad eyesight, and had to wear very thick eyeglasses. When he was to be in Haifa to meet with the beloved Guardian, he was very embarrassed about his thick glasses. To an African's way of thinking, it is especially important to put forward your very best when meeting with an esteemed person.

After Mr Olinga's first day, it came time to have dinner with the beloved Guardian. It was always customary for any special guest to sit near Shoghi Effendi at the table. The Guardian would share the latest on the World Crusade with the visitor, and would ask the visitor for any news about the city or country from which he or she had come.

Because Shoghi Effendi was the Guardian, he knew the secrets of hearts. He knew that Mr Olinga was ashamed of his eyes and the thick glasses. So some time during the dinner the Guardian caught Enoch's gaze, and he stared at him – and stared and stared. From that time onward, Mr Olinga never wore glasses again. He no longer needed them to see.[14]

In a letter written on behalf of Shoghi Effendi to Músá Banání, the Guardian expressed his pleasure with the visit on his pilgrimage of the first African Bahá'í of the Ten Year Crusade – in fact, the first Negro Bahá'í from Africa. Enoch Olinga has achieved many victories for the Faith; first in his work in Uganda; then by pioneering in the British Cameroons, becoming a Knight of Bahá'u'lláh there. Five of his spiritual children went from the Cameroons, to virgin areas of the Ten Year Crusade, thus becoming themselves, Knights of Bahá'u'lláh. He himself has confirmed 300 souls, with five Assemblies. The Guardian considers this unique in the history of the Crusade in both the East and West; and he had blessed the one who so selflessly served, and won these victories for the Cause of God, by naming him 'Abu'l-Futúh, the 'Father of Victories'.[15]

Rúhíyyih Khánum greatly loved Enoch, particularly his 'great, joyous, consuming and contagious laugh', which was so enjoyed that the other Hands would save up funny stories all year to tell him at the Conclaves after the Guardian's passing just so they could hear it. Rowshan Mustapha remembered that under normal circumstances, Enoch had a 'calm and serene face [that] hid entirely both thoughts and feelings. With the exception of a slight rise of his eyebrows, there was no sign of his inner reactions . . . except, when he laughed. Anybody who has seen and heard Mr Olinga laugh will remember it for life . . .' [16] 'Alí Nakhjavání later vividly recalled one story that cured Enoch of illness:

We arrived in Ethiopia, in Addis Ababa. There was a very active Bahá'í community there and wonderful pioneers there. They were longing to see this African . . . Hand of the Cause of God. But Mr Olinga fell ill. Already the announcement had been made that he was going to come . . . The meeting was held in the house of Mr Jamshid Monajem. It was full – all the friends had come. Next to this house was . . . the house of Mr Foad Ashraf. That is where Mr Olinga was staying . . .

I was in the room talking with Mr Olinga when I saw Mr Monajem come to the room to see how his condition was so he can report to the friends. Mr Monajem loved jokes himself, so he said, 'Mr Olinga, I understand that you like very much jokes. Do you mind if I tell you a joke?' He said, 'Very good!' So, he started telling him this little story:

He said there were two friends and these friends were talking about their own servants. They said that their servants were so stupid, so uneducated, they just didn't understand so many important things. Each was telling the other that his servant was more stupid than the other. Finally, they agreed that they would have a test. The two servants were outside, so they called them in one at a time. So, one of them came in. His boss told him, 'You know where the Volkswagen garage is?' He said, 'yes'. 'I want you to go there and reserve for me a car, a Volkswagen car. If they want any payment, here'. He pulled out some money and he gave it to him. It was only ten Ethiopian dollars, it was really only one or two American dollars. He said, 'Yes, sir!. I will go and do what you say.' So he went out.

Mr Olinga, of course, was following this story to see how it was developing. The boss said, 'You see, he doesn't think. I give such little money – how can anyone accept such money to reserve a car? He doesn't realise that. He said, "I would go"'.

His friend said that is nothing. Give me a chance to test my own servant. So, he called his servant and he came in. He said, 'Do you know where my club is that I go to every day?' He said, 'Yes'. He said, 'I want you to go there, although it is a little bit far, to see whether I am there or not.' The servant listened. He said, 'Yes, sir. I will do that.'

Mr Olinga was very surprised at such a question and such a stupid answer. He sat up in his bed, at this point. So this man went out. So, you see it was obvious the second fellow was more stupid then the first one. But what they did not know, Mr Monajem said, that the two servants outside were also having an argument. Their argument was: Which of our two bosses is the most stupid. Now, Mr Olinga really became interested at that point. He was all eyes and all ears. He wanted to know what was going to happen. The first one said, 'He gives me money to go and reserve a Volkswagen car for him. He doesn't realise that today is Sunday and all the shops are closed!'

Mr Olinga exploded at this point. He laughed from the depths of his heart. But he was still in bed. But he was laughing, and when Mr Olinga laughed, the walls vibrated, so deep was his laughter, so loud was his laughter! Anyway, the other man was telling him, 'This was nothing! Sunday, so he has forgotten it is Sunday. Look, he tells me to go all the way to his club to find out whether he is there or not. Okay, there is the telephone. He can just can call and ask for himself.'

At this point, Mr Olinga could not bear it anymore. He jumped out of his bed and he rolled. He actually, physically rolled over the carpet laughing all the time, holding his sides and laughing from the depths of his whole being. He could not resist this story. But as a result, he perspired. This laughter, this movement on the floor, he perspired. He said, 'I must have a shower.' We all waited. He went to have a shower. He came out and said, 'I'm fine! My fever is gone. I don't feel anything. I feel strong and I am ready to go and meet the friends.' And he went to the meeting and he gave a wonderful talk to the friends.[17]

Rúḥíyyih Khánum recalled one night in Bahjí when there was a plague of snails devouring the gardens. She talked all of the eight Hands of the Cause overnighting at the Mansion to come out and collect snails, giving each a bucket or a bowl to put them in. It was a bright moonlit night when they started in front of the Shrine. After a while, Rúḥíyyih Khánum looked around and found that 'everyone had sneaked off, only faithful Enoch and I were still gathering snails!'[18] In October of the year of his pilgrimage, Enoch, at the age of just 31, was named a Hand of the Cause.

Aileen Beale, from Bournemouth, England, was on pilgrimage in February at the time when the United Nations Armistice representative of the Israeli Government, General Burns, visited Shoghi Effendi. The Guardian gave him a tour of the Shrine of the Báb, the Archives building and the gardens. Afterwards, the General and his entourage all came for tea. Aileen talked with a Colonel's wife and she was very interested in the Faith.[19]

'Alí Nakhjavání

'Alí Nakhjavání came on pilgrimage from Africa and saw a striking example of the Guardian's humility. 'Alí and the five other male pilgrims saw Shoghi Effendi arrive and start walking toward the Shrine of the Báb. The pilgrims excitedly ran over to him so that they could walk with him to the Shrine. 'Alí noted:

> One of the pilgrims was an elderly believer residing in Turkey, and possibly because of the running, when we reached Shoghi Effendi he began coughing repeatedly. Shoghi Effendi turned to him and said, 'You are tired.' This dear friend said in response, 'Beloved Guardian! We were tired but now that we are in your presence all our fatigue has vanished.' This sentence was in praise of the Guardian. He stopped, and when he turned his face towards us, I saw that the Guardian was not happy. With great gentleness he said, 'Why did you say this?' With bowed head, the disoriented pilgrim kept silent. Shoghi Effendi then proceeded to say, 'What you should have said was that you were tired but since we were approaching the precincts of the Shrine, this brought relief to you . . . You did not come here to see me. You came here to visit the Shrines . . . The friends should not fix their gaze on individuals.'[20]

In this way, the pilgrims understood their true reason for being on pilgrimage.

The Passing of George Townshend

George Townshend passed into the Abhá Kingdom on 25 March. Shoghi Effendi thus lost one of his greatest literary helpers. In a cable, Shoghi Effendi wrote: 'His high ecclesiastical position unrivalled any Bahá'í Western World entitle him rank with Thomas Breakwell Dr Esslemont one of three Luminaries shedding brilliant lustre annals Irish English Scottish Bahá'í communities.'[21] Two days later, the Guardian appointed Agnes Alexander to replace him as a Hand of the Cause.[22]

The codification of the Kitáb-i-Aqdas

Shoghi Effendi spent three weeks during the spring working on the codification of the Kitáb-i-Aqdas. This document, along with 'Abdu'l-Bahá's Will and Testament, the Guardian said, was the 'chief depository wherein are enshrined those priceless elements of that Divine Civilization, the establishment of which is the primary mission of the Bahá'í Faith'.[23] Shoghi Effendi said that it was so difficult to translate that only the infallible Head of the Faith, could do it. The final result was not 'a legal codification of the provisions in the Aqdas but rather a compilation, placing subject with subject, which would enable the Bahá'ís to comprehend the nature of the laws and ordinances given by Bahá'u'lláh to His followers.'[24] Rúḥíyyih Khánum was with him as he did this work and remembered him saying several times that he didn't think he could ever finish it. When he died six months later, she wondered if that was what he meant. After his passing, his notes 'for the preparation of the Synopsis and Codification of the Laws of the Kitáb-i-Aqdas' were found in his papers and published by the Universal House of Justice in 1973.

Alice Dudley, John and Vera Long, Sally Saynor

Alice Dudley, an American pioneer to France, arrived at Lydda Airport on 15 April, welcomed by a glass of orange juice and a temperature of 98°F (37°C). As she waited to go through Customs, Leroy Ioas suddenly walked into the room. Leroy had been part of her San Francisco community when she declared 18 years before and had no idea Alice would be there; he had come to collect Milly Collins. When Alice finally reached the Customs official, after the usual interrogation she mentioned that she was a Bahá'í, whereupon the official quickly apologized, saying, 'Why didn't you say you were a Bahá'í in the first place, we wouldn't have kept you waiting.' A short while later when she had to write down her address for another officer, she wrote, 'No. 10 Persian Street, Haifa'. Upon seeing the address, the officer brightly said, 'You are a Bahá'í!' [25]

When Milly arrived, she, Alice and Leroy climbed into the Guardian's new Chrysler. Alice was amazed to find herself being chauffeured to Haifa in the Guardian's personal car. Alice had known Milly for many years and wrote that she always looked the same:

Lovely blue eyes in a face once framed with golden curls, now snowy white. An expression of great sweetness, yet gentle authority and dignity were worn like a garment. Her life style – austere. I once heard her tell about her early married life when living in mining camps with her husband – that a simple element like water, was so precious that not one drop could be wasted. Later, after her husband had amassed his great fortune, she grew accustomed to the comforts supplied by money, but not dependent upon them. Her life in the Holy Land was lived in the utmost simplicity and her wealth was used only in the service of Bahá'u'lláh. [26]

Alice greatly enjoyed the trip from the airport to Haifa and was fascinated by the diversity of the human panorama they passed:

Along the highway were all kinds of transportation trucks, cars, donkeys, bicycles. We passed an Arab village and people along the highway in groups, waiting for rides, dressed in garments of all descriptions, the differing styles of apparel indicating their origin and background. Bedouins wore flowing white robes (jellabas) under brown cloaks with camel wool sleeves, and a headpiece, the ghuta, covered by a large kerchief held in place by a twisted cord, called the iqal. These white headcloths falling to the shoulders were often black-banded. Their women appeared in the traditional qamis, shapeless cloaks of black or dark blue, covering a simple cotton dress. This costume was completed by a shawl covering the head and often the face. Moroccans dressed as their ancestors – the men in loose, wide trousers (seraweel) or long, cotton shirts (kumsan) reaching their ankles and gathered at the waist with a sash. Large, hooded cloaks served as an outer garment; sometimes worn with a tarboosh – a tall brimless, red felt, black tasselled hat. The women appeared in linen shirts called bloozat, tied at the waist with silken sashes, under body length cloaks (haraks) which covered their faces, except for the eyes. Striped kilts (futa) indicated men from Yemen; on their heads the ubiquitous tarboosh, while the women, in the typical qami, were often tattooed on their faces and arms, with tribal marks. Kurds were distinguished by shirts and baggy trousers with wide sashes; the women in long cotton gowns worn over pants gathered at the ankles. Like the Kurds, the Jordanian men wore shirts and baggy pants but the women sported embroidered dresses of bright blues, reds, pinks, greens, with multi-colored scarves and metallic ornaments. Religious scholars were identified by a garment resembling a night shirt either of cotton or silk. Men and women both wore leather sandals and the women were often bedecked with silver anklets, bracelets and coins.[27]

Alice was impressed by many things on her first pilgrimage. She carefully described the Western Pilgrim House with its 'yellow sandstone' exterior and the Oriental interior of white and black marble pillars, Moorish angles, high ceilings, Persian rugs on the floor and silken hangings on the walls. She admired the photographs and paintings of 'Abdu'l-Bahá, Mírzá Mihdí and the Greatest Holy Leaf as well as the urns full of peacock feathers. Leroy and Sylvia Ioas had a three-room suite in the house. Mason Remey and Milly Collins had rooms as well, though Milly lived in the House of the Master.[28]

Ethel Revell met Alice at the door and introduced her to the only other pilgrims, Vera and John Long from Leicester, England. After a rest, the pilgrims gathered to await the arrival of Shoghi Effendi for dinner. While they were waiting, Rúḥíyyih Khánum called and said that Isfandíyár, 'Abdu'l-Bahá's 'much loved coachman', had just died.[29] Isfandíyár, who had originally come from Burma, had been in charge of the Master's horse-drawn carriage since at least the late 1890s. The funeral of Isfandíyár was held in the House of the Master the next afternoon, with men in one room and women in another. After prayers and tea, the Baháʼís followed the Guardian and Leroy Ioas, who walked immediately behind the casket, to the cemetery. At dinner that night,

Shoghi Effendi eulogized Isfandíyár for his 60 years of loyal service to the Faith in spite of the efforts of those who broke the Covenant. The malcontents had even tried to persuade Isfandíyár to kill 'Abdu'l-Bahá by driving His carriage off the road into a deep ditch. They offered him a very large sum of money, but he had flatly refused.[30]

At eight o'clock on Alice's first night in Haifa, Shoghi Effendi arrived for dinner. Alice was the first pilgrim to enter the dining room and the Guardian seated her at the head of the table on his left. He was dressed in dark clothing with a white shirt and black necktie. Alice noted that his dark brown hair was 'immaculately groomed', and he wore a black tarboosh. After welcoming her, his first question was if she knew that there were 30 Bahá'í centres in France. She didn't.[31]

Vera, John and Alice arranged to meet at four the next morning to go to the Shrine of the Báb for prayers. At 4:15, they walked up the terrace steps, collected the key at the Eastern Pilgrim House and entered the Shrine just as the first 'opalescent' light of morning filled the sky. Later when she met with Shoghi Effendi, he was surprised that she had gone up so early and jokingly said that 'it was because I was a Scandinavian. He expected it of the English, but not the Americans.'[32]

That night, Shoghi Effendi praised George Townshend's latest book, *Christ and Bahá'u'lláh*, saying that it should be sent to all church leaders in America, England, Germany and France, to Catholics, Protestants, Lutherans. He repeated his claim that George and Dr John Esslemont were the greatest Bahá'í writers of the West. Mírzá Abu'l-Faḍl, he said, was the greatest Bahá'í writer in the East.

Shoghi Effendi had proposed a world congress to be held in Baghdad in 1963 to commemorate the hundredth anniversary of the Declaration of Bahá'u'lláh and the successful completion of the Ten Year Crusade. But to successfully complete the Ten Year Crusade, the Bahá'ís had work to do. He brought out three maps. The first map showed all the goals which had been exceeded. The other two displayed supplementary goals. He noted that all the goals for virgin areas had not only been completed, but had been greatly exceeded. Home front goals, however, were lagging behind.[33]

Sally Saynor, another San Francisco Bahá'í Alice Dudley had known, arrived on 17 April. Soon after she arrived, Leroy took her, the Longs and Alice up Mount Carmel to the Temple site, which Shoghi Effendi called the 'Head' of Mount Carmel, as opposed to the Shrine of the

Báb being the 'Heart'. The ground had originally been purchased by German Crusaders because of its proximity to the Cave of Elijah, and later the monastery and nunnery were built. The Carmelites had owned the ground for 900 years. When Bahá'u'lláh visited the site, He had proclaimed the Tablet of Carmel in 'such ringing tones' that the monks heard Him.[34]

One day Rúḥíyyih Khánum visited Sally and Alice and brought them three dresses that had been donated to her by believers in other countries, but which Shoghi Effendi didn't care for. Alice accepted a 'beautiful purple silk suit'. They then helped her straighten out the linen closet, which contained a hundred sheets and pillow cases sent by Eastern believers. Rúḥíyyih Khánum had many jobs. She assisted her husband with his correspondence, planned menus for the Eastern and Western Pilgrim Houses plus the House of Abbúd, assigned sleeping accommodations to the pilgrims and oversaw the household staff. She also wrote books, most recently *Prescription for Living*, and did furniture upholstering.[35]

Shoghi Effendi's memory and rapid response to changing conditions were obvious to all around him. Alice noted:

> One of the characteristics of the Guardian was his amazing memory. He has statistics of every kind pertaining to activities in all areas of the world at his finger tips and he quotes them constantly. He was especially happy over the progress of the Faith in the Pacific area. It surpasses even Africa now. The beloved Guardian kept reiterating the goals of the various areas, stating what progress had been made, what goals had been surpassed or when they had lagged.[36]

Isobel Sabri

Isobel Sabri, an American married to an Egyptian, Hassan Sabri, and pioneering in Uganda, arrived in Haifa on 19 April. On her first night with the Guardian, he brought out his statistics saying that Uganda had been open for six years and now had 1,200 believers. He teased her by saying the Mentawai Islands, off Indonesia, had only been open for four years, yet already had 1,100 believers and two schools. Four Regional Spiritual Assemblies had been elected in Africa the year before and Isobel asked when they would be 'deregionalized'. Shoghi Effendi said that before National Assemblies could be formed, the African believers had to gain experience in administration and be trained as administrators.[37]

On 20 April, 1,542 people visited the Shrines of the Báb and 'Abdu'l-Bahá between nine in the morning and noon. Alice was able to serve as a guide for the visitors. In the afternoon, two carloads of pilgrims, nine Persians and the three Americans, Alice, Sally and Isobel, went to Bahjí. Dr Lotfullah Hakím was their guide and they learned the fascinating story of his grandfather's discovery of the Faith of the Báb:

> Dr. Hakím's grandfather was doctor to the court of the Shah. He went to Mecca on a pilgrimage with the Shah. On the way back, he heard Ṭáhirih talking to mullás in a house in Baghdad. He was curious and listened to her. He became her follower. When he returned to Ṭihrán, the prison keeper came and asked him to treat the Bábís who were ill in the prison. All the Muslim doctors had refused because they considered Bábís dangerous – they were 'infidels' and 'unclean'. Dr. Hakím eagerly accepted. When he saw the Bábís in the prison, they converted him. He became the first Jewish believer of the Báb and Bahá'u'lláh and received many Tablets from Bahá'u'lláh although he never came into Their Presence. While treating the Bábís in the prison, he noticed a little boy in the prison who was the same age as his own son (the father of the present Dr. Hakím). He could not bear to see the child in prison and asked permission to take the child to his own home during the day. Permission was granted, so each day this Bábí child would be called for and spend the day at the home of the physician and each night would be returned to prison to sleep. The present Dr. Hakím first met 'Abdu'l-Bahá in London in 1911 and the Master asked him to come to Haifa . . . Recently Dr. Hakím was pioneering in England when the Guardian sent for him. The doctor thought it was for a visit but he has been in Haifa ever since. Dr. Hakím says the Guardian is just like the Master except that 'Abdu'l-Bahá has become young.[38]

On the way to Bahjí, the pilgrims passed a hill where Bahá'u'lláh once pitched his tent, near the old Roman viaduct. At Mazra'ih, they were greeted by the caretaker, Salah Jarrah, and his wife. Salah was a member of the family of Colonel Aḥmad Jarrah whose duty it had been to stand guard before the cell of Bahá'u'lláh in 'Akká. He had

> witnessed the majesty of Bahá'u'lláh in the barracks, but it was some years later that his heart was touched, when Bahá'u'lláh . . . was taken to the Governor's house and kept in custody for about three days . . . this humiliating treatment resulted from the murder of three Azalis in 'Akká. Aḥmad-i-Jarráḥ was one of the officers present in the case and it was then that the majesty and glory of Bahá'u'lláh made a deep impression upon his soul. The mighty and powerful words He uttered on that occasion enabled Jarráḥ to realize that the Prisoner in his custody was not an ordinary man but One endowed with divine authority. After reading some of the Writings and becoming fully conscious of the station of Bahá'u'lláh, he entered the rank of the believers.
>
> Amín Effendi, a brother of Jarráḥ and the head of the municipality of 'Akká, also recognized the truth of the Faith and became a believer. An interesting incident happened which confirmed their faith. One day, Amín and Aḥmad sought permission to attain the presence of Bahá'u'lláh. Permission was granted and they came. They wanted particularly to complain and seek advice about a certain superior officer by the name of Áqásí who was a bitter enemy of theirs. Before they were able to utter a word, Bahá'u'lláh turned to them and said, 'Praise be to God who has rescued you from the evil doings of Áqásí!' The two brothers were surprised to hear this. Only two days later, the officer was dismissed by the order of the Sultán.[39]

Salah had a photograph of his ancestor in his uniform on the wall of the house. After the pilgrims had prayed in the room of Bahá'u'lláh, Salah's wife had a surprise for them: a pudding flavoured with attar of oranges on top of which was written in Arabic in chocolate, 'Welcome'.[40]

When the pilgrims arrived at Bahjí, they were taken to the Shrine of Bahá'u'lláh and then to the Mansion, where they were to stay for the night. Dr Hakím gave them a tour and told them that Shoghi Effendi had asked Effie Baker, the Australian photographer who had served as host in the Western Pilgrim House for ten years and whom he had sent to Iran to photograph all the Bábí historical sites in 1930, to go to the

Mansion during the time it was occupied by the Covenant-breakers and photograph it so he would know how to restore it later. In Bahá'u'lláh's room were His táj, a cloak, a summer suit, shirt, socks, nightcap, hand-kerchiefs and a camel hair aba that the Greatest Holy Leaf had saved from the Covenant-breakers after His ascension. In one room there was a chart showing images of all the Popes, with the two who ruled during the time of Muhammad circled in green and Pope Pius IX, to whom Bahá'u'lláh had written, circled in red. Another chart showed images of all the Sultans of Turkey with Bahá'u'lláh's nemesis, 'Abdu'l-Hamíd circled. A final photo was of the Shahs of Persia with Muhammad-'Ali and Násiri'd-Dín Sháh circled. The display also included the original order for the execution of the Báb and a picture of the officer in charge of the soldiers who martyred Him.[41]

The pilgrims and resident Bahá'ís celebrated Ridván on 21 April. An elderly Persian, 'Ináyat 'Isfáhání, who as a young boy had lived in Akka in Bahá'u'lláh's household was also present. His wife, before they were married, had served the Greatest Holy Leaf. They were to be married just when one of the Commissions of Enquiry descended upon Akka and 'Abdu'l-Bahá sent all the Bahá'ís away for their safety. But he insisted that 'Ináyat and his fiancée be married before they left, performing the ceremony Himself, so there would be 'no unfinished business'.[42]

Others present that night at Bahjí included Rúhíyyih Khánum, Milly Collins, Sylvia Ioas and Jessie and Ethel Revell. Rúhíyyih Khánum shared the news that groups of up to 50 Bahá'ís could now meet together in Tehran, something not possible the year before, and that 1,000 telegrams had arrived announcing the formation of Local Spiritual Assemblies. The Rome Local Assembly election was held in the apartment of a great-grandson of the arch-enemy of Bahá'u'lláh, Násiri'd-Dín Sháh in Iran. The great-grandson was a Bahá'í.

After eating at a table used by 'Abdu'l-Bahá, the pilgrims all entered the Shrine, women going into one room and men into another, after which Shoghi Effendi chanted. A young Black boy had come from Akka to take part, insisting that he was a Bahá'í, and that when he grew up, he was going to Persia and would marry a Persian girl.[43]

Alice felt the power of the Shrine:

The Shrine of Bahá'u'lláh is indescribably beautiful. A court in the center was filled with ferns which were as large as trees. Four urns of illuminated alabaster stood on white marble pedestals, filled with golden tulips, at each corner of the court. In the center was a huge white marble urn filled with marble roses, so life-like it was almost unbelievable. Costly rugs adorned the walls and floors. A gold velvet hanging was in front of the Inner Shrine where the body of Bahá'u'lláh lies entombed in the earth. This velvet hanging was drawn back, revealing a gold mesh curtain which gave a slightly veiled appearance to the Inner Shrine. Priceless rugs covered the floor upon which were placed daily, in urns, myriads of fresh roses, their scent permeating the air. Lighted alabaster lamps illumined exquisite objects d'art. After prayers, we walked back to the pilgrim house for dinner. I was so filled with joy I found it difficult to concentrate on such mundane things as food . . .[44]

That night, Sally and Alice shared a room. The next morning, they awoke refreshed, 'as if a divine elixir had been quaffed which heightened one's perceptions'. During the day, they were taken to the Most Great Prison and to the House of Abbúd before returning to Haifa.

After dinner on 22 April, the Guardian brought up a subject that he had consistently broached with American believers. Isobel's notes of that talk were interesting:

Europe is not the seat of the Christian civilization – not by any means. It is the seat of material civilization. And America is the stronghold of material civilization – the center of gravity of material civilization. (The Guardian was here speaking in the strongest terms <u>against</u> the excesses of materialism.) Bahá'u'lláh established His Faith in Persia – the most decadent nation on earth. The Persians were more barbarous than the savages of Africa. The World Order of Bahá'u'lláh will be established and has been started in America because it is now the most corrupt politically. The American nation is not altruistic in what it does. The American government lends money to other nations only to protect itself. Other nations know this and resent it, but they take the money. America is trying to buy friends . . .

'Abdu'l-Bahá went to America to warn the nation and appeal to the believers. The Master was very sad at the lack of response of the American nation and the American Bahá'ís. This is why he was so sad when he died. If you want to know the truth, history will record that the Master's mission to America was a failure because of the lack of response of the nation and the believers (The beloved Guardian was here speaking with considerable emotion . . . The impact of his grief in rendering this verdict was truly heart-wrenching.)

It is a sign of the times that the Faith in America is stagnant. The American Bahá'í community will pass through a period of transition when the believers will almost be spectators instead of participants. Look at them even now. How many items of American news are in my Convention message – as compared to Africa and the Orient? Their news bulletin contains only programs, agendas, marriages, death, etc. And they do not even know how to present the news of the victories of the Faith in other areas . . .

The black and brown races will lead the world. They will rise up – through materialism, education and other means . . . The white race will go down . . .

The American people are too fond of their central heaters, their comforts. They are not willing to sacrifice. Victories only come through self-abnegation and sacrifice. The American believers should not only leave their homes and go pioneering; they should go . . . to the other ends of the earth. Otherwise they will go as refugees – bankrupt both materially and spiritually. The Baha'is should be willing to lower their standard of living in order to teach and serve the Faith . . .

There is a great distinction between pioneering and dispersal. In the past I appealed to the American Baha'is to pioneer – to arise and sacrifice for the sake of the Faith . . . But when I saw that they did not respond to my appeals and saw in what danger they were, as a loving father I urged them to disperse to the farthest corners of the earth – and to take with them all those things which they love more than the Faith: their money, their cars, their refrigerators . . . But this is dispersal and it is very different from pioneering which is done with sacrifice and for the love of the Faith.[45]

Alice too remembered Shoghi Effendi saying that:

the U.S. was chosen as the cradle of the World Order (Administrative Order) not because of its spiritual qualities but because of its corruption, the same as Persia was chosen for the Revelation because they, the Persians were worse than Africa's savages, far more barbaric.

After the coming calamity, the U.S. will fulfil the prophecy of Abdul Baha that the U.S. will lead all other nations – because of its suffering . . . The message of Baha'u'llah has been in the world for over 100 years and has been rejected.[46]

After Shoghi Effendi retired for the night, Rúḥíyyih Khánum and the members of the International Council said that they 'had never heard him speak with such force or so decisively.'

Florence Mayberry, who had arrived on 23 April, mentioned child education and the Guardian replied:

It is good to have Baha'i children's classes, but the machinery is not as important as to know the principles involved. The machinery is a means to an end, and you should know what the end should be.

The parents, especially the mothers who are with the children more than the fathers, are responsible for the Baha'i education of their children. The parents must be strict in all matters. The mothers must exercise their influence when the child is young – not wait until it is too late. The parents must teach the children the difference between right and wrong, between good and bad! They must insist that the children do what is right and good. If the mothers neglect their duties, the children, when they come to the age of decision-making, will make the wrong decisions. All that parents think about today is ensuring the child's future financial success, security and position in the world – but not their spiritual character. The principal purpose of Baha'i children's classes is the training of the children to have a spiritual character.[47]

When the pilgrims were exchanging stories with the Ioases about Shoghi Effendi's sense of humour, Sylvia told how, one day, she had made some pickles. At dinner, Shoghi Effendi declined them. Rúḥíyyih Khánum mentioned that Sylvia had made them herself, but still he would not eat one, saying 'with a twinkle in his eyes', 'I do not like dead cucumbers.' At another time when eating chocolate candy, he rhapsodized, 'What delicious poison'.[48]

Isobel's last day was 28 April. Before she left, Shoghi Effendi gave her a piece of the plaster from the cell of the Báb in Mákú. The bit of plaster was in a 'small, beautifully inlaid Persian mosaic box wrapped in a many-colored Persian silk handkerchief.' Isobel was to take it back to Kampala and give it to Músá Bánání. Músá was to place the plaster with the foundation stone for the Temple, which he did.[49]

Florence Mayberry

At 12:30 a.m. on 23 April, Florence Mayberry (later to become a Counsellor member of the International Teaching Centre) arrived at the Western Pilgrim House. When her taxi driver knocked on the door, two heads appeared, one belonging to the tiny Jessie Revell and the other to Isobel Sabri. After some sleep, Florence joined Alice and Sally for a visit to the Bahá'í Archives at the Shrine of the Báb. Lotfullah Hakím was their guide and the first thing he showed them was the photograph of Bahá'u'lláh. Florence was mesmerised until a voice suddenly whispered, 'Get Mrs Mayberry out of there!' Startled, she wondered what she had done wrong. She was told that before she could see the Archives, she had to meet her Host, who was the Báb. She was taken to the Shrine of the Báb and left alone inside. Florence had heard the many stories of tears, powerful emotions, visions and other reactions to being in the Shrine so was wondering how she would react.

> I knelt before the raised entrance to the inner shrine where beneath its floor rested the Body of the Gateway of this Revelation. I laid my forehead upon its carpet, longing to have its touch release some intimate connection with this Source of Power. Prayed. No vision came, no flash of intuition.
>
> I stood, backed away, gazed upward at the ceiling in that instinctive human and physical reach for unearthly heights. Still no voice, no illumination, no anything.
>
> I wanted to cry, like a disappointed child. But a stern, monitoring warning reverberated within my head, 'Don't ask for something special – if you had earned it, it would have appeared, remember, greediness does not belong in this shrine, you just accept what comes!'
>
> I whispered, 'I will, I will.' Backed to the outer door. Then, as I touched its handle, a lovely, astounding transformation came over me. Suddenly I felt so young, so pure, so noble. Not a transformation of myself, not an ego change arising within me. This feeling, this youth, purity and nobility belonged to the Báb. For an instant

it had radiated upon my soul, like a blessing. As though the Báb was aware of me, knew that I loved Him.[50]

That afternoon, Florence and the other pilgrims were invited to the House of the Master for tea by Rúḥíyyih Khánum. There she found Alice Dudley, Sally Sanor, the Persian women pilgrims, Amelia Collins, Sylvia Ioas and Jessie Revell. Rúḥíyyih Khánum spoke to the Western pilgrims in English and the Eastern pilgrims in Persian, translating for both. Then the tea arrived. Florence did not like tea so was in a bit of a quandary about what to do. She finally decided to drink it no matter what is tasted like.

> I accepted the fragile glass contained in a cloisonné holder, brought it to my lips, the exotic fragrance rising from the hot brew. Sipped it – cautiously – sipped it again. This was tea? Real tea? No, it was ambrosia, delicious, to think I had deprived myself of tea all those years. Now at last I could have a go at England's teapots, so long envied . . . However, England's tea, I was to discover, was somewhat different. This was Persian-style samovar tea, a strongly steeped brew transformed by scalding water and sugar lumps into scented, heart-lifting delight.[51]

That night when dinner was called, Milly leaped up and Florence breathed a sigh of relief at not being the first to enter the room where Shoghi Effendi waited. Her relief was short-lived as she was quickly pushed to the front of the line as the newest pilgrim. Normally, the newest pilgrim sat at the head of the table with the Guardian on their right, but Florence had long hoped to be able to sit across from him, though she had not breathed a word of this desire to anyone there. When she entered the room, Shoghi Effendi warmly greeted her, then pointing to the chair directly across from him, said, 'Mrs Mayberry, please sit here.' Now the tears wanted to come, but Florence desperately held them back by biting her lip, clenching her hands and swallowing. She was also speechless. Shoghi Effendi then began to talk to everyone and Florence was able to regain her composure.[52]

Florence had met a university professor who had once taught Shoghi Effendi at the American University of Beirut. He described Shoghi Effendi as 'beautiful' and she had thought that to be a very strange word to describe a man. But as she sat at the table that night, she realized what he had meant:

> Shoghi Effendi was beautiful. Not in any way an effeminate beauty, rather one totally masculine, its delicacy and sensitivity coupled with great strength. His eyes were large, round and glowing, with the slightly almond contour seen so often in Persian miniature paintings. Rather than piercing as had Bahá'u'lláh's eyes appeared in His photograph, His great-grandson's eyes were absorbing, magnetic, as though drawing within them whatever they gazed upon. His nose was well formed in harmony with the strength of the oval face. And the mouth . . . if I were wealthy, able to commission the world's finest etcher . . . to create the most perfect masculine mouth, this would be it.[53]

Then came her day to visit the Shrine of Bahá'u'lláh. She arrived after dark with Isobel and Lotfullah Hakím to find the garden lights on and illuminating the red pathways. After a brief visit to the Shrine followed by dinner at the pilgrim house, Lotfullah took them to the Mansion where they saw the room of Bahá'u'lláh. Florence was amazed at how small the Manifestation's bed was. That night, Florence slept across the hall from the room of Bahá'u'lláh in the room Shoghi Effendi occupied when he visited the Mansion.

The next morning, Florence had the chance to enter the Shrine alone. After kneeling at the threshold, she moved to a spot where she could see both the garden and the inner shrine – and waited. When nothing happened, she resigned herself to the apparent reality. She had no sooner accepted that when

> it happened. Richness flooded me throughout every vein, bone, atom. I was suffused with an intangible richness, a veritable butter-richness of mystic wealth. Not my richness, not a personal wealth, but a wealth awaiting whoever longed for it and opened the human spirit to accept it.[54]

When Florence first arrived, she'd been told that she had missed Shoghi Effendi chanting. Since he rarely chanted during those times, she was told not to expect to hear him. On the Ninth Day of Riḍván, Shoghi

Effendi led the men to the Shrine of the Báb while Rúḥíyyih Khánum led the women. When the men were all gathered in one chamber and the women in the one opposite, someone began to chant the Tablet of Visitation:

> Out of the silence arose a strong, lyrical chant, soaring up into the vaulted ceiling, seeming to escape into the freedom of the sky. This was the Guardian's voice, in the chant I feared I would never hear! As the prayer vibrated the air I felt I had never before experienced the impact of this Tablet of Visitation, entirely had missed its inner potency. Somehow it was transformed in my hearing into a plea of the Báb Himself, grieving for humanity, those poor troubled creatures too blinded by self and tradition to comprehend the Gift offered by their Creator.[55]

Then everyone moved to the Shrine of 'Abdu'l-Bahá and the Guardian chanted again. After leaving the Shrine, everyone gathered informally in the gardens. Florence looked down on the unsuspecting city wondering why they couldn't feel the spiritual vibration.

One night, Florence was at dinner and the Guardian was speaking forcefully about the station and duties of the Hands of the Cause. Over a decade later, in 1969, she recalled:

> He spoke on their most important role as protectors of the Faith. He spoke of enemies who would arise both within and without the Faith, and said the Hands of the Cause must be ever watchful. As my original notes state, the Guardian said one does not have to associate with Covenant breakers to catch the disease, one has only to be near it, this is why the Faith does not grow in New York – not only the New History group, but other groups, they are spreading over the country and tainting the country.
>
> Then Shoghi Effendi turned to me, fixed me with his luminous and piercing gaze and asked in a powerful voice, which seemed to impale one, 'WHAT ARE THE HANDS DOING TO PROTECT THE CAUSE! This is their chief function. THEY ARE PROTECT-ING THE CAUSE!'
>
> At this time I was the sole pilgrim present at the Guardian's table. Others there were Amatu'l-Bahá Rúḥíyyih Khánum, Mrs.

Amelia Collins, Mr. Leroy Ioas, Mrs. Sylvia Ioas, Jessie Revell. And serving the Guardian was Fujita. Charles Mason Remey, the Hand of the Cause, was sitting opposite the Guardian. As the lone pilgrim present, I sat at the head of the table, the Guardian at my right, Remey at my left.

The Guardian looked across the table at Remey. Remey was eating steadily, his eyes fixed on his plate, his face smooth and unmoved. The ringing, wrathful voice of the Guardian cried, 'MASON, ARE YOU LISTENING? DID YOU HEAR ME?'

The old man raised his head, startled, like an upbraided child. He nodded his head and said, 'Yes sir, yes sir!' At the time, having such respect for him as a Hand of the Cause, it was a poignant experience. For the old man was like a school boy before his school master, who was so much younger a man.

And I heard that often Remey, who was very deaf, turned off his hearing aid because it bothered him. I had a twinge of compassion for him, excusing him. Then, like a tape recording running through my mind, went the phrase: 'The Guardian is the scion of the House of God. Whatever he says is right, right, the old man is a boy before his master.'[56]

Shortly after this event, Mason Remey visited Wilmette and stayed with Dorothy and Harvey Redson. Amelia Collins was also in Wilmette at that time and Shoghi Effendi wrote to her saying that she should not leave Mason alone with any of the Bahá'ís. Consequently, Amelia also stayed with the Redsons during his visit.[57] Within three years, he would be one of those attacking the Faith.

For the last two nights of her pilgrimage, Florence was the only pilgrim at Shoghi Effendi's table. During her last evening, he brought out the long scroll of the Knights of Bahá'u'lláh, and pointed out the few blank goals left, telling her to offer the friends in America the priceless chance to have their names inscribed there in that Roll of Honour. Then he mentioned Marion Jack in relation to the Knights of Bahá'u'lláh. 'They are Knights of Bahá'u'lláh,' he said, 'but Marion Jack is the General! She was different than many of the pioneers now. She would not leave her post even when I asked her to do so for her own safety.' At the end of the evening, the Guardian told Florence, 'I thank you for all your work,' then turned and walked away. When she saw him from the back, for the first time she saw the shoulders stooped as though 'weighted by an unseen heavy burden'.[58]

Riḍván 1957

The results of the Ten Year Crusade that had so pleased Shoghi Effendi became very apparent at Riḍván with the election of 12 Regional and National Spiritual Assemblies. In Europe, Regional Spiritual Assemblies were elected: for Scandinavia and Finland, based in Stockholm, Sweden; for the Benelux Countries (Belgium, the Netherlands and Luxembourg), with its seat in Brussels; and for the Iberian Peninsula (Portugal and Spain), with its seat in Madrid. South Americans elected Regional Spiritual Assemblies for Mexico and the Republics of Central America, which operated from Panama City; for Argentina, Chile, Uruguay, Paraguay and Bolivia, based in Buenos Aires, Argentina; for Brazil, Peru, Columbia, Ecuador and Venezuela, seated in Lima; and for the Greater Antilles and the Caribbean in Kingston, Jamaica. North-East Asia and South-East Asia also formed Regional Spiritual Assemblies, based in Tokyo, Japan, and Jakarta, Indonesia, respectively.

In addition to the Regional Assemblies, National Spiritual Assemblies were elected in Pakistan, New Zealand and Alaska. Alaska was different than the rest. Though technically a territory of the United States at that time (it would become a US state two years later), Shoghi Effendi split it off for its own National Spiritual Assembly. It was the first time that a part of a single national community was given a separate National Spiritual Assembly.[59] In 1953, a letter had been written on Shoghi Effendi's behalf to the Anchorage Local Spiritual Assembly containing a surprising passage: 'The future of Alaska is so important that he has set as one of the goals of the Ten Year Crusade, the establishment of a National Spiritual Assembly in Alaska.'[60] Of that goal, Pat Moul, the newly elected chairman of that Assembly, said:

> That there is a National Assembly in Alaska is a miracle. Fifteen years ago the first Assembly was formed in Anchorage. In 1953 Alaska was a consolidation goal. We thought we had ten years, but the Guardian had other plans. When we learned that we were to have a National Assembly by Riḍván 1957, our collective gasp must have been heard round the world.[61]

Alaska, along with Uganda, shared the distinction of leading the Bahá'í world in numbers of goals accomplished.[62]

The Faith had spread to 251 countries and 4,200 localities by Riḍván 1957. Translations of the Writings were available in 230 languages.[63]

Completion of the exterior of the Archives Building

A year after its design had been announced to the Bahá'í world, construction of the International Archives Building had begun with excavation of the basement. And as usual, Shoghi Effendi didn't follow conventional building techniques. Normal construction would have involved erecting the building, then planting the gardens around it. But Shoghi Effendi, before actual construction began, started laying out gardens, pathways, hedges, trees and flower beds on three sides of the building. All construction, therefore, had to be done from the back and inserted into the already developed gardens. The result was that when construction was completed, the gardens looked as though they had always been there.[64]

Ugo Giachery, in Italy, coordinated all the various activities there. Andrea Rocca, Professor Emeritus of the Beaux Arts Academy of Carrara, who had been the supervising architect for the stonework of the Shrine of the Báb, did the same job with the Archives stone. Leroy Ioas, in Haifa, was put in charge of the Archives project in addition to all his other work. Local architect S. Rosoff was contracted to do the actual construction. The first shipload of carved stone had arrived in Haifa in August 1955 and things were so well organized that Mr Rosoff told Leroy that there was no need for an on-site architect.[65]

The basement itself was interesting. Shoghi Effendi also looked to economize when possible and he did so in the basement. Bedrock was not far below the surface on Mount Carmel and in order to create a uniform basement floor, the rock would have had to be blasted. Shoghi Effendi avoided that by simply leaving a 'great stone shoulder jutting up from the floor in one half of the basement'.[66]

The most difficult final job was the ceiling. The ceiling, made of concrete, had to cover the entire hall supported only by the surrounding walls. To do this, a first ceiling six centimetres thick was poured. On top of this, 37-centimetre-high beams were poured then they were covered by a second ceiling layer eight centimetres thick. This was all done so that there would be no cracks.[67]

At Riḍván 1957, the Guardian was able to announce that the exterior of the Archives Building had been completed. Completion of the interior was delayed, however, because of the floor inside the building. A floor made of green tiles of compressed concrete was first laid down, but it bleached out and had white salt deposits form on its surface, so an alternative had to be found. A company in England was able to provide 450 square metres of almond-green vinyl tiles that worked well.[68]

During the summer of 1957, Shoghi Effendi and Rúḥíyyih Khánum went to England to purchase furnishings for the building, a task he finished just before he died.[69] Since Rúḥíyyih Khánum had heard Shoghi Effendi describe how he planned to place the furniture and display the many revered objects, she, over the course of the next years, organized the displays as best she could.[70] The first pilgrims were able to view the displays in 1961.

1957

SHOGHI EFFENDI'S LAST VISITORS

Ian Semple

Ian Semple made his first pilgrimage between 4 and 16 May. Ian was then a member of the National Spiritual Assembly of the United Kingdom and was later elected to the International Bahá'í Council in 1961, and then to the Universal House of Justice in 1963. In his diary, he wrote:

> I well remember that first lunch in Haifa. I sat to Rúḥíyyih <u>Kh</u>ánum's left and we had cheese on toast, which she toasted in a little portable grill beside her. We had the same lunch on my last day. I still felt rather nervous and a little unreal.
>
> Much of my first evening at Shoghi Effendi's table is blank in my mind. He embraced me welcome and sat me opposite him. I am sure I lost a lot of what he said because of the thoughts that coursed through my mind.
>
> More than once in the nights that followed I had a feeling of being with God. I know that, in a way, it is blasphemous to say so, but in Shoghi Effendi I saw God and heard Him speaking. He showed me God as I have never before seen Him, and what I saw filled me with wonderment and tranquillity, and kindled the fire of love in my heart. If I had never even heard of Bahá'u'lláh or 'Abdu'l-Bahá, I would go to the ends of the earth for Shoghi Effendi.[1]

Ian also learned that Shoghi Effendi spoke quite freely, and sometimes bluntly, in front of pilgrims. One night, a pilgrim asked the Guardian to confirm his understanding of what Shoghi Effendi had said. Rúḥíyyih

<u>Kh</u>ánum thought the pilgrim had misunderstood and said, 'Oh no!' But the Guardian immediately turned to her and said, 'Oh yes!'[2]

Anna and Hermann Grossmann

Hermann and Anna Grossmann went to Haifa for their second pilgrimage on 7 May in response to a cable from Shoghi Effendi that read, 'You must come now, otherwise it will be too late.' While in the Athens airport en route to Haifa, they met Ezzat Zahrai, a Knight of Bahá'u'lláh for Southern Rhodesia who was then living in Kenya.

Anna wrote that the Guardian was

> fresher, more energetic and more joyful than he had been during our last pilgrimage twenty years earlier. The unexpected successes of the Ten Year Plan, especially in Africa and in the Pacific Ocean, made him happy. 'The so-called backward peoples are more receptive than the so-called civilized peoples,' he said with a gentle smile.[3]

Hermann and Anna, acting on behalf of the National Spiritual Assembly of Germany, spent many hours talking with Shoghi Effendi about the plans for the House of Worship near Frankfurt. There were several possible designs for the Temple, but the Guardian preferred a design by an architect named Rocholl, which was indeed the one chosen. At one point, Rúḥíyyih <u>Kh</u>ánum

> sent for some of the other drawings submitted for Germany and Persia. They were monstrosities. Shoghi Effendi said one looked like a frog, at which Anna broke into uncontrollable laughter, tears streaming from her eyes. This set Shoghi Effendi off. He chuckled deep down and tucked his chin into his collar. I have never seen him laugh so. It was delightful.[4]

After a few days, a group of five European pilgrims, including the Grossmanns and Ian Semple, went to Bahjí. Anna shared a room with Rúḥíyyih <u>Kh</u>ánum and Hermann and Ian shared another room, one dominated by a portrait of the Purest Branch. Ian wrote that he could say very little about the visit except that it was 'beautiful and moving . . . then we each read a prayer and Rúḥíyyih <u>Kh</u>ánum chanted the

Tablet of Visitation. It was now quite dark. So we went and walked in the Harám-i-Aqdas, up the Guardian's hill. It was magnificent and crickets were chirping in the background.'[5]

Ezzat Zahrai

Ezzat Zahrai met the Grossmans in Athens and flew with them to Israel. When he arrived at the airport, he was confronted by a 'stern-looking' customs officer who, as he prepared to inspect Ezzat's luggage, asked why he was there. When Ezzat replied that he was there as a guest of Shoghi Effendi, the man waved him through without checking anything. Soon after arriving in Haifa, he was taken to meet Shoghi Effendi. His host was

> about 60 years old, he had a gentle voice and kind eyes but there was about him an aura of natural dignity . . . I felt as if I had come home and one of my brothers was asking about my trip . . . I soon felt quite at ease. Whatever my failings, the man opposite me seemed to possess immeasurable quantities of love and understanding.[6]

There were no other Eastern pilgrims for the first part of Ezzat's pilgrimage, so he had Shoghi Effendi to himself in the afternoons. Ezzat had many questions, but was afraid to take up too much of the Guardian's time. Lotfullah Hakím, however, told him not to worry – whether there was one pilgrim or ten, he always came. And, Lotfullah told him,

> You must ask questions. You must ask as many questions as possible. And record the answers to those questions. Shoghi Effendi will not always be with us and we will never have the answers to the questions you don't ask him . . . The more questions you ask, the more answers posterity will have from Shoghi Effendi.[7]

The Guardian sent Ezzat to Bahjí for two nights. On the way, they stopped at the Most Great Prison where the authorities allowed him to enter the cell of Bahá'u'lláh. That night, Ezzat stayed in Shoghi Effendi's room in the Mansion. Being a voracious reader, he looked over the Guardian's bookshelf and selected *Christ and Bahá'u'lláh*, by George Townshend, to read before going to sleep. The first thing the Guardian asked him on his return was, 'Did you find something to read?' Ezzat wondered if Shoghi Effendi could read his thoughts. This idea was further strengthened a couple days later when, while walking in the gardens, Shoghi Effendi suddenly turned to him and stated, 'You're not planning to go to Iran after your pilgrimage, are you?' Ezzat admitted that he was because he hadn't seen his mother for several years. The Guardian said no, that it would be better if she went to live with him in Africa.[8]

Ezzat was a Knight of Bahá'u'lláh for Southern Rhodesia because of 40 days he had been able to spend there before being forced to leave. When he told the Guardian that it bothered him that he had won such a big title for so little time spent, Shoghi Effendi just smiled and replied that 'Today I have received a cablegram that the Assembly in Salisbury [the capital of Southern Rhodesia, now Harare, Zimbabwe] has been formed and registered.'[9]

Before he left, Shoghi Effendi asked Ezzat to go to Egypt after his pilgrimage. The young pilgrim, of course, quickly agreed without thinking. The Suez war had cut off communication between the Egyptian Bahá'ís and the Holy Land and the Guardian wanted them to know that he had not forgotten them and to remind them of their pioneering goals. The more Ezzat thought about going to Egypt, however, the more difficult it appeared. First, it was impossible to go from Israel to Egypt and even more so if there was an Israeli stamp in one's passport. As he walked with Shoghi Effendi, he began to worry about what he would have in his suitcase when he went through Egyptian customs. Suddenly, Shoghi Effendi stopped and looked at him, saying, 'Yes, you will have to be very careful.' Ezzat was now sure that the Guardian could read his mind.[10]

Ezzat decided to go to Istanbul in Turkey and try to get a new passport, one without an Israeli stamp. Arriving there, the Bahá'ís said that it would be impossible because the Persian consul did not like Bahá'ís. But Shoghi Effendi had given him the task, so he went to the Persian consul and asked for the new passport, explaining that he had been in Israel and couldn't enter Egypt with his current one. 'Why the hell did you have to go to Palestine?' the consul asked. Ezzat said he was a Bahá'í and had gone on pilgrimage. He needed the new passport to do some important business in Egypt. 'Are you out of your mind?', was the consul's next question. Ezzat then said that he could have said he had lost his passport and gotten a new one, but then he would have lied. The consul calmed down a bit and asked why he had left Persia. He replied that he had read about Africa and wanted to find work there. The consul ruffled through his passport, noting Ezzat's travels through Mozambique, Rhodesia, Congo, Kenya and Tanganyika. He began asking questions about the countries. Finally, the consul said he had been to Palestine and had visited the Persian Gardens in Haifa. He then gave him a new passport.[11]

Ezzat flew from Istanbul to Cairo on a four-engine plane that carried just two passengers. He had no problems at Customs and managed to contact the Bahá'ís, who were thrilled that the Guardian was thinking about them. He spent two weeks travelling from city to city, telling the Bahá'ís news from the Ten Year Crusade, assuring them of Shoghi Effendi's prayers for them, and collecting statistics which he later sent to Haifa.[12]

Elmer and Gladys Beasley, and others

On 8 May, Elmer and Gladys Beasley arrived at the Western Pilgrim House from Spokane, Washington. They were met by Fujita who welcomed them 'with outstretched arms and immediately served tea'. They described Fujita as the 'little Japanese with a great big sense of humor'. After tea, Fujita took them up to the Shrine of the Báb. The day was a holiday in Haifa and 600 people came to visit the Shrine before noon. The Shrine of the Báb was open to all, but only Bahá'ís were allowed to visit the Shrine of 'Abdu'l-Bahá. The Beasleys remembered one woman who went into the Shrine of the Báb with her two children. When they came out, her daughter, who was about six, said, 'I feel this is a Holy Place.' They noted that many people asked questions, but since the Guardian had prohibited the teaching of the local people, the Bahá'ís had to be very careful.[13]

At dinner that night, the Beasleys met Mason Remey, Milly Collins, Jessie and Ethel Revell and a pilgrim from New York, Marie Nadler. Like many others, the Beasleys tried to describe the Guardian:

I think he must be a lot like 'Abdu'l-Bahá and walks like Him. He was shorter than I had expected him to be, olive complexion and a small moustache. His eyes, of course, are brown and very expressive and one has the feeling the Guardian sees everything. His hands are small, and without any doubt, the most beautiful hands I have ever seen. He is dressed in a black aba which fits more closely than those we have seen in pictures, and he wears a small cap about 3 inches in height rather tipped over one eye very striking and his hair is gray over the temples.[14]

The pilgrims were surprised to find that the Guardian did not have private audiences and that all of his work with others was done at the dinner table. They weren't surprised at Shoghi Effendi's command of statistics. He noted that the Spitzbergen goal had finally been filled and that there were three new National Spiritual Assemblies in Africa with 3,000 new believers. Because Africa was on fire, he suggested sending Africans to America to teach. Shoghi Effendi was not happy with the American Bahá'í community because it was not responding to his entreaties. The Americans wanted to be captains, he said, which showed their immaturity.[15]

During the rest of their pilgrimage, the Beasleys learned a number of interesting things. First, they learned that when Bahá'u'lláh first moved to Bahjí, He took all His relatives with Him except for His wife, Navváb, 'Abdu'l-Bahá and the Greatest Holy Leaf. All the relatives who went with Him became Covenant-breakers, while those who stayed in Akka remained steadfast. When asked when Bahá'ís should observe the Sabbath, Shoghi Effendi noted that each religion had its own day of rest: the Muslims on Friday, the Jews on Saturday and the Christians on Sunday. Some people, he noted, took advantage of all three days. Bahá'ís should observe whatever day was considered the Sabbath in the country they lived in. Prayer was also brought up. It was said that there were so many different ways and forms of prayer: wearing long sleeves, head coverings, veils, kneeling, standing, etc. Shoghi Effendi said that there should be no ritual. He noted that the Persians prostrate themselves when they enter the Shrines and are upset when Westerners do not. The Guardian said that their being offended was good because they could then develop their own spirituality. He said he didn't want the Persians to think that the Bahá'í Faith was a Persian Faith.[16]

When it came time for the Beasleys to leave, Shoghi Effendi said they should go back to New York City and tell the Bahá'ís to 'get out'. In particular, they should pioneer to France, but not to Paris. He also told them that the Faith must come first in everything, 'regardless of what hardship it entails. We must remember all the world forces are against the Bahá'í Faith, so the Bahá'ís must learn to lean on one another and show forth such love that people will be attracted'. The Americans, he said, were too lethargic, that there was too much committee activity and that 'hampers the teaching work and kills the spirit'. Just as the Beasleys were leaving, two New York pilgrims, Bob and Keith Quigley, arrived.[17]

Sometime in May, Mary Magdalene Wilkin came on pilgrimage. Shoghi Effendi warned her about the flood of Persian students who were entering the United States. He noted that Americans were 'too naïve, too gullible, too welcoming' and that Covenant-breakers were 'very sweet, smooth and subtle'. He said that the best way was always to check their Bahá'í credentials and then to be vigilant. Shoghi Effendi also mentioned Bahá'í summer schools and said that they should not be for parties, picnics or dancing, but should be more serious. He also told her that 'THIS is the faith of persecution. Tell the friends! Stir them up!'. On her way home, Mary had gone to Jerusalem where a hotel clerk had told her that there was to be a World Conference there the next year. When she informed the Guardian, he said it was Ahmad Sohrab's doing, but warned that the greatest danger was not from outside of the Faith, but from inside.[18] Shoghi Effendi's warnings went unheeded because in 1960, Mary became a follower of Mason Remey.

The Guardian, the year before, had told the Bahá'ís in Britain to simply ignore the Sohrab conference. He wrote that it was

unwise to seek to clarify the relationship of the Bahá'ís to the advertised holding of Ahmad Sohrab's conference in Jerusalem. Having a very shrewd eye to his own advantage, it has become obvious that one of the means by which he hopes to promote interest in his conference is to arouse active opposition from the Bahá'ís and create a source of discussion in the press. In view of this, the Guardian has been very careful to have the friends avoid rising to this bait. They should, in their personal contacts with people, and in a quiet manner, point out when occasion arises that the Caravan activities have nothing whatsoever to do with the Bahá'í Faith and are indeed unfriendly to it. Whatever he does cannot but end in failure, because he has cut himself off entirely from the living tree of the Faith and is wholly insincere in his motives.[19]

Shoghi Effendi's last visitors, Thelma and Bill Allison

The last pilgrims to visit Shoghi Effendi were Thelma Allison and her son, Bill. Bill was the one who asked for pilgrimage, but when the reply came, it read: 'Come and bring your mother.' For Thelma, it was very difficult to raise enough money for the trip. She 'begged, borrowed, and saved enough money to get there', but their excursion tickets gave them only two hours for refuelling the plane in Paris and another hour stop in Rome. But, Thelma said, 'women want to see Paris and to see some of the smart things there. Maybe I had no business to think of those things – maybe I should just think of my pilgrimage and not let that worry me. But you know it did just a little.' Flying was no problem for Bill because he had been in the army and had flown many times before. Thelma, though, had only been on a plane once before and she was terrified. But it wasn't just the flying that terrified her. She was also terrified that Shoghi Effendi would ask: 'Why, Mrs. Allison, aren't more Negroes in the Faith'. She was black and didn't have a good answer. On the long flight over, she and Bill tried to come up with a reasonable reply.[20]

When they reached Tel Aviv, Thelma was relieved to find that the people looked pretty normal: 'Israeli women looked just like the people in America . . . They were bustling along . . . and very relaxed looking.' Bill and Thelma took a sherut to Haifa and arrived at the Western Pilgrim House in time for lunch.[21] Thelma thought the Pilgrim House was 'a very lovely place' and much more elaborate than where Shoghi Effendi lived. She described Shoghi Effendi's rooms as fairly spartan:

> They live very simply and to think that Amelia Collins, the beautiful Amelia who has all of this money, all of this stuff who lives in this one little cramped room with a basin and a single bed and the beds are something to talk about . . . your worst enemy wouldn't be able to get a good night's rest on them. But she sleeps there and is so happy to be in the house with Shoghi Effendi and who can blame her. Today Shoghi Effendi is the last . . . remnant of God on earth and she was just radiant all day every day all night just to be near him.[22]

Thelma was famished from the long journey and was not overly happy with egg soup, cucumbers and bread for lunch, but their warm welcome more than compensated for that. After lunch, the Allisons were shown to their rooms and left there to rest. About nine that evening, Fujita called them to dinner. Thelma wrote that she was

going to come behind all the rest of them. When we got there there was a Canadian pilgrim there, the Grossmanns from Germany were there, Mrs. [Sara] Kinny [Kenny], I know she's an American but she's in France now, was there and there was a young Persian pilgrim there. Then the regular household which is made up of the Revell sisters, Mr. Ioas and his wife, and Ruhiyyih, and Mason Remey. So when he came for us I started getting in the back, getting myself back of Bill, back of anybody I could get back of because I knew this was the time and I just didn't want to get out in front, I just didn't want him to see that I was scared . . . but I was pushed forward . . . 'Every new pilgrim has to get in front so you get in front and Bill comes behind you', and that's the way they shoved me into the dining room.

Well, it was too late then to get nervous. I just had to go forward. There comes a time when you just have to moooove and I moved and there was this beautiful man standing there . . .

I don't know what I was looking for but I certainly wasn't looking for the beauty, the beautiful piece of humanity that I saw. The Guardian was a beautiful man . . . To me he looked like a tan Nordic – he didn't look like an oriental to me. His eyes were, I know they weren't black, they weren't oriental eyes – they were blue and grey, and he was tan with the most delicately chiselled features . . . his lips were thin and his nose was carved and he was just angelic . . . And he stood there until I came into the room. He embraces the men, he doesn't embrace the women. He put his hands on your shoulders and takes your hand and the greatest love on his face and he says 'Won't you sit down here Mrs. Allison . . .?' The newest pilgrims, of course, are given the honor of sitting at the head of the table and I was the newest pilgrim.[23]

So, Thelma sat at the head of the table next to Shoghi Effendi. Mason Remey sat across from the Guardian, because his hearing was poor, and the remaining 15 people filled in around the table. For the first two nights, Thelma was tongue-tied and spoke not a word. Finally, on the third night, she was able to ask a question. For those first two nights, when the Guardian asked her something, she would just nod. But when she looked at him, the light of his eye blinded her with its beauty. 'He would just look at you with compassion and love and the whole thing was there and the lashes were black and they were just beautiful and you would just be lost in that eye . . .'

The next day, the Allisons went to the Shrine of Bahá'u'lláh and that evening Shoghi Effendi asked her about it:

> 'Mrs. Allison, did you go to the Shrines today?' I said, 'Yes, Shoghi Effendi, I went.' He said, 'But what did you feel? What did you feel when you went into the Shrines to pray? How did you feel? What struck you?' Well, I sat there for a minute and I said, what should I say to him; to sound as if I were really impressed – what shall I say – there was no feeling. I just laid there without any life at Bahá'u'lláh's Shrine. Just lay there for 20 minutes – just laid there with no thought, no nothing, and I said that to him. I said 'Shoghi Effendi I just didn't feel anything. There was no life in me even. I just lay there with no feeling'. I don't know what I expected him to say but he said, 'Mrs. Allison, you old people are fine people. They are talented people, they are still asleep and pure.' Now I don't know what that meant. Maybe because I didn't fabricate, because I just said what was true. I just don't know. That's what he said to me. Well the next time I went to the Tomb it was different, of course . . .[24]

And Thelma's fears about the race question were justified. She wondered if Shoghi Effendi talked so much about race because they were black. He said, 'I don't blame the Negroes in the South for not being Bahá'ís. Maybe if I were a Negro and in the South in America, I would not be a Bahá'í either.' Then Bill asked, 'The youth in Chicago told me to ask you a question . . . They want me to ask you how to promulgate the Word in Chicago – how better to attract the youth . . .' Before he could finish, the Guardian threw up his hands and said, 'You are wasting your time in Chicago.' Bill was shocked and didn't speak much during the next couple of days. Shoghi Effendi bluntly told him to get out of Chicago.[25] When Bill returned, he only stayed in Chicago for a couple of months and then left as Shoghi Effendi had said.

Thelma was very impressed with the Eastern pilgrims. She wrote that they were much more reverent than the Americans and that, at dinner, they always asked permission to ask a question before humbly asking it. The Americans, she said, were 'just gabbering and talk and carry on'. One Persian family greatly impressed her:

> On this pilgrimage we had a gentleman from Persia and his family
> . . . his wife and his daughter and his small son . . . They had tried
> to live in Turkey to pioneer but he hadn't been able to make a living
> for his family so he went back – he had to go back to Persia and he
> learned how to make wigs and then he went back to Turkey again
> and made these wigs and he had accumulated enough to bring his
> family on pilgrimage.[26]

Bill was taken with Shoghi Effendi's logical thinking. When he explained that the coloured races would gradually gain ascendancy over the white race, it was because most of the people in the world were darker skinned. One night the Guardian talked about the future World Order of Bahá'u'lláh:

> He began by saying that the Báb had announced the 'Plan'.
> Baha'u'llah established the laws of the 'Plan'. Abdul Baha laid out
> the 'blue print' for the erection. Now the Baha'is are in the forma-
> tive phase of establishing the administrative order of the 'Plan'. He
> pointed to the establishment of the Divine 'Arc' of Salvation being
> likened to the 'Arc' which the Baha'is are erecting on Mount Carmel
> with the Shrine of the Báb, the Archives Building, the House of
> Justice and the Temple. Outside of this arc the Baha'is are carrying
> out this plan by their widespread teaching activities which is part of
> the 'Arc of Salvation'.[27]

But the Guardian was not happy with America's lack of growth. With his tremendous knowledge of statistics, he told the pilgrims that 4,000 people had come into the Faith in Africa during the previous four years and that 3,500 had become Bahá'ís in the South Pacific. America had not done anywhere near as well. He said that 'In every country except America the Faith is growing.' (The United States National Bahá'í Archives give the number of Bahá'ís in December 1953 as 6,395. In 1955, 1956 and 1957, respectively, there were 7,754, 7,578 and 7,984 Bahá'ís.[28] So, after an initial 8% jump, growth had indeed slowed.).

He stated: 'There is not enough difference between the Baha'is & non-Baha'is – no distinguishing characteristics – no high mark of spirituality to mark the Baha'is from the non-Baha'is.' Shoghi Effendi said that the knowledge of the American friends was 'much too superficial'.[29]

> American friends must study harder, read more & read clearly the signs of the times. They must become more like the Germans & the British, more deeply immersed in the Faith. This is the day of martyrdom & persecution. Martyrdom integrates and disintegrates. It repels & gets rid of the lukewarm believer & draws closer & refines the true-hearted. The faint-hearted will drop off like dead leaves from a tree but the ordeal of fire will only make the flames glow higher in the hearts of a true Baha'i.[30]

The Allisons went to Bahjí for the weekend and stayed for two nights at the Mansion, 'a beautiful place. Great vaulted halls and a bedroom off each . . . about 10 bedrooms'. Lotfullah Hakím was their guide and he gave Shoghi Effendi's room to Thelma and she was 'dumbfounded' at the privilege. The pioneers from Turkey were given a room which had photos of Covenant-breakers on the wall. The man and his wife didn't get any sleep that night. 'He prayed and hollered all night because he said those eyes were following him. All night the eyes of the Covenant-breakers.' Jessie Revell left the next day so the family was able to take her room and escape the gaze of those lost souls.[31]

One day, Leroy asked Thelma if she could cook chicken for Shoghi Effendi and the pilgrims. It was common that the women pilgrims would make something in the kitchen. When Leroy said that Shoghi Effendi loved chicken, Thelma, of course, said she would. But

> when they brought the chickens out and I saw them I said 'My Lord, Bahá'u'lláh. You are going to have to help me . . . They had been in the freezer for about a month and they were just about the color of [a] fireplace brick . . . they were just two small chickens and then they had a turkey that had been there for a long time. So they dumped the three things in my lap and said now 'You see what you can do with them – Shoghi Effendi likes them with gravy.'
>
> I said Bahá'u'lláh You are going to have to help me. I did do a lot of praying with my cooking because I had a lot of children and I had

to make the oatmeal and prunes go around all my life . . .

Well, I started with these chickens . . . and I prayed and I cooked and I prayed and I cooked. And then . . . Ruhíyyih said 'He likes onions Mrs. Allison – do you suppose you could put some onions in there?' I said 'Yes, I'll fix it up as best I can.' Well, I stewed and I stewed and I put the onions in last so that they would be just crunchy and right and Bahá'u'lláh really was with me because when we got to the table, the chickens were just nice . . . they were stewed so that I put them all together the turkey and the chickens so that it didn't taste like turkey and it didn't taste like chicken but it was a mixture of the two. But the gravy was delicious and Shoghi Effendi . . . had two or three helpings.[32]

On their last night in Haifa, Thelma fell ill at dinner and a doctor was called. She had a temperature of 104°F (40°C) and the doctor ordered her to bed for five days. Since the other pilgrims had left, that meant that Bill had a week alone with the Guardian. The silver lining for Thelma came when the only way the airlines could get them home required a two-day stay in Paris. When they arrived in Paris, they found themselves in the 'grandest hotel you could imagine'. They immediately wondered how they were going to pay for such luxury, but an airline representative said, 'You've been the guest of Air France.' So Thelma got to see Paris after all.[33]

The final cleansing of Bahjí

On 8 May, Leroy Ioas returned from Jerusalem where papers had just been signed allowing him to remove the final three Covenant-breakers who were living at Bahjí. Leroy was quite elated after all the hard work, but the Guardian told him: 'Now, Leroy, we must be generous and we must be patient.'[34] The Covenant-breakers appealed the expropriation order, but on 3 June Shoghi Effendi cabled to the Bahá'í world that an 'epoch-making' victory had been won over the band of Covenant-breakers who had been infesting Bahjí since the Ascension of Bahá'u'lláh in 1892. The Guardian was able to announce to the world the news that, after 65 years, Bahjí was free of Covenant-breakers:

With feelings of profound joy, exultation and thankfulness,

announce on morrow of sixty-fifth Anniversary of Ascension of Bahá'u'lláh, signal, epoch-making victory won over the ignoble band of breakers of His Covenant which, in the course of over six decades, has entrenched itself in the precincts of the Most Holy Shrine of the Bahá'í world, provoking through acts of overt hostility and ingenious machinations, in alliance with external enemies under three successive regimes, the wrath of the Lord of the Covenant Himself, incurring the malediction of the Concourse on high, and filling with inexpressible anguish the heart of 'Abdu'l-Bahá.

The expropriation order issued by the Israeli government, mentioned in the recent Convention Message, related to the entire property owned by Covenant-breakers within the Haram-i-Aqdas, recently contested by these same enemies through appeal to Israel's Supreme Court, now confirmed through adverse decision just announced by same Court, enabling the civil authorities to enforce the original decision and proceed with the eviction of the wretched remnants of the once redoubtable adversaries who, both within the Holy Land and beyond its confines, labored so long and so assiduously to disrupt the foundations of the Faith, sap their loyalty and cause a permanent cleavage in the ranks of its supporters.[35]

The Israeli Supreme Court had decided that all the lands around the Shrine of Bahá'u'lláh and the Mansion were the property of the Bahá'í Faith and that the remaining Covenant-breakers had no right to live there. Shoghi Effendi called this 'the final, shattering and most humiliating blow' and that

> The implementation of this order will, at long last, cleanse the Outer Sanctuary of the Qiblih of the Bahá'í world of the pollution staining the fair name of the Faith and pave the way for the adoption and execution of preliminary measures designed to herald the construction in future decades of the stately, befitting Mausoleum designed to enshrine the holiest dust the earth has ever received into its bosom.[36]

On 6 September, Shoghi Effendi announced that the 'complete evacuation of the remnant of Covenant-breakers and the transfer of all their belongings from the precincts of the Most Holy Shrine, and the purification, after six long decades of the Haram-i-Aqdas from every trace of their contamination' had been accomplished.[37] The Guardian had planned to supervise the removal of the Covenant-breaker's final habitation himself, but his passing in London left that task to the Hands of the Cause. The long two-storey structure that blocked the whole of the north side of the Mansion was destroyed. When the gardens Shoghi Effendi had designed were laid out, it was found that they were 'so accurately measured out and planned' that they fit right up to the Mansion wall.[38] In addition to completing the gardens, a third terrace, composed of material from the demolished building, was added to the two the Guardian had raised.[39]

The final call to the Americans

On 21 September, Shoghi Effendi wrote his last letter to the National Spiritual Assembly of the United States. In it, the Guardian plainly stated that with a high destiny came a great responsibility:

> The Bahá'ís are the leaven of God, which must leaven the lump of their nation. In direct ratio to their success will be the protection vouchsafed, not only to them but to their country. These are the immutable laws of God, from which there is no escape: 'For unto whomsoever much is given, of him shall be much required.'
>
> They cannot be the chosen people of God, – the ones who have received the bounty of accepting Him in His Day, the recipients of the Master's Divine Plan – and do nothing about it. The obligation to teach is the obligation of every Bahá'í, and particularly, the obligations of the American Bahá'ís towards humanity are great and inescapable. To the degree to which they discharge them will they be blessed and protected, happy and satisfied.[40]

American pilgrims had been hearing this message for five years, but the Bahá'ís of the North American continent, though they had accomplished amazing things during those years and 40 per cent of the Knights of Bahá'u'lláh were American,[41] still hadn't risen to the heights of servitude, detachment and dedication the Guardian had expected of them, given their station as the recipient of the *Tablets of the Divine Plan*. Fortunately, this was about to change.

New Hands of the Cause

Shoghi Effendi's last message to the Bahá'í world was the announcement in October of a new group of Hands of the Cause. These included Enoch Olinga, William Sears, John Robarts, Hasan Balyuzi, John Ferraby, Collis Featherstone, Raḥmatu'lláh Muhájir and Abu'l-Qásim Faizí. The Guardian pointed out that this group represented 'the Afnán, as well as the black and white races and whose members are derived from Christian, Muslim, Jewish and Pagan backgrounds'. This brought the total of Hands of the Cause to 27. With his usual prescience, Shoghi Effendi, for the first time, called the Hands of the Cause the 'Chief Stewards of Bahá'u'lláh's embryonic World Commonwealth'.[42] After the Guardian's passing, this phrase became very important to the Bahá'í world.

Bill Sears heard the congratulations before he heard the news of his elevation. On the day the announcement was made, the Sears had driven to Johannesburg to collect their mail and were surprised to see four cablegrams. On the way home, with Bill driving, Marguerite began reading the cables. The first one read, 'Loving greetings honor well received.' The next two, including one from Aziz Yazdi, contained similar congratulations. The Sears were baffled. Then Marguerite read the last one: 'Following message just received from beloved Guardian quote inform Enoch Olinga William Sears John Robarts their elevation rank Hand Cause'. Bill abruptly stopped the car and said, 'You drive.'[43]

When they got home, Bill, remembering that Shoghi Effendi would lie down and cover himself with one of Bahá'u'lláh's blankets when he was distressed, did likewise – and stayed there for a long time. Bill later said that he opened his prayer book at random and read, 'I have risen from my couch . . .' but noted that he was actually in bed. Then he read, 'the hair of my head declareth . . .', and thought of his rapidly balding head. He decided it meant that to be a Hand of the Cause would mean changing his life. Afterwards, being a Hand came before all other projects.[44]

John Robarts also received the cable from a friend addressed to 'Robarts, Bulawayo, Rhodesia'. John opened it and read 'Loving congratulations elevation Hand Cause God'. Until he read the cable, John thought it was to him. But after reading it, he suddenly decided it must be addressed to Audrey so he gave her the cable saying, 'Audrey, you are a Hand of the Cause!'

She replied, 'I certainly am not!'

And John said, 'Neither am I.' It was two more hours before they knew which Robarts was now a Hand of the Cause.[45]

Enoch Olinga was in the house of 'Alí and Violette Nakhjavání when he was handed the cable announcing his elevation to Hand of the Cause. Upon reading it, 'he prostrated himself flat on the floor, a mark in Africa of deep submission to one's Liege'.[46]

Knights of Bahá'u'lláh

During 1957, two more of the Guardian's island goals were filled. Pouva Murday managed to find work on the privately-held Chagos Islands in the Indian Ocean, and the mother and daughter team of Margaret Bates and Jeanne Frankel managed, with great difficulty, to spend two weeks on the Nicobar Islands.

1957

THE PASSING OF THE GUARDIAN

During the summer, Shoghi Effendi and Rúḥíyyih Khánum left the Holy Land, as they usually did, and visited many of the Guardian's favourite places in the mountains. Rúḥíyyih Khánum wondered about this at the time, but was 'only happy to see him happy, forgetting, for a few fleeting moments, the burdens and sorrows of his life'.[1] Shoghi Effendi also had the joy of announcing to the Bahá'í world, on 17 July, that the remains of Mírzá Buzurg, Bahá'u'lláh's father, had been successfully found and transferred to the Bahá'í cemetery in Baghdad, fulfilling another of the Guardian's goals for the Ten Year Crusade.[2]

Shoghi Effendi was planning to return to Haifa in November, but first he went to London, arriving on 20 October. He went there because it was possible to find furniture and objects from many different countries in one city at cheaper prices than anywhere else. He did not contact the Bahá'ís while in London, but just went about his business. On the 24th, Rúḥíyyih Khánum came down with the flu and was in bed. Three days later, Shoghi Effendi told his wife that he had pain in his hands and fingers, adding, 'I feel so tired, so tired.' By the next day, his temperature was up to 39°C (102°F) and a doctor was called. He diagnosed the Asian flu. The Guardian had long suffered from high blood pressure due to the stress of his work, but in London it was not elevated. The doctor prescribed rest, in any case.[3]

There was to be little rest. A huge amount of mail and a large number of cables had come in by Tuesday and, by Wednesday, Shoghi Effendi couldn't stay idle so spent the next few days reading the mail and the cables and sending answers. The doctor came every day to check on the Guardian and 'invariably found him sitting in bed reading, surrounded by papers, his brief-case beside him'. On Saturday, 2 November, Shoghi Effendi asked for a large table so he could work on a big map, called 'The Half-Way Point of the Ten Year Crusade'. He had started this particular map in September, when he had a bad cold. On that day, he was told to rest, but instead spent ten hours working on the map. Now, ill again, Shoghi Effendi wanted to make sure the map was correct. Rúḥíyyih Khánum tried to get him to wait until he was stronger, but he said 'No, I must finish it; it is worrying me. There is nothing left to do but check it. I have one or two names to add that I have found in this mail, and I will finish it to-day.'[4]

> In the early afternoon he stood in front of the table and worked for about three hours. The table was strewn with pencils and files of papers which constituted the Guardian's lists of languages, tribes, countries, Temples, Haẓiratu'l-Quds, work completed, work being carried out, and a tremendous amount of data. At one time, while Rúḥíyyih Khánum was checking over with him the various lists and totals, he said to her, as he had said many, many times during the last year: 'This work is killing me! How can I go on with this? I shall have to stop it. It is too much. Look at the number of places I have to write down. Look how exact I have to be!'[5]

Shoghi Effendi had many enthusiastic plans for the winter in Haifa as he lay in his bed. He would put the new furnishings in the Archives Building, oversee the demolition of the buildings by the Mansion formerly occupied by the Covenant-breakers, using the rubble to enlarge the mound at Bahjí, and expand the gardens at Bahjí. But suddenly, he said:

> Who is going to go back and do all these things? I have no strength left. I am like a broken reed. I can't do anything more. I have no spirit left to do anything more. Now we will be going back – who is going to go up that mountain and make all those plans and stand for hours and supervise the work? I can't do it. And I am not going to do anything about the houses in Bahjí. Let them stay like that until I see how I feel. And I am not going to furnish the inside of the Archives this winter. It can wait another year, until everything that is needed to furnish it is collected. I shall just see the pilgrims

and stay in my room and rest and do the few things that I have to do. I am not even going to take the telegrams back from Jessie and make copies of them and keep all the receipts the way I have done all these years. She did this in the summer, she can go on doing it in the winter. I am too tired.[6]

The next day, Sunday, Shoghi Effendi continued to work on his correspondence. That evening, Rúḥíyyih Khánum and Shoghi Effendi talked until 9:30, when she asked if he was tired. He was quite awake and asked her to stay longer and talk. Finally, at 10 o'clock, he was ready for sleep so she left him. Rúḥíyyih Khánum did not sleep well that night, feeling that her heart was 'heavy and sad'. The next morning, Monday, 4 November, she went to his room and knocked. But he did not answer. She then went in and found him

> lying on his left side facing her, with his left hand folded over towards his right shoulder and his right arm over his left one, in a most relaxed and comfortable position. His eyes were three-quarters open and she thought he was drowsy – in that state when people wake up and lie comfortably beginning to think of their day's work. She asked him how he had slept, and if he felt better. When he neither moved nor replied, and he seemed unnaturally still, a wave of agonizing terror swept over her; she leaned over him and seized his hand. He was ice-cold and absolutely rigid . . .[7]

Within two minutes, Rúḥíyyih Khánum was on the phone to the doctor. He arrived very quickly and determined that death had been caused by coronary thrombosis, a blood clot in the heart.

Rúḥíyyih Khánum wrote about the Guardian's last days:

> Life and death are so closely allied that they are the two halves of one heartbeat and yet death never seems very real to us in the normal course of events – who therefore awaited Shoghi Effendi's death! He had been in very good health that last summer, better than for a long time, a fact that he not only mentioned himself but which his doctor commented upon at the time he examined him some weeks prior to his passing. No one dreamed that the time clock inside that heart was reaching the end of its allotted span. Many times people

have asked me if I did not notice indications that the end was near. My answer is a hesitant no. If a terrible storm comes suddenly into the midst of a perfect day one can later imagine one saw straws floating by on the wind and pretend they had been portents. I do remember a very few things that might have been significant, but certainly they meant nothing to me at the time. I could never have survived the slightest foreknowledge of the Guardian's death, and only survived it in the end because I could not abandon him and his precious work, which had killed him long before any one believed his life would end.

One of the goals of the Ten Year Plan associated with the World Centre, a goal the Guardian had allotted to himself, was what he termed the 'codification of the laws and ordinances of the Kitáb-i-Aqdas, the Mother Book of the Bahá'í Revelation'. Any work involving a book of this magnitude, which Shoghi Effendi had stated was, together with the Will and Testament of 'Abdu'l-Bahá, 'the chief depository wherein are enshrined those priceless elements of that Divine Civilization, the establishment of which is the primary mission of the Bahá'í Faith', would certainly be unsuitable for any one but the Head of the Faith to undertake. Shoghi Effendi worked on this for about three weeks or so in the spring of 1957 prior to his departure from Haifa. As I often sat in the room with him while he worked, reading out loud and making notes, I realized from what he told me that he was not planning at that time a legal codification of the provisions in the Aqdas but rather a compilation, placing subject with subject, which would enable the Bahá'ís to comprehend the nature of the laws and ordinances given by Bahá'u'lláh to His followers. It was at this time that Shoghi Effendi remarked more than once that he did not feel he could ever finish this task he had undertaken. I attached no particular importance to this, as he sometimes fretted under the terrible load of his ever-increasing work, and attributed it to his great fatigue at the end of the long, exhausting, unbroken stretch of labour he had passed through during his months at home. After his death I remembered and wondered . . .

But the strains and pressures of his life had been too many and early in the morning of 4 November he suffered a coronary thrombosis. Death must have come to him so gently and so suddenly that he died without even knowing he was ascending to another realm.

When I went to his room in the morning to ask him how he was I did not recognize that he was dead. His eyes were half-open with no look of pain, alarm or surprise in them. He lay as if he had wakened up and was quietly thinking about something in a relaxed and comfortable position. How terribly he had suffered when he suddenly learned of the death of his grandfather! Now he had been called softly and quickly away to join Him. The suffering and shock were this time to be the portion of someone else.[8]

Rúḥíyyih Khánum, of course, was traumatized as well as terrified of having to announce such a shocking blow to the world. She temporized, sending a cable to the International Bahá'í Council in Haifa that said, 'BELOVED GUARDIAN DESPERATELY ILL ASIATIC FLU TELL LEROY INFORM ALL NATIONAL ASSEMBLIES INFORM BELIEVERS SUPPLICATE PRAYERS DIVINE PROTECTION FAITH.' A few hours later, having fortified herself, she sent a second cable to the World Centre detailing the passing of the Guardian and requesting them to relay it to the world. She felt that the official announcement should come from the World Centre. During those few hours between cables, Rúḥíyyih Khánum phoned the two British Hands of the Cause, Hasan Balyuzi and John Ferraby.[9] Dorothy Ferraby was at home when, suddenly

at about 10 o'clock in the morning John rushed up from the office to our flat and said that he was going out and didn't know when he would be back. And I wondered what was the matter with him? He came back late in the afternoon and said that he had been with Ruhíyyih Khánum. We didn't know she was in London but we did know that the Guardian and Ruhíyyih Khánum came there sometimes, although they never contacted us. Anyway, he said that she was in a hotel in London and that the Guardian was dead. It was a terrific shock.[10]

Rúḥíyyih Khánum kept making phone calls. She called Ugo Giachery in Rome and Leroy Ioas in Haifa. Ugo arrived in London that night. On Tuesday, she called Adelbert Mühlschlegel, who as a physician and a Hand of the Cause, she wanted to perform his last service for the Guardian by washing his body and preparing it for burial. He, along with the other German Hand, Hermann Grossmann, arrived that night.[11]

Between phone calls, Rúhíyyih Khánum had to take care of all the material aspects of the burial. She had to talk with the undertaker so that he completely understood the Bahá'í laws for burial: no embalmment, no preservative injections, and nobody was to wash the Guardian's body, except Adelbert. And she had to find a suitable burial site in keeping with the Bahá'í law that burial must be within an hour's travel from the place of death. The first idea was to find a piece of land in London, but that proved impossible because of land-use laws. On Tuesday after-noon, Rúhíyyih Khánum, Hasan Balyuzi and Ugo Giachery went to examine possible sites within an hour's travel. The first cemetery had only a single suitable plot and it was opposite a 'massive, depressing vault of a family of the British nobility, and prohibitively expensive, in addition to being very near the entrance gate'. The trio continued into the gathering twilight until they came to the Great Northern Cemetery at New Southgate. There they found 'a beautiful, peaceful spot on a hill, surrounded by rolling country, where birds sang in the trees and which had an entirely different atmosphere from the pomp and worldliness of the first'. It had good access, was quiet and adjacent to a forested area, and Rúhíyyih Khánum immediately arranged its purchase. After consultation with the Hands, a lead coffin that could be hermetically sealed, and a bronze casket, were chosen as the Guardian's final vehicle. They chose the sealed coffin, thinking that one day, with faster trans-portation methods it would be possible to transfer the sacred remains to Haifa.[12]

Milly Collins arrived from the Holy Land on Tuesday night to support Rúhíyyih Khánum. On Wednesday, Milly went to the cem-etery and arranged for flowers for the funeral. On Thursday morning, Rúhíyyih Khánum and Adelbert Mühlschlegel went to the undertak-ers. Rúhíyyih Khánum had bought nine yards of the best and heaviest silk she could find, plus another nine yards of lighter material for the shroud. She waited in the anteroom while Dr Mühlschlegel washed Shoghi Effendi's body, wrapped it in the shroud and sprinkled it with attar of rose. Adelbert Mühlschlegel was powerfully affected by his task:

Something new happened to me in that hour that I cannot, even after a few days, speak of, but I can mention the wisdom and love that I felt pour over me. In that room – which to worldly eyes would have appeared no different – there was a tremendous spiritual force such as I have only felt in my life in the holy Shrines. My first impression was the contrast between the body left behind and the majestic, transfigured face, a soul-stirring picture of the joyous victory of the eternal over the transient. My second impression, as I prayed and thought and carefully did what I had to do, was that in this degree of consecration to the work of God I should work all my life, and mankind should work a thousand years, in order to construct 'the Kingdom' on earth; and my third thought was, as I washed each member of his body and anointed it, that I thanked those beloved hands which had worked and written to establish the Covenant, those feet that had walked for us, that mouth that had spoken to us, that head that had thought for us, and I prayed and meditated and supplicated that in the short time left to me, the members of my body might hasten to follow in his path of service; and my last thought was of my own distress because I felt how unworthy my hands were to anoint that blessed brow with attar-of-rose as the Masters of old were wont to do to their pupils; and yet what privileges, what duties fall to us, the living, to watch over what is past and mortal, be it ever so exalted. A great deal of mercy, love, and wisdom were hidden in this hour.[13]

When he was finished, Rúḥíyyih Khánum went in alone to say her final farewell:

He was our Guardian, King of the world. We know he was noble because he was our Guardian. We know that God gave him peace in the end. But as I looked at him all I could think of was – how beautiful he is, how beautiful! A celestial beauty seemed to be poured over him and to rest on him and stream from him like a mighty benediction from on high. And the wonderful hands, so like the hands of Bahá'u'lláh, lay softly by his side; it seemed impossible the life had gone from them – or from that radiant face.[14]

Then the Guardian's body was placed in the coffin and covered with flowers brought by Milly from the threshold of the Shrine of the Báb. The next day, in a room full of flowers, the Hands kept a vigil and prayed.

As much as the Bahá'ís were affected, those who were not Bahá'ís, but who were associated with the moment, also seemed to feel something for this 'stranger who had passed away in their country so suddenly'. When Rúḥíyyih Khánum and Milly Collins went to the grave on Friday, the florist had already planted the four small cypress trees, ordered by Rúḥíyyih Khánum, at the four corners of the site. The alcove in the Chapel was

> filled with a bank of chrysanthemums and asters, beginning with deep shades of purple and running up through violet, lavender and orchid tones to white at the top. Like two arms reaching out, garlands of lavender chrysanthemums ran along a cornice which framed the raised upper part of the Chapel. Above this, from wall to wall, was a beam of wood, in the centre of which a framed Greatest Name was hung. Beneath this, in front of the alcove of flowers, the coffin was to rest on a low catafalque covered by a rich green velvet pall, the colour to which the descendants of Muhammad are entitled by their illustrious lineage, and which the Guardian, as a Siyyid himself, through his kinship to the Báb, had every right to bear with him to the grave.[15]

The funeral

Initially, the funeral was to be a private one, but it quickly became apparent that it wouldn't be. There were 18 Hands of the Cause and, seemingly, most British Bahá'ís, plus National Spiritual Assembly members, eight members of the American National Spiritual Assembly, Auxiliary Board members and individual Bahá'ís from many countries. Leroy Ioas had remained in the Holy Land to inform the Israeli authorities, but felt it was safe enough so he, too, went to London, bringing with him a small rug from the innermost Shrine of Bahá'u'lláh. The rug was to be placed on the floor of the vault in Shoghi Effendi's grave.

At 10:40 a.m. on Saturday 9 November, more than 60 automobiles left the National Bahá'í Centre at 27 Rutland Gate carrying over 360 people. Shortly they joined the hearse carrying Shoghi Effendi to his final resting place. When they arrived at the cemetery, a large crowd of believers awaited them. One of the very few of the participants who were not Bahá'ís was the Chargé d'Affaires from the Israeli Embassy in London, Mr Gershon, sent at that Government's request.[16]

The Guardian's coffin was carried into the Chapel.

> The casket was covered by a blanket of flowers of red roses, lilies-of-the valley, and white carnations. It bore these words in the hand of our precious Amatu'l-Bahá, whose every thought embraced each one of us in her grief and loss:
>
> 'From Rúḥíyyih and all your loved ones and lovers
> all over the world whose hearts are broken.'

She took her place amidst the Hands of the Cause on the right of the casket. The friends filled all the chapel, seats and aisle, and more than half stood reverently without. The service began with Bahá'u'lláh's long prayer for the departed, an unforgettable chant in the timeless voice of the East [chanted by Abu'l-Qásim Faizi]. There followed Hidden Words, other prayers, chants, and passages of Scripture, read with great clarity and beauty by his 'servants', and at the close the sweet unbearable words of the Will and Testament –

> Salutation and praise, blessing and glory rest upon that primal branch of the Divine and Sacred Lote-Tree . . . the most wondrous, unique and priceless pearl that doth gleam from out the twin surging seas . . . Well is it with him that seeketh the shelter of his shade that shadoweth all mankind.'

> Came now the final and irrevocable scenes. The casket was carried outside, placed again in the car as she stood watching at the chapel door, and was borne slowly down a long avenue, each silent believer taking his place to follow on foot and for the last time on this earth our first and unique Guardian.[17]

The coffin was then carried to the grave and 'there is a moment of hushed silence, and then moaning and sobbing are heard again . . . It is a struggle to remain standing erect, when the weight of sorrow bends us down . . . nearer to him whom we loved so much.'[18]

> It was now the hour of farewell. The casket rested at the head of the grave, facing the Qiblih, the Point of Adoration . . . It was by the wish of Ruhiyyih Khanum that each single believer had the blessing

of approaching the Guardian's casket, of saying farewell in his own way, of adding his tears to the drops which even the heavens shed. No one will ever forget that time. No one can ever truly describe it.

She comforted us throughout – a queen, a sister, a mother to those too much overcome, a tower of strength, the wife of our Guardian.[19]

Lois Gregory remembered the 'sea of umbrellas that surrounded the grave' because of the rain.[20] As people filed slowly past the coffin, most knelt, some kissed the edge or the handle of the coffin. 'Children bowed their little heads beside their mothers, old men wept, the iron reserve of the Anglo-Saxon – the tradition never to show feelings in public – melted before the white-hot sorrow in the heart.' The Israeli representative, Mr Gershon, was deeply and obviously moved.[21]

When the last person had passed by the coffin, Rúḥíyyih Khánum approached, kissed it, then knelt in prayer. Orange and olive leaves, brought from the Garden of Riḍván in Baghdad by Ṭarázu'lláh Samandari, the only living Hand of the Cause who had met Bahá'u'lláh, were then spread on the grave along with flowers brought by Leroy from Bahjí. 'Then the mortal part of our Beloved was laid to rest, the last chants were raised and attar of rose sweetened all the air.'[22] A woman chanted with a broken voice, followed by 'Alí Nakhjavání and Hasan Balyuzi.

Later, when the believers had dispersed, and a cover of concrete had sealed the vault in which the casket rests, Amatu'l-Bahá Rúḥíyyih Khánum came again to the grave, bringing with her the revered Hands of the Cause, and the members of the National Spiritual Assemblies and Auxiliary Boards. Flowers sent from all the world were lovingly placed around; magnificent flowers, more than we had ever seen, ennobled this last resting place of a King of Kings. At the four corners of the blessed Spot four cypress sentinels stood guard. She asked for prayers in the languages of many lands. All was now done that could be done for our Beloved. We watched with full hearts as her car slowly drove away. Then we too departed.[23]

Madeline Hellaby, an English Bahá'í who was present, wrote:

Our beloved Guardian is dead. I cannot believe it. I, who have only been a Bahá'í for nine months, and have never set eyes on him, I did not realise how much I had come to love him, nor how much the name Shoghi Effendi was wedded to the name Guardian in my mind . . . And yet we must go on – we who are left behind to carry on the work for which he burnt himself out. He would not wish us to mourn. Now is our time of testing. He has given his life in death, and we must do the same – death of all that is bad in us. We must rise with renewed ardour, devotion and self-sacrifice to attain the goals he has promised us.

O God! That this should take place in London! What blessedness is this? . . . Is it not strange that he who received his call to take on the Guardianship while sojourning in our country should be called to relinquish it here also? – and at two most critical stages in the development of the Faith . . . This is 1957 – the year in which 'the signs of the rise, the glory, the exaltation, the spread of the Word of God throughout the East and the West shall appear'; the beginning of the period at whose culmination 'the Teachings of God' will be 'firmly established upon the earth and the Divine Light shall flood the world from the East even unto the West'. . .

And what shall I say of Saturday? Has London ever witnessed such a funeral? Surely the most highly-respected leader, the best-loved king of all time mourned by all his countrymen, cannot have united so many hearts in such love and grief. What other international gathering could have been so utterly devoid of barriers or caused so much amazement? Passers-by stopped and stared. They did not merely look – they stared. Their wonderment was plain: Who can this be? Such a long procession, so many nationalities represented, and all mingling together without segregation, and yet we know not who it is they mourn . . . O wondering bystanders! You will not find it in your newspapers, the time is not ripe.

And as we went along I had a curious sense of detachment from my surroundings. This, the Cause of God, was real. The roads, the people, the shops, the traffic, all the noisy restlessness of the city, was the dream, the illusion. O heedless Londoners! Little did you know what blessedness was passing through your streets! . . .

O coffin-bearers! You who witnessed all, were not your hearts moved to tears and wonderment by what you saw? . . . You who are used to tears, were not even you moved, to see men weep like this? Did you notice how, after a warm and sunny morning, at the very moment when the first believer collapsed in tears at the head of his coffin, the heavens also wept? Did you notice how cold it went suddenly? – and did you notice how, at the moment of the coffin being lowered into the grave the heavens wept again? And did you not marvel at what was sprinkled over the grave? – not dismal earth, but perfume. O heavenly fragrance! Small wonder that you have found your way so often into the Writings of Bahá'u'lláh! May the fragrance of our lives be wafted through the world as you, O attar of rose, were borne upon the winds of heaven from that blessed spot![24]

A few days after the funeral, John and Rose Wade, who lived nearby, visited the grave

because we thought that maybe the flowers had died and were beginning to look a bit untidy so we went up to see what it looked like. At that time there were planks across the actual grave and there were lots of flowers placed around and on the planks and they were a bit bedraggled so we cleaned them up and tidied it. I remember that we bought some more and then we thought about what were we going to do. We felt it couldn't just be left so we started going up there fairly frequently, often two or three times a week, and at times we would buy flowers. Then without permission from anyone and because the friends wanted to get to the grave to pray but it was difficult for them because it was wet and muddy, we made a little path all the way around it, and then we made paths to it so that people could get there and kneel and pray. We put the flowers around to make it look nice, so actually we undertook to be caretakers of the grave, and ultimately Rúḥíyyih Khánum became aware of this and later we were appointed official custodians of the Guardian's grave until we went to Haifa . . .[25]

Ian Semple mirrored the feelings of most of the world's Bahá'ís:

It is difficult now, looking back, to convey the tremendous uncertainty and sense of loss of those days. All the Bahá'ís had lived all their lives in the Faith under the guidance of Shoghi Effendi, some there still were, who remembered 'Abdu'l-Bahá, and a tiny handful from the days of Bahá'u'lláh. But always there had been a clear, firm hand at the helm of the Cause of God, always someone to turn to. And this not an abstract, remote, figure, but a person who inspired the greatest love and loyalty and admiration. Of course for some time some friends had been uneasy and curious about the Guardian's apparent lack of a son. Some people even thought that there might be a son who was concealed to protect him from the Covenant-breakers. I remember Marion Hofman telling me that she had asked Rúḥíyyih Khánum, who had replied 'There are no secrets in this house, Marion,' which was sufficiently ambiguous to leave Marion still wondering. In any case we were all serenely confident that the Cause was in the hands of God and that the Guardian would give us the necessary guidance. Then, suddenly, the Guardian had been taken from us at the early age of 61 and we suffered not only the crushing blow of separation from Shoghi Effendi whom we loved so deeply, but the uncertainty of a future for which we could only hope there would be some clear guidance.[26]

And the Faith moved into uncharted waters.

The Chief Stewards chart a course

Transitions in the progress of the Faith of Bahá'u'lláh had always been fraught with dangers. Bahá'u'lláh had left the Kitáb-i-Áhd which specifically designated 'Abdu'l-Bahá to be His Successor. 'Abdu'l-Bahá, at His passing, left His *Will and Testament* clearly appointing Shoghi Effendi and the Universal House of Justice to be His heirs. But Shoghi Effendi left no will or obvious guidance on what was to happen after his passing and, since there was no Universal House of Justice in 1957, it fell to the Hands of the Cause, whom he had carefully selected himself, to find the path into the future. In *Ministry of the Custodians*, Rúḥíyyih Khánum wrote:

the unique accomplishments of an unpretentious group of world religious officials who, with no forewarning or preparation, suddenly, under the most tragic circumstances, found themselves called upon to seize the helm of their Faith, protect it from dissolution and schism, win the goals of an ambitious, far-flung world ten-year-teaching campaign, which had only reached its half-way point, and steer it to the victory of unitedly electing its Supreme Body in 1963![27]

In his final messages, Shoghi Effendi had made it obvious to whom fell the task of guiding the Bahá'í world community after his passing. On 4 June, when writing about the Hands of the Cause and the Auxiliary Board members, he explained:

> The security of our precious Faith, the preservation of the spiritual health of the Bahá'í communities, the vitality of the faith of its individual members, the proper functioning of its laboriously erected institutions, the fruition of its worldwide enterprises, the fulfilment of its ultimate destiny, all are directly dependent upon the befitting discharge of the weighty responsibilities now resting upon the members of these two institutions . . .[28]

Then in October, when he appointed eight new Hands of the Cause, he called them his Chief Stewards and gave them specific tasks:

> the designation of yet another contingent of the Hands of the Cause of God, raising thereby to thrice nine the total number of the Chief Stewards of Bahá'u'lláh's embryonic World Commonwealth, who have been invested by the unerring Pen of the Center of His Covenant with the dual function of guarding over the security, and of insuring the propagation, of His Father's Faith . . .[29]

The first Conclave of the Hands of the Cause

On 15 November, Rúḥíyyih Khánum, Milly Collins, Mason Remey and Leroy Ioas entered Shoghi Effendi's apartment and sealed his safe with tape and wax. The key was placed in an envelope, which all those present signed, and then locked in Leroy's safe. Three days later, on 18 November, all but two of the 27 of the Hands of the Cause met in the upper hall of the Mansion at Bahjí after having prayed at the Shrine of Bahá'u'lláh. Corinne True, who was 96 and frail, was the only Hand not in the Holy Land, but Clara Dunn, who was in Haifa, at 88, was not well enough to travel to Bahjí.

It was a worried group of people who gathered upstairs in the Mansion for the eight days of the first Conclave of the Hands. Rúḥíyyih Khánum began the Conclave by telling about the illness and passing of the Guardian. It was a difficult meeting because, of the Western Hands, only Rúḥíyyih Khánum spoke Persian and her skills were not capable of handling the nuanced consultations that ensued. So, it fell to Hasan Balyuzi and 'Alí-Akbar Furútan to translate every word anyone spoke. All those present, 'conscious of the frightening responsibilities resting upon' them, insisted that every word be precisely translated.[30] Later, Mr Samandarí said that Rúḥíyyih Khánum was a 'Westerner imbued with Eastern understanding' whose 'horizons had been widened and stretched by Shoghi Effendi'. Because of this, she acted as a bridge between the cultures and, 'as a result of her deep sense of fairness and her ability to see clearly both sides of any argument, the gaps were gradually narrowed and negotiated'.[31]

Jalál Kházeh said that it 'was a dark day for us. No sign of happiness . . . all of us were not aware of what was going to happen. We never expected anything like this.' Rúḥíyyih Khánum was asked if she knew anything about a will left by Shoghi Effendi. She responded that she had asked him several times, but he just said, "Don't worry, everything will settle out alright and there is nothing in my heart".'[32] Rúḥíyyih Khánum and eight other Hands of the Cause, Mason Remey, Milly Collins, Ugo Giachery, Leroy Ioas, Hasan Balyuzi, Horace Holley, Músá Banání and 'Alí Muhammad Varqá, then went to Shoghi Effendi's office in Haifa, examined the seals to make sure they were untouched, and opened the safe to look for a will. No will was found.[33] The only things in the safe were the original *Will and Testament* of 'Abdu'l-Bahá and the original of the *Kitáb-i-Aqdas*. They then took all the files in the office and divided them up between the nine Hands, each looking in his or her pile for any sign of a will. None was found.[34]

When the group returned to Bahjí at 1 p.m., Jalál Kházeh said, 'We didn't find any sign of happiness in their faces.' The Hands then went to the Shrine of Bahá'u'lláh to pray, followed by lunch in the Pilgrim House. After lunch, they returned to the Mansion and went in to Bahá'u'lláh's room to pray for His help. After about 20 minutes of prayer, the Hands reconvened in the Hall. At an impasse, they decided to split up into groups and study the *Book of the Covenant*, the *Will and Testament* of 'Abdu'l-Bahá, the *Dispensation of Bahá'u'lláh*, and the writings of Shoghi Effendi in Persian and English that mentioned the House of Justice.[35]

After a day and a half of reading, the Hands questioned each other about what they had discovered in the Writings. The Hands wanted all their decisions to be unanimous, and after considerable consultation they agreed that, since Shoghi Effendi was required to appoint his successor within his lifetime and then have an elected body of nine Hands approve his choice, and since no body of Hands had been elected during the life of the Guardian, there was no apparent way to appoint a second Guardian. In this, and the fact that he had left no will, the Hands were unanimous.[36]

But through their study of the Guardian's writings, they realized that he had, indeed, written a will, but it wasn't a single document. Leroy Ioas wrote:

In the Will and Testament of 'Abdu'l-Bahá He has provided that nine Hands of the Cause should be elected by all the Hands of the Cause throughout the world and that these nine should be continuously in the service of the Guardian.

When the twenty-six Hands of the Cause met in the Holy Land after the passing of the Guardian, they consulted very deeply, in a consecrated manner, with utmost humility, to try and find the pathway which would lead to the unity of the friends throughout the world, and which would ensure the protection, the development and the success of the Ten Year Crusade.

It became evident that the Ten Year Crusade was the mandate of the beloved Guardian to the friends of the world. Therefore it was most logical, and indeed absolutely necessary, that the Hands of the Cause elect that body of nine referred to in the Will of the Master. That is the action which was taken, and the body of the Hands in the Holy Land, now increased to nine, and elected by all of the Hands of the Cause, will be continuously in the service of the beloved Guardian.

It is their hope that they will be helpful to the friends throughout the world in carrying out all the duties and obligations of the Cause and in winning this great and glorious victory which will resound as the greatest spiritual crusade in the history of mankind . . .[37]

Shoghi Effendi had added the last group of Hands just weeks before his death so there was a total of 27. In his last message to the Bahá'í world, the Guardian called the Hands of the Cause the Chief Stewards of Bahá'u'lláh's embryonic World Commonwealth. This led to consultation on what a 'steward' was. The term was unfamiliar to the Persian contingent. Only when they began travelling the world did they become acquainted with the stewards on planes and boats. Jalál <u>Kh</u>ázeh wondered, 'We [were] looking at what kind of steward we are.' Through their consultation and their examination of the Writings, they realized that the stewards of the Faith were the Spiritual Assemblies. The Guardian called the Hands the Chief Stewards because their job was to care for the assemblies. It was understood that Shoghi Effendi's designation of the Hands as the Chief Stewards was part of his unconventional will. This led to the understanding that the Hands, in the words of Mr <u>Kh</u>ázeh, were to be the 'midwives' of the Universal House of Justice.³⁸

Up to this point, the Hands had maintained their unanimity. But when they came to the question of electing nine Hands to serve in the Holy Land as indicated in 'Abdu'l-Bahá's *Will and Testament,* they struggled without universal agreement. Some Hands said that since the *Will and Testament* called for the elected Hands in the Holy Land to serve the Guardian, since there was no Guardian there was no one to serve. After much consultation, Horace Holley finally broke the impasse by telling a story, as recounted here by Mr <u>Kh</u>ázeh:

> When Christ was crucified, the Disciples, by fear, ran away and hid themselves and the Faith was not improving for three days. Then Mary Magdalene went and gathered all of them and said, 'What's the matter with you? Why don't you teach?' They said, 'The one for whom we were teaching has disappeared from the surface of the earth.'
>
> She said, 'I have three questions. The first is: What was in Jesus Christ that you were worshipping him?' They said, 'The Holy Spirit of God was in Jesus Christ.'
>
> The second she asked was . . . who they were going to follow or worship. They said the one who has the Holy Spirit. Then she asked if when Jesus was crucified and nails went into his hands and feet, did the nails also go through the hands of the Holy Spirit, too? They said no. So she said, is the Holy Spirit alive? They said yes.

'So, get up. Let's go and serve for the Holy Spirit. That is the original thing. Not the body of flesh of Jesus.' So they got up and they went and served.[39]

Horace then asked:

Do we want nine Hands to be elected to come brush the clothes of the beloved Guardian or brush his shoes or cook food for him? Or to serve his Cause? He has brought the Ten Year Crusade. Four and a half years he himself supervised . . . let us elect nine people that they should carry out that. We are not going to say that we are inspired from on High. We are not going to change anything in the Bahá'í Faith.[40]

After more prayers, the Hands unanimously decided to elect nine Hands to serve in the Holy Land. They quickly decided to keep the four Hands who were already serving in Haifa who had been appointed by the Guardian. These were Rúḥíyyih Khánum, Leroy Ioas, Mason Remey and Milly Collins. To elect the other five, they divided into three groups. Each group selected five Hands. Any Hands that appeared on all three lists were elected. They did this until they had the full complement.[41] The five new members were Hasan Balyuzi, Jalál Kházeh, Músá Banání, 'Alí-Akbar Furútan and Adelbert Mühlschlegel. Adelbert was unfortunately unable to serve in the Holy Land so he was replaced by Abu'l-Qásim Faizí. These nine became known as the Custodians.

The next big problem was how to transfer all the Bahá'í properties from the name of Shoghi Effendi into the name of the Custodians, something the Israeli authorities wanted to know. Since this was a legal question, they brought in Shoghi Effendi's lawyer, Dr Weinshall. After researching the problem, he returned and said that they only needed six copies of 'Abdu'l-Bahá's *Will and Testament*, six copies of the cables that contained the appointments of the Hands of the Cause, six copies of the declaration naming the Custodians, and six copies of the names of each Custodian along with a biography. With all these documents, the Custodians were recognized as the head of the Bahá'í Faith and the Israeli Government forwarded 54 cables they had received from world leaders and outstanding people.[42]

Another question was about the funds of the Faith, which had been blocked pending the resolution of the leadership question. That was solved the next day when a letter arrived from the bank saying that the Government had written to them saying that the accounts should be transferred to the Custodians. All they needed to do this were the signatures of the Custodians.[43]

On 25 November, at the end of the Conclave, the Hands issued their first Proclamations as the guiding body of the Faith. The first Proclamation told the Bahá'í world that the body of nine Hands specified in 'Abdu'l-Bahá's *Will and Testament* had been formed. It named them as the Custodians and gave them the task of coordinating world-wide Bahá'í activities. The document was signed by all 26 Hands present in the Holy Land. Corinne True declared her agreement in an Affidavit five days later, making the Proclamation unanimous. The Hands also issued two Resolutions that described the relationship between the Custodians and the rest of the Hands and the duties and responsibilities of the Custodians.[44]

The second Proclamation summarized what had occurred during the Conclave and their realization that Shoghi Effendi had not appointed a successor. The document noted that their despair was ameliorated by the knowledge that the Guardian had left them with an active, ongoing plan in the Ten Year Crusade, plus a world administrative centre, the Hands of the Cause and the International Bahá'í Council. Calling for steadfastness from the Bahá'ís, they declared their intention to carry on with the Guardian's announced plans so that the Universal House of Justice could be elected. That body could then re-examine the issues surrounding the lack of a Guardian and decide what could be done. This Proclamation was signed by all Hands of the Cause.[45]

Ian Semple had been dismayed to find that Shoghi Effendi had left no will and was worried about attacks, but a talk by Hand of the Cause Hasan Balyuzi calmed his fears of Covenant-breaking:

> Nor was my mind eased until Hasan came to read the paragraphs beginning 'In our capacity of Chief Stewards…' and 'As to the International Bahá'í Council'. Then the realization dawned upon me of the miraculous way the Covenant had been preserved. I looked across the table at Marion [Hofman] and she smiled at me, her eyes shining.
>
> Hasan finished reading the proclamation and then spoke to us of

many things which he said were for the ears of the N.S.A. alone. He described the anguish of the Hands at the tremendous responsibility placed upon them, of their seven days of prayer and deliberation which culminated in complete unanimity and the painstaking formulation of the proclamation.

He spoke of the commemoration of the passing of 'Abdu'l-Bahá and the feeling of tragedy that overcame him to realize that not one member of the Master's family was present. As he described these events I could not restrain the tears. The Master once said that if Muḥammad-'Alí had not broken the Covenant the pilgrim kings would have made the pilgrimage in His own lifetime. What then must be the effect upon mankind of this subsequent Covenant breaking which had, for a number of years, deprived mankind of its source of Divine Guidance? And how great the suffering inflicted upon Bahá'u'lláh to see this outcome.[46]

Hand of the Cause Dhikru'lláh Khádem also addressed the lack of a will. He said that a Bahá'í will had two parts: 1) a testimony to the oneness of God; and 2) the disposition of worldly possessions. One day when talking with Mr Khádem, Shoghi Effendi said that he had 'written a [testimony] about the belief of the Bahá'ís'. He said that this testimony was the book, *The Dispensation of Bahá'u'lláh* (now a chapter in *The World Order of Bahá'u'lláh*). He added, 'Indeed, that is my will and testament.' He then gave Mr Khádem a copy and said again, 'This is my will.'[47]

A monument for the Guardian

During the Conclave, Rúḥíyyih Khánum had brought out a sketch she had made for a monument for Shoghi Effendi's resting place. Just before leaving London, she had made one final visit to his grave, which was covered with flowers but nothing else. As she drove away, Rúḥíyyih Khánum said that suddenly, 'in front of my eyes, I saw the whole thing – I saw the foundation and the column, and the globe and the eagle . . ., and I made a little sketch, I remember, in the car. . .' When she showed the Hands the sketch, it was quickly decided that it would be an appropriate monument to the Guardian. But she wondered where she could find an appropriate eagle for the top. Then she remembered visiting an antiques shop on Princes Street in Edinburgh where Shoghi Effendi had discovered a beautiful sculpture of an eagle. Rúḥíyyih Khánum said that

> he liked that eagle, and he put it on a table near his bed in his bedroom, which was also his office. I couldn't get him to separate the two, because he would sit at his desk and work, and when he was too tired to sit up any more, he would get into bed and work . . . So this eagle was in that room, and he enjoyed it so much.[48]

Rúḥíyyih Khánum continued:

> he wanted a Corinthian column, and of course he'd seen them in Italy and other places, and although he had the Archives building, he wanted one; and I said, 'Well Shoghi Effendi, I don't see how you can have one, I don't know where you'd put it – you just can't put a column like that, you know, all by itself!' And he accepted that, but he looked a little dubious about it, as much as to say, 'I still want my column!'[49]

In her sketch, Rúḥíyyih Khánum had a Corinthian column topped by a globe and an eagle. She went up to Shoghi Effendi's office for the eagle

> and carried this thing down in my arms, and the Hand of the Cause Mr Faizi was there, and Alice Kidder, who was living with me at that time; and Faizi got off in a corner, and stood on something; and he held this eagle way up like that, and then I looked at it, and I realised that it was perfect! So I took it in my arms, and wouldn't let anybody else carry it, and took it to Rome with Dr Giachery. We got the architect who had helped in building the Shrine and the stones for the Archives and so on, and he came up and we showed him what we wanted, so he made the design, brought it full scale while I waited in Rome so we could approve the proportions, and then I left the eagle there to be enlarged to the appropriate size.[50]

After the Conclave had ended, only Hands of the Cause Faizí and Furútan remained in Haifa and they did all they could to help Rúḥíyyih Khánum with her grief. Mr Furútan began teaching her Persian writing and dictation while Faizí played chess with her and taught her calligraphy, the art Shoghi Effendi had introduced her to shortly before their marriage. They were surprised at how quickly she mastered the calligraphic art. During the summer of 1958, Rúḥíyyih Khánum spent most of her time in the Mansion at Bahjí with Milly Collins and Dr Alice Kidder.

1958

On 12 January, Hand of the Cause Hermann Grossmann spoke to a meeting of delegates organized by the National Spiritual Assembly of Germany in Frankfurt in order to calm fears. It was a powerful talk:

When our beloved Guardian passed away unexpectedly, the older believers among us who remember hearing the equally unexpected news thirty-six years ago of the passing of 'Abdu'l-Bahá will undoubtedly have recalled the heavy burden of uncertainty that shook the Bahá'í world until the Will and Testament of the Master was made known and they began to recognize his loving and wise provisions. 'Abdu'l-Bahá had left us a Plan and a Guardian who was to provide us with unerring guidance for the prosecution of the Plan. Hence, the mists of fear for the young Faith began to lift, but it was to be a long time before we started to recognize Shoghi Effendi, the Guardian, in a position to which he had been appointed in the Will and Testament of the Master. It was not a mere continuation of the time of 'Abdu'l-Bahá when we had been able to cling like children to the hand of the beloved father, but a time when we were to become independent and learn to stand on our own feet, feel with our own senses and think and perceive with our own minds. Only gradually did we begin to learn the lesson, it took us a long time to comprehend, or even to realize, that there was a Divine Plan from the pen of 'Abdu'l-Bahá and that we – with the exception of a few individuals – had failed to recognize this Plan as something that affected each and every one of us. It was the Guardian who, initially in close collaboration with the 'master builders of the Administrative Order of the Faith of Bahá'u'lláh', the National Spiritual Assembly of the United States and Canada, and later with the other countries in the world, laid the basis for an ever-expanding Bahá'í community throughout all five continents in a series of individual Plans, establishing an Order that in the words of Shoghi Effendi himself was to be the foundation and the model for the future World Order of Bahá'u'lláh . . .

And yet now that our Guardian has left us, we wonder whether we learned everything we should have learned and whether we have taken it all in as was intended in 'Abdu'l-Bahá's Will and Testament and in the 'Divine Plan'. Have we not been waiting too eagerly for the green and red lights we expected to guide us? Did we not burden the Guardian too often with problems that we could, with some effort, have solved ourselves, as we did in the time of the Master, thus overwhelming him with an even greater burden of work than 'Abdu'l-Bahá's Will and Testament already placed on his shoulders? Did we consider thoroughly enough the words of that very Testament, which called upon us to 'take the greatest care of Shoghi Effendi . . . that no dust of despondency and sorrow may stain his radiant nature, that day by day he may wax greater in happiness, in joy and spirituality, and may grow to become even as a fruitful tree'?

Do we not also ask ourselves what would have happened if we had acted more swiftly in performing all the tasks entrusted to us by the Guardian, if we had understood more quickly and enabled the Cause to progress more rapidly? The Guardian did once consider establishing the Universal House of Justice, the pillar that, according to the Will and Testament of 'Abdu'l-Bahá, is destined to uphold the Order of Bahá'u'lláh along with the pillar of the Guardianship, and he evidently regarded this as feasible. Events prevented this from happening, but was it really only the fault of those events and not perhaps also our own failings? . . .

Now that the shock of the unexpected passing of our Guardian has given way to calm reflection, we are beginning to understand that he has certainly not left us in a state of obscurity and uncertainty, but rather that every detail that we will need to consider when the time comes to establish the Universal House of Justice has been taken care of. Although Shoghi Effendi is no longer with us physically, his spirit lives on in his books and plans, which culminate in the world-wide Ten Year Plan of teaching and consolidation, the basis for the mighty Bahá'í World Crusade, the climax of which will be the great Bahá'í Congress marking the hundredth anniversary of the Declaration of Bahá'u'lláh. We must identify ourselves fully with this Crusade and make the joys and difficulties arising from it completely our own, and we must not hesitate to take action and implement it . . .

Shoghi Effendi left us suddenly, but he did not leave anything undone or unsaid that we will need on our way to the establishment of the World Order of Bahá'u'lláh and to the ultimate firm foundation of the Order set out in the Will and Testament of 'Abdu'l-Bahá.[1]

In early February, the Custodians in Haifa had to deal with a misinterpretation by the National Spiritual Assembly of the United States of their Proclamation from the First Conclave. A pamphlet entitled *A New Bahá'í Era* had been published that made reference 'to the door being closed to any hope for a future second Guardian'. After sending an urgent cable on 4 February requesting that the pamphlet be withdrawn from circulation,[2] the Custodians in the Holy Land explained their reasoning in a letter two weeks later. The American National Assembly had drawn the fairly obvious conclusion that since the Hands of the Cause could find no way to create a second Guardian, there never would be one. This missed the two important points that were also in the Proclamation: that only the Universal House of Justice was infallible and that only they could decide if there was or was not a way to select a second Guardian. The problem was not particularly the interpretation made by the National Assembly, but rather that it was not done in consultation with either the Hands of the Cause or the Custodians. The Custodians were highly worried that 'continental' interpretation could result in divisions within the Faith:

> There are in our World Community eastern and western believers. Their backgrounds are different, their approach to a test of this nature different – the answer however must be uniform the world over; otherwise grave differences may arise and the marvellous accomplishment of our beloved Guardian in unifying this diversified Community be lost temporarily and its efficiency impaired.[3]

In a letter to Hand of the Cause Horace Holley on 10 March, the Custodians said that after working with correspondence from all over the world, they were extremely conscious of the need for unity in the 'approach to fundamental matters affecting the structure and future development of the Cause', and hoped that Horace understood their 'delicate' position.[4]

The problem of the Guardianship, however, did not go away, because the widely disseminated pamphlet troubled many, so in June, the Custodians were compelled to restate what the Hands of the Cause had declared in their Proclamation at the end of the First Conclave: basically, since only Shoghi Effendi could appoint a new Guardian and he did not do so, the Hands saw no way of appointing a second Guardian.[5]

*   *   *

During 1958, five Intercontinental Conferences planned by Shoghi Effendi were held in Kampala, Uganda; Sydney, Australia; Wilmette, United States; Frankfurt, Germany; and Jakarta, Indonesia (later moved to Singapore).

Intercontinental Conference for Africa

The Intercontinental Conference for Africa was held in Kampala from 23 to 28 January, attended by Hands of the Cause Ṭarázu'lláh Samandarí, Músá Banání, Enoch Olinga, John Robarts and William Sears, in addition to Amatu'l-Bahá Rúḥíyyih Khánum who had been appointed by Shoghi Effendi as his representative.

So soon after Shoghi Effendi's death, Rúḥíyyih Khánum at first did not want to go, but was convinced that she should. Lotfullah Hakím and Rúḥíyyih Khánum's cousin and her husband, Jeanne and Challoner Chute, travelled with her. Though it was the custom that people in mourning wear black for a year, Rúḥíyyih Khánum wore a white suit that had been previously approved by the Guardian. As she entered the conference hall for the first time on 24 January, the 900 participants all stood in shared grief. Then the 400 Bahá'ís in the audience began softly singing 'Alláh-u-Abhá'. When Rúḥíyyih Khánum spoke, her voice occasionally broke and there were tears, but the palpable love from the Bahá'ís, she later said, was 'like a balm to her soul and a healing for her grief'. She said that Africa was especially close to the Guardian's heart and that was why, on the globe atop the monument at his grave, Africa faces to the front.[6]

Rúḥíyyih <u>Kh</u>ánum centred her talk on the Guardian:

We take too much for granted in this world, all of us. I took the
Guardian for granted before I went to live in Haifa. I don't know
what I thought, I must have thought that he just sat there and all
the time heard 'Abdu'l-Baha speaking into his ears, and that it was
a lovely, peaceful experience. My observations, naturally, are those
of an ant looking at the sun. But nevertheless I did observe certain
things, and I believe that the nature of divine inspiration is not like
something that is written up that these great souls read constantly
before their eyes. It is rather in the nature of intermittent pulsations
– flashes of lightning.

The Guardian was always guided and always protected, but that
doesn't change the fact that he had agonizing moments of anxiety,
of sorrow, of despair perhaps, over certain situations, and that he
suffered terribly. Then came these tremendous impulses. He always
said the right thing; he always did the right thing. God never abandoned him for a second. But it was not a constant process – it was
flashes, and in between those flashes, there was room for infinite
suffering . . .

The Guardian was never prevented from accomplishing anything
because there were obstacles in the way. He charged them full on,
he never tried to avoid them or go around them – he flew at them.
His ingenuity in accomplishing the work in Haifa particularly was
phenomenal. He devised ways of doing things which he himself had
never seen done, and had never heard of being done.

For instance, he used to build terraces and gardens. People would
come to him and they would say 'A tree can't grow in one meter of
soil – a tree can't grow on top of a roof of a cistern – you cannot
plant a tree in the ground and pile up earth all around up to its
crown, it will die,' and so on. He did all of those things, he planted
trees on tops of cisterns and nothing happened to them, he covered
trees up to the crown and it looked as if three beautiful trees would
grow out of the soil instead of one. He was not intimidated by the
opinions of other people.[7]

On 26 January 1958, the foundation stone for the African Temple was
laid. On that day, 'a long line of private cars and taxis, followed by 14

huge buses' went up to Kikaya Hill. Once there, Rúḥíyyih Khánum placed a small silver box and a silk bag, both wrapped in silk scarves, beneath the foundation stone. The bag, made by the Greatest Holy Leaf, was of hand-sewn silk and contained a small piece of plaster from the ceiling of the cell of the Báb at Mákú, the cell in which the Báb had written His Book of the Covenant and His Laws. The box contained dust from the Threshold of the Shrine of Bahá'u'lláh.[8]

Following the Conference, Rúḥíyyih Khánum went to the Teso region, 200 miles from Kampala. There were 1,400 Bahá'ís and 42 Local Spiritual Assemblies in the area. She spent 24 hours enjoying the 'life of Africa – eating curried turkey and soup, millet, rice, and matoke (cooked green bananas), drinking what became her favourite African beverage, "smoked water", and sitting on hand-woven grass mats to watch the evening programme of traditional dancing and singing'.[9]

Intercontinental Conference for Australasia

Between 21 and 24 March, another conference was held in Sydney, Australia, and was attended by 300 Bahá'ís from 19 countries, including native believers from Tonga, the Solomon Islands and seven other island groups in the Pacific. Mason Remey, Clara Dunn, Agnes Alexander, Collis Featherstone, and Dhikru'lláh Khádem represented the Hands of the Cause. The Conference raised over £30,000 sterling for the Temple Fund and other projects around the Pacific.[10]

When Hand of the Cause Mason Remey, the Guardian's representative to the Conference, addressed the participants, he recalled 'the beloved Guardian's repeated warnings of the tests and dangers which would beset the believers ere "this Ark of human salvation is safely launched"', and reviewing the tremendous tasks which lay ahead of the Australian and New Zealand communities, concluded the message of the Custodians in these words:

> We are assured that the ultimate victory will be ours, ours the glory of having served and sacrificed for this Most Holy Faith, ours the crown of having remained steadfast in the path laid down for us by our well-beloved Guardian, ours the reward of his radiant smile when we meet him face to face in a better world, ours the joy of hearing him say: 'Well done, thou good and faithful servant.'[11]

This powerful statement came from the man who two years later would break Bahá'u'lláh's Covenant. Remey also presented the Conference several gifts from the Guardian including a portion of the earth from the inmost Shrine of Bahá'u'lláh, a lock of His precious hair, and a reproduction of His portrait. The Hand then anointed each Bahá'í as they passed by the gifts.[12]

On the second afternoon of the conference, 250 Bahá'ís travelled in 'three omnibuses and a fleet of cars' to Mona Vale, site of construction of the Mashriqu'l-Adhkár, for the Foundation Ceremony. As in Africa, Shoghi Effendi had sent a fragment of the cell of the Báb in Mákú and some earth from the Shrine of Bahá'u'lláh. Mason Remey and Clara Dunn carefully placed the small silver caskets in the centre of the Temple dome where they were sealed with concrete.[13]

In addition to showing two films about the Shrines and Holy Places at the World Centre, the Bahá'ís hosted a public meeting in downtown Sydney. Almost fifty people listened to three Bahá'í speakers who talked about how the Faith fulfilled the Christian and Muslim prophecies.[14]

Intercontinental Conference for the Western Hemisphere

Over 1,600 Bahá'ís coming from Alaska to Chile attended the conference at the Eighth Street Theater in Chicago from 2 to 4 May. The Hands in attendance included Ugo Giachery (earlier appointed by the Guardian as his representative), Corinne True, Horace Holley, Leroy Ioas, John Robarts and Mason Remey. Shoghi Effendi's words dominated the conference: '. . . these communities are now called upon . . . to play a preponderating role in the systematic propagation of the Faith, in the course of the coming decade, which will, God willing, culminate in the spiritual conquest of the entire planet'.[15]

On the first morning, at exactly 10 o'clock Chicago time, all those gathered paused with heads bowed in tribute to Shoghi Effendi, while at that moment in London, Hand of the Cause William Sears placed a wreath at the grave of the Guardian. Later, Horace Holley tried to get the participants to understand the importance of arising to serve, saying:

There are not many Bahá'ís who know the difference between the condition of the Faith at the time of 'Abdu'l-Bahá's ascension and today. Step by step the Guardian guided the Baháʼí world into World Order and into a profounder understanding of the Baháʼí Faith. In a letter in 1929 the Guardian mentioned '. . . that Divine Civilization, the establishment of which is the primary mission of the Baháʼí Faith'.

In the past it was thought the sole purpose of religion was to guide people into spiritual understanding which would lead to cooperation and peace. Shoghi Effendi was to us then a bright light illumining the path. He outlined the evolution of the Administrative Order in which the spiritual assemblies of today will become the Houses of Justice . . .

In another letter of March 21, 1930, the Guardian wrote, . . . 'I cannot refrain from appealing to them who stand identified with the Faith to disregard the prevailing notions and the fleeting fashions of the day, and to realize as never before that the exploded theories and the tottering institutions of present-day civilization must needs appear in sharp contrast with those God-given institutions which are destined to arise upon their ruin. I pray that they may realize with all their heart and soul the ineffable glory of their calling, the overwhelming responsibility of their mission, and the astounding immensity of their task.'[16]

Ugo Giachery told the audience that they were the only ones who could do the job, echoing what the Guardian told virtually all Western pilgrims in his disappointment at their lethargy and reluctance to arise:

For this Crusade we have an immensely potent instrument in the Divine Plan. Every act of obedience brings a victory; every victory leads to new spiritual life. The Western Hemisphere was singled out by ʼAbdu'l-Bahá. Attendants at this Conference must feel the weight of this responsibility. The greatness of this affliction, which has filled all hearts with grief and longing, must make us wiser, more consecrated than ever before. There can be no escape from duty for any believer, least of all for any American believer. We must ponder the critical state of the home front that we may rescue it from its precarious position. 'The individual alone must assess its character . . . shed attachments . . .' We must not allow 'this one remaining opportunity to be irretrievably lost.' God will make of this dire deprivation a leaven. Let us strive to gladden the heart of the beloved Guardian in the Abhá Kingdom; something we did not always do while he was alive.[17]

On the second day, Shoghi Effendi's Ten Year Crusade map was brought out and over 150 pioneers who had arisen were brought up on the stage. The next day, a hundred more pioneers volunteered to follow in their footsteps.[18] The United States began to step out of its lethargy.

Intercontinental Conference for Europe

Between 25 and 29 July, 2,300 Bahá'ís from 57 countries gathered in Frankfurt, including Hands of the Cause Amelia Collins (appointed by the Guardian as his representative), Hasan Balyuzi, Músá Banání, John Ferraby, Ugo Giachery, Hermann Grossmann, Jalál Kházeh, Dhikru'lláh Khádem, Adelbert Mühlschlegel, Enoch Olinga and John Robarts.

Milly Collins talked about the Guardian during his final years:

In 1951, when the Guardian called some of the friends to serve him in Haifa, I began to learn of some of what he had passed through. His face was so sad, one could see his very spirit had been oppressed by the agony he went through for years during the period when the family pursued their own desires and finally abandoned the work of the Faith and their Guardian to go their own way. I can truthfully say that for a number of years, we who served in the World Centre seldom saw him smile, and very often he poured out to us his woes and confided some of the things he had passed through . . .

The Guardian had a profound and innate humility. Whenever the Faith was involved, he was fiery in its defence, king-like in the loftiness of his bearing, the authority with which he spoke. But as a human being he was self-effacing, would brush aside our adulation and praise, turn everything we wished to shower on him towards the central figures of our Faith. We all know this characteristic of his, how he would never allow any photographs to be taken of himself, or give any of himself, but invariably encouraged the friends to place the Master's picture in their rooms; how he would not allow anyone to have his clothes or personal things lest they might be regarded as relics . . .

After the years of sorrow and trial he went through with the family, after his final separation from them, there came a new joy and hope to our beloved Guardian. The rapid progress made in the attainment of so many of the goals of the World Crusade lifted him up. How can I ever describe to you his eyes when he would come over to the Pilgrim House and announce to us a new achievement; they sparkled with light and enthusiasm and his beautiful face would be all smiles. Often he would send over one of his maps and when it was spread out on the dining room table, his finger, full of infinite strength, insistence and determination, would point out the new territory, the new Ḥaẓíratu'l-Quds purchased, the new language translated, as the case might be. I feel it would be no exaggeration to say that it was the progress of the Ten Year Plan that gave him the encouragement to go on working so hard, for he was very tired. More than once he said during the last year of his life, that his ministry had lasted longer than that of either Bahá'u'lláh and 'Abdu'l-Bahá, and complained of the crushing burden, but none of us could foresee it presaged his release, that he was burned out with thirty-six years of struggle, of constant work, of sorrow and self-sacrifice.

His conscientiousness was like a fire burning in him; from his earliest childhood he showed the sensitive, noble, painstaking qualities that characterized him, and grew stronger as he matured and throughout his Guardianship . . .

When 'Abdu'l-Bahá passed away, the Shrine of the Báb consisted of six rooms surrounded by a small piece of land. The Mansion of Bahjí and most of its lands were in the hands of the Covenant-breakers or their friends, except for the Holy Tomb itself, which covers a very small area, and two pilgrim houses, one rented. The Master Himself, though so widely loved and respected, was not known as the Head of an independent religion, but rather regarded as a Moslem notable and Holy Man. The young Guardian, freed by his very youthfulness, armed with the power conferred on him by his Grandfather, cut with one stroke the bonds still holding in appearance the Bahá'ís to Islam – he refused to go to the Mosque . . . Shoghi Effendi began to do all the Master had hoped to accomplish and to carry into effect His Words when He hinted that after Him the veils would be rent asunder. The Perfect Exemplar, the loving and forgiving Father, had passed away and the Order of Bahá'u'lláh was now to take shape under the guidance of the Champion of Divine Justice.

With wistful eyes the Blessed Master had gazed up at the Shrine of the Báb and said that it was not possible to build the Shrine of the Báb, but God willing, it would be done. The Guardian first added three rooms . . . to make the building a nine-roomed edifice. In 1944, the model of the completed Shrine was unveiled . . . By 1953 it was all built. Year after year the Guardian increased the size of the Shrine gardens . . . Patiently, persistently, he had the lands about it bought . . . He got the Mansion of Bahá'u'lláh away from the arch Covenant-breaker . . . and turned it into a Museum and Holy Place; he had all the Bahá'í properties exempted from government and municipal taxes . . . he secured . . . recognition of the fact that this is a World Religion . . .

The Administrative Order . . . Shoghi Effendi set out to build. When the Master passed away, there were few Spiritual Assemblies in the world, and only one national body functioning in a very rudimentary manner. The builder, however, had been provided by God; the Great Administrator, with an almost unique capacity for organization, with a wisdom vouchsafed from on High, with a world-encompassing vision, set about his task. Patiently, persistently, painstakingly, Shoghi Effendi reared strong national bodies . . . When he had created the system and reared the machinery of the Bahá'í Administrative Order, he suddenly shifted the whole mechanism into gear; he called for the first Seven-Year Plan . . . Plan followed plan. The scattered diversified followers of the Faith began to take shape as the army of Bahá'u'lláh; guided by the National Spiritual Assemblies. The pioneers, the vanguard as he called them of this great host, began to march out and over the world . . .

What gifts he had, what gifts he gave: *Gleanings from the Writings of Bahá'u'lláh, The Dawn-Breakers – Nabil's Narrative, The Kitáb-i-Íqán, The Hidden Words,* and the *Epistle to the Son of the Wolf,* translations of superlative style and power, making available the essence of Bahá'u'lláh's Message to the western world . . . What life he breathed into us through his own writings, beginning with his World Order letters . . . To such a long list of distinguished works was added the finest flower of his mind . . . *God Passes By.*[19]

Intercontinental Conference for Asia

The Intercontinental Conference for Asia was supposed to be held in Jakarta, Indonesia, in September 1958. As they were preparing for the conference, Hand of the Cause Rahmatu'lláh Muhájir warned the organizers not to use extensive publicity because Muslim fundamentalism had just awakened in the country and also because the conference was for Bahá'ís only. Unfortunately, his advice was not heeded and a media blitz was launched announcing the imminent arrival of hundreds of Bahá'ís. Interviews were given to newspapers and meetings arranged with high government officials. This did not last very long before suspicions were aroused and the permit for the conference was cancelled. Dr Muhájir immediately returned to Jakarta and tried to resolve the problem, but with no success. Two of those involved with the proclamation met with him and told him that he was too cautious and didn't understand the value of publicity, but he was able to stop them from continuing with it.[20] This was the beginning of a period of severe repression of the Faith in Indonesia, leading, in 1962, to the banning of the Faith in the country.[21]

Leroy Ioas, the Guardian's representative, arrived in the middle of the chaos. He immediately understood the gravity of the problem and 'became like a general in command, planning the next move for the forces of Bahá to triumph over the crisis that had been created'. They visited the Prime Minister, the Foreign Minister and the Minister of Religion, but to no avail.[22]

Hands of the Cause Collis Featherstone and Tarázu'lláh Samandarí were in Jakarta and joined the consultation; it was decided to move the conference to Singapore. When Leroy addressed the conference in its new venue, he noted that the forced move actually had a positive side. He said that there were now three countries, strangely all beginning with the letter 'I', which now knew a lot about the Bahá'í Faith: Iran, Israel and now Indonesia. Another plus to moving the conference to Singapore was that the Malaysian Bahá'ís, who had not been able to get visas to go to Jakarta, were now able to attend.[23] On 23 September, chartered planes took all the delegates from Jakarta to Singapore.

The conference started on 27 September and lasted for three days. Three hundred Bahá'ís attended along with Hands of the Cause Leroy Ioas, Collis Featherstone, Agnes Alexander, Enoch Olinga,

Raḥmatu'lláh Muhájir, Ṭarázu'lláh Samandarí, 'Abu'l-Qásim Faizí, and 'Alí Muḥammad Varqá. When Leroy first addressed the conference, he said, 'This Conference is so important it had to be held in two cities'.[24]

The Feast of Mashíyyat was held on the estate of Mrs George Lee and 180 people were there. One was Ho-San Leong, a new Bahá'í from Malacca, and he was by the main door when Leroy walked in.

> I was standing close to the main entrance of the very large room when Mr. Ioas and several of the friends walked in. He turned to me, extended his hand in a firm manner, and said 'I am Leroy Ioas and I am from the Holy Land', in such a natural style, warm and friendly. I shook his hand and introduced myself as a new Bahá'í from Malaysia. I had no idea then who he was or what he was doing in the Holy Land . . . He gave the keynote address on the work of the beloved Guardian spanning thirty-six years. The talk was so powerful and with every word and sentence you could sense his great love and devotion to the Guardian. I don't believe there was a dry eye in the audience when he ended. Young and inexperienced as we were, we were taken to new heights of belief and vision of the greatness of this faith of ours, and that we had indeed joined a religion that would one day unite all mankind on this planet. We also saw a glimpse of the services and dedication of those great and self-effacing souls who labored day and night to bring joy and happiness to the Guardian . . .
>
> He was a giant on the stage. He spoke in a powerful voice and in a flowing style, and I do not recall him talking about his achievements, on the achievements and victories that were won, one by one and so painstakingly, by the beloved Guardian. We knew so little then of the Guardian and his mission on earth, but Mr. Ioas in the course of his masterful talk described the Guardian in such vivid detail, it was almost as if Shoghi Effendi was present himself that day in spirit. And he gave us such a vision of the Holy Land . . . In the course of the conference we soon learned who Mr. Ioas was and of his selfless work in the service of the Faith.[25]

Ho-San was also impressed with the

spectacular entrance into the large hall of Miss Agnes Alexander walking arm in arm with Mr Enoch Olinga, a magnificent sight to behold. Everyone stood up in awe and respect and we were all overcome by this magic moment, a white American lady with a handsome black African, walking together with humble dignity that spoke of their stature and rank in the worldwide Bahá'í community.[26]

The Custodians emphasized the importance of opening the Intercontinental Conferences with the one in Africa and closing with the one in Asia, saying:

It is significant to ponder that the first, the opening Conference of this half-way point of the World Crusade was chosen by him [Shoghi Effendi] for the heart of Africa, and that the last, the closing Conference, was set midway in the Pacific-Asian region. He did not thus honour the old world and the new. No, he chose the black people and the brown people for this distinction. He visualized the African and the Pacific peoples vying with each other in the spread of the Faith.[27]

Ridván 1958

Ridván came half-way through the Conferences. Only one National Spiritual Assembly was formed in 1958, that of France, but the number of Local Spiritual Assemblies elected reached 1,100. There were also Bahá'ís in 4,500 different places in the world and the Writings could be read in 244 languages.[28]

Audacious pioneers who were not Knights

Many people pioneered during the Ten Year Crusade who did not earn the coveted title of Knight of Bahá'u'lláh for the simple reason that they chose goals that were outside of those named by the Guardian. But their efforts matched those of the Knights. Two of these were Adrienne and Dempsey Morgan, black American Bahá'ís who pioneered to Vietnam in 1958. Dempsey was one of the famous Tuskegee airmen, the black American pilots who gained renown for their bravery during the Second World War. Racism, however, affected him strongly. Appointed to the

American military academy at West Point, racism drove him to resign and become a pilot. Serving in Europe during the war, he flew 181 missions. His white commanding officer, who only flew 72 missions, gave Dempsey credit for just 70.[29]

Dempsey and Adrienne met in Washington DC and were married in 1953. Two years later, they became Bahá'ís. With the Ten Year Crusade in full swing, the young couple decided to play their part and pioneer, choosing Cambodia as their goal. Landing in Saigon, Vietnam, they were met by Jim Fozdar, brother of Knight of Bahá'u'lláh John and son of Knights of Bahá'u'lláh K.M. and Shirin Fozdar. Jim convinced Adrienne and Dempsey to stay a while in Vietnam. Jim had been in the country since 1954 and had helped almost 400 people accept the Faith. Jim, Dempsey, Adrienne and another black Bahá'í, Rodney Edward, each contributed part of their salaries to the teaching effort and by 1962, the Saigon Bahá'í community consisted of 1,000 souls.[30] The pioneers faced rampant government corruption as well as the beginnings of the Vietnam War.

In 1959, the Morgans, unable to extend their visas, moved to Thailand and found work as teachers in the International School in Bangkok. Thailand was a much more difficult country in which to teach the Faith than Vietnam and they concentrated on translating books into the Thai language. Charles Duncan, a Knight of Bahá'u'lláh for Brunei and who had arrived in Thailand in 1956, worked with them.[31]

In 1961, visa problems again forced the Morgans to move, and the Vietnamese National Spiritual Assembly asked them to go to Cambodia, their original goal. Initially, it was a difficult time to find work, but Adrienne managed to acquire a job as a secretary. Later, they both became teachers at the Cambodia American English Institute. The Morgans' teaching activities took them back into Vietnam on occasion. Adrienne described the exciting return from one such trip in verse:

Close Encounters

On returning to Cambodia
From a meeting in Vietnam,
We boarded an early taxi –
The trip was eight hours long.

1958

To avoid a confrontation
With fighting along the route
Twixt raiding Communist forces
And the government, in pursuit.

Ten passengers in an old Ford
That had once seen better times.
We two and the driver up front,
Five women with babies behind.

At one point on the highway,
With a line of cars ahead,
The traffic slowed down to a crawl
Then came to a halt instead.

We had a premonition
That something might happen here;
Too quiet, ominous silence.
One could sense the mounting fear.

I looked off toward the lush rice fields
Where some farmers were at work.
They stopped, looked up, and stood quite still.
Our driver began to jerk.

He quickly threw the car in gear,
Jammed the accelerator,
And sped around the line of cars.
Scarcely a few moments later

There was a barrage of gunfire.
His instincts hadn't been wrong.
All breathed a sigh of relief, because
We'd escaped the Viet Cong.

In 1963, Dempsey attended the election of the first Universal House of Justice and served as one of the nineteen tellers. He then joined Adrienne for the Jubilee in London.[32] When they returned to Cambodia, the Vietnam War was spilling over and there were anti-American riots in Phnom Penh. The Bahá'ís, too, were targeted, with some imprisoned and beaten. Then the Faith was banned. Dempsey wrote that

> a politician from Indonesia had come to Cambodia and told the wife of the Minister of Interior that Bahá'ís caused trouble and participated in politics in Indonesia. This caused the Cambodian government to close the Bahá'í Center and outlaw the Faith. I was summoned to the police department and obliged to write a letter saying that I would never send any Bahá'í teachers outside the capital city. When the take-over of the country by the Communists was imminent, we left for Thailand in the nick of time, a day or so before everything fell apart. We were in Cambodia many times because when there was a serious Communist threat we left for Thailand, and when the threat had passed we would return.[33]

The Morgans left South-East Asia in 1964 and pioneered to Africa, first to Uganda, because that was where Hand of the Cause Enoch Olinga was, and then to Chad in December 1967. Settling in Fort Lamy (now known as Ndjamena), during the first year they were only able to bring in six new believers. Then they began teaching people who passed in front of their house, and between April and July 1968 one hundred people declared their Faith in Bahá'u'lláh. By the end of the year, Chad had 1,000 Bahá'ís. Soon a third of Fort Lamy's population of 9,000 had become Bahá'ís and Dempsey said that he was being greeted with 'Alláh-u-Abhá' by people he didn't know. By the time the Morgans left Chad in 1971, there were 10,000 Bahá'ís.[34]

The Morgans continued their pioneering efforts after leaving Chad, going to the southern United States, Martinique, Zaire and Belize. Their arising to serve during the Ten Year Crusade resulted in thirty-two years of pioneering service to the Faith.

Pilgrimage reopened

On 24 August, pilgrimage was again opened to the believers of the world[35] and the Hands kept things exactly as they had been before. Each pilgrimage was restricted to 18 pilgrims, nine from the East and nine from the West and it was the Hands who met with them instead of the

Guardian.[36] But something was different. Obviously, Shoghi Effendi was not there and that had an impact on how the pilgrims were affected by their pilgrimage. Seven months after pilgrimage was restarted, the Custodians wrote that 'The flow of pilgrims has been steady, and the spirit they bring with them deeply touches our hearts . . .'.[37] What was strikingly different between this time and the time when the Guardian was there is that the pilgrims stopped sharing pilgrim notes. Those personal remembrances almost disappeared until after the conclusion of the Ten Year Crusade and the election of the Universal House of Justice. Previously, the notes which many pilgrims took and shared contained the words and thoughts of the Guardian. Without those words and thoughts, pilgrimage became a more personal time, more about spirituality and less about a single person. For 36 years, Shoghi Effendi had pushed the Bahá'í world to grow up, so to speak, and to learn to stand on its own two feet. His passing forced the pilgrims to reorient themselves from a titular head to the source of the Bahá'í Faith, the Revelations of the Báb and Bahá'u'lláh. The Shrines of the Báb and Bahá'u'lláh now became the most important aspect of pilgrimage.

Monument to Shoghi Effendi

On 1 November, the Custodians announced that the monument designed by Rúḥíyyih Khánum for the Guardian's grave had been completed. As envisioned by Rúḥíyyih Khánum, the monument consisted of a single column of white Carrara marble surmounted by a Corinthian capital on which sat a globe of the world. Perched on the globe was a golden eagle, either just about to spring into flight or just settling in after landing. Dust from the Shrine of Bahá'u'lláh was placed in the foundation. The monument was surrounded by a white stone balustrade, on each corner of which sat an ornate stone urn. The entrance to the gravesite was through a gate, then up a path of crushed red brick between two cypress trees. Two weeping holly trees, two white pedestals with flower-filled marble vases adorned the small garden.[38]

The Second Conclave of the Hands

The Second Conclave of the Hands of the Cause, during the first week of November, went well until two hours before the end. They had already extended the Conclave for two days to cover things that needed to be discussed, but suddenly Mason Remey brought up things he did not like, in part relating to a second Guardian. He knowingly waited until the very end for his own reasons, even though the rest had plane reservations already made. The Hands were quite upset because it was a subject that could require hours of consultation. Rúḥíyyih Khánum later said that Remey

> got up and introduced a very negative element – that he was very dissatisfied, that he didn't think the Hands had the right spirit and so on. And we said, 'Mason, why did you say this now? Why in God's name couldn't you have said it in the beginning and then we could have thrashed this out.' Now we were just leaving. People had airplane reservations for that night to go out. We couldn't meet any longer, as I say we already postponed it two days. 'Why on earth didn't you say all this?' 'Well I was hoping somebody else would get up and say it.' Well, we said that, 'We think that you should have said it.' And we gave him the floor for an hour and all of his thoughts were very much along the line that we were not properly guided, we didn't have the right ideas and we were wrong. We shouldn't do this, we shouldn't do that. And criticism. And we said 'Well Mason, we don't know why on earth you didn't say this before but if you still feel this way next year why, you can have the floor and talk about these things as long as you like and would you accept that?' 'Yes.' And so on and so we parted.[39]

The United States rises to the challenge

By the end of 1958, the North American Baháʼí communities were rising to the challenge set before them by Shoghi Effendi. More people arose in the Baháʼí year 1957/58 than in any previous year. Ninety pioneers went to Latin America, 15 to Asia and the Pacific, and 5 to Africa. A total of 359 American pioneers were at their posts by the end of 1958. Eleven National Spiritual Assemblies had been elected under the auspices of the US National Assembly.[40] One goal, however, still eluded them. Shoghi Effendi had called for the United States to have 300 Local Spiritual Assemblies by the end of the Crusade. The country had started with the Crusade with 169 Local Assemblies, but by Riḍván 1959 had only achieved 195.[41]

Knights of Bahá'u'lláh

One further goal of the Ten Year Crusade was filled in 1958 when Paul Adams, a young British Bahá'í from London, found work as a hunter's apprentice in Spitsbergen and spent a dark and lonely winter there.

1959

Persecution in Turkey

At Naw-Rúz, just one month before the Bahá'ís of Turkey elected their first National Spiritual Assembly, Turkish police arrested the whole Local Spiritual Assembly of Ankara. One of the prosecutors in the case declared that the Bahá'ís were 'Tarighat', or a sect of Islam 'whose rituals, practices and forms of worship are forbidden by the law of the country'. The Court requested three experts on comparative religion to examine the case. Two found that the Bahá'í Faith was an independent religion while the third agreed with the prosecutor that the Bahá'ís were 'Tarighat'. The Court then appointed three 'outstanding religious scholars' to review the affair and all three agreed, in a report submitted two years later, on 17 January 1961, that the Bahá'í Faith was indeed an independent religion.

The case received considerable publicity with most of the main newspapers coming out against the action. With the unanimous statement by the scholars, most people expected the case to be dropped, but on 15 July 1961, the Court baffled everyone by declaring that the Bahá'í Faith was 'Tarighat'. Even stranger, with that verdict, the Bahá'ís were then 'forgiven, on the grounds that their gathering [the Local Spiritual Assembly meeting] constituted a criminal case and under the general amnesty provisions of the law they could be released . . . the case against them dropped'.

The Custodians urged the National Assemblies of the United States, the British Isles, Germany, Italy and Switzerland to 'appoint [a] well-qualified delegation' to call upon their Turkish ambassadors in a 'friendly' way to educate them about the Bahá'í Faith.[1]

Riḍván 1959

By Riḍván 1959 there were almost 6,500 Baháʼís and 238 Local Spiritual Assemblies in the Central and East Africa area, the third largest Baháʼí population in the world after Iran and the United States This was exceptional growth from 1,400 Baháʼís and 61 Local Assemblies in Uganda and Kenya just three years earlier.[2]

Two National Spiritual Assemblies were split to make four new ones at Riḍván: Germany, Austria, India and Burma. In addition, the National Spiritual Assembly of Turkey and a new Regional Spiritual Assembly of the South Pacific Islands, with its seat in Fiji, were elected. With four years left in the Ten Year Crusade, 31 National and Regional Spiritual Assemblies had been formed. Across the world, there were now 1,275 Local Spiritual Assemblies and 5,200 localities in 255 countries. The Writings had been translated into 261 different languages. [3]

Pilgrims: Carol Bowie and William Maxwell

Carol Bowie, from Niagara Falls, Canada, a very active Baháʼí who had found the Faith two years before, was on pilgrimage in May at the same time as William Maxwell. When Carol and the other pilgrims stayed in the Mansion at Bahjí, Amatuʼl-Bahá Rúḥíyyih Khánum was also there. One night at dinner, the group was talking about world events. In making a point, Carol quoted the first paragraph from Shoghi Effendi's *The Promised Day Is Come*. This sparked a surprising response from the Guardian's wife: 'Rúḥíyyih Khánum jumped up from the table, came around and hugged me and said, "At last, a North American who reads Shoghi Effendi!"' Carol explained that her husband, David, would always read the Guardian's works to her as she cared for their children.[4]

William Maxwell, a member of the first Regional Assembly of North East Asia, arrived in Tel Aviv from Korea in May on a plane that was 'a madhouse of excitement', being filled mostly with newly arriving Jews. Their arrival was quite chaotic until 'a real sergeant of a lady' learned that he was a Baháʼí, whereupon he was rapidly taken through Customs. William asked if he could call the Baháʼí World Centre and five minutes later, he was talking with Hand of the Cause Paul Haney. William was soon on his way to Haifa in a 'jitney' (sherut), which he shared with a government worker who was quite proud of his country and kept up a running commentary:

> 'See those apartment houses over there, none were there a couple of years ago. See this new highway? Just finished.' He further explained that before the 1948 war broke out Israel imported nearly all her vegetables from her Arab neighbors. Now she exports vegetables, eggs, etc., to Turkey and even to Europe. So he continued for nearly an hour.[5]

When the man found out that William was a Bahá'í, he stated that Israel was the 'most developed, the most beautiful country', that Haifa was 'the most beautiful city in Israel' and that the Bahá'í Gardens the most beautiful spot in Haifa. The driver insisted that he knew exactly where the Western Pilgrim House was, but at 8 p.m. he dropped William off in front of the Eastern Pilgrim House.

The door was opened by Hand of the Cause Jalál Kházeh. Inside he was greeted by an arc of pilgrims and Hands, including 'Alí-Akbar Furútan and 'Abu'l-Qásim Faizí. In short order, William and his luggage were loaded into Mr Kházeh's Volkswagen and taken down to the Western Pilgrim House, where he was welcomed by the Haneys, Mrs Wilks from Seattle, Cora Oliver (Knight of Bahá'u'lláh from British Honduras, now Belize), Carol Bowie and the Revell sisters. Though William protested that he had already eaten four times that day, Mrs Haney had dinner ready for him. Sitting at that table where Shoghi Effendi had sat with the pilgrims was a very emotional moment for William – Paul Haney had to calm him down before Rúḥíyyih Khánum arrived so that his tears didn't release hers.[6]

William and Carol wanted to go to the Shrine that first night, but since it was after 11 p.m. by that time, they were encouraged to wait until the next day. William was awake by 4 a.m. and, after waking Carol, headed impatiently up the still dark mountain, up 'scores of endless steps'. Arriving at the Eastern Pilgrim House, he found everyone still asleep and the gate to the Shrine locked. William climbed over two fences, but was then restricted to praying 'on the cool marble steps' at the door to the Shrine. Carol soon arrived with keys she had been given by Mr Kházeh, who had probably been awakened by William's effort to get the keys himself.[7]

The pilgrims returned that night to the Shrines in the company of the Hands. William wrote:

> We entered first the Shrine of the Báb. It was night, the air was cool. The hillside had the quiet serenity of a tired devoted mother. We entered in turn. Knelt, walked to the threshold and knelt again. This, fortunately, took a long time. No one hurried . . . Crystal, Persian carpets, lights hidden in alabaster. Majesty. Quiet. Awe.
>
> Then after each had knelt and after we had backed away to the wall, one of the Hands directed prayers. The blessed were we. Ruhiyyih Khanum chanted the Visitation Tablet of Baha'u'llah in the original. No words can describe that beauty. Exquisite is inaccurate. Painfully beautiful is as close as I can come. Her voice was like the finest of tuned 17th century Venice goblets. I never knew a woman's voice could be so compellingly simple, unassuming, yet so extraordinarily melodic. Her crystal voice was reinforcement of the already crystal nature of the room. I feel sure today that one minute more of it and my feet would have left the floor . . .
>
> To add too much to too much, Mr Faizi then chanted . . .
>
> Prayer that night was real . . .
>
> My mind had limited capacity. Thus after we left the Room facing the Báb's Chamber and our feet went to the section of Abdu'l-Baha's remains . . . I cannot remember what happened there that night.
>
> On other occasions . . ., the impression that Abdu'l-Baha's sector of the tomb leaves is . . . quite different, it is cooler, more soothing. I do not know how to express the 'feeling' of this place . . . [8]

Later, the pilgrims went to the Archives. William was really looking forward to seeing the photograph of Bahá'u'lláh because, though he had seen it before, he couldn't remember a single detail of His face. So, it was with great anticipation that he looked at the photograph. But what he saw wasn't what he had expected:

> I could read nothing in the eyes. The lips whispered nothing. The forehead said nothing to me . . . it was as if I was an ant looking at a blue-print. I saw the lines, the shadings and shadows, but the story, the meaning of the lines, was over my head . . . My ignorance

was manifest to me. I left the portrait, came back, looked again, left again, came back. [9]

Then the pilgrims went to Bahjí, driving in the old station wagon, and were met by Rúḥíyyih Khánum and Mr Faizí. In the Mansion, William saw a photograph of those who had participated in the 1953 Intercontinental Teaching Conference in New Delhi. He remembered the photograph from *The Bahá'í World* (vol. XII) because it had been taken with a panoramic camera that turned on a stand to take such a wide photo. One enterprising young fellow, taking advantage of the time it took the camera to pan the length of the believers, had managed to run from one end of the group to the other and thereby be seen in the picture twice. In his framing of the photo for the Mansion, Shoghi Effendi had neatly eliminated him from both ends. [10]

That night, William shared a room with Eric Blumenthal, a German pioneer in Greece and an Auxiliary Board member. William couldn't sleep, but in the morning he felt that his brain had been scrubbed clean. When he went to the Shrine of Bahá'u'lláh and tried to pray, he found that he could not. When he later told Rúḥíyyih Khánum about that, she laughingly replied: 'Well, it's probably because you had too many prepared speeches for God.' Everyone laughed, but William decided that it had the 'ring of truth'. [11]

Some of the pilgrims helped at the Shrine of the Báb with visitors. William found that when he spoke of the Faith to Americans and Europeans, they accepted what he said without the least argument. One day, two boys arrived just as they were locking up. It was their first visit, so they were allowed in. William was quite surprised when they returned a short while later, backing out with great reverence. One, who spoke English, said, *'Now,* I understand a great man is buried there.' [12]

William noted that the Hands of the Cause were not concerned with what would happen to the Administrative Order in the future. Everything they did was focused on carrying out the specifics of Shoghi Effendi's plan. At that time, the Hands were very concerned with forming National Spiritual Assemblies:

> They explained: If the International House of Justice is to be formed in '63, the NSAs which are the pillars of it, must be formed in '62. The LSAs which must be the pillars of the NSAs must be formed in

'61. [Which] means that the seeds for these LSAs must be planted in '59. Time is running out. There was worry that if these goals were not met, the Jubilee could not rightly be called.

It is interesting to note that Shoghi Effendi stipulated precisely how many LSAs were necessary for each country.[13]

The pilgrims were very impressed with how the Hands in the Holy Land did their work. They exercised great frugality. Milly Collins, who was quite wealthy, lived in a tiny room with no bath facilities. Mason Remey also had just a small room and he shared a bathroom with the Haneys, the Revell sisters and the pilgrims. In spite of their frugality, the Hands had gained great respect from the Israeli Government. When the group of nine Hands was selected to handle the affairs of the Faith, the Israeli Government had pledged its cooperation and accepted them as the supreme body of the Faith.[14]

On his last day, William went alone to the Shrine of the Báb. After kneeling at the threshold, he stood and began to recite the Tablet of Visitation aloud. The moment he started, the melody used by Rúḥíyyih Khánum and Mr Faizí when chanting the Tablet filled his mind and he found himself chanting it. 'At last,' he wrote, 'I entered the condition of prayer. And I was happy. And I wanted nothing else.'[15]

The Third Conclave of the Hands

The Third Conclave of the Hands of the Cause was held at Bahjí from 23 October to 1 November. Twenty-three Hands attended and consulted about the remaining goals and how to achieve them by the end of the Crusade. Shoghi Effendi had defined what had to be done during the Crusade, so they knew what to do until then. But he had left no guidance about what to do afterwards. Jalál Kházeh said that they asked themselves what would happen when the Crusade was completed:

. . . we are not inspired from on High. What shall we do? Who is going to guide the friends throughout the whole world? We wanted to bring to existence the embryo that was in the womb of the world, to create the Universal House of Justice, but we found that we had no authority to do that.

But one miracle happened that some of the Iranian Hands,

especially Mr Samandari . . . when they meditate on the Writings of Bahá'u'lláh and the Tablets which he has gathered. He brought one Tablet from 'Abdu'l-Bahá [and] in that Tablet it is written [that] 'Abdu'l-Bahá said that 'I am in a great danger now. There is not a single minute that I should be alive. They may drown me in the ocean or hang me or send to the desert of Fezzan in Africa.' And therefore, in that [Tablet] He explained the station of the Báb and Bahá'u'lláh and the Universal House of Justice . . . There is nothing in that Tablet about the Guardian or the Guardianship because . . . Shoghi Effendi at that time was about six years old.

In that Tablet, He says, if the time is proper and there is no danger, the central assembly of Iran and the central assembly of the United States, and India and Burma, and Iraq and Egypt and some other central assemblies – you know what central assemblies means? There were no national spiritual assemblies in the time of the beloved Master. The Local Spiritual Assembly of Tehran, the capital of Iran, was the central assembly to supervise all the assemblies throughout Iran. The same in England, the same in the United States and the others. So, He called these local assemblies of the capitals as central assemblies. He said they should gather and elect nine people from the whole world and that is the Universal House of Justice.[16]

Hasan Balyuzi, 'Alí Nakhjavání and 'Abu'l-Qásim Faizí translated the Tablet into English for the American and British Hands and that became the foundation on which they set the date for the election of the Universal House of Justice. At Riḍván 1962, there would be 56 National Spiritual Assemblies and they would elect the House of Justice at Riḍván 1963. But first, they had to achieve the goals, so they called for Latin America to elect 21 National Spiritual Assemblies at Riḍván 1961. They had hoped to elect an additional 11 National Assemblies in Europe at the same time, but it was obvious that that goal could not be reached, so it was postponed until Riḍván 1962. [17]

The Conclave called for another milestone on the road to the Universal House of Justice when it announced in its Conclave Message that the International Bahá'í Council would, for the first time, be elected at Riḍván 1961. Hand of the Cause Mr Furútan, in a talk to pilgrims at the World Centre, described a meeting of the Hands at which they were consulting on the idea of asking not to be elected to the first elected

International Bahá'í Council. Mason Remey was incensed at the idea that he wouldn't be elected and all others in the room sat with heads bowed because of the extreme tension. Except Rúḥíyyih Khánum. She stood up to Remey, and the Hands asked not to be voted for.[18]

This Conclave was a pivotal moment for Mason Remey. Because of his actions the previous year, he was put at the top of the agenda 'so he could talk all he wanted to'. He spoke, however, very little. At the end of the Conclave when the Hands had written the Conclave message, Mason surprised everyone by refusing to sign it:

> 'I won't sign it.' And we were very surprised. He said, 'No, no, no, no, I won't sign it, I don't agree with it. I don't agree with the plans that have been made. I don't agree with electing a [International Baha'i] Council . . . I don't agree with the formation of the [Universal] House of Justice at this time. The Hands are on the wrong track. You are violators [of the Covenant]. You are in the path of violation.'[19]

This stance shocked the other Hands. Though there had been differences of opinion between individual Hands, their desire to follow Shoghi Effendi's plan and bring about the election of the Universal House of Justice was such that they had never caused disharmony. Suddenly, they were faced with the rebellion of a Hand who disagreed with all the rest. Mason Remey said that he would take part in meetings, but that he would no longer sign any communication or document put out by the Hands. He even refused to meet with the pilgrims. The Hands realized that this made his position as one of the nine Hands in the Holy Land untenable and they told him that he would have to be replaced. Rúḥíyyih Khánum said, 'that didn't upset him at all. He wasn't a bit hurt by it.'[20] As they were to find out within a few months, he already had plans in motion.

Despite Mason Remey's accusations of violation, Leroy Ioas thought that overall, the Conclave had gone well. Writing to Dhikru'lláh Khádem afterwards, he said, 'We had a very wonderful Conclave, even though it was fraught with many difficulties, and was very exhausting. Yet as we look back, history was made – and really speedily. Never in the history of religion were so many important decisions taken and with such unified action.'[21]

But that same month, when Philip and Lois Hainsworth were returning to their pioneering post in Kampala from a visit to London they stopped in Orleans, France, and stayed with Joel Marangella, an Auxiliary Board member. While there, Marangella closely questioned Philip about the possibility that the Guardian had left a will, which had yet to be found, and about the Guardianship. The Hainsworths continued to the town of St Jean de Luz where they stayed with John Carré. John also was very interested in the possibility of a second Guardian. Philip thought little of it at the time, but it was a portent of what was about to happen, because both Marangella and Carré ended up following Mason Remey and became Covenant-breakers.[22]

Pilgrims: John and Rose Wade

In December, John and Rose Wade made their first pilgrimage. They were the caretakers of Shoghi Effendi's resting place in London, and were met by Rúḥíyyih Khánum. The Wades stayed in the Western Pilgrim House along with Paul Haney, William Sears, Horace and Doris Holley and John and Dorothy Ferraby. John Wade remembered that they all shared a downstairs bath and the 'funny little kitchen'. The laundry hung from the downstairs ceiling to dry. He noted that

> At this time pilgrimage was not organised. It was a very informal visit, but Jessie Revell made sure that we went to the right places and so this is what we did. We were taken to Bahjí and other places connected with Bahá'u'lláh . . . Rúḥíyyih Khánum took us to several places herself. She had arranged a dinner for us so we and the caretakers had dinner in the Pilgrim House. I also remember something special that took place. Rose had taken some roses from London for Rúḥíyyih Khánum and gave them to her. On that pilgrimage we slept in the Mansion of Baha'u'llah in Bahji for two nights. During the night I got up and went into Bahá'u'lláh's bedroom and said prayers. When I went into the bedroom I noticed that Rúḥíyyih Khánum had placed one of [the] roses in a vase on the table in the room. It was such a lovely gesture.[23]

Near the end of their pilgrimage, John mentioned that they were going to Iran afterwards to see their daughter, Christine, who was living there at the time. Jessie Revell looked serious and said,

> 'Oh John, this will have to be discussed.' Well I can tell you that I was a bit nonplussed; I couldn't see the reason for discussing my private affairs, such as where I went after pilgrimage. Anyway it was discussed and we were called to meet with, I think, Paul Haney.
>
> He told us, 'John, I'm sorry, there's no way the Hands can allow you to do this.' Of course I asked 'Why?' and he said 'Well only because the Guardian had stated that no one could go to Persia, other than Persians, that this was not allowed at this time, because of the problems.' So he said 'You can't do this, it's impossible for us to give you permission.' Well, of course, I didn't know how to take this because it was my cheque book that I had used to pay the fare! Nevertheless we went to the Shrines and prayed and came to the conclusion that we were Bahá'ís and obedience was one of the big things so we would have to be obedient and do this. So we went back and said OK, it's fine, we will have to cancel, and do you know what the Hands did? They arranged for us to go to Turkey and for Christine to come to Turkey and meet us.[24]

Gathering the Guardian's correspondence

Shoghi Effendi never kept copies of the thousands of letters he sent to all corners of the globe, which potentially meant the loss of a huge amount of guidance. On 4 December, the Custodians requested that all National Assemblies return or send copies of any original letters from Shoghi Effendi. Additionally, they asked the Assemblies to forward copies of all correspondence they had sent to the Guardian over the years.[25]

Knights of Bahá'u'lláh

Two more of the Guardian's goal areas were achieved during 1959 when John Chang managed to visit Hainan Island for two weeks, and Catherine and Cliff Huxtable settled in the Gulf Islands, between Vancouver Island and the British Columbia mainland. These were the last virgin territory goals to be won during the Ten Year Crusade.

1960

On 11 February, the Custodians wrote to the Bahá'í world with news of the world-wide activities of the Faith. They noted that Ugo Giachery was touring in Central America, John Robarts had gone to Canada, Adelbert Mühlschlegel was in Scandinavia, 'Alí-Akbar Furútan was on a lengthy trip in Iran, Shu'á'u'lláh 'Alá'í was travelling in India, Japan and the north Pacific, and Hermann Grossmann was assisting in South America. Collis Featherstone had been invited by a group of Maori chiefs in New Zealand to present the Faith in an area where religious teaching had been forbidden because of the conflicts caused by competing Christian sects. They reported that Uganda, Kenya and the Malayan Archipelago were seeing an 'extraordinary' number of enrolments. German pioneers had arisen to teach in neighbouring countries and South Americans were pioneering to their own goal cities. The Ten Year Plan was going well.[1]

Geertrui Ankersmit

About the time the Custodians sent their message, Geertrui Ankersmit (later Bates) came on pilgrimage from Luxembourg. Geertrui was a Knight of Bahá'u'lláh who had pioneered to the Frisian Islands off Holland in 1953, then had moved to Luxembourg to help them elect their first Regional Spiritual Assembly. She flew to Tel Aviv on a plane filled with South American Jews who were so excited that they kissed the ground when they landed. Since it was one o'clock in the morning when she arrived, Geertrui went looking for a hotel, but the only place she could find was a bed on a stair landing of the floor the hotel employees lived on.[2]

Geertrui's train to Haifa was filled with German-speaking Jews. Once in Haifa, one of them helped her get a sherut to the Western Pilgrim

House at 10 Haparsim where she was greeted by Jessie Revell. Geertrui was very impressed with the frugality of those living in the Pilgrim House. John Ferraby, Paul and Margery Haney, Leroy and Silvia Ioas, and Horace and Doris Holley all lived there and shared a single cold-water shower. There was only a solitary kerosene heater in the dining room to provide warmth, something very much needed in February. Doris Holley and a housekeeper took care of the Pilgrim House. Milly Collins lived in the House of the Master where she had to bathe herself with a bowl of warm water.[3]

Sylvia Ioas took Geertrui to the Shrine of the Báb for her first visit. Before she could even pass through the door, Geertrui was in tears, but the physical world intruded once she had entered and saw a curtain, unmended and which had come loose from its rings. Recomposing herself, she said her prayers, then went to the Shrine of 'Abdu'l-Bahá where she was surprised to find a completely different feeling. Hand of the Cause Jalál Kházeh took her to Bahjí and she greatly enjoyed his company and sense of humour. Being the only pilgrim, Geertrui had the Shrine of Bahá'u'lláh to herself and was able to sing to her heart's content. While there, she also met the custodians, Dr Forsyth and Janet Ward. They were the parents of Alicia Cardell, wife of Knight of Bahá'u'lláh Ted Cardell, and had been on their way to visit them when they stopped in Haifa to visit the Holy Places.[4] They had been asked to stay and care for the Shrine at Bahjí, which they did for ten years.[5]

An English meteorologist living in Libya, Ray Humphrey, arrived on pilgrimage and Mr Kházeh took them to Akka, the Temple land on top of Mount Carmel, and the new Archives building. The Archives building had only just been completed, but was not yet ready for pilgrim use. All the furniture inside was covered with sheets and the Archive materials were still being displayed in the three back rooms of the Shrine of the Báb. Lotfullah Hakím showed Geertrui and Ray the historical artefacts and even let them hold the blood-stained clothing of Mírzá Mihdi and the sword of Mullá Husayn.

One day, Mr Kházeh told Geertrui that, as a pioneer, she should be married. Geertrui answered: 'Yes, I will marry an Englishman when I am 35', which was still a year and a half away and which usually ended that type of conversation. Mr Kházeh, however, replied that maybe she should marry Ray, her pilgrimage companion, adding, 'You can have my car to go on honeymoon. Just cable your parents for permission.'

Geertrui and Ray later asked Rúḥíyyih Khánum about marriage and she explained that 'there was something to be said for arranged marriages' when the families knew each other's backgrounds. Geertrui and Ray didn't get married, but six weeks later, when Mr Kházeh visited Geertrui in Luxembourg, he exclaimed, 'What, you are still not married? And I said prayers for you to be married.' But within a year, and before her 35th birthday, Geertrui met and married an Englishman, Ronald Bates, who had, interestingly, been on the pilgrimage immediately after hers.[6] The Bates family later served in Haifa at the World Centre.

Business at breakfast

Near the end of February, Richard Mereness came on pilgrimage from his pioneering post in Seward, Alaska. What struck him about life in the Holy Land was how the Hands conducted some of their business:

> Breakfasts were very informal, attended by those Hands living in the Western Pilgrim House: Mr. Ioas and his wife Sylvia, Mr. Holley and his wife Doris, Mr. Ferraby and his wife Dorothy. Mr. Ioas presented the agenda, which consisted of correspondence from the English speaking sectors of the Baha'i World. Imagine this scene to which I, as a lone pilgrim, witnessed. All were gathered . . . drinking their tea or coffee and eating corn flakes or toast while various letters from individuals and assemblies were read and discussed, and when there was consensus to a response then another topic was brought forth. So on it went, each Hand offering his opinion frequently supplemented by wifely comments. Mr. Ioas, with his white hair, had a very kind looking, rather square face behind his spectacles and a measured, strong even-tempered voice. He was a man with determination and conveyed authority. Mr. Holley, an aging diplomatic gentleman with an erect posture, neatly trimmed white mustache and slender build, housed a brilliant mind. He was rather paucilloquatious in his comments, but always directly to the point.
>
> Mr. Ferraby, whom I had always imagined to be one of the most conversational writers about the Faith that I had experienced, was to my amazement, rather quiet. He sat such with his head lowered paying all the while close attention to the conversation. And so it went, this gentle conversation from topic to topic while I sat

spellbound by the procedure, scarcely wanting to munch my corn-flakes, which noisily interfered with my riveted attention. But then of a sudden, Mr. Ferraby would dislodge himself from his meditative posture, sit upright and offer a thought regarding something already discussed to which the others listened intently and some thoughts were offered again about the topic, thus altering a decision previously settled by reason of his introspection. This experience has led me to think that many of us have minds that operate in what I would describe as a horizontal mode, rather lineal; one darn thing after another. Mr. Ferraby's mind operated in a vertical fashion; he would twist his way down through possibilities, examining consequences and then, having examined the subterranean channels of thought, emerge to the surface with a piece of gold, a glittering gem of truth.[7]

Riḍván 1960

The Riḍván Message from the Custodians to Bahá'í National Conventions around the world illustrated the unstoppable power of the Faith. Local Spiritual Assemblies were elected in 1,275 localities in 256 countries. Bahá'ís were living in 5,800 places and could read the Writings in 268 languages.[8]

The Custodians were completely unaware of the lightning that was about to strike. In describing how well the Guardian's Ten Year Plan was progressing, they wrote:

Not only has the unity of the Faith been protected, the plans of the enemies forestalled and its properties safeguarded, but the spirit of the believers has not faltered in the darkest hours of test. We may truly say that it is this great pact of faith in the hearts of the friends that has held the Cause steadily on the course chartered for it by its Guardian, and has been the magnet attracting so many new souls to the Faith during the past two years. It is this force of faith in Bahá'u'lláh and love for Him that has swept the Bahá'ís of the world forward to such astonishing victories . . .[9]

Mason Remey declares himself second Guardian

On 8 January, the Custodians had sent a message to all the Hands of the Cause saying that they had

> received word that some of the Hands have not been sufficiently careful in strictly observing the understandings we reached [at the First Conclave], particularly that no comment whatsoever would be made concerning the Guardianship or its future except as outlined in our . . . messages.
>
> We call this to your attention because we are fearful that the least infraction of this most important matter on the part of any Hand may lead to very serious consequences throughout the Bahá'í world.[10]

Just five days into the Riḍván period, on 26 April, Ian Semple collected the mail from inside the front door of the Ḥaẓíratu'l-Quds in London and found a letter from Hand of the Cause Mason Remey addressed to the National Spiritual Assembly. When he opened it, he was 'profoundly shocked' to find a document in which Remey declared himself to be the 'Second Guardian of the Bahá'í Faith'. The proclamation, he said, was 'a pitiful document' and 'utterly baseless'. Ian bolstered himself with the Tablet of Aḥmad, then called the members of the emergency subcommittee of the National Spiritual Assembly. The trio immediately wrote to the Custodians declaring their faithfulness. Three days later, the Custodians announced Remey's perfidy to the world.[11]

Remey's 'Proclamation' was devastating to the other Hands. As Rúḥíyyih Khánum told the Bahá'ís in New York on 5 June:

> We had been having for a period of about a month very strange communications from Mason . . . We began to get these communications from him attacking the Hands and on practically every page calling us violators. And this distressed us very much. We couldn't understand what on earth had happened to him. And if you analyze the documents [sent by Remey] they're not that sound as far as arguments go. And we were very upset . . . we never dreamed that when something like this happened it would come again from *inside* the Cause. All of us had been waiting in Haifa for an attack. Because

we knew that 117 years of [Bahá'í] history couldn't suddenly change overnight. We knew that somehow, something would crop up. Was it reasonable that we should have all this, relatively speaking, peacefulness after the passing of the Guardian? But it never occurred to us in our wildest dreams that anything like this could happen, or that it should come from dear old Mason Remey. But he seems to be persisting in these ideas and he is going further and further in his statements. He is calling all of the Hands Arch Covenant-Breakers, which he has no right in the world to do. Whatever his claims he certainly has no right to do that. And of course his claims are absolutely untenable. They are ridiculous. Anyone in their right mind, as the Hands said in that cable they sent to the friends, [knows] they are preposterous.[12]

But the shocking surprise of Remey's defection was just the first jolt. Ian Semple was soon called by Hand of the Cause Hasan Balyuzi and asked to go to France where eight members of the National Spiritual Assembly, excepting only Colonel Barafrukhtih, had joined Remey in his defection. Ian was perplexed that he was being sent because, though he was an Auxiliary Board member, Joel Marangella was also an Auxiliary Board member and he was already there in France. The blow fell when Mr Balyuzi said that Marangella was a ringleader of the Covenantbreakers. Evidently he and Bernard Fillon, a French National Assembly member, had French translations of Remey's declaration ready for distribution the moment Remey declared himself. Hand of the Cause Abu'l-Qásim Faizí and Auxiliary Board Member for protection 'Aziz Navidí were sent to Paris to attempt to bring the errant members back into the fold.[13]

Mr Faizí arranged a meeting with the breakaway National Assembly for 2 o'clock on 6 May. Upon his arrival at the meeting, the chairman informed him that the assembly wanted to meet privately first. Normally, Mr Faizí was obedient to the institutions and very loving and gentle. Not this time. He told them that they had agreed to meeting at that time, that he was there and that they would sit down and start. They sat down and started. When he questioned the assembly members, their responses left him with his 'whole body trembling' and his 'mouth was frozen'. Mr Faizí then asked who supported Remey and, when five hands were raised, Mr Faizí told them the meeting was over. That night,

Mr Faizí worried about what had to be done next. He had been told that if a majority of the members of the French Assembly remained as Covenant-breakers, then the body would have to be dissolved and he wondered how this could be done while maintaining the dignity of the Faith. His dilemma was solved the next morning when one of the loyal Assembly members brought him five resignation papers from Remey's followers. That meant that since the Assembly only had four members, a new election could be called. Following his meeting with the National Assembly, Mr Faizí travelled throughout France and visited every Bahá'í centre to ensure they understood what was happening.[14]

Bill Sears heard the news in Jamaica. He and Marguerite had just landed at the airport and were being collected by a member of the Regional Spiritual Assembly. As the Assembly member walked with Bill to the taxi, he quietly informed him of Remey's declaration. Unfortunately, the taxi driver was not a Bahá'í and a two-hour driving tour had already been scheduled so the stunned visitors were forced to feign interest for what felt like a lifetime. Soon, Bill was on his way to Haifa.[15]

The Hands of the Cause now faced their greatest challenge since the Guardian's passing. On 28 April, the Custodians in the Holy Land had warned the Bahá'í world that Mason Remey had proclaimed himself as the second Guardian of the Faith. Remey was sending copies of his declaration as the second Guardian to everyone he could think of. In this document, he arrogantly proclaimed his rationale for claiming the Guardianship:

> He who is the President of the Universal House of Justice is the Guardian of the Faith for he who is the Guardian of the Faith is President of the Universal House of Justice. These two offices are one and the same. Therefore, when the beloved Guardian Shoghi Effendi appointed me President of the Bahá'í International Council, that, he explained, was the forerunner of the Universal House of Justice that was the Embrionic [sic] Universal House of Justice that would eventually develop into the Universal House of Justice. I or one of my successors in Guardianship would be President of this divinely instituted infallible body the Universal House of Justice; therefore the Guardianship of the Bahá'í Faith and the Presidency of the Universal House of Justice are one and the same position in the Faith.[16]

Remey's claim was laughably transparent. First, Shoghi Effendi had appointed the International Bahá'í Council and he, the unquestioned Guardian, had not been its President at any time. Using Remey's thinking, that would have meant that there were two Guardians at the same time, Shoghi Effendi, appointed by 'Abdu'l-Bahá, and Mason Remey as the President of the International Bahá'í Council.

Then there were the terms of the Will and Testament of 'Abdu'l-Bahá. They stated very clearly the manner in which a new Guardian was to be appointed. First, the Guardian himself had to appoint his successor. Remey claimed that Shoghi Effendi had done just that, but that he had just not done so in writing. Secondly, according to the Will and Testament, any Guardian had to be a lineal descendant of Bahá'u'lláh, an Aghsán. Remey obviously was not a descendant of Bahá'u'lláh and all the other possible candidates had either died or been declared Covenant-breakers. Third, during the lifetime of the Guardian, a group of nine Hands of the Cause had to accept that choice. That obviously had not happened, either. Remey also seemed to forget that on 19 November at their first Conclave, all 27 Hands of the Cause, including himself, had signed the Proclamation that confirmed that

> Shoghi Effendi had left no Will and Testament. It was likewise certified that the beloved Guardian had left no heir. The Aghsán (branches) one and all are either dead or have been declared violators of the Covenant by the Guardian for their faithlessness to the Master's Will and Testament and their hostility to him named first Guardian in that sacred document.[17]

In 1957, Remey had agreed that there could be no Guardian. The Hands, including Remey, stated that it was up to the Universal House of Justice to re-examine the question when it was formed. Two years later, Remey called the other Hands 'violators' for not appointing a second Guardian. Less than five months after that, Remey publically proclaimed himself to be the second Guardian.

The Hands of the Cause were in unknown terrain. On 10 May, the Custodians wrote, 'It is clear that by claiming that he is the Guardian, Mr Remey has abandoned his station as a Hand of the Cause, and therefore cannot receive recognition as a Hand until he renounces the self-conferred title of Guardian.'[18] At the first Conclave in November

1957, it had been decided that the Hands in the Holy Land, the Custodians, would have the power to expel people from the Faith, but 'only on the recommendation of the Continental Hands concerned'. The Hands of the Cause had never dreamed that a Hand of the Cause might do something like this.[19]

By the end of May, 24 countries had announced their loyalty to the Custodians and ultimately all others followed suit, except for France. As the Hands examined the Bahá'í world, they were gratified to find that the numbers who chose to follow Remey were very small. By 15 June they had identified ten in France and five in the United States. Remey had sent a copy of his declaration to the President of Israel and consequently the Bahá'í Department of the Ministry of Religions in Israel contacted the Custodians. The Israelis saw the claim for what it was worth, but the Hands sent them a letter explaining the situation in any case.[20]

What to do with Remey and his associates was the question of the hour and the Hands were divided on what should or could be done. Jalál Kházeh wrote to Leroy Ioas on 12 June saying the he 'had suggested from the very first days that we should expel this mad man'.[21] Mr Faizí cabled 'SAKE GOD PROTECTION CAUSE EXPEL IMMEDIATELY'. Mr Ioas sided strongly with Mr Faizí, writing, 'With his continuing destructive activities I do not see how we can dismiss them – by simply asking the Friends not to associate with him. As I have cabled previously, he must be put out of the Faith entirely – as a Covenant-breaker – and the same action must be taken with regard to those who uphold his blasphemous claims.' Bill Sears also supported this view:

> I completely agree that all the Hands should unite in this action, as they (the entire body) are the ones who must accept this responsibility as 'Chief Stewards'. However, to await a meeting this Fall would be to delay it too long, I feel. Surely if all the Hands repudiate Mason and call for his expulsion if he does not repudiate, it is sufficient.[22]

Hasan Balyuzi, however, responded that 'Mason's claim is laughable, preposterous, abominable . . .', but then asked:

> Where do the Hands obtain the authority to expel anyone from the

Community? . . . These are the exact words of the Master, which I have read and read, and which I quote: 'My object is to show that the Hands of the Cause of God must be ever watchful and so soon as they find anyone beginning to oppose and protest against the Guardian of the Cause of God, cast him out from the congregation of the people of Bahá . . .' nowhere else have I found the express authority given to the Hands of the Cause to expel people for any reason other than opposition to the Guardian.[23]

Adelbert Mühlschlegel was also against expulsion at that time.[24] Ugo Giachery wanted the five members of Remey supporters on the dissolved French National Assembly to be expelled as well, but the other European Hands preferred to simply remove their voting rights.[25]

The problem came down to whether the Hands of the Cause had the power to expel people from the Faith. The Master had given the Hands the power to 'cast out' anyone who 'opposed' the Guardian or caused a 'division'. Hasan Balyuzi and Adelbert Mühlschlegel thought that if there was no Guardian, no one could oppose him. But Bill Sears wrote:

Mason has 'opposed' the beloved Guardian for two years, insisting, as you well know, that we the Hands should choose a Guardian. He called us 'violators' at the last meeting because we wouldn't choose a Guardian, in spite of the beloved Guardian's written words that the Hands could not choose a Guardian, and against the sacred Will and Testament that only the Guardian could choose his successor. Mason has truly caused a 'division' however small by appointing himself, declaring himself infallible, circulating the National Spiritual Assemblies and the Bahá'ís, sending out his encyclical letter, and now approaching the Government of Israel. He has 'opposed' the Guardian and caused a 'division' and under our sacred right as Hands, we should 'cast him out' and 'accept no excuse whatsoever' from him.[26]

Jalál Kházeh wrote to Leroy Ioas to say that 'this kind of thoughts and conflicts between Hands really disturbs me & the remedy to my understanding we should form our Conclave as soon as possible & I think we should do it at July because these different ideas gives good material to Mason . . .'[27]

On 7 July, the Custodians told the rest of the Hands that Remey had released what he called his first 'Encyclical' as Guardian. In it, he declared that the rest of the Hands were violators of the Covenant, that the believers should cut off contact with them and withhold financial support, and that they should turn only to him for guidance. Most of the Hands strongly supported the expulsion of Remey and his followers, but a few were not sure they had the power to do so. They did instruct the Bahá'ís to avoid all association with them, but stopped short of expulsion.

By 26 July, their uncertainties were gone and all National Spiritual Assemblies were cabled with the message that Remey had been declared a Covenant-breaker. On 3 August 1961, the Custodians added John Carré, Bernard Fillon, Moneer Darakhshan, Joel Marangella, Jacques Soghomonian, Donald Harvey and John Byers in France and Mary Wilkin in America to the list of Covenant-breakers.[28] In a letter dated 9 August, the Custodians explained their actions to the rest of the Hands:

It seems that this agitation, far from ceasing and far from being . . . the evidence of great emotional disturbance and unbalance – is a persistent and well-thought-out campaign. Not only does he personally continue to send out communications asserting his claim and adding ridiculous arguments to support it, but his attacks on the Hands and all who support them are becoming more violent and insidious all the time, and his chief supporters in France, Joel Marangella, Don Harvey and others, have now been joined by Mary Magdalene Wilkins in the United States. These henchmen are circularizing the Bahá'í world widely with violent attacks on the Hands, their decisions and their right to carry on the beloved Guardian's Crusade while at the same time deducing so-called 'proofs' of the authenticity of Mason's claims and position.

In view of this critical situation and the urgent need to close this door through which spiritual pollution was pouring unhindered into the Bahá'í world . . . we expelled both him and his supporters from the Faith. We felt we could not take the risk of deferring this drastic action until the time when we all meet together . . .[29]

Remey's attack on the Faith, however challenging in the beginning, fizzled out within a short time. Two years later, a former believer in

Cameroon and another in Mauritius left the Faith to become supports of Remey and were subsequently expelled.³⁰ In July 1961, however, the Custodians were able to report the good news that five supporters of Mason Remey in Pakistan had abandoned him and returned to the Faith.³¹

A letter from Leroy Ioas to David and Marion Hofman summarized the bafflement of those who knew Remey;

> How Mason could have been so misled, I don't know . . . but it shows his insincerity when with the Guardian and explains many things that he did and that occurred, which I did not understand. That one who was so highly honoured by the Master and by the Guardian should end his days as the outstanding Covenant-breaker of this period is, alas, altogether too sad. How great is the Cause of Bahá'u'lláh that one of Mason's stature and wide field of service should defect and it have such an insignificant response. It shows how well 'Abdu'l-Bahá and Shoghi Effendi have built the structure of the Faith and how deep is the faith of all the friends. It also shows that one must be firmer than a rock and unto the last breath pray for humility and confirmation.³²

John Eichenauer, an American soldier who had helped re-establish the German Bahá'í community after the Second World War, was also baffled by Remey's defection. 'You just don't know how it was then for us. Everything went through Remey, he was like Shoghi Effendi's right hand and he helped us so much!'³³ In a letter dated 24 October, Agnes Alexander wrote to Marion Hofman, 'God surely has used Mason to strengthen His Cause & draw us all nearer together.' It was an insightful comment and proved to be true.³⁴

Remey went on in 1963 to form a group called the National Spiritual Assembly of the United States under the Hereditary Guardian. The next year, he created the Second International Bahá'í Council and appointed Joel Marangella President, apparently forgetting that he had previously based his claim to be the second Guardian on the premise that the President of the Bahá'í International Council was also the Guardian. Two years later, in 1966, however, Remey disbanded the Council and expelled Marangella, who then went on to form his own split of the Covenant-breakers by saying that Remey had appointed him the third Guardian. Over the following years, the Covenant-breakers continued to split into more, smaller and increasingly acrimonious groups, all fighting with each other over their assorted claims.[35] Remey's delusions continued to grow. Initially, he simply appointed himself the second Guardian to continue what Shoghi Effendi had started, but by the end of 1966 he had thrown out everything Shoghi Effendi had done, claiming that Shoghi Effendi had so misconstrued 'Abdu'l-Bahá's Will and Testament that the Administrative Order he built was based on the Bábí Faith, not the Bahá'í Faith, and that the only way to save it was to 'discard all which Shoghi Effendi did and to institute a New Faith which shall be the Orthodox Faith of Bahá'u'lláh under the Holy Name of ABHA in order to carry out the conditions that will lead to the establishment of the TRUE Bahá'í Faith (of Bahá'u'lláh) which Faith has not yet been established in the world.'[36] Remey died in Italy in 1974, just short of his one hundredth birthday, and was buried without any religious rites, abandoned by almost all his followers.[37]

Other activities at the World Centre

Early in the year, Hand of the Cause Ṭarázu'lláh Samandarí began the immense task of identifying the authors of 10,000 Tablets written or dictated by Bahá'u'lláh and 'Abdu'l-Bahá. It wasn't an easy task, but luckily Mr Samandari knew the handwriting of both Bahá'u'lláh and 'Abdu'l-Bahá as well as that of their amanuenses. The job took many months, but he was ultimately successful. During this work, he unearthed some surprises, such as a letter written by eleven-year-old Ḥusayn-'Alí (Bahá'u'lláh) to the Shah of Iran in which the Youth offered to answer any questions the Shah might have.[38] He also found a Tablet written about the Hands of the Cause, which (in the translation made by Hands of the Cause Mr Balyuzi and Mr Faizí and 'Alí Nakhjavání)[39] reads:

> May My praise, salutations, and greetings rest upon the stars of the heaven of Thy knowledge – the Hands of Thy Cause – they who circled round Thy Will, spoke not save after Thy leave, and clung not save unto Thy hem. They are servants whose mention and praise are recorded in the Holy Writ, Thy Books and Tablets wherein are extolled their services, victories, and high resolve. Through them the

standards of Thy oneness were raised in Thy cities and realms, and the banners of Thy sanctity were uplifted in Thy Kingdom. They utter not a word on any subject ere Thou hast spoken, for their ears are attuned to hear Thy Command, and their eyes are expectant to witness the effulgence of Thy Countenance. They are servants who have been well-favoured, have attained Thy good-pleasure, and have arisen in Thy Cause. The people of the world, the denizens of the Kingdom, and the dwellers of Paradise and the Realm on High, and beyond them, the Tongue of Grandeur send salutation upon them. Praise be to Thee, O my God, that Thou hast aided me to make mention of them and to praise them and their stations in Thy Cause and in Thy days. No God is there save Thee, the Reckoner, the All-Knowing, the All-Wise.[40]

The Custodians continued the Guardian's efforts to renovate and restore places of special interest to the Faith. In their newsletter of 21 July, they announced that both the House of Abbúd, where Bahá'u'lláh had lived for seven years and where the *Kitáb-i-Aqdas* was revealed, and the palace of Mazra'ih, where Bahá'u'lláh first lived when He left Akka, had both been restored and beautified.[41]

Persecution in Egypt

Further complicating the work of the Hands of the Cause, the Government of the United Arab Republic (a short-lived coalition composed of Egypt and Syria) issued a decree in August that prohibited all Bahá'í activity, closed all Bahá'í centres in both countries and made it possible for the Government to confiscate Bahá'í property. On 27 August, the Custodians wrote to all National Assemblies requesting that they stop all further correspondence with Egypt and Syria, but not to publically protest. They stated that the Bahá'í International Community would, instead, take the matter to the appropriate agencies at the United Nations.[42]

The Fourth Conclave of the Hands

At their annual Conclave, held in 1960 from 18 to 27 October, the Hands of the Cause looked toward the looming date of Riḍván 1963 and evaluated what was left to be done. In its Conclave letter to the Bahá'í world, the successes of the previous years were proclaimed:

> Our beloved Guardian led us year after year, along the most arduous paths, to victories which, to the people of the world, must have appeared impossible of achievement. Yet victory was ours at every step of the way. Before we muster our strength for the tasks that lie immediately ahead, let us for a moment contemplate what has already been accomplished by the followers of Bahá'u'lláh since the inception of the Ten Year Plan: The banner of the Faith has been unfurled in the astounding number of two hundred and fifty-six countries of the globe; the Mother Temples of both Africa and Australia are to all intents and purposes completed; at long last the soil has been turned on the site of the Mother Temple of the European continent and its corner-stone will be laid this month – just three years after the passing of our most beloved Guardian, an event which culminates seven years of heart-breaking effort to secure a property where permission to build could finally be obtained, and which marks another great victory of the Cause of God over the consistent opposition of certain ecclesiastical elements. Well nigh three thousand pioneers have left their homes since 1953 and scattered over the face of the planet, to the barren lands of the world, to regions within the Arctic Circle, to distant deserts and lonely islands, to populous cities and jungle villages. Heroes and martyrs, individuals drawn from every stratum of society, old people and young children, representatives of not only the Asiatic and European civilizations, but Africans, American Indians, Pacific Islanders and Eskimos, have swelled the ranks of pioneers, each in his own way and in his own part of the world, contributing to this glorious testimonial of belief in the Manifestation of God in this day. The initial evidences of that great wave of mass conversion which must sweep the planet have been seen through the enrolment, since the inception of the Crusade, amongst the Africans, the people of Indonesia, and the Indians of South America, of over 30,000 believers, almost 20,000 of whom have embraced the Faith since the passing of the beloved of our hearts; the centres where believers reside have been more than doubled since 1953; hundreds of new Spiritual Assemblies have been formed; schools opened and run by Bahá'ís

have been multiplied, not only in the Pacific area and in Africa, but more recently in India and in Latin America; the first dependency of the Mashriqu'l-Adhkár in Wilmette – harbinger of the great cultural and humanitarian centres that will cluster about Bahá'í Houses of Worship in the future – has been completed. And last but not least, the Spiritual Assemblies specified by the beloved Guardian for Latin America have been elected and upon this firm foundation can now be erected next Riḍván the twenty-one new pillars of the Universal House of Justice. All these are but a part of the tremendous victories won for the Cause of Baha'u'llah by His small band of devoted, heroic followers in less than eight years.[43]

This unprecedented string of victories forced the Hands to re-evaluate how they organized themselves to best accomplish their tasks. Up to that time, the Hands had served on a continental scale; from this point on, their arena of service became global. Examining the tasks that still lay ahead, the largest were the election of the 21 new National Spiritual Assemblies in Latin America and the first election of the International Bahá'í Council at the next Riḍván. Unfortunately, as the workload of the Hands increased, their numbers decreased. Horace Holley passed away on 12 July and was replaced in the Holy Land by William Sears. Then just three weeks after the Conclave, Clara Dunn passed away.[44] Clara was followed by Corinne True in February of the next year.

There was not one word about the amazing but ineffectual defection of Mason Remey.

John Kolstoe's pilgrimage

In December, Alaskan John Kolstoe arrived on his first pilgrimage. He reached Tel Aviv late at night and didn't get to Haifa until 2 a.m. Because of the lateness of the hour, he booked into a hotel for the night. In the morning, he headed off in search of the Bahá'ís. Spying the Shrine of the Báb between buildings, he headed that way and soon began his pilgrimage. Jessie Revell took charge of him and

> marched me down town the day after my arrival to make sure my return reservations were in order. She took care of the many practical details that a traveler can easily overlook – including pointing

out which gift shops to patronize and which ones to avoid. She was short, but always in full command of what needed to be done. In those days the pilgrims guided at the Shrine of the Báb during the hours when it was opened to the public. The pathway consisted of small, smooth, white pebbles that were no longer available because of political turmoil. They were appealing and it would be tempting to pick one up as a souvenir. She warned me of this and told me if anyone tried to pick one up to say, 'Azures'. This is Hebrew for forbidden. Then, this under-five-feet tall dynamo added, 'If anyone gives you any trouble, just call for me.' I didn't even want to think about how she might handle it, but I knew the pebble would remain.[45]

There were only two other Western pilgrims there at that time, and Rúḥíyyih Khánum invited John to lunch:

As I entered the large foyer of this well-known house, I noticed off to the right an alcove where an aviary had been constructed, reflecting her love for birds. A table for two was set next to the aviary and we enjoyed a light lunch with her birds fluttering and chirping away at our sides. This 29-year old received a priceless education during an hour and a half lunch. She shared her wisdom on a wide range of matters. Among the gems was her response to my youthful impatience at the slow development of the Faith. Placing things in timeless perspective, she said, 'Well, five hundred years really isn't very long in the history of man.'[46]

She also showed him Shoghi Effendi's typewriter on its 'wobbly typing stand' and said that he made five carbon copies of each page, having to put in all the diacritical marks by hand.

John met several of the Hands of the Cause. John Ferraby took the pilgrims to Bahjí, where they stayed for two nights. Abu'l-Qásim Faizí returned from a trip while he was there and John encountered him in the Eastern Pilgrim House. Fourteen Persian Bahá'ís were staying there and John greatly enjoyed being with them. At one point, Mr Faizí

turned to me and thanked me for being there among the Persian pilgrims. I protested that no, it was such a great privilege for me. He said, 'No, you don't understand.' He then motioned to a woman sitting next to me who spoke no English and said, 'She comes from a small village in Persia where there is severe persecution of the Bahá'ís and they cannot teach the Faith. All that gives them hope is what little they can learn about what is happening in other places. You have no idea what it means to her to sit next to you, a Bahá'í from Alaska. You are living proof of what she has only been able to read about and dream.'[47]

John was at the Shrine of the Báb when 'Alí-Akbar Furútan came out of it. It was evening and the Shrine was illuminated. They sat together and Mr Furútan asked him if he knew why the Shrine was lit up at night. When John confessed his ignorance, Mr Furútan explained that it was because of the nine months that the Báb had been kept in darkness at Mákú. Mr Furútan had a great sense of humour. John remembered that he had first met him at the dedication of the Mashriqu'l-Adhkár in Wilmette. Upon being introduced, Mr Furútan had said, 'I'm humble.' John didn't know how to respond to such a strange proclamation. Mr Furútan then added, 'Yes, in Persian, *furútan* means humble, so I can honestly say 'I'm humble.' A number of years later, John was introducing Mr Furútan at a large meeting in Alaska and 'waxing eloquently about his many accomplishments'. He suddenly noticed that the audience was not paying attention to him. Later he found out that Mr Furútan, who was sitting behind John on the stage, had 'rolled his eyes and made the sign of the cross on his chest', completely capturing the audience's attention.[48]

One day, John hiked up above the Monument Gardens with Fujita to plant some almond trees:

I was 29 and in reasonably good shape. Fujita was over 70. None-theless he ran circles around me climbing the steep slope of Mt. Carmel. When we returned, Col. Kházeh was in the cactus gardens in front of the Eastern Pilgrim House. Exhausted, I told him, 'You guys should put an escalator over there.' In mock horror he threw his arms in the air and said, 'Here we are, nine Hands of the Cause, knocking ourselves out just trying to keep up with what the Guardian was doing and you want us to do more!'[49]

John returned from his stay in Bahjí on 25 December. When he arrived at the Pilgrim House, he found 'Jessie Revell was lustily singing the Protestant Doxology. I said, "Jessie, what are you singing that for?" She replied, "It's Christmas Day . . . They just came to get the last of Mason's things. I feel as if the place has been sanctified."'[50]

1961

First Irish Bahá'í pilgrim

In early March, brand new Bahá'í Dermod Knox, an Irishman living in England, cabled asking permission for pilgrimage. The return cable said that he would be welcome on 15 March. Dermod had only been a Bahá'í for about six months when he arrived in Tel Aviv, and was trying to keep the Fast:

> It was my first Fast and I arrived late at night and, in those days having no money, I stayed in the cheapest possible hotel. I hadn't the nerve to say to anybody, give me breakfast at 4 am, so I went out and bought a sandwich and set my alarm, which I had bought specially for that purpose. I got up at 4, turned on the tap (and [the water] came out rusty), had a drink of water then went to my sandwich which was then all curled up from the heat, dried up.[1]

Arriving in Haifa on the bus, he didn't have any idea where the Pilgrim House was. When he asked people on the street about Bahá'í, they all pointed to the Shrine of the Báb. Finally, he found the Pilgrim House:

> On arrival, Jessie Revell at the Western Pilgrim House welcomed me at the door. 'We have been waiting for you, you are very welcome, what will you have for breakfast?' I was a bit amazed and replied hesitantly, 'Well, nothing, thank you!' She repeated the question twice, so I felt it must be some sort of test – so eventually I replied, 'Well actually I'm fasting!' To which she replied 'Nonsense. On pilgrimage you don't have to fast. How many eggs do you want with your bacon?'[2]

Dermod discovered that he was the only Western pilgrim there, though there were about 20 Eastern pilgrims from Persia and Turkey. After breakfast, Jessie took Dermod up to the Shrine of the Báb, where he met the other pilgrims as well as Hands of the Cause Rúḥíyyih Khánum, Mr Furútan, Mr Faizí, Mr Ioas and Mr Kházeh. The Hands took the pilgrims into the Shrine. After coming out, Rúḥíyyih Khánum walked back down to the Pilgrim House with Dermod, as he noted, to '"watch" me have lunch'. The Revell sisters, Jessie and Ethel, and Mrs Doris Holley (widow of the Hand of the Cause Horace Holley) also joined him to watch.[3]

One day, Rúḥíyyih Khánum invited Dermod to her house for dinner:

> Then one night, she invited me to supper and I accepted. Now I would be in awe of all of this; then I just thought it was all normal. She cooked the meal because it was the night her cook was off. I didn't think anything of it. I had tea with Amelia Collins . . . Being a new Bahá'í, I didn't appreciate all this.[4]

Lotfullah Hakím took the pilgrims to the Archives, which were still housed in the back three rooms of the Shrine of the Báb. Lotfullah would pick up an item and say, '"That's 'Abdu'l-Bahá's cup", and he would pass it around. "And that's Bahá'u'lláh's glasses", and he would pass it around.'[5]

Dermod also spent a night in the Mansion at Bahjí. He was able to visit the room of Bahá'u'lláh at any time he wished during that night. He found, however, that he could not stay in that room for more than 20 minutes at a time 'because the "power" in the room became so over-powering'. After returning to England, Marion Hofman told him that he was the first Irish pilgrim.[6]

The Mother Temple of Africa

The dedication of the Mother Temple of Africa, in Kampala, Uganda in January 1961 was the culmination of an eight-year effort to accomplish one of Shoghi Effendi's goals for the Ten Year Crusade. In February 1953, when the Guardian's map of pioneering goals was unveiled, there were few Bahá'ís in Kampala, but he had chosen the site himself and it was the British National Spiritual Assembly which initially took charge of the project.

Originally, on 20 April 1954, six acres of land were purchased for £987 on Kibuliriza Hill, a site overlooking Kampala. The site, however, became problematic when the owner of land adjacent began causing difficulties about the access road, a supposedly reliable source of water was found to be uncertain, and a new housing development was planned that would ultimately encircle the site. Shoghi Effendi had also requested that endowment land be purchased in the area. This endowment land, 13 acres on Kikaya Hill three miles north of Kampala, had been acquired by Riḍván 1956. In August of that year, the temple location was moved to Kikaya Hill when it was found that additional acreage was available. Ultimately, the new temple site consisted of over 21 acres. Work began in October 1957. Water initially appeared to be a big problem when a government geologist said that a well on the site would probably not find water. A local driller, however, proved him wrong, finding a very good water supply at a moderate depth. One day, Rex Collison, who was a soil chemist, geologist and archaeologist, found man-chipped flint and a stone axe on the site. They turned out to be 30,000 years old.[7]

The first design possibilities were submitted to the Guardian on 28 October 1955, but he thought they were too 'modern'. In August 1956, a design by Mason Remey was accepted, though it had to be modified for the local weather conditions and cost. Remey's design called for an open plan, but the high wind and rain at certain times of the year required the building to be well sealed.[8]

The Mother Temple of Africa was dedicated over the weekend of 13–16 January 1961 with Amatu'l-Bahá Rúḥíyyih Khánum and almost 500 Bahá'ís attending. On 13 January, the Uganda Broadcasting Service presented a 15-minute programme about the Faith, and a Unity Feast was held at the Makerere College Main Hall.[9] The official dedication took place at the Temple the next day. In the morning there was a Bahá'í-only event. The Bahá'ís were taken by bus to the bottom of the hill, from where they walked to the Temple. It was a perfect day with 'beautiful flowering bougainvillea (red, orange, yellow, mauve, purple, pink and white) splashing down the slopes of the hill along each of the nine great gardens which ray out from each door of the temple'. The floor of the House of Worship, where those who were to speak stood, was covered by a large and beautiful Persian carpet, oriented towards Akka. Two other carpets, gifts from the Persian friends, flanked the main one. Inside the door opening toward the Qiblih, Rúḥíyyih Khánum had hung a Persian carpet from the Shrine of Baháʼuʼlláh. Eighteen iron flower stands held flower-filled silver vases sent by the Hands in the Holy Land. After prayers in Persian, Arabic, Ateso, Luganda, Swahili, Lubukusu, Acholi and English, every believer came forward to view the portraits of the Báb and Baháʼuʼlláh, each being anointed by Rúḥíyyih Khánum with attar of rose as they approached.[10]

Later that afternoon, at 3:30, 1,500 people, including 500 Baháʼís, came for the public dedication, including Prince Henry Kalemera, the brother of the King of Buganda, and the Mayor of Kampala. The local newspaper that day published a special eight-page supplement with stories and photographs of the Temple. The organizers had managed to squeeze eight hundred seats into the sanctuary and more chairs were set up at each open door. A choir, composed of Kampala's best singers, including four Baháʼís, sang selections by Baháʼí musician Daniel Jordan.[11]

The next month, Rúḥíyyih Khánum wrote a letter to the National Spiritual Assembly of the Baháʼís of Central and East Africa extolling their sacrificial efforts and the place of African Baháʼís in the world:

> I want to thank you all for your great victory; how happy you must be that your efforts to obey the wishes and fulfill the plans of our beloved Guardian have been so successful, and that your labours have been so richly blessed. This I know is a victory of the pioneers and the newly converted African believers. Together, and through the tireless labours of your Assembly and its many committees, you have succeeded in bringing about the largest mass conversion since the Heroic Age of our Faith.
>
> And you have built the Temple, our glorious Mother Temple of Africa! When I see what has been accomplished since the Conferences called by our Guardian in 1958 I realize how undefeatable our Faith is, how it moves forward impelled by the bounties of Baháʼuʼlláh, how He seizes on every instrument, however weak, and confirms every effort, however inadequate, made in His Faith . . .
>
> I firmly believe now is the time for you to press on with mass conversion . . . I fully realize that capable and mature (relatively speaking! for I think we are all very immature still) Baháʼí administrators shy away from this prospect, foreseeing about one thousand

possible headaches which may arise. But our religion is based on faith, not logic, and we have never failed to witness that in a mysterious manner new people, great servants of the Faith, are raised up, problems are solved in miraculous ways, means found we never dreamed of, mass conversion will bring both its own problems and its own solutions . . .

I remember a conversation the Guardian had with a Japanese Bahá'í pilgrim. He said the majority of the people of the world were not white and in the future the majority of the Bahá'ís would not be white either, in other words, they would be a cross-section of the world. This must mean all races will come into the Faith and bring their own contribution. Our motto is not unity producing uniformity but unity in diversity, something much richer and more interesting. If we ponder Bahá'u'lláh's words about civilization and freedom if carried to excess, etc. and the Guardian's repeated and vehement denunciations of present materialistic Western civilization we must come to the conclusion that one of the biggest changes that must come about in the future is in the white man's thinking, standards and way of life. Let us white Bahá'ís never make the mistake of so many other white people who try to make other races over in their own image![12]

Rúḥíyyih Khánum takes up the Guardian's banner

In March 1961, Rúḥíyyih Khánum wrote a second letter, this one to the National Spiritual Assemblies of Canada and the United States, reflecting on her observations during a trip through those countries in 1960 and her experiences at the dedication of the House of Worship in Kampala. The letter bluntly looked at racism and the attitudes of the white Bahá'ís, bringing up Shoghi Effendi's statements that the darker-skinned races of the world would move to the forefront of spreading the Faith around the globe. Her reflections are powerful:

Bahá'u'lláh warned us against the evils of civilization when carried to extremes. The Master, and particularly the Guardian, elaborated on this theme until the end of his life. Shoghi Effendi fairly thundered against our civilization – particularly the American variety of it. The future Bahá'í culture and civilization is therefore scarcely likely to be patterned on it! It occurs to me (speaking for myself) that we have confused the things so highly praised in our teachings, such as freedom of speech, the democratic method of election, the ideal of justice for all and integrity in administrating affairs, with our materialistic civilization which the Guardian stigmatized as corrosive and corrupt in western civilization and against the dangers of which he constantly warned us . . .

I remember when we had the first Japanese pilgrim here, Shoghi Effendi said to him that the majority of the human race was not white and that the majority of Bahá'ís would not be white in the future. As up until very recently the Bahá'ís of the world were almost exclusively white it is only natural that their virtues and their faults should have colored the Faith and its community life. It is illogical to suppose that what we have now is either mature or right; it is a phase in the development of the Cause; when peoples of different races are incorporated in the world-wide community (and in local communities) who can doubt that it will possess far greater power and perfection and be something quite different from what we have now? And yet let us ask ourselves frankly if we do not believe that what we North American Bahá'ís, what we Western white Bahá'ís have, is the real thing, practically a finished product, and it is up to the rest of the world to accept it?

It seems to me we are confusing the fact that North America is the cradle of the Administrative Order with the old order that already exists there. Perhaps we forget sometimes that just as Bahá'u'lláh appeared in Persia because it was the worst country in the world, the Administrative Order was given to America to develop because she was politically the most corrupt. I remember when the Guardian was writing 'The Advent of Divine Justice' and elaborated on this theme how astonished I was. I thought we had been given the Administrative Order because we already had the best democratic system in the world and were therefore best qualified to elaborate it!

. . . He . . . repeatedly stressed teaching the American Negro and the Indian people. It has been borne in on me, at least to a limited degree, during my trips in America and Africa, the vast significance of two statements in our Writings. Bahá'u'lláh said the black people are like the pupil of the eye and sight is in the pupil; the Master said when we converted the American Indians to the Faith they would be like the original inhabitants of Arabia. The Words of these Divine Beings, we know, are the very essence of Truth. When Bahá'u'lláh likens the Negro race to the faculty of sight in the human body – the act of perception with all it implies – it is a pretty terrific statement. He never said this of anyone else. I thought the American Negro's humility, his kindness, friendliness, courtesy and hospitableness were something to do with his oppression and the background of slavery. But after spending weeks, day after day in the villages of Africa, seeing literally thousands of Bahá'ís and non-Bahá'ís, I have wakened up to the fact that the American Negro has these beautiful qualities not because he was enslaved but because he has the characteristics of his race. I learned why the Guardian so constantly spoke of the 'pure-hearted' Africans.

The non-white world is stirring. Africa is awakening; our civilization is beginning to crumble. I believe the responsibility we Bahá'ís (most of us still white) have at this time is tremendous. We must make haste to obey the instructions of the Master and the Guardian and teach in active, determined campaigns, by every means in our power, the American Negroes and Indians.

In the first place, it is a duty placed upon us in writing; in the second place, we need them in our communities for their characteristics of mind and heart can greatly enrich our Bahá'í community life; and in the third place, we cannot estimate at this time how far-flung will be the repercussions of bringing these two races in North America into the Faith. I am convinced that if we start mass conversion of the Indians and Negroes, mass conversion of the whites will follow. The people of the world are tired of words, words, words. They don't really pay any attention to what we say about 'oneness, unity, world brotherhood', although many of them agree with this. What they need is to see deeds, to see Bahá'í communities, local and national, full of people of different races working together, in love, for their common belief . . .

. . . are we for the most part absorbed in playing with the Administrative Order, criticizing, judging and disputing with each other? Do we constantly bear in mind that as early as the start of the first Seven Year Plan the Guardian told us that now that we had built up the Administrative machinery, we must put it into operation, for teaching the Cause? That Bahá'u'lláh has commanded all His followers to teach the Faith? . . . Forgive me if I seem impassioned on this subject, but I am very distressed because I feel we are in a race and not conscious of it. What answer are we all going to give in the next world if Bahá'u'lláh, the Master and the Guardian say to us: 'but We told you all about it, we told you what to do, why didn't you do it?' . . .

The foundation of all religions is to accept the Manifestation of God and believe what He taught is God's truth. If one believes this, then the moment one comes across a teaching one has not heard about before, one accepts it because Bahá'u'lláh is the Mouthpiece of God and God is always right. It is this quality of faith the African believers are being taught and are capable of. The doctrine of salvation through accepting the Manifestation of God exists in our Faith just as much as in Christianity. But are we teaching the Cause this way in the West? I am afraid not. I remember talks I have given (and listened to) which were a sort of intellectual jargon that went on and on elaborating on the working of a society which does not yet exist, giving supposedly full details of a system a little over a hundred years old but which must evolve during at least a thousand years!

Over and over again the Guardian told the Bahá'ís to study the talks of 'Abdu'l-Bahá and teach by His methods, simple language, parables, stories, examples. It is teaching through this method that is bringing about mass conversion in Africa and Indonesia, and can do the same, I believe, not only amongst the red Indians and the Negroes, but amongst the white people as well.[13]

Riḍván 1961

This was a big year for South and Central America. All the Regional Spiritual Assemblies were broken up and 21 new National Spiritual Assemblies were formed. The new National Assemblies were in Argentina, Bolivia, Brazil, Chile, Colombia, Costa Rica, Cuba, Dominican Republic, Ecuador, El Salvador, Guatemala, Haiti, Honduras, Jamaica, Mexico, Nicaragua, Panama, Paraguay, Peru, Uruguay and Venezuela.

In their Riḍván message to the Bahá'í world, the Custodians outlined the history of the North American Bahá'í community and its charge, beginning with the *Tablets of the Divine Plan*, to take the Faith to Latin America. This lengthy historical summary described the goals of the first

Seven Year Plan which opened in 1937 and led to the second Seven Year Plan in 1946 and then the Ten Year Crusade. The result of these plans was the election of the 21 National Spiritual Assemblies in 1961.[14]

There were now 48 National or Regional Spiritual Assemblies and 1,850 Local Spiritual Assemblies and the Faith had spread across 6,500 localities.[15]

Election of the International Bahá'í Council

At the end of 1960, the Custodians had sent out nine ballots to every National Spiritual Assembly then in existence for the election of the International Bahá'í Council. This Council had originally been appointed by Shoghi Effendi in January 1951 and had at that time consisted of seven members: Mason Remey, Amelia Collins, Ugo Giachery, Leroy Ioas, Jessie and Ethel Revell and Lotfullah Hakím. Rúḥíyyih Khánum was quickly added to liaise between the Council and the Guardian, then Sylvia Ioas was added in May 1955. Until 1961, the members had all been appointed.

The International Bahá'í Council was now, at Riḍván, to be elected for the first time and was considered to be a transitional body to the Universal House of Justice. Like the House of Justice, it was to be elected by the members of all of the National Spiritual Assemblies of the world, but unlike that body, the election was by postal ballot instead of at an International Convention, and election was open to both men and women.[16] It was almost like a 'practice' election for the Universal House of Justice. In their Conclave message of 1960, the Hands of the Cause had written:

> We shall witness for the first time in the history of the Faith an election on a global scale, and the hearts of the believers will echo the words of the beloved Guardian at the time when he appointed the first International Baha'i Council: 'Hail with thankful, joyous heart' this historic moment. This Council, which the beloved Guardian characterized as the 'most significant milestone' in the evolution of the Administrative Order since the Master's passing, will now undergo, in his own words, its 'transformation into a duly elected body'; it will be international in character, and have its headquarters at the World Centre of the Faith. In addition to those functions

which were announced last year, it will be given certain administrative duties to discharge in facilitating the work at the World Centre
in relation to National Assemblies abroad. It would be well for the
believers, pondering at this time the importance of the step that is
being taken through this election, to bear in mind that however significant this first universally elected body may be, it must never be
compared with that Supreme Body upon which we are promised the
Twin Manifestations of God will confer infallibility in the discharge
of those duties ordained for it in the Holy Text.[17]

The Hands of the Cause had requested that they not be elected to the
Council and that they be allowed to continue their own tasks as Hands:

> the Institution of the Hands, different in both nature and function
> from the structure constituting the elected administrative bodies of
> the Faith, placed us in a separate category and we requested the
> believers not to vote for the Hands of the Cause in Bahá'í elec-
> tions. We Hands burned in the fire of this weighty decision until it
> became clear to us that greater strength, diversity, and breadth lay in
> keeping these two aspects of the system of Bahá'u'lláh separate and
> therefore more mobile, each free to function in its own field.[18]

The ballots were counted at Riḍván and the results were announced on
25 April. Those elected were: 'Alí Nakhjavání, Jessie Revell, Lotfullah
Hakím, Ethel Revell, Charles Wolcott, Sylvia Ioas, Mildred Mottahedeh, Ian Semple and Borrah Kavelin.[19]

Ian Semple was in Stockholm for their National Convention on 28
April and at one point went to the post office. When he returned, Scandinavian Auxiliary Board member Modesta Hvide excitedly pulled him
aside and showed him a cable announcing his election to the International Bahá'í Council. Luckily, he later said, the cable wasn't made
public for several days so he had time to get used to his elevation before
attention was turned on him.[20]

The Council met for the first time on 25 June at the House of
'Abdu'l-Bahá. Joined by the Hands of the Cause in the Holy Land, they
first went to the Shrine of the Báb. Afterwards, the Hands explained
their duties. The Council was to:

1. Forge link with authorities of newly emerged State [of Israel].

2. Conduct negotiations related to matters of personal status with civil authorities.

3. Legal protection of the international endowments of the Faith at the World Centre and completion, circumstances permitting, plans made by the beloved Guardian for their extension.

4. Supervision of income-producing properties at the World Centre.

5. Assist the Hands in preparing for the World Congress to be held in Baghdad in 1963.

6. Assist the Hands in arrangements for the election of the Universal House of Justice.

7. Issue News Letter from the World Centre of the Faith.

8. Financial responsibility for work at the World Centre exclusive of affairs of the Hands of the Faith.

9. Handle guiding at Shrines.[21]

'Alí Nakhjavání was elected President, Sylvia Ioas Vice-President, Jessie Revell Treasurer, Charles Wolcott Secretary-General, and Ian Semple Assistant Secretary.

A schoolgirl's life in Haifa

Teenaged Brigitte Ferraby spent three summers in Haifa with her parents, John and Dorothy Ferraby. She was there from June into September and stayed in the Western Pilgrim House. The family lived in the round room at the south end of the building where the first Universal House of Justice would later meet. At dinner, she would eat with Jessie and Ethel Revell, Ian Semple, William and Marguerite Sears and Paul Haney. Rúḥíyyih Khánum would often come over and tell stories of the Guardian and Brigitte remembered that there was a lot of interesting conversation. During 1962, Brigitte was joined by May and Naysan Faizí. The next year she had the company of Bahiyyih and Mehran Nakhjavani.

One day, Brigitte and May helped Rúḥíyyih Khánum clean the interior of the Shrine of Bahá'u'lláh:

> There were the Persian ladies in the pilgrim house at Bahji. We placed the ornaments and the little chandeliers on the grass near the Pilgrim house and they would clean them. I remember when we went back to Haifa Rúḥíyyih Khánum said: 'Since you have been so good you can take anything you like out of the stores for supper.' We had a tin of oysters – we had never seen them before.[22]

The girls also helped Lotfullah Hakím at the Shrine of the Báb. Every morning when everyone was allowed to visit the Shrine, Lotfullah sat at the entrance with his clicker, counting the number of visitors. The girls helped by answering questions and asking the visitors not to take photographs inside. When the Hands of the Cause arrived to pray, the girls would join them.

Brigitte described going to Bahjí to help Rúḥíyyih Khánum:

> In those days it was not so easy to get to Bahji or to Akka. The road was alright, but it wasn't built up and there was still a big rubbish dump in the bay there; it was one part that wasn't so pleasant . . . During the first year they were still placing objects in the central part of the Mansion. Rúḥíyyih Khánum had all the incorporation certificates from Local Spiritual Assemblies and she wanted them stuck on big pieces of cardboard, so she gave me the job of arranging them carefully. It was fantastic then as we would be staying in Mirza Abu'l-Faḍl's room or John Esslemont's room and the atmosphere would be absolutely incredible. It was like nothing else.[23]

The Mother Temple of the Antipodes

On 16 September, the Mashriqu'l-Adhkár in Sydney, Australia, was dedicated. The first steps in the development of this House of Worship had been taken eight years earlier, in March 1953, when a piece of land was purchased for £2,000. Unfortunately, the site was also wanted by the Education Department. In 1955, the Bahá'ís sold the land for £2,500 and bought Mona Vale, where the Temple now stands. As he did for Africa, Mason Remey had created the design. Construction began in 1957. The exterior of the building was covered with a crushed quartz aggregate that appeared to change colour with varying light. When the skies are blue, the temple sparkles a dazzling white from the quartz. At other times, the Temple can be 'a soft pearly gray, and the six turquoise stars on each of the wrought-iron doors glow with a peacock brightness'.[24]

The foundation ceremony was held on 22 March 1958 during the Intercontinental Conference in Sydney. About 250 people attended and watched as Remey and Hand of the Cause Clara Dunn placed the small silver box containing a plaster fragment from the cell of the Báb in Mákú and a second box with earth from the Shrine of Bahá'u'lláh directly under the centre of the future dome. The lantern which caps the dome was placed by helicopter on 27 April 1960.

On the morning of 16 September 1961, Rúḥíyyih Khánum and Jessie Revell were in Sydney for the dedication. Over 300 Bahá'ís attended, including Fred Murray, the first aboriginal Bahá'í, whose reaction was: 'I joined the Faith two months ago and when I saw the Temple, the tears came to my eyes. Dear friends, yes, I would like to see my friends, my colored people, join this Faith.' Inside the Mashriqu'l-Adhkár, Persian rugs, again gifts from the Persian believers, covered the floor. On the door facing the Qiblih, a green silk carpet from the Shrine of Bahá'u'lláh was hung, the gift of the late Guardian. As they had done for Africa, the Hands in the Holy Land sent silver vases filled with orchids. At 2:30, the first public services began. So many came to participate that two services had to be conducted, each with 900 people present.[25]

Opening the International Archives

In the autumn of 1961, the first pilgrims were able to visit the newly completed International Archives. The exterior of the International Archives Building had been completed by Riḍván 1957, but Shoghi Effendi never had time to fill it with the collected treasures of the Faith. That task fell to Rúḥíyyih Khánum. Luckily, the Guardian usually told Rúḥíyyih Khánum about everything he did each day and that included conveying to her his ideas for the Archives Building, including the placement of every piece of furniture. He told her, for example, to put the Chinese rug he had bought in the centre of the long room and then to put a certain table on the rug and that a certain ornament should be placed on the table. The furniture from the original Archives in the back three rooms of the Shrine of the Báb, she knew, were to go on the balcony in the new building. When the task fell to her to furnish the Archives Building, Rúḥíyyih Khánum realized that she knew where everything was to go.[26]

The floor had

> green tiles, the immense deep blue Chinese rug in the centre . . . ; the large multi-coloured Persian carpets before it; and beyond the twin eighteenth century console tables with their gilded legs placed back to back and forming one large square table in the centre, their green marble tops surmounted by a Chinese cloisonné incense burner; the rows of Japanese gold lacquer and Chinese black carved teak wood cabinets with their stencilled green glass doors, set back to back and forming groups on either side, standing free from the walls in the centre space; the accents of red from carved Chinese cinnabar lacquer vases and ornaments; the beautifully illuminated Tablets, with their brilliant green mats and gilded, ornate frames; the vases, candelabra, photographs, calligraphy, and bibelots; the bronze-gilt electric wall brackets; the overhanging balconies running down each wall with their cabinets and ornaments and more framed and illuminated Tablets on the walls – all glows with an inexpressible sense of warmth and beauty and peace.[27]

From the ceiling hung the six crystal chandeliers to illuminate the displays which contained relics and historical objects from the Báb, Bahá'u'lláh, 'Abdu'l-Bahá, the Greatest Holy Leaf, the Purest Branch, Shoghi Effendi and others. Shoghi Effendi never paid too much for anything and always preferred beauty over antiquity. He purchased many fragile and delicate ornaments whose only purpose was for decoration and beauty.[28] Sutherland Maxwell had collected many rare and antique items and Rúḥíyyih Khánum appropriated them and other family heirlooms for the Archives Building.[29]

The portraits of the Báb and Bahá'u'lláh were in a closed cabinet which was opened for the pilgrims. The small painting of the Báb displayed in the Archives was done in Tabríz at the time when the authorities gave the Báb a wild horse to ride, hoping to humiliate him. Unfortunately for them, under the Báb's hand, the horse was completely docile and this brought many people to see him during the following three days. An artist was one of those who came. Even though the artist and the Báb had not met before and never spoke, each time the artist saw Him, the Báb would 'fix his attire and take the same position . . . as though he were posing and knew it'. The artist made pencil sketches of the Báb and then painted the portrait. After becoming a Bábí, the artist sent the portrait to Bahá'u'lláh. Later, Bahá'u'lláh returned the portrait to the artist, asking him to add as much colour as he could recall. In addition to the photograph of Bahá'u'lláh taken in Adrianople, there was also a painting of Bahá'u'lláh by an Armenian artist. This artist was Christian, so painted Bahá'u'lláh in an attitude of benediction, much like the pictures of Christ. The colours of the portrait were reported to be very accurate, including His lips, which were said to be very red.[30]

Bahá'u'lláh's nightcap and a small skull cap were on display and described as 'worked with the needle on white cotton, so finely that one wonders what eyes could see to make stitches so infinitesimal into a web of pattern'. The Báb's prayer mat and dust from His casket were also on view,[31] as was a piece of the shirt the Báb was wearing when He was martyred. The remains of the Báb had been transferred from place to place over a period of 50 years, with only a few people knowing their whereabouts. From time to time Bahá'u'lláh, and later 'Abdu'l-Bahá, would send instructions saying, 'Change the place – there is danger.' At one point, the remains were in a small mosque and robbers broke into the casket looking for precious stones, something commonly included in those days. Because of this attempted robbery, a non-Bahá'í family came to possess the piece of shirt. Initially, they refused to part with it, but when a Bahá'í doctor helped them, they gave him the sacred relic.[32]

Many of Bahá'u'lláh's Tablets were displayed, including some to 'Abdu'l-Bahá, the Greatest Holy Leaf, and Navváb. A Persian artist came to Haifa at one point and spent six months illuminating the Tablets by adding artwork around the margins. Bahá'u'lláh wrote many letters to 'Abdu'l-Bahá while living at Bahjí, primarily because 'Abdu'l-Bahá, who lived in Akka, rarely went to visit Him. 'Abdu'l-Bahá stayed away primarily because when He did visit, the love and honour

Bahá'u'lláh exhibited towards Him created great jealousy in the other family members. In order to entice His Son to visit, Bahá'u'lláh wrote such excuses as, 'Your son is here – he is happy but he wishes to see you' and 'A wonderful pilgrim is here and giving a banquet and wished to have Abdu'l Baha there, too'.[33]

In addition, among the archives were dried blood and hair from Bahá'u'lláh. The Greatest Holy Leaf used to collect every hair from His comb and carefully preserve it.[34] Also displayed were Bahá'u'lláh's *kashkúl*, the begging bowl He owned in the mountains of Sulaymani-yyih. Visitors could also inspect His copper bowls, wooden clogs and towels as well as His marriage certificate.[35]

The section on 'Abdu'l-Bahá included letters written to His sister and mother, His binoculars, travelling bag and the Arabic-Persian-English dictionary which contained His own handwritten notes. From the Greatest Holy Leaf there were head scarves, clothes, boxes, slippers, combs, dresses, plus a special brocaded box somehow preserved from her life in Tehran before her Father was thrown into the Síyáh-Chál. From the Purest Branch, Mírzá Mihdí, there were the now blood-stained clothes he was wearing when he fell through the skylight in the Most Great Prison.[36]

Apart from the Holy Family, the cabinets contained the sword of Mullá Ḥusayn, a turquoise ring that had belonged to Quddús, and a portrait of Bahá'u'lláh's father. There was also a cannonball extracted from the ruins of Shaykh Ṭabarsí where the Bábís made their stand. Finally, as Rúḥíyyih Khánum pointed out, there was the new cabinet which contained things from Shoghi Effendi: the last photograph taken of him, showing 'the ineffable sweetness, at the end of a road too long and a burden too heavy'. With it, there were his gloves, the coloured pencils he used for his maps, a watch, a tie and his clothes.[37]

Within that beautiful building, Rúḥíyyih Khánum had laid out the history of the Faith in material bits and pieces – bits and pieces that evoked the spiritual battles fought during earlier times. Each item in the Archives included a written history describing where it came from and who donated it. The Guardian certified each precious artefact to ensure it was genuine.[38]

Conclave of the Hands 1961

The annual Conclave of the Hands was held between 15 October and 5 November. When Collis Featherstone arrived, he was shown to his room by Jessie Revell. When he re-emerged, he saw Bill Sears sitting in the hall. Collis at first sat across from him, but Bill quickly got up, crossed the room to sit by him, then humorously demanded, 'Come on now, inspire me!'[39]

It was during this Conclave that the Hands changed the location of the World Congress to be held after the election of the Universal House of Justice, from Baghdad to London. Conditions in Iraq were not conducive to hosting thousands of Bahá'ís from around the world, so London was selected in its stead. It would also allow participants to visit the grave of Shoghi Effendi. The Hands were reluctant to change anything that the Guardian had set in motion, but since Shoghi Effendi himself had expressed doubts about the feasibility of holding the Congress in Baghdad, they made the change.[40]

The Custodians reminded the Bahá'í world of three things that still had to be accomplished before the Universal House of Justice could be elected. Special emphasis was placed on as yet unmet home-front goals:

> The first of these is to bring the teachings of Bahá'u'lláh to the waiting masses at this critical time, this unique juncture in human history, when the hearts of so many of the less privileged peoples of the world are ready to receive His Message, and to be enrolled under His banner 'in troops' as foretold by 'Abdu'l-Bahá. The second is to win the remaining home-front goals in five of those original twelve stalwart, long-established, much-loved national communities which, at the inception of the Ten Year Plan, received the unique and priceless honour of having the spiritual conquest of no less than an entire planet entrusted to their care. Wherever the army of Bahá'u'lláh was free to march, in their totality, and with the greatest distinction, these global goals have been won. It is inconceivable that the home-front goals, given to them at the same time and forming an integral part of the World Crusade, should not also be triumphantly achieved. The third is undoubtedly the pivotal one at this point of the Crusade and comprises the heavy, pressing, inescapable duty of every single believer to assist in providing an uninterrupted

and greatly amplified flow of that 'life blood' of material resources without which construction of the Mother Temple of Europe and other vast undertakings now gaining momentum all over the world, in old and new Bahá'í communities alike, will either cease to go forward, come to a standstill or, in important areas of mass conversion, stand in danger of losing the precious ground won through so much heroic effort and sacrifice. There can be no doubt that the discharge of these three paramount duties at this time can alone provide a suitably strong and unshakeable foundation for the future activities of that glorious and august Institution, so soon to be elected, Bahá'u'lláh's long-anticipated Universal House of Justice.[41]

Near the end of the Conclave message, the Hands asked, again, that they not be subject to election: 'The Hands of the Cause do not limit the freedom of the electors. However, as they have been given the explicit duties of guarding over the security and ensuring the propagation of the Faith, they ask the electors to leave them free at this time to discharge their duties.' In *Century of Light*, the Universal House of Justice writes:

In asking that their own members be left free from election to the Universal House of Justice, so as to perform the services assigned them by the Guardian, the Hands also endowed the Bahá'í world, as a second great legacy, with a spiritual distinction that is without precedent in human history. Never before had persons into whose hands the supreme power in a great religion had fallen and who enjoyed a level of regard unmatched by any others in their community, requested not to be considered for participation in the exercise of supreme authority, placing themselves entirely at the service of the Body chosen by the community of their fellow believers for this role.[42]

1962

On the first day of January 1962, Milly Collins, the first living Hand of the Cause appointed by Shoghi Effendi, passed from the physical world. She had been growing weaker every year and had been spending each summer in Arizona for her arthritis. Then, in 1961 in Wilmette, she fell down some stairs, but even that couldn't prevent her from returning to Haifa to do her part in the annual Conclave. Following that meeting, although she was confined to bed in the House of the Master, she continued to work – until one day, when signing a letter, she could get no farther than the letters, 'Am . . .' She soared into the Abhá Kingdom while in the arms of Rúḥíyyih Khánum.[1]

Pilgrims from the United Kingdom

In March 1962, Charles and Yvonne Macdonald decided that they should go on pilgrimage with their 15-year-old son Iain. The family flew from Northern Ireland to England, sailed across the Channel to Belgium and then spent three days on a train travelling to Greece, one of which was spent without water. From Greece, they sailed to Haifa. When they arrived, Iain remembered,

> It was morning, and as we glided into the harbour, the golden dome of the Shrine of the Báb gleamed against a cold blue sky. This was how so many of the early pilgrims arrived, but without the golden dome or Archives building until the early fifties, however it had a romance now denied pilgrims.
>
> We were met at the quay by Jessie Revell, our pilgrim guide, and taken to the Western Pilgrim House opposite the House of 'Abdu'l-Bahá. There was a large hall from which our rooms branched off and at each end were the small apartment homes of Leroy and Sylvia

Ioas and John and Dorothy Ferraby . . .

I was pushing my suitcase under my bed which faced the open door of my room when I spied shoes standing the other side of the doorway. I popped my head up above the side of the bed and found myself looking at Rúḥíyyih Khánum. She said 'Hello. Do you know anything about bubbles in varnish? I have just varnished a table, and it has dried out with these little bubbles on the surface.' I hesitated for a split second, realising that if I did know about bubbles on varnished tables, Khánum was about to ask me to accompany her across the road to the House of 'Abdu'l-Bahá, her home. I brightly said 'I'll have a look for you,' with as much false expertise as I could muster.

There then followed for a fifteen-year-old boy a quite surreal experience as I trotted behind Rúḥíyyih Khánum, and up the steps to the great hallway of 'Abdu'l-Bahá's house, to check out a table with bubbly varnish. My expert opinion was that she should re-sand it and start again.

She was truly wonderful. She was so elegant yet accessible, so dignified yet unpretentious, with a sharp sense of humour. A highly intelligent, engaging lady who later in the pilgrimage invited me and my parents for lunch with her. All these years later I am still in awe of what happened.[2]

In addition to Iain and his parents, the only other pilgrims were Ian Semple's parents and Dr Edris Rice-Wray. The small group had the bounty of daily contact with the Hands of the Cause who lived there: Leroy Ioas, Paul Haney, John Ferraby, Mr Faizí and Mr Furútan. Then came the day they went to Bahjí and stayed overnight. Iain remembered that he

slept in what had been, the scholar Abul Fazl's room. The bed was bang in the middle of the room – rather strange and unsettling sleeping in a bed isolated in the middle of a room! Jessie Revell asked me the next day how I had slept. I told her badly! Indeed on waking in the middle of the night I felt impelled to leave the room, cross the great central hallway of the Mansion, and enter the far room where Bahá'u'lláh had received Edward Granville Browne. A light burned all night just above the door of Bahá'u'lláh's room, and I remembered as Browne had entered it, he did not at first see Bahá'u'lláh, as he was seated to the side of a long divan. I froze at the doorway quite unable to move, as I sensed that Bahá'u'lláh might be sitting, hidden within! Quite unable to move forward or backward for some seconds, I eventually retreated very nervously back to Abul Fazl's room and the rather spooky bed. The sight of Bahá'u'lláh's fez and cloak in the room, earlier in the day, made for me that night, one of the most compelling and awesome experiences of that teenage pilgrimage. You can't do that any more! Nor can you hold the sword of Mullá Ḥusayn nor the original Bayan as I was able to do in the Archives Building. Those items were shortly to be sealed up for protection.

The impact of that pilgrimage on me was immense. I was not only walking through a history I had been told about through countless talks and conversations with Bahá'ís, but I was enamoured by the love, friendship, wisdom and humour of some extraordinary human beings, whose vision, selflessness, courage and dedication left a print on me for life. Real people who simply sacrificed their daily lives for this nascent Faith.[3]

Jeremy and Denise Fox also went on pilgrimage in 1962, immediately after their marriage. They first flew to Nicosia in Cyprus and met a few of the Bahá'ís, then took the boat from Limassol to Haifa. They arrived at dawn and had their 'first glimpse of the Shrine of the Báb's golden dome'. Hand of the Cause Mr Faizí was their guide to Akka and Bahjí. Jeremy had the privilege of sleeping in Paul Haney's room in the Mansion, notable because, since Paul was very tall, the bars at the end of the bed had been cut off to give room for his feet. Mr Samandarí told stories about meeting Bahá'u'lláh. Jeremy said that

Lotfullah Hakim advised us how to pray at the Shrines and Rúḥíyyih Khánum invited us to tea. While we were having lunch in the House of Abbúd, Mr Faizi showed us how to tell whether a boiled egg was hard or soft by spinning it.

Jessie and Ethel Revell looked after us and a guided visit to the town with Jessie was memorable – seeing her reach up on tiptoe to collect the mail from P. O. Box 155, buying cards and booking our return boat to Cyprus. Everywhere we entered she would be greeted 'Good morning Miss Revell' to which she would reply in a firm clear voice, 'Good morning – Bahá'í pilgrims'. 'When will the tickets be ready?' 'In two days time.' I'll call for them tomorrow morning' – 'Very good, Miss Revell.'[4]

Riḍván 1962

In 1962, the eleven European National Assemblies that were initially to have been formed the year before came into existence. These were the National Spiritual Assemblies of Belgium, Denmark, Finland, Italy, Luxembourg, the Netherlands, Norway, Portugal, Spain, Sweden and Switzerland. In addition, the National Spiritual Assembly of Ceylon was elected.

In their Riḍván message, the Custodians took a final look at the state of the Bahá'í world as it entered the last year of Shoghi Effendi's Ten Year Crusade. The Faith was established in 257 countries, islands and dependencies around the globe. The next year would give some of the various Bahá'í communities 'an opportunity to add to the trophies they themselves have already piled so high', but laid bare areas where some communities were struggling. Those who were piling up trophies included India, where 13,000 new believers had enrolled since the previous Riḍván; Bolivia, where 2,500 souls, mostly from indigenous tribes, had entered the Faith; the Pacific region, which had doubled its Bahá'í population to 15,000; and Africa, where 10,000 new believers had bolstered the ranks of the Faith during the year. The Custodians hoped that these successes would spur into action the older communities of Germany, the British Isles, the United States, Canada and Australia who 'had not yet won the all-important home-front goal of forming the number of Local Assemblies he [Shoghi Effendi] had specified as an essential part of the tasks entrusted to their care under the provisions of his Crusade'. Though successes were many, challenges still remained. The goal for National Spiritual Assemblies had, however, been achieved, thus allowing for the election of the Universal House of Justice the next year.[5] Over 2,000 Local Spiritual Assemblies were also formed and Bahá'ís had spread out into 7,500 localities.[6]

The American Bahá'í community, whose pilgrims had returned chastened from the Guardian's talks, were also exhibiting their passion. By 1962, the American community had increased by 27 per cent from

1957, going from 7,984 in May 1957 to 10,095 in September 1962.[7] As mentioned earlier, the number of pioneers had risen dramatically after the Guardian's passing compared to the numbers before.

A special call went out to all pioneers to remain steadfastly at their posts and not abandon the tremendous amount of sacrifice that had gone into their establishment. This was reemphasized on 27 July when the Custodians wrote:

> The greatest care must be taken, however, that the triumphal conclusion of the various national Plans in April, 1963 is not succeeded by an anti-climax in which pioneers leave their posts, Assemblies are lost and the work and sacrifices of the last ten years are marred by setbacks to the progress of the Cause.
>
> Pioneers who have performed such noble services by leaving their home to open territories, establish Assemblies, or consolidate what has been achieved at home and abroad should make every effort to remain at their posts after Riḍván 1963, until their services can be dispensed with, remembering the appeal of the Guardian in one of his last messages that they should 'remain at their posts', and bearing in mind that at the glorious yet critical juncture of the formation of the International House of Justice, any weakening of the administrative structure and depletion of the ranks of the vanguard of the faithful holding distant and difficult outposts of the Faith, would place in jeopardy the fruits of the World Crusade we have achieved so gloriously and in no small measure through the labours of the host of valiant pioneers.[8]

On the same day, the Custodians sent a message to all the Hands that the next Conclave would be postponed until 9 April 1963. The message urged all the Hands to plan to stay for at least a week or two after the World Congress for initial consultations with the Universal House of Justice.[9]

Commemorating the Ascension of Bahá'u'lláh

For the Commemoration of the Ascension of Bahá'u'lláh, Ian Semple went to Bahjí with a group that included Hand of the Cause Mr Samandarí. It was an eye-opening moment for Ian:

In those days we would go out there in the evening and have a meal together, and then we would spend the evening either dozing or walking around or sitting, talking, and then we would probably go to sleep for a while and, finally, in the morning hours gather for the commemoration of the Ascension of Bahá'u'lláh. Well, that particular night, while we were sitting around the table where we had been eating, the Hand of the Cause Mr Samandarí, who was there with us, said how moved he was to be there on that evening because it was the first time he had been in Bahjí on the night of the Ascension since it took place. And we realised he had been a pilgrim in the presence of Bahá'u'lláh when Bahá'u'lláh had ascended. And here he was sitting with us.[10]

He suddenly realized how short Bahá'í history was.

Persecution in Morocco

On 7 December 1961, an article had appeared in the Moroccan national newspaper *Al Alam* that worried about the decline of the Faith of Islam and blamed, in part, the Bahá'í Faith:

> These [Christians and Jews] are the movements which have schools and institutions, but there is another community which was driven out of the Islamic East and came to Morocco with its destructive ideas. These are the Baha'is . . . All this is taking place and no one raises a hand to defend [Islam]. Where are our men of religion? They are asleep.[11]

The Moroccan Ministry of Islamic Affairs responded to the article by thanking those who had written about the 'nefarious' activities of the Bahá'ís. The effects of these attacks began to be felt by the Bahá'ís on 25 January 1962 when Fawzi Zaynu'l-Ábidín, Professor of Fine Arts at the University of Tétuan and a Knight of Bahá'u'lláh, was fired from his job and ordered not to associate with other Bahá'ís. On 10 April, five Bahá'ís were arrested in Nador. Three days later a special commission of inquiry arrived and examined the affair. It found the Bahá'ís innocent and they were released. Only hours later, however, the men were rearrested and thrown back into jail. In June, three more Bahá'ís were arrested, one of whom was hung upside down and tortured. Though he remained silent, his jailers found a letter from another Bahá'í who was in turn promptly arrested. In mid-July, French Lawyer Jacques Vallet and Muslim lawyer Maître Triqui took on the case of defending the men, but though no formal charges had been filed, their efforts to gain the freedom of their clients were unsuccessful.[12]

The first foreign public report of these unjust actions was in the French newspaper *Le Monde*, which mentioned the arrests on 10 August. On 22 August, the Custodians announced the arrests in a letter to the National Spiritual Assembly of the United States. This new wave of persecutions mirrored events in Iran in 1955 when the Muslim clergy and the Government had also combined to attack the Bahá'ís. The fanaticism was primarily based on religion, but the fact that the Bahá'í World Centre was in Israel further inflamed the matter.[13]

The Bahá'í International Community, which represents the worldwide Bahá'í community to the United Nations and its agencies, brought the arrests to the attention of Roger Baldwin, Chairman of the International League for the Rights of Man, who wrote in October to Ahmed Taibi Benhima, the head of Morocco's Mission to the United Nations, saying:

> According to information emanating from Morocco these persons are being held without any formal charges which could bring them before a court of justice. Our informants also declare that these persons have been subjected to brutal treatment in prison. They have lawyers but the latter are unable to bring the case into court. We have the names and know the places of detention of all the prisoners on whom reports have been made up to now.[14]

Following Baldwin's contacts, however, the court in Nador formally indicted the prisoners for 'rebellion, disorder, attacks against public safety, formation of an association of criminals, attacks against the religious faith, and illegal formation of an association'. Those charged were:

1. Kebdani Mohammed Mohammed Ali, age 22, Moroccan, resident of Nador;

2. Ben Chillal Abderrahman Hamida, age 22, Moroccan, official of the Nador Post, Telegraph and Telephone Department;

3. Bou Arafa Maanan Mohammed, age 28, Moroccan, Inspector of Police, at Nador;

4. Mustapha Mohammed Taib El Mitoui, age 24, Moroccan, of Nador;

5. Abdelaziz Abdallah AI Waryachi, age 21, Moroccan, Bursar of the Institute of Higher Studies in Nador;

6, Mestari Miloud El Houssein, age 23, Moroccan, teacher from Tétuan;

7. Jabbari Mohammed Hassan, age 24, Moroccan, teacher from Tétuan;

8. Abdessalam Hadj Salem El Sebti, age 31, Moroccan, Customs Inspector in Nador;

9. Mohammed Mohammed Said El Bekkali El Amrani, age 26, Moroccan, tailor from Fez;

10. Abdessalam Ahmed Barrada, age 28, Moroccan;

11. Houssein Mohammed Chamlal, Moroccan, teacher from Tétuan;

12. Mohammed Ahmed El Sebti, age 32, Moroccan, official of the Agriculture Service in Tétuan;

13. Fouad Mohammed Jaouad Tahhan, age 37, Syrian, Director of the Centre d'Etudes de Tannerie in Tétuan.

14. Abdessalam Miloud El Choukri, age· 27, Moroccan, official of the Public Works Service in Fez.[15]

The indictment illustrated the moral dishonesty and the true reason for the persecution. It stated that on 14 April 1962, 'numerous' complaints were made to the police in Nador about the Bahá'ís. Strangely, this was four days after the initial five Bahá'ís were arrested and one day after the commission of inquiry had exonerated them. It also stated that the commission of inquiry that had visited Nador on 13 April had not even been ordered until after the 14th. The true motive of the indictment was included: 'It is clear from the report, attached to the file, addressed by the Minister for Islamic Affairs to His Majesty, the King, that Baha'i is a religion whose goal is to undermine the precepts of Islam and the commandments which Mohammed . . . has brought.' Then followed a list of factually wrong statements about the beliefs of the Bahá'í Faith. The only thing the indictment actually established was that the 14 prisoners had 'read Bahá'í books, discussed Bahá'í philosophy in private, and professed belief in the Bahá'í Faith.'[16]

The so-called trial began on 10 December with the Bahá'ís accused of 'rebellion, disorder and other crimes against the state'. Of the accusations listed in the indictment, not a word was said. The whole trial concentrated on the religious beliefs of the defendants. Very quickly, the trial was seen as a sham by the populace of Nador and the large crowd of onlookers soon began to ridicule the Court to such an extent that one man was arrested for 'showing his disgust'. Then the people of Nador, who had supposedly flooded the police with complaints about the Bahá'ís, began 'expressing their disapproval of the trial and their sympathy for the defendants'. The defence lawyers tried to object to the nature of the trial, but met a brick wall everywhere they turned. In frustration, the four lawyers submitted a written protest to the Court, then quit, saying that the outcome had been decided before the trial had even started. Their protest stated that not one of the charges had been addressed and 'that it was in fact sufficient to read . . . [the indictment] to see that the defendants are essentially charged with having spread a religious doctrine'.[17]

A week later the Custodians cabled that the trial had ended and three of the Bahá'ís, Kebdani Mohammed Mohammed Ali, Bou Arafa Maanan Mohammed, and Fouad Mohammed Jaouad Tahhan, had been condemned to death, five more to life imprisonment, and one to ten years imprisonment.[18] The world was aghast at what was patently religious persecution. On 9 January 1963, the London *Times* wrote: 'The recent death sentence on three Bahá'ís by a provincial court shocked Moroccan as well as foreign opinion.' That same month Mr Baldwin appeared before the United Nations Subcommission on Prevention of Discrimination and Protection of Minorities. He stated:

One charge . . . the one from which the other stemmed . . . was of injuring the Islamic faith . . . During the trial . . . the only evidence was that they practiced their faith and ignored the faith of Islam. So far as we know, this is the only case in recent history in any country where members of a religion have been condemned to death solely for holding and expressing religious views regarded as heretical.[19]

The *New York Herald Tribune* illustrated the hypocrisy of the trial by saying, 'Ironically, the trial began last December 10, which is the U.N. Human Rights Day, and was finished December 14, the day when a new Moroccan constitution was promulgated guaranteeing to all free practice of their Faith'.[20]

The world-wide outcry obviously upset a few people. Mr Mohammed Berrada, assistant at the Ministry of Islamic Affairs, let the true nature of the attack on the Bahá'ís out of the bag when he

published a long statement in which he violently attacked not only the Baha'i Faith but all those who dared to come to the defence of the nine men condemned at Nador. 'The Baha'i Faith,' Mr. Berrada claimed, 'makes common cause with Zionism. Its "Vatican" is in Israel and is an instrument in the Zionist game for the destruction of the Arab world and of its holy places. Morocco,' Mr. Berrada stated, 'will not tolerate the violation of freedom in the name of freedom. Baha'ism is not a religion, it is a heresy . . . which, unless stopped, would continue its inhuman ravages.'[21]

On 24 December, the Bahá'í International Community learned that the three Bahá'ís condemned to death would be executed on the 26th. The National Spiritual Assembly of the United States immediately telegraphed President John F. Kennedy and many scholars, lawyers and religious leaders from around the world who then sent messages to Morocco. On 27 December 1962, the Bahá'í International Community sent a letter to the United Nations delegations who had signed the Genocide Convention, pointing out the

flagrant violation by Morocco of the U.N. Declaration of Human Rights . . . We request that you urge your Government to take appropriate steps to remove this threat to the Convention by a State which has signed and ratified it. We also appeal for your personal intervention, in the manner you consider most effective, to save our co-religionists in Morocco from sentences of death and life imprisonment at hard labor imposed upon them on the charge of heresy.[22]

World pressure obviously was having an effect. The Moroccan Secretary of Information back-peddled, saying that the verdict was 'not definitive' and that the condemned had the right of appeal to the Supreme Court of Appeals.[23] But the 14 Bahá'ís remained imprisoned.

The King of Morocco, King Hassan, made extremely derogatory remarks about the Bahá'í Faith during a television interview in America with NBC's *Meet the Press* on 14 March 1963, declaring that the Bahá'í Faith was not a religion and was 'against good order and also morals'. Before the broadcast, Nathan Rutstein, who had been heavily involved with the media campaign against the persecution for the American National Spiritual Assembly, contacted the producer of the programme, Larry Spivak, who knew about the Faith and sympathized with its peaceful nature, and explained what was happening in Morocco. When the programme began,

King Hassan, dressed smartly in a military uniform, was handling the journalists' questions with confidence and authority through about three-quarters of the program. He had a profound grasp of world affairs, especially of what was going on in the Middle East. The king's assurance, however, disappeared as soon as Mr. Spivak brought up the Baha'i situation in Morocco. Mr. Spivak's first question was a zinger, because before asking it he gave a brief but powerful description of the peaceful nature of the Bahá'í Faith. It was obvious the king had not expected the question. The closeup of his face revealed to the viewer a person caught off guard, grasping for ways to get out of a trap. A number of newspapers wrote about the king's embarrassing moments on Meet the Press.[24]

Shortly after the *Meet the Press* show, Nathan Rutstein had an opportunity to meet Dr Martin Luther King. After King gave a speech, a group of reporters clustered around him, full of questions about the American civil rights movement. Nathan, however, asked Dr King if he had heard about the Bahá'ís in Morocco. Dr King moved closer to me, his eyes reflecting deep concern . . . it was as if we were having a private conversation. He wanted to know the scope of the persecution and what had set it off. He asked what form the persecution had taken, and if anyone had been harmed . . . An aide came by, pointing to his watch, but Dr. King didn't turn away from me. He continued to listen and told me that he knew some Bahá'ís and he was impressed with them and the Faith's teachings . . . He promised to write to Morocco's prime minister.[25]

World pressure began to tell on King Hassan and on 2 April, he magnanimously promised a royal pardon for those condemned to death if their appeal to the Supreme Court upheld their convictions. The French newspaper Le Monde quoted the King as saying, 'I am not personally in agreement with the condemnation to death of the Bahá'ís in Morocco . . . If I am asked to pardon them, I shall do so.' The Bahá'í opinion was that 'men cannot be pardoned for a crime they did not commit. They should be completely exonerated.' The British Manchester Guardian wrote that

> Now three men who profess Bahá'í have been condemned to death by a regional court at Nador, in Morocco, and five others sentenced to life imprisonment . . . simply, so far as one can see, because of their religion. It is astonishing enough that the Courts should still be condemning men to death for their religion anywhere in the world; that this happens in Morocco is, Le Monde put it, a matter for stupefaction. The people of that country just voted themselves a bright new constitution which 'guarantees freedom of worship to all'.[26]

The Economist quoted a leading Moroccan journal saying, 'Significantly, the newspaper attacked the verdict as a medieval barbarity, unworthy of modern Morocco. And many educated Moroccans have been shocked by what seems a reflection of their good name for religious tolerance . . . a tolerance enshrined in their new constitution'.[27]

The case of the 14 Moroccan Bahá'ís lasted 20 months until the Moroccan Supreme Court fully exonerated them and had them released on 13 December 1963. Surprisingly, some of the Bahá'ís were paid compensation for their loss of two years of earnings and a few were given jobs with the Government.[28] But with the intense pressure of world opinion and the obvious hypocrisy of having freedom of religion enshrined in their constitution while persecuting the Bahá'ís simply because they were Bahá'ís, maybe the change wasn't so surprising.

The Covenant-breakers

On 7 September, news reached Haifa that Mason Remey's supporters were sending out a 'flood of correspondence' and had gained a foothold in Chile. Bernardo Fillon, a former member of the dissolved French National Spiritual Assembly, went to Chile in order to influence the Bahá'ís there. He went to the village of Loncoche and managed to sway seven members of the Local Spiritual Assembly and a long-time member of the National Assembly, Fabienne Guillon. The group wrote to the Chilean National Assembly declaring their support for Remey. Auxiliary Board member Mas'úd Khamsí made an initial assessment in Loncoche, then was joined by Hand of the Cause Mr Faizí and National Secretary Alexander Reid. By 10 October, after meeting with the defectors, all seven understood their error and renounced Remey, writing a letter to the National Assembly declaring their complete loyalty to the Faith. Guillon, however, remained defiant and was expelled as a Covenant-breaker, along with his daughter and son-in-law, and four others.[29]

In a letter to Leroy and Sylvia Ioas dated 20 September, Bill Sears reported that 'Remey is flooding the Bahá'í world with his documents, particularly the 52 page printed copy of his so-called "last appeal"'. He added that John Robarts wrote that the National Assemblies in Africa were receiving 'voluminous materials' and that the Covenant-breakers had held a conference in France the previous July. Finally, he mentioned that John Carré had gone into a 'retreat' in Spain, then had sent a letter to Pope John XXIII, addressed to 'His Worship' and informing 'the Pope that the "Infallible Guardian" of the Bahá'í Faith, Charles Mason Remey, wished to warn his "Most Excellent Excellency" the Pontiff that he should flee to his Castel Gondolfo estate, as that was the only place he would be safe. Madness!'[30]

The Custodians on the state of the Plan

On 31 October, the Custodians gave the Bahá'í world an update on the Ten Year Crusade, noting that every territory named by the Guardian as a goal had been filled, except for those few behind the Iron Curtain of the Soviet Union, and that almost all his supplementary goals had been attained. In this message, they explained Shoghi Effendi's use of the term 'Spiritual Assembly' and how they would become Houses of Justice:

> Over the face of the globe he ensured that those Local Spiritual Assemblies, which he characterized as 'the chief sinews of Baha'i society, as well as the ultimate foundation of its administrative structure', should be elected on a firm foundation; he said they were presently 'designated as "Spiritual Assemblies" – an appellation that must in the course of time be replaced by their permanent and more descriptive title of "Houses of Justice" . . .'; he informed us the National Assemblies, which the Master Himself had designated as 'secondary Houses of Justice', would constitute 'the electoral bodies in the formation of the International House of Justice'; he assured us that 'Abdu'l-Bahá Himself had 'established beyond any doubt the identity of the present Bahá'í Spiritual Assemblies with the Houses of Justice referred to by Bahá'u'lláh', and explained that 'it has been found advisable to bestow upon the elected representatives of Bahá'í communities throughout the world the temporary appellation of Spiritual Assemblies, a term which, as the position and aims of the Bahá'í Faith are better understood and more fully recognized, will gradually be superseded by the permanent and more appropriate designation of House of Justice'; he stated that: 'Upon the National Houses of Justice of the East and the West devolves the task, in conformity with the explicit provisions of the Will (of 'Abdu'l-Bahá), of electing directly the members of the International House of Justice.'[31]

The Bahá'í Faith was on the 'threshold of what . . . is an event of incalculable spiritual significance. We are entering what Shoghi Effendi termed the "tenth part" of that majestic process which was 'set in motion at the dawn of the Adamic cycle".'[32]

On 4 November, the Custodians sent out ballots and instructions to all National Spiritual Assemblies for the election of the Universal House of Justice.[33]

1963

The Mother Temple of Europe

Within Shoghi Effendi's goal of three continental Houses of Worship during the Ten Year Plan, Germany was given the challenge of building the Mother Temple of Europe. Rúḥíyyih Khánum believed that if Shoghi Effendi had asked the Baháʼís where the European temple should be constructed, they would not have wanted it in Germany, because that country had started two devastating wars, the second of which had only ended a few years previously. The Guardian, however, was 'unafraid, unhampered by worldly considerations' and the 'standards of the world were never his index, only the standards enshrined in the teachings'.[1] Shoghi Effendi knew how much attention ʻAbduʼl-Bahá had given to Germany and he followed suit in 1933:

> Germany has a glorious future under the banner of the Faith of Bahaʼuʼllah. Its mission is to champion the cause of God in Europe and establish it firmly in the heart of that continent. The tests and trials which have beset the Faith in that land were necessary and providential. It is for the German believers, who have weathered the storm, to arise and promote the Cause, to proclaim the non-political character of their Faith, to establish its nascent institutions and prove by their words and acts their freedom from every taint of particularism and prejudice.[2]

Shortly after the end of the Second World War, Shoghi Effendi wrote of the German Baháʼí community:

> The German Baháʼí community, dearly beloved, highly honored by ʻAbduʼl-Bahá, and destined to play an outstanding role in the spiritual revival of an oppressed continent, has abundantly demonstrated

in the course of ten years of severest tribulations, dire peril and complete suppression, the high character of its indomitable faith.[3]

The sufferings which the German Baha'is have passed through have grieved his heart very much – but he is very proud of their loyal and devoted spirit, and the way their faith in Baha'u'llah has come out of the fire of these war years pure and unstained and stronger than ever! They have a great future, promised them by the beloved Master . . .[4]

The next year, the Guardian wrote of the 'astounding resurgence' of Germany and that the country had the largest number of believers of any country in Europe.[5]

Shoghi Effendi had initially sent the German National Assembly a design for the House of Worship that he had chosen, but according to Rúḥíyyih Khánum,

there was already so much strong church-aroused opposition to the erection of a Bahá'í House of Worship that the National Assembly had informed him they felt the conservative nature of the design he had chosen would, in a land favouring at the moment extremely modern-style buildings, complicate its erection, as a building permit might be refused on this pretext. Shoghi Effendi therefore permitted them to hold a competition . . .[6]

The initial submissions from this competition did not make Shoghi Effendi happy:

the recent drawings submitted in competition in Germany . . . were all highly modernistic and undignified and a lot of money and time was spent for nothing. There was only one he considered at all possible, and this was not chosen by the judges; necessary qualifications: a building nine sides, surmounted by a dome. Note – circular building. Seating capacity 500 with possible additional seating in a balcony at a future date. Height 40 to 45 meters. Note: no assembly hall is to be included, only auditorium for worship, with no surrounding rooms, is necessary. Extra rooms for maintenance, toilets, caretaker, can be in basement.[7]

Unlike the Houses of Worship in Kampala and Sydney, the Temple in Frankfurt was not completed by the end of the Ten Year Crusade. But this was not the fault of the German Bahá'ís; it was caused by the opposition of the German Christian churches and the German bureaucracy. In October 1953, the Bahá'ís had applied for a piece of city-owned land in Frankfurt, but were rejected because the Bahá'í community was regarded as being too small. Then, in July 1954, they tried to purchase land in Eschborn, but a month later the Protestant Church in the town, supported by the Catholic and Protestant churches from the area, strongly objected, claiming that the erection of a Bahá'í Temple 'in a community of Christians constitutes a challenge to Christianity'. Again, the sale was rejected by the authorities. Two subsequent appeals were ultimately denied by July 1956. Another site, this time in meadow land near Diedenbergen, was purchased in March 1957, but in August of that year this sale, too, was blocked.[8]

During all of these attempts, six protest meetings were called; five by the Protestant and one by the Catholic churches. Even when the local residents supported the project, the churches were still able to get the permits denied. Opposition from the churches, however, resulted in about 600 articles appearing in various newspapers, most being sympathetic. Even the churches, in their attempt to illustrate the supposed dangers of the Bahá'í Faith, brought 'the Revelation to their own adherents'. On 23 December 1956, a thirty-minute radio programme focused on the question of tolerance and featuring a Protestant, a Catholic and a Bahá'í speaker.[9]

Then, in October 1957, a parcel of land was purchased near the village of Langenhain. This time, despite needing at least 13 permits, including one from the Air Traffic Control Board and another from the Defence Ministry, the land was successfully purchased. Even so, the Bahá'ís still had a very rocky road. On 5 January 1958, the building contract was submitted, but by July the Bahá'ís were appealing to higher authorities for help in acquiring the approvals. Then, on 16 December, the application was rejected on the grounds of 'landscape planning and legal aspects with a view to construction'. Within days the National Spiritual Assembly, together with the community of Langenhain where the Temple was to be constructed, lodged a complaint against the rejection. Finally, on 7 April 1959, the rejection was reversed and by the end of the year the National Spiritual Assembly of Germany was officially listed as owning the Temple site. But the struggle was not over yet. In July 1960, the permit was granted, but with 'special provisions, subject to prior fulfilment of numerous conditions'. It wasn't until October 1960 that contracts could be signed to start construction.[10]

The foundation ceremony had been held on 20 November 1960. Hand of the Cause Milly Collins represented the World Centre of the Faith and summarized the frustrating years of work:

> For seven years, work on this important goal of the World Crusade has been delayed. Indeed there have been times when the outlook was so dark we wondered whether it would be possible to fulfil it within the allotted time. Now, however, we see that the mysterious forces latent in the Revelation of Bahá'u'lláh have once more been demonstrated, and yet another great victory won in His name.[11]

As he had for the other temples, Shoghi Effendi had sent some of the dust from the Shrine of Bahá'u'lláh to be placed with the foundation stone. Once the permits were finally obtained, work began rapidly. On 16 November 1962, the shell of the dome was completed. The Mayor of Langenhain, as well as members of the National Spiritual Assembly, the architect and the contractors, addressed a crowd consisting of Bahá'ís, the builders, townspeople and the press. At Riḍván 1963, thousands of visitors came to see the almost finished House of Worship. The Mother Temple of Europe was dedicated on 4 July 1964.[12]

Election of the Universal House of Justice

As the election of the Universal House of Justice drew near, the Hands of the Cause could bask in a job well done. Shoghi Effendi had drawn up a map before he died, showing 4,000 dots, each one representing a location where Bahá'ís lived. His goal was to have 5,000 dots on the map at the end of the Ten Year Crusade.[13] But the Bahá'ís of the world, under the guiding hands of Shoghi Effendi, the Hands of the Cause and the Custodians, put over 11,000 dots on that map by the time the Crusade finished.

Everything they had worked for was drawing to a close, but the Hands of the Cause were still very concerned that nothing should go wrong. Two problems arose: where could they host the election; and what should they do about a few men who appeared to be making themselves obvious? For the first problem, Rúḥíyyih Khánum suggested using the House of the Master for the election. One night, 'Alí Nakhjávání and Ian Semple were with her in the House and they thought they could make enough room for all the delegates if they took all the doors in the central hall off. To make sure, they removed all the doors and measured the resulting open space. There was just enough area for all the delegates to be seated.[14]

The second problem, apparent electioneering, was more troublesome. A few men were travelling the Bahá'í world making donations and thereby raising their visibility before the election. The Hands were worried that their generosity was not genuine, but aimed at making themselves popular. Ian Semple noted that

> the Hands were very worried, because they were deeply concerned that nothing should go wrong in that election. There were some Bahá'ís at that time, one or two, who had obviously set out to tour the Bahá'í world, donating things here and there and making themselves very popular and very well-known, and the Hands were worried that in some cases it was not genuine. Some people are very generous people, but in other cases there was a little electioneering going on. But the Hands thought 'What can we do? If we interfere it is the same thing, we must just trust to Bahá'u'lláh.' And they did, and none of those who were fiddle-faddling got elected. So the delegates were sensible enough and Bahá'u'lláh looked after His Cause well enough that the problem went away.[15]

To further reduce any hints of electioneering, the Hands decided that none of the male Bahá'ís resident in Haifa would have any contact whatsoever with the delegates until after the election. It was left to the women to meet the delegates and conduct their pilgrimages. This rule caused Ian Semple some difficulty because, as a member of the International Bahá'í Council, he had to get a message to Borrah Kavelin, who was also a member of the International Council; but Borrah was also the Chairman of the American National Assembly and, therefore, a delegate. Borrah was staying at the Lev HaCarmel Hotel on top of Mount Carmel, so Ian went up at night and sneaked up through the bushes to an open window through which he passed the message to a member of the hotel staff to deliver.[16]

Just before the election of the Universal House of Justice, Rúḥíyyih Khánum ordered thousands of roses and carnations. With a few helpers, she then spent a full day and a night cutting off the buds and culling the blossoms with which she carpeted the inner sanctuaries of the three Holy Tombs.[17]

The delegates arrived on 18 April and had three days to visit the Shrines and prepare themselves for what was about to happen. The Shrines were closed to the public and made available only to the delegates. Periods of time had been set aside each evening for designated groups of delegates to visit the Archives. Never before had so many come on pilgrimage.[18] Florence Mayberry remembered that the Shrines

> and Holy Places were crowded with believers from every clime and ethnic group. When they scattered over the side of Mount Carmel it resembled a giant ballet of joy, much running to and fro, embracing, bending and kneeling in prayer, all shades of skin, costumed in saris, lava-lavas, Chinese, Japanese, African tribal adornment, Persian, Arabian, and Western dress. When this unchoreographed ballet clustered for group photographs, the ballet was momentarily transformed into a rainbow-hued human bouquet.[19]

A report by the Alaskan delegates said that

> we were divided into groups of about 30. Arrangements had been made so that everyone would have the privilege of pilgrimage. On Saturday morning we first visited Bahji – walking through the Milly Collins gate and through the gardens to the Most Holy Shrine of Bahá'u'lláh. Removing our shoes, we filed reverently into the outer shrine where the Tablet of Visitation was chanted, following which individuals made their way to the threshold of the inner shrine where people would kneel or prostrate themselves as the spirit moved them – and empty their hearts in praise and gratitude for this bounty of pilgrimage, asking that they may be worthy instruments of the Faith of Bahá'u'lláh, beseeching that they be made worthy of the name Bahá'í, and asking for guidance in the forthcoming election of the Supreme Bahá'í body. . .
>
> . . . we moved to the Mansion of Bahá'u'lláh where we visited the rooms in which Bahá'u'lláh and 'Abdu'l-Bahá had lived and moved.

We entered the room of Bahá'u'lláh where Professor Browne was entertained and tried to recapture the feeling that Browne so ably expressed at his meeting with Bahá'u'lláh . . . one wished so much to instill the feeling and every detail of the room into his heart and mind . . .

From Bahjí we moved to Akka and visited the walled city – walking over the bridged moats to the prison building and up the steps to the cell where our Beloved Bahá'u'lláh was imprisoned for so many years. Many prayers were read in different languages as we tried to imagine the dire conditions under which Bahá'u'lláh was imprisoned and to see the window from which Bahá'u'lláh would wave his handkerchief to the pilgrims who had travelled for months and on foot to know that Bahá'u'lláh was still comparatively safe . . .

Thence to the House of Abbúd – where Bahá'u'lláh first lived after leaving the prison and also where 'Abdu'l-Bahá was married, and where the Most Holy Book, The Kitáb-i-Aqdas, was revealed. Here again it was difficult to believe we were actually in these Holy Places.

The afternoon was left free so we made our first visits to the Shrine of the Báb. We were greeted at the gate to the gardens by that legendary figure – Fugita – that tiny but mighty man who was so close to the heart of the beloved Guardian, Shoghi Effendi . . .[20]

The Hands of the Cause had decided they 'would not put themselves forward in any way at the time before the election of the House of Justice'. In order to alleviate the possibility of being voted for and to complete the work required to be prepared for the Universal House of Justice, the Hands went into session for the duration of the time from the arrival of the delegates until the end of Riḍván.[21]

As noted above, the election was held in the House of the Master. To accommodate the 288 participating National Spiritual Assembly members, all 12 doors around the main hall were removed. The International Convention began at 9:30 on the morning of 21 April. All 56 National Spiritual Assemblies participated, though some, such as Arabia, Burma, Cuba, Haiti, Iraq and Nicaragua, were unable to attend and were forced to send in postal ballots.[22] Shirley Macias was there as a member of the National Assembly of Honduras and remembered that she and her companions sat in an alcove with the representatives from

Guatemala, India and Iran. Just outside the window were Rúḥíyyih Khánum's peacocks in 'full feather'. The Hands were seated across from Shirley and, while she was filling out her ballot, she looked up and saw Mr Faizí smile and blow her a kiss.[23]

John Wade attended as a member of the National Spiritual Assembly of the British Isles and he described the event:

> The excitement of the event was something that you can't very well describe because this was the first ever event of its kind in the world. It wasn't just another event, it was the first time ever that such an institution had been elected by people who themselves had been elected and I remember sitting with the British contingent. Ernest Gregory was a teller and he stood up in front of everyone with the box. Rúḥíyyih Khánum was sitting there too. One of the most impressive things about the delegates was when the black delegates came by, extraordinarily happy looking. I don't know what it is about these people that they can express a happiness that you and I can't. They walk with 'a happiness' and have a way of expressing happiness that we have lost.
>
> It was a very difficult situation because who did we know? Many of us didn't know many people and it was very difficult to think of who we should vote for. This reflects the fact that it is up to Bahá'ís to go to as many different meetings and summer schools as they can because it is only in this way that you can get to know people. . . .
> I remember when we were leaving London Airport with the British contingent, we saw the American contingent and I said to one of our members: 'That black gentleman over there, what's his name?' and I was told that he was Mr Amoz Gibson. I made a mental note of this and he became one of the members of the House. The impression I got was so strong that I knew without saying a word to him that there was a man who had qualities of suffering and I felt instinctively that he would be good.
>
> Anyway, the voting took place and then it took a long time to count the votes . . .[24]

Amatu'l Baha Rúḥíyyih Khánum welcomed the delegates and presided over the election. An Alaskan participant wrote:

Prayers were read and chanted by Hand of Cause Agnes Alexander and other ladies to open the meeting. Then Ruhiyyih Khanum, after making sure that every delegate had a ballot, read the instructions for Bahá'í elections, then stated that delegates would have all the time they needed and not to hurry. Ruhiyyih Khanum also pointed to two daffodils which had been graciously brought by delegates from England from the grave of Shoghi Effendi and expressed how these flowers brought the spirit of the Guardian close to this historic election, and told us that this was the house in which 'Abdu'l-Bahá had lived for 11 years and the Guardian for 36 years.

The completion of ballots began at 10:00 a.m. and it was significant to notice the complete silence and attitude of prayer which ensued during the hour of voting. Ruhiyyih Khanum asked twice if anyone needed more time and then at 11:00 a.m., when everyone had completed their ballots, she outlined the method of naming the National Spiritual Assembly or Regional Spiritual Assembly and the dropping of the ballots into the box. Ruhiyyih Khanum then called the names of 18 tellers – six groups of three, and three supervisory tellers. Then Alaska, as the first National Spiritual Assembly (alphabetically) was called, the nine delegates rose and moved forward, and as the individual's name was announced, he would drop his ballot into the box. This method, although slow and taking a good deal of time, ensured complete order and control of the assembled delegates' ballots and those ballots of the absentee delegates. As each assembly was announced, Ruhiyyih Khanum would make some appropriate remark about each – their teaching work, difficulty in attending convention, mass conversion area, cradle of the Faith, etc.

This registration of the ballots continued through the 56 National and Regional Spiritual Assemblies until the last ballot of the Venezuelan Assembly had been passed into the box and the first stage – the voting – was over for the election of this Supreme Bahá'í Administrative body. After closing prayers, we . . . returned to our hotels in preparation for the Most Great Feast of Riḍván to be held at Bahji that afternoon at 4:00 p.m.[25]

The first person to vote for the Universal House of Justice was Howard Brown from Alaska. As each country's delegation deposited their ballots, applause would explode in the packed hall.[26]

Philip Hainsworth noted that before the election, the Hands appeared to be much older than he remembered them being because of the stress of bringing the Bahá'í world to this point. As the delegates flowed to the ballot box, Philip said that 'the Hands became visibly brighter, less strained, even younger as they realised what a weight was being lifted from their shoulders'.[27] The 18 tellers, each from a different country, worked all through the night to complete the count. John Wade noted:

> It is interesting and surprising that 254 delegates had chosen people who were all from different backgrounds and from different countries and yet when you saw these nine they were all highly intelligent and experienced men; and imagine their sacrifice!

The celebration of Riḍván was held inside the arc of cypress trees at the Mansion of Bahjí, facing the Shrine of Bahá'u'lláh. Prayers were said in the languages of Uganda, Eskimo, Bolivian Indian, Togo, Japan, Malaya, Sarawak, Persia, Germany, France, Navajo and English, then the Tablet of Carmel was read by Hooper Dunbar. The celebration closed with the chanting of the Tablet of Visitation by Hand of the Cause Dr Muhájír and the singing of 'Alláh'u'Abhá' by the Africans.[28]

The next day, the Convention reconvened at Beth Harofe Auditorium at the Israeli Medical Headquarters and was opened by Rúḥíyyih Khánum. At 11 a.m., after Hand of the Cause Ṭarázu'lláh Samandarí had chanted and thirteen prayers had been said, the tellers, who had worked all night counting and rechecking the ballots, entered the hall to great applause:

> After the tellers had announced the nine members receiving the highest number of votes, there was a standing ovation for these nine friends who were to constitute the members of this nascent institution. They were embraced by the Hands of the Cause and by the friends and then asked to assemble on the platform. There was not a dry eye in the room as Ruhiyyih Khanum shook hands with each of the nine members of the Universal House of Justice. There was a motion made by one of the delegates that the report of the tellers be accepted. A show of hands revealed that the motion was carried unanimously. As the morning session came to a close, it

was emphasized that we had witnessed the birth of a new Body; we should not look back on what they have individually accomplished or not accomplished, but start from new.[29]

After all the names had been called, nine men stood on the stage with Rúḥíyyih Khánum: Charles Wolcott, Borrah Kavelin, Hugh Chance, Amoz Gibson, Hushmand Fatheazam, Lotfullah Hakím, 'Alí Nakhjavání, David Hofman and Ian Semple.[30] Martha Kavelin said that many of those elected had been aware that they could be elected, but that Hugh Chance was 'completely overwhelmed'.[31]

The Hands of the Cause, who knew from the beginning that they were not an infallible body, were finally to pass on the burden they had carried for five and a half years to the body which, by Bahá'u'lláh's explicit proclamation, was divinely guided and freed from error. With one exception, the Hands of the Cause of God had lived up to the highest standards of the Faith. Now, they could let Bahá'u'lláh's divinely-ordained Administrative Order take charge.

On the night of the day the Universal House of Justice was elected, the new members of that body had their first meeting. That night, they made some decisions, then asked the Custodians to meet with them the next morning. Five of the newly elected members of the Universal House of Justice had been on the International Bahá'í Council and they were accustomed to getting their direction from the Custodians, so when the Custodians arrived, the House of Justice began asking about whether they should do this or do that. These questions brought tears to the eyes of one of the Hands. When asked why, he replied, 'Please do not ask any questions from us. We are in obedience to your decisions . . . You are not the same people of yesterday. You are the Universal House of Justice inspired from on High. We Hands now are obedient to you.' Charles Wolcott agreed that they were no longer subservient to the Hands of the Cause. But then he said that when he walked out of that meeting, he would be just another Bahá'í. At the next election of the House of Justice, he might no longer be a member of the House. The Hands, on the other hand, were Hands of the Cause for their lifetime, until they passed into the Abhá Kingdom.[32]

Concluding the Ten Year Crusade

Shoghi Effendi had set a monumental task before the Bahá'ís of the world at the beginning of the Ten Year Crusade that had challenged every Bahá'í individual and institution. But people tend to work best when set a challenge with a deadline. In all but a few cases, the Bahá'í world had accomplished all of Shoghi Effendi's goals. Those goals not completed all involved political problems beyond the control of the Bahá'ís and their institutions.

The goals set for the World Centre, as listed earlier in this book (p. 17) were:

1. Adoption of preliminary measures for the construction of Bahá'u'lláh's Sepulchre – Result: land around the Shrine was acquired and the Covenant-breakers and their structures were completely removed. Shoghi Effendi greatly beautified that area around the Shrine with extensive gardens.

2. Acquisition of land for a Mashriqu'l-Adhkár on Mount Carmel – Result: through the unstinting efforts of Leroy Ioas and the financial help of Milly Collins, this was accomplished.

3. Development of the Institution of the Hands of the Cause – Result: twenty-seven Hands were appointed and their areas of responsibility defined. They were named the Chief Stewards of the Faith which allowed them to guide the Bahá'í community from the passing of Shoghi Effendi to the election of the Universal House of Justice. An Auxiliary Board was created to assist the Hands.

4. Establishment of a Bahá'í Court in the Holy Land – Result: this was not done, mostly because Israel was changing from religious courts to secular civil ones.

5. Codification of the Laws and Ordinances of the *Kitáb-i-Aqdas* – Result: Shoghi Effendi completed this.

6. Extension of the International Bahá'í Endowments on Mount Carmel and the plain of Akka – Result: substantial endowments

were acquired throughout the region. The size of Bahá'í land holdings in the area increased from 354,000 square metres to 487,000 square metres.[33]

7. Construction of the International Bahá'í Archives – Result: this was completed.

8. Reinforcement of the ties between the Bahá'í World Community and the United Nations – Result: these ties were greatly reinforced.

9. Convocation of a World Bahá'í Congress in Baghdad on the Centenary of Bahá'u'lláh's Declaration in the Garden of Riḍván – Result: because of the political situation, the World Congress was moved to London.

The goals for national communities were:

1. To the American, British, Indian and Australian Bahá'í communities: more than doubling the number of languages into which the Writings of the Faith have been translated – Result: Shoghi Effendi called for the Writings to be translated into 91 additional languages and they were actually translated into 220 more.

2. To America: Erection of the first dependency of the Mashriqu'l-Adhkár in Wilmette – Result: this was completed with the construction of a Home for the Aged.

3. The construction of a Mashriqu'l-Adhkár on both the Asian and the European continents – Result: because of the religious persecution in Iran, the Asian Mashriqu'l-Adhkár that was to have been constructed in Tehran was replaced by two, one in Africa and one in Australia. The European Temple was completed in 1964.

4. Purchase of land for eleven future Temples – Result: sites for 46 Temples were purchased.

5. Establishment of National Bahá'í Courts in Tehran, Cairo, New Delhi, Baghdad, Karachi and Kabul – Result: these were not

accomplished because of political considerations.

6. To Iran: Construction of the tomb of the Wife of the Báb in Shíraz – Result: because of the political and religious persecution, this could not be done.[34]

7. To Iran: Identification of the resting places of Bahá'u'lláh's Father and of the Mother and Cousin of the Báb and their reburial in a Bahá'í cemetery near the Most Great House in Baghdád – Result: five months before Shoghi Effendi's death, the remains of Mírzá Buzurg, Bahá'u'lláh's father, were moved to the Bahá'í cemetery in Baghdad. It was not possible to transfer the remains of the Báb's mother and cousin because of the situation in Iran.[35]

8. To Iran: Participation of women in the membership of the National and Local Spiritual Assemblies – Result: by the end of the Crusade, women were serving on both local and national bodies. Nine other Muslim countries, including Iraq, Egypt, Sudan, Tunisia, Libya, Arabian Peninsula, Jordan, Lebanon and Turkey, did the same.[36]

9. To Iran: Establishment of a National Bahá'í printing press – Result: this was not done because of political and religious persecution.

10. To Iran and Iraq: Acquisition of the Síyáh-<u>Ch</u>ál in Tehran, the site of the Báb's incarceration at Chihríq, the site of the Báb's Martyrdom in Tabríz, and the Garden of Riḍván in Baghdád – Result: the site of the Síyáh-<u>Ch</u>ál was purchased in 1953 and the site of the Báb's incarceration at Chihríq was purchased before 1958, but both were later confiscated by the Iranian authorities. Acquiring the site of the Báb's martyrdom and the Garden of Riḍván proved to be impossible at that time.[37]

11. Sevenfold increase in the number of National Ḥaẓíratu'l-Quds (National Centres, 49 new) – Result: this was accomplished.

12. More than quadrupling the number of National Spiritual Assemblies – Result: this was accomplished.

13. Framing of national Bahá'í constitutions and establishment of national Bahá'í endowments in capital cities – Result: this was accomplished.

14. More than quintupling the number of incorporated National Spiritual Assemblies – Result: the number of incorporated National Assemblies was quadrupled.

15. Establishment of six national Bahá'í Publishing Trusts – Result: seven Publishing Trusts formed.

16. Establishment of seven Israeli branches of National Spiritual Assemblies – Result: this was accomplished.

The goals for individual believers included:

1. Doubling the number of countries open to the Faith (131 new countries) – Result: 132 new areas were opened.

2. Inclusion in the Administrative Order of the Faith of 11 republics in the Soviet-dominated region – Result: the Administrative Order was established in four republics.[38]

Of the pioneering goals initially set by the Guardian and for which the title of Knight of Bahá'u'lláh was awarded, ten were found to have already been opened. Five of the goals were not opened until after the Ten Year Crusade: Romania (1968), White Russia (1978), Moldova (1984), Mongolia (1988) and Sakhalin Island, Russia (1990). A total of 255 people earned the title of Knight of Bahá'u'lláh. Two people, however, each fulfilled the Guardian's goals for two different areas. Many lists, therefore, contain 257 Knights. The Knights were almost evenly split by gender with 131 men and 126 women.[39]

The basic results of the Ten Year Crusade are tabulated on the next page:

	National and Regional Assemblies	LSAs	Countries	Localities	Languages
1953	12	681[40]	129[41]	2,500[42]	91[43]
1954	12		228[44]	2,900[45]	130[46]
1955	12		236[47]	3,200[48]	167[49]
1956	16	over 900[50]	247[51]	3,700[52]	190[53]
1957	24		251[54]	4,200[55]	230[56]
1958	25	1,100[57]	254[58]	4,500[59]	244[60]
1959	31	1,275[61]	255[62]	5,200[63]	261[64]
1960	31	1,500[65]	256[66]	5,800[67]	268[68]
1961	48	1,850[69]	257[70]	6,500[71]	270[72]
1962	56	over 2,000[73]	257[74]	7,500[75]	296[76]
1963	56	3,549[77]	259[78]	11,210[79]	300[80]

With the completion of the Crusade, there were 56 National and Regional Spiritual Assemblies, and 3,549 Local Spiritual Assemblies. Shoghi Effendi had hoped to have 5,000 localities opened to the Faith by the end of the Crusade, but the Bahá'ís greatly overran that mark, reaching 11,210. The Faith was at that point in 259 countries and the Writings had been translated into 300 languages.[81] The above table illustrates the amazing decade of Shoghi Effendi's Ten Year Crusade. The number of localities where Bahá'ís lived was multiplied 4.5 times, while there were 5.7 times as many Local Spiritual Assemblies in 1963 as there were in 1953. After a slow start, the United States, which began the Crusade with 171 Local Spiritual Assemblies,[82] ended the decade with 332[83] and accomplished all its goals. At the beginning of the Crusade, India had just 34 Local Assemblies.[84] It managed to increase that to 58 by February 1961 with a total of 850 Bahá'ís, but then Hand of the Cause Raḥmatu'lláh Muhájír came and a teaching campaign was organized for the State of Madhya Pradesh, in central India. Two years later, there were 87,000 Bahá'ís and 675 Local Assemblies.[85] Africa, too, demonstrated the amazing power of the Crusade. At the beginning, in 1953, there were 17 Local Spiritual Assemblies and 200 Bahá'ís in all of sub-Saharan Africa. When the Universal House of Justice was elected, there were 861 Local Assemblies serving 40,000 Bahá'ís.[86]

THE MOST GREAT JUBILEE

Shoghi Effendi had called for a World Congress to close the Ten Year Crusade, specifically using the word 'Congress', a word he had never used before. When asked why he called it a Congress, he replied that a Congress was a more formal event where formal things were done.[1] Shoghi Effendi had planned for the Congress to be held in Baghdad, but with the trouble in that part of the world, it was held instead at the Royal Albert Hall in London from 28 April to 2 May.

In 1961, an international committee was set up to organize the Congress and Dorothy Ferraby was appointed its secretary. Other members, some short-term, included John Wade, Mildred Mottahedeh, Edna True, David Hofman and John Long.[2] Mildred Mottahedeh, the Bahá'í representative to the United Nations in New York, widely experienced and with great artistic taste, said one day to the English committee members, 'Now, we want to do things properly, none of your typical British understatement.' 'Oh,' replied David Hofman, 'You mean understated like the Coronation . . .?'[3] The committee spent considerable time in the Royal Albert Hall 'deciding where to house everything and how to arrange admission for the Bahá'ís etc.' The hall had been designed by a naval commander and had many levels and circular hallways.[4] The committee had the task of finding accommodation for 6,000 people and simultaneous translation so that they could all understand what was said.[5]

In the two weeks prior to the Congress, Jan Mughrabi worked at the British National Centre serving refreshments to the Hands of the Cause and the members of the Universal House of Justice, who were meeting to prepare a new teaching plan. Bahá'ís began arriving from all over the world a week in advance.[6] Ten chartered flights, each carrying 150 or more Bahá'ís, came from the United States. Nineteen-year-old Letifeh Anvar (now Rowlands) had the job of meeting arriving Bahá'ís from around the world, many of whom were Persian. She wrote that on one occasion I was with May Hofman, meeting Bahá'ís coming from different parts of the world; the majority were from Iran, many of whom had never travelled abroad before so it was essential to have someone Persian-speaking there. Some already had hotels booked so we found them taxis or directed them to the underground and on to their destinations. Those who were still looking were guided to a hotel in Russell Square where other volunteers there helped them find accommodation . . . It was quite amusing to remember London taxi drivers standing and looking at me in bemusement asking for guidance as we found taxis for different groups and asked for them to be taken to different places.[7]

More Bahá'ís poured in by train or ship. Many of these early arrivers took advantage of their time to explore London. Most went to the grave of Shoghi Effendi to pay homage to the one who had guided the Bahá'í community to this point; so many wanted to go that groups of 40 were sent every half hour for ten hours a day. Harriet Cruver, from Canada, was one and she remembered the Persian chanting and three birds singing in trees north, south and west of the grave. Each person who visited the grave was given a small packet of pressed flowers.[8] These were collected and packaged by Rose Wade and her 17-year-old daughter, Margaret. Rose, who with her husband, John, were the caretakers of the site, had collected the flowers from Shoghi Effendi's resting place, dried them at home, then filled hundreds of envelopes. During the Congress, each visitor was given a small envelope of petals. It soon became apparent that there were going to be many more visitors than they had prepared for, so Margaret spent much time sitting in a small hut which was just inside the original entrance to the cemetery, filling more envelopes with petals.[9]

This was the hut where Bahá'í youth volunteers had their 'headquarters' to meet the many coaches of arriving pilgrims. Among the volunteers were Mark and May Hofman, 14 and 16 years old. May remembered:

As we stood outside the hut greeting a group of American Bahá'ís, one lady asked us, 'And who are you two dear little children?' We were not too pleased, as teenagers, to be called 'little children', but told her our names, whereupon her jaw began to drop. It seemed to take forever, and I remember noticing her very red 'American' lipstick. 'Why, don't you know what's happened to your Daddy?' she said – as she said this my stomach began to fall through the ground, Mark and I exchanged looks and before she got to the end to the sentence – we knew. In these days of instant communication, this seems odd, but in 1963 there would have had to be a telegram or a phone call from Haifa, and my mother had decided it would be inappropriate to tell us the news of the election of the House of Justice before the official announcement. So it was from this lady – Helen Hornby – that we discovered our father had been elected.[10]

Over 6,000 Bahá'ís from all parts of the world, 'many in native costumes, thronged across Knightsbridge, halting the traffic on this busy thoroughfare, crowding up the steps of the huge hall, eager to witness the opening of the first Bahá'í World Congress'. The streets around the Albert Hall were so full of hugging and kissing friends, either reunited or just meeting, that a London newspaper described it as 'out where the kissing begins'.[11] Brigitte Ferraby remembered that

> May Faizi (now May Moore), Aziz Yazdi's daughters, and myself were given the job, by Masoud Khamsi, of accompanying the two Bolivian Indian representatives back and forth to their hotel as they did not speak English and were not used to travelling. I had learned a little Spanish at school. They were Andreas Jachakollo and Julian Ugarte and they wore their South American costume which was very colourful and drew some looks on the underground trains. Julian was very concerned because he should have been at home in the Andes planting his crops. Andreas spoke Spanish, but Julian only spoke Quetchua. One day everyone who could was urged to come in national costume, and it was a wonderful sight, and they were photographed beside the Albert Memorial on the opposite side of the road from the Royal Albert Hall for the London Evening News, which brought out a souvenir edition. There were also posters about the Congress pasted on the sides of London buses, a publicity we had never dreamed of before. Everyone had to wear their World Congress badge during proceedings, and when on the underground one could somehow sense if fellow travellers were Bahá'ís as they stood out, and looked so happy. Outside the Albert Hall were

parked some Iranian buses, which had brought people all the way from Iran. One evening I went to visit my Mum who was at a hotel opposite Kensington Gardens where all the Canadian Bahá'ís were staying. I remember also meeting a young Bahá'í who had pioneered to the north of Canada in the Arctic circle. We also met Uncle Fred, an aboriginal Bahá'í from Australia, who gave my Mum a boomerang, and I met a Bahá'í from Malaysia who was an artist.[12]

The Bahá'ís were accommodated in many hotels near the hall. Harriet Cruver stayed at the Prince of Wales Hotel and was amazed at the people she saw in the lobby or at dinner. There were ten Hands of the Cause and two members of the newly elected Universal House of Justice staying there, and others passed through. At one time or another, she sat in the lobby talking with Marguerite Sears, Rosemary and Emeric Sala, and Ruth Moffett. Leroy and Sylvia Ioas, Paul and Margery Haney, 'Alí-Akbar Furútan, and Hushmand Fatheazam sat near her at mealtimes and Enoch Olinga was sometimes in the lobby. She also sat near a 'waxed-mustached Britisher who ummphed!' in the dining room.[13]

A group of more than 30 Bahá'ís from Wales, including Knight of Bahá'u'lláh Charles Dunning, Beatrice, Mary and Flo Newman, Sally Tempest and Eric and Beatrice Kent, travelled to London, some going in a caravan of cars, while others filled a train carriage. The Kents' daughter, Corinne, who was seven, wore a Welsh costume and met a Japanese girl wearing her own national dress.[14] Corinne said that her father filmed 'the Japanese girl and myself in our national dress. He made us walk away from the camera because he wanted to film the huge bow at the back of her kimono . . . She didn't speak a word of English and I don't speak Japanese but amazingly we made friends.' Corinne also remembered that all the people wearing national costumes sat together near the podium for one session. She said that she was the only one from Wales in a Welsh costume and was very proud to represent her country. She did admit that it was a little difficult, though, as a seven-year-old, having to sit quietly though the whole session.[15]

Sally Tempest and her group arrived at the Albert Hall expecting to see huge numbers of Bahá'ís. Being quite early, they were dismayed to see none at all. Returning from dinner some time later, their expectation was realized:

The police were holding back the traffic for hordes of Bahá'ís crossing the road from the Albert Memorial to the Albert Hall. We ended up in a huge queue, trying to get into the conference. We ended up in the highest seats in the Albert Hall, known as the Gods. I can remember looking down at the scene, which consisted of people of all different colours in various different costumes, and thinking that this is the world of which I wished to be a part.[16]

Sally specifically remembered how a young Bolivian Indian, 'in his peaked hat, in broken English, told how his tribe had collected money together, to send him as their representative to the Congress. All my life, I have remembered his last words: "I go back to my people and tell them that everybody loves them."'[17]

The *London Evening Standard* reported on 28 April that

There must be something in a religion that prompted an old Cypriot woman to sell her cow to help pay her passage to England.

Others had been saving for ten years. Many others of course could afford the trip. But however they managed to converge on London, the thousands of Baha'is who are meeting at the Albert Hall this week present one of the most astonishing examples of international unity that can be imagined outside Utopia.

Their religion, Baha'i, which began in Persia in 1844, has now spread throughout the world and countries were represented today at the Albert Hall conference.

It was a colourful scene, but mingling mantillas, sombreros, saris and other national clothing is only an outward semblance of international unity.

There is something else, but it would be an impudence to define what it is on a brief acquaintance.[18]

Vivian Roe, who acted as a German and French interpreter at the entrance gates, wrote:

The celebrations were a shock, I am sure, for a lot of people in London, for the Bahá'ís walked in the middle of the road outside the Royal Albert Hall, oblivious to all the traffic – especially people who came from South America and so on, who had never seen a bus in their lives. It was charming and almost childish in a way, and lovely – and the general public just didn't understand it. There was a Souvenir edition of the London Evening News (the cover and special insert).[19]

Iain Macdonald recalls: 'There were occasions when the London police became irritated by chatty Bahá'ís stopping in the middle of the pedestrian crossing (running between the Albert Hall and Hyde Park) and cheerfully holding up the London traffic.' One policeman who was watching the chaos, heard the Bahá'ís greeting each other with 'Alláh'u'Abhá!'. When he repeated the greeting to the Bahá'ís in an attempt to get them to move on, he was hugged enthusiastically.[20]

The Royal Albert Hall was filled 'to capacity, but those who were obliged to find seats in the topmost rows under the ceiling had the advantage of seeing spread before them, as a colorful garden, believers of every race and color, many in the national or native dress of the countries from which they came.' Twenty-year-old Liz Morley (later Emerson) was there that first day and

> joined the unbelievably large throng outside the hall, a throng that was stopping traffic and causing quite a stir. There were newspaper headlines everywhere. 'Where the kissing begins', I think was one national newspaper headline, together with photos of Bahá'ís from all over the world, many in national costume. Inside the hall I sat with my parents in this vast sea of friends. It seemed that the whole Bahá'í world was here right before our eyes and the dream was becoming a reality.[21]

Audrey Rogers remembered the opening speaker welcoming the thousands of Bahá'ís. Malaysia's political situation was very difficult for Bahá'ís and getting visas to attend the Congress had been extremely difficult. The speaker said, 'Friends, we have Bahá'ís here from every part of the world, except Malaysia . . .' Those words had barely left his mouth when he was interrupted by a cry of 'We're here from Malaysia!' Audrey looked down from her seat in one of the balconies and saw, far below in the main part of the auditorium, two men standing and waving to everybody, to tumultuous applause.[22]

The focus of all those present was the platform, beautified with many flowers, on which sat the Hands of the Cause and the members of the newly elected Universal House of Justice (who were not formally introduced until the following Tuesday).[23] Enoch Olinga, the youngest Hand of the Cause, welcomed the great ensemble of humanity with his 'deep, warm voice'. Iain Macdonald was there in the Royal Albert Hall and remembered

> the awe-struck moment of entering an empty Royal Albert Hall, and raising my gaze ever slowly upward, taking in tier upon tier of gilt and red velvet. I could not comprehend that this vast auditorium would be filled with Bahá'ís from all over the globe, but filled it was!
>
> When the very newly elected, first Universal House of Justice stood before a packed Hall, I had deliberately taken myself up to the very highest gallery, so that I might look down on this stagger-ing sight. Those distant nine figures, heads bowed, stock still, as thousands upon thousands of encircling world Bahá'ís stood and applauded them.[24]

John Wade was almost overwhelmed: 'I remember very distinctly that I was deeply impressed by the fact that they had no badges, nothing to distinguish them but were all dressed in ordinary suits and I thought then "Well, if this is the Faith, then this is really it".' John had to occa-sionally make announcements to those in the hall:

> I had a little place up in the boxes near the top of the main hall from where I had to speak to the assembled friends, using a loudspeaker every now and again. As a matter of amusement I remember that my voice and what I said became quite well known because I used to say, when things were getting a bit out of hand, 'Can I have your attention please' twice and 'This voice requests' and they used to respond. It was pretty good![25]

Later, Audrey Rogers was walking along a corridor on one of the upper levels of the hall when she suddenly found herself looking at a sign on a door that read 'The Universal House of Justice'. The sign caused her to abruptly step back. She had been telling everyone for years that this day was coming, just as Bahá'u'lláh had ordained, but the realization that it had finally occurred was very moving.[26]

To cope with so many languages, there was simultaneous translation into Persian, German, French and Spanish. Those needing translation purchased headphones and this created some interesting problems. Dorothy Ferraby wrote,

> We knew exactly how many headphones we had got and there-fore how many we could book because we were charging for them. But when we came to handing them out, the man who had been entrusted to do it in Persia had not stopped when he got to his number and had just gone on selling them. So there were Persians turning up with tickets and Spanish people and Spanish-speaking people from Latin America competing with each other for these headphones. Poor John Wade was plunged into the middle of it and had to sort them out. In the end we had a lot of the Bahá'ís sitting in pairs, each with one ear phone on, sitting there with their heads close together – at least they did hear! All the translators were up in the top gallery. It went fairly well. They didn't get a full transla-tion – they got a summary, and that was about as much as could be hoped for.[27]

The translators only had one day of training before the Congress began and none were professional translators. One was Denise Fox, who was French but married to an Englishman, Jeremy. One of the speakers 'recalled Mullá Husayn's resounding cry "Mount your steeds, O heroes of God!".' For some reason, Denise instinctively modernized the phrase to 'Get into your cars (en voiture!), O heroes of God'. Simultaneous translation into French was temporarily paused while the three French translators 'were speechless with laughter'.[28]

The programme for the Congress had some great themes: The Day of Victory, the Mission of Bahá'u'lláh, The Unfoldment of the Divine Plan, The World Centre of the Faith, The Spiritual Conquest of the Planet, and Shoghi Effendi, the Sign of God. Amatu'l-Bahá Rúḥíyyih <u>Kh</u>ánum spoke on that first day about the Guardian.[29] Adrienne and Morgan Dempsey, black American Bahá'í pioneers, noted that she also 'pointedly mentioned that since the majority of the human race is not white, there is no reason why the majority of the peoples in the Bahá'í Faith should be white. We now have Australian aborigines, Bushmen of Africa, Dyaks of Borneo, Eskimos of North America, Gypsies, Hamitic peoples, Laplanders, Pigmies, Zulus, Ainus of Japan, and many other indigenous groups.'³⁰

To most Bahá'ís, Rúḥíyyih Khánum was a well-known figure. But to Graham Waterman, who had only recently become a Bahá'í, his first meeting with the famous lady was memorably embarrassing. He had offered to help at the Jubilee and had been asked to be a doorkeeper at the Albert Hall, with the job of ensuring that everyone had the proper credentials before being allowed inside. When a lady came who had no credentials, Graham denied her entrance – until he was told that it was Rúḥíyyih Khánum. There were obviously no hard feelings because soon afterwards, when he married a daughter of Hand of the Cause Collis Featherstone, Rúḥíyyih Khánum attended the wedding.³¹

Jeremy and Denise Fox attended the Congress, staying with Marianne Mihaeloff in her flat in the basement of the National Centre at 27 Rutland Gate. Of the Congress, Jeremy wrote that it was

> an unrepeatable experience. For most of us it was the first time we saw before our eyes a glimpse of united humanity. The successful fulfilment of the Guardian's plan and the election of the first Universal House of Justice with the presence of so many Hands of the Cause together and iconic figures like 'Uncle Fred', from Australia, a Dyak ex-head-hunter and the first Bolivian Indian Bahá'í – all these things and many others touched and exhilarated our hearts.³²

Denise had the privilege of taking a tray of tea into the first meeting of the Universal House of Justice at the Centre. Iain Macdonald was also given that privilege, but the power of that body overwhelmed him:

> . . . back at 27 Rutland Gate, the Universal House of Justice was going to meet in the National Assembly's Meeting Room. Betty [Reed] decided that her golden teapot and prize china were to grace their refreshment break. 'And you are going to carry it in', she cheerfully instructed. I was part-excited and part-terrified. My great friend Marianne Mihaeloff, who was Betty's secretary, assisted me with the tea preparations in the back kitchen of Rutland Gate. I set off up the stairs with a tray gripped in sweating palms, the golden teapot glowing amongst the china. As I neared the door something akin to my feelings outside the Bahji room of Bahá'u'lláh overwhelmed

me. I froze and slowly retreated having to ask Marianne to do the honours rather than me. So a unique experience was lost, but I have never been so sure of the station of the Universal House of Justice, as at that moment![33]

At the end of the morning session on the second day, Dhikru'lláh Khádem introduced Hand of the Cause Ṭarázu'lláh Samandarí as the one whom Bahá'u'lláh 'held in store for this Most Great Jubilee as a gift to us, the precious soul who belongs to the oldest family which starts from the time of Shaykh Aḥmad-i-Ahsá'í, and as 'one of the few souls who met Bahá'u'lláh'. Mr Khádem concluded his introduction saying, 'I don't know how to call him. The Blessed Beauty called him Taráz Effendi. The Centre of the Covenant called him Mírzá Taráz. Our beloved Guardian called him Jináb-i-Samandarí'. With that, one of the few people alive who had met Bahá'u'lláh told his stories of what he had felt, at the age of 16, during the three times he was in Bahá'u'lláh's presence.[34] When he stood before the microphone, Mr Samandarí said that he didn't need it – and proved that he didn't as his booming voice reached all corners of that great hall.[35]

Mr Samandarí called for an 'expression of appreciation and love for the beloved Guardian' and 6,000 people stood in complete silence.[36] Then he told of his first meeting with the One Who had caused those thousands of people to be there that day:

As Bahá'u'lláh says, this is the Day which all the Prophets of God and His Messengers have prophesied on behalf of the Lord of mankind, and in like manner, They have all foretold the advent of the Speaker on the Mount. The proof of Moses was His Staff. The proof of this Oppressed One is His Pen. Now, see what the Pen of Bahá'u'lláh did from His prison. The Pen of Bahá'u'lláh has subdued the world.

For your pleasure I will tell you how I went to Bahá'u'lláh, without capacity, at the age of sixteen. It was in a room that you all know – those of you who have been to Bahjí – and I, with four people, was in that room on the first day of Riḍván; and it is there that I saw Him. One of these people was the late Nightingale – his name was the Nightingale. He had been a prisoner two years in that prison of Rasht, and he was one of the very first of Bahá'u'lláh's disciples. He had many volumes of Tablets from the Báb and Bahá'u'lláh. Another went in the ship with Bahá'u'lláh on the Mecca pilgrimage and his name was Haji Abu'l Hasan. I don't know who the others were, but we five were the first on the first day of Riḍván to come into the presence of Bahá'u'lláh.

He sat on a chair and we kneeled down before Him. There was only a straw mat on the floor. It was a prison; there were no beautiful carpets. For twenty minutes, or perhaps half an hour, He read from the Tablet which He had revealed for Násiri'd-Din Sháh, in a heavenly voice. And He was in two conditions as He read – one the condition of Divine Might; one that great meekness, that humility that you have felt as you read His Words.

Then, He said: 'Taraz Effendi, rise.' There beside Him were flowers, fragrant flowers, and He said to me, 'Take these flowers and give one each to the friends who are present.' To each one of those other four who were in the room I gave a flower. And then in a very special way He said, 'And give Me My share, too.' Therefore, I offered Him one of the flowers, too. I rose and He said, 'And you take one, too.' Then He dismissed us and trusted us to God.

Well, this was one of my Riḍván days. This is how it began and how it ended.[37]

At the end of the morning session on 30 April, a gathering of a large number of those who had arisen to fulfil Shoghi Effendi's initial pioneering goal, and who had won the title of Knight of Bahá'u'lláh for doing so, came to the stage, where House of Justice member Borrah Kavelin announced that a scroll with the names of all the Knights of Bahá'u'lláh would be interred at the entrance door to the inner sanctuary of the Shrine of Bahá'u'lláh. Then 'Azíz Navídí read a message from the still-imprisoned Bahá'ís in Morocco. This was followed by a tape recording of those same prisoners chanting prayers.[38]

That afternoon came the moment all the thousands of Bahá'ís had been waiting for, the introduction of the Universal House of Justice. Florence Mayberry watched as

the Bahá'ís wept and applauded as the nine members of their first Universal House of Justice stood before them. This was a goal they and all the friends back home in the many countries had helped to achieve, each in his or her own way, whether it was the elderly ladies in the small towns who braved newspaper offices and radio stations with news items about Bahá'í firesides or the sole Bahá'í child in a school where anyone with 'different' religious affiliation was a target. The Persian farmer threatened with death by Muslim neighbors, the Jew, the Catholic, the Hindu, the Buddhist who had faced an orthodox family's wrath, the plodder and the gifted – all had accomplished this. The great Albert Hall, with its magnificent organ as backdrop for the platform, was packed. Above the floor of the auditorium ranged the boxes and balconies. I sat in a center box, whipping my vision side to side to catch everything . . .[39]

The newly elected Universal House of Justice, whose members had all worked with the Hands of the Cause during the previous years, showed their appreciation for the work of this stalwart body in their first ever message to the Bahá'í world:

The paeans of joy and gratitude, of love and adoration which we now raise to the throne of Bahá'u'lláh would be inadequate, and the celebrations of this Most Great Jubilee in which, as promised by our beloved Guardian, we are now engaged, would be marred were no tribute paid at this time to the Hands of the Cause of God. For they share the victory with their beloved commander, he who raised them up and appointed them. They kept the ship on its course and brought it safe to port. The Universal House of Justice, with pride and love, recalls on this supreme occasion its profound admiration for the heroic work which they have accomplished. We do not wish to dwell on the appalling dangers which faced the infant Cause when it was suddenly deprived of our beloved Shoghi Effendi, but rather to acknowledge with all the love and gratitude of our hearts the reality of the sacrifice, the labour, the self-discipline, the superb stewardship of the Hands of the Cause of God. We can think of no more fitting words to express our tribute to these dearly loved and valiant souls than to recall the Words of Bahá'u'lláh Himself: 'Light and glory, greeting and praise be upon the Hands of His Cause, through whom the light of long-suffering hath shone forth, and the declaration of authority is proven of God, the Powerful, the Mighty, the Independent, through whom the sea of bestowal hath moved and the breeze of the favour of God, the Lord of mankind, hath wafted.'[40]

Two years later, they reemphasized the monumental nature of what the Hands had done:

> From the very outset of their custodianship of the Cause of God the Hands realized that since they had no certainty of divine guidance such as is incontrovertibly assured to the Guardian and to the Universal House of Justice, their one safe course was to follow with undeviating firmness the instructions and policies of Shoghi Effendi. The entire history of religion shows no comparable record of such strict self-discipline, such absolute loyalty and such complete self-abnegation by the leaders of a religion finding themselves suddenly deprived of their divinely inspired guide. The debt of gratitude which mankind for generations, nay, ages to come, owes to this handful of grief-stricken, steadfast, heroic souls is beyond estimation.[41]

On the fourth day of the Congress, the wife of one of the Moroccan believers who was under the sentence of death, Fouad Tahhan, stood in front of the assembled Bahá'ís. She and her young son, Essam, chanted prayers.[42] Then 'Alí Nakhjavání, now a member of the supreme Bahá'í body, said that 'Here at this moment of great joy and jubilation, we see reason for broken hearts, and we hope that everything that is happening will result in the ultimate triumph of the Faith of Bahá'u'lláh'. His words were prophetic because the imprisoned Moroccan Bahá'ís were all completely exonerated before the year was done. But it did give the new House of Justice a look at the world its task was to conquer.[43]

Alvin Blum, Knight of Bahá'u'lláh for the Solomon Islands, gave one of the many other talks. He spoke of the experience of pioneering and of the 'secret of pioneering'. The secret, Alvin said,

> is being willing to give everything of yourself. The secret is willing to be sick, be lonely, willing to cry, give up, give up yourself and be willing for God to help. That's the secret. Believe me, you go into strange places. You're hungry, you're tired and you're just fed up. But if you have the faith, everything works. The power of prayer, friends, is dynamic. You can't believe what has happened.[44]

Fred Murray, an 87-year-old Australian Aborigine who was there at the express invitation of Rúḥíyyih Khánum, talked about flying across the ocean in 'a great new flying kangaroo'. He said he was 'glad to see the people here, all like a flower. . . Bahá'u'lláh has given me a good life . . . I have joy in my heart'. Shirin Boman, an Auxiliary Board member from India, spoke of the Indian believers. She told about an illiterate Bahá'í woman who, when asked to explain how she remembered God in her everyday life, said that it was like a woman carrying a jug of water on her head while walking and talking with her friends. All the while as she walked and talked, she was remembering that jug. Alvin Blum talked about a group he met in the Philippines who had become Bahá'ís by reading a pamphlet left in a local library by a passing Bahá'í. A Quechua Indian from Bolivia, Andrés Jachakollo, told the assembled Bahá'ís, 'In the name of the Indians of Bolivia I greet and salute you. I am not a literate man, and I am very happy to be here and to see my brothers from all over the world . . . We want unity and love for the whole world . . . When we go out from here, we have to teach all that we have learned . . . We have to help each other through prayers all over the Bahá'í world . . . The Holy Spirit is the power that propels us in our lives . . . This is the way we can find unity, love and universal peace'.[45]

While the Jubilee was going on, a 14-year-old was stuck in a traffic jam in front of the Royal Albert Hall with his family. The lad, Paddy Vickers, saw a big banner proclaiming a World Congress of the Bahá'í Faith and asked his father 'what the B word was'. His father told him that it was a religion that recognized Krishna, Muhammad and Jesus, 'but then they go and spoil it all by adding their own prophet, called Bahá'u'lláh'. Although slightly disappointed by his father's version of Bahá'í beliefs, he was fascinated as he 'watched the people coming out of the Albert Hall, a great variety of colours and many in national costumes, and remembered thinking, that although there couldn't be too many in any part of the world . . ., they clearly were very well distributed around the world!' Paddy had never heard of the Bahá'í Faith before, but his mother said that her best friend from high school, Audrey Rogers, was probably in the Hall since she was a Bahá'í. Paddy had always liked Audrey and thought that her being a Bahá'í was a point in its favour. Audrey was indeed inside. There she met an American Bahá'í, Jonathan Reynolds, whom she soon married.[46] Together Jonathan and Audrey spent the rest of their lives pioneering to American Indian reservations in the Dakotas and New Mexico before pioneering to Alaska. The couple later became, in 1994, the first Bahá'í pioneers to Petropavlovsk-Kamchatski where Audrey served as probably the oldest Auxiliary Board member in the world for a time.

Paddy wasn't the only one of the wider community affected by the masses of Bahá'ís. Earl Cameron, an actor originally from Bermuda but living in Britain, was studying the Faith with Roy Stines. Roy invited him to the public meeting during the Jubilee. Earl, who was initially reluctant to go, described his amazement at what he saw:

When Roy and I arrived for the public meeting at the Royal Albert Hall on the night in question (Hand of the Cause William Sears was the speaker), I was enthralled to see all the radiant faces. I turned to Roy and said: 'This is different, the people are different'. There were something like 6,000 people there. What I had expected was a lot of rather bland-looking faces which was what I had formerly experienced on a Good Friday when I was desperately in need of some kind of spiritual sustenance. At the time, I had ventured into a church near to where we were living only to find a congregation of people who appeared to be somewhat down-hearted and certainly not as happy, cheerful and so full of joy as the scene that evening at the Royal Albert Hall.

We arrived about 20 minutes before the start so we went to the cafe area. While standing at the counter, an African-American said to me 'Isn't it fantastic? Isn't it great?' I replied: 'Yes, it's wonderful!' I added that I wasn't a Bahá'í. He replied cheerfully, 'Oh yes, you are, you just don't know it yet'.

John Long gave an introduction as Chairman of the NSA, then Philip Hainsworth gave a wonderful talk about Uganda. Philip said that 74,000 people in Uganda had become Bahá'ís. Then I heard a most brilliant talk by Hand of the Cause William Sears and the evening drew to a close. On returning home, I couldn't wait to tell Audrey about the experience. About three months later, we started going to the Bahá'í Centre at Rutland Gate almost every Thursday night and we were getting very close to declaring our belief in Bahá'u'lláh.[47]

Hyde Park was a convenient place for the Bahá'ís to gather and relax. Steve Jenkerson remembered picnicking alongside a Persian family from

Iran. The Persians 'were so pleased to know that we were British Bahá'ís (the first they had met). We could not understand each others' language but felt a great affection in meeting at such a special occasion.'[48]

One day during the Congress, Bill Sears was walking across Hyde Park thinking about the amazing event:

> All of the exciting things about that World Congress were running through my mind. The Press had described the Bahá'í Congress as one of the greatest cross-sections of humanity ever assembled under one roof. Nearly seven thousand Bahá'ís from almost every country, skin color, previous religious conviction and station in life had come to London from every corner of the earth: The Bushman, the Eskimo, the African tribesman, the Maori, the American Indian, the ditch-digger and the Harvard psychiatrist, the Oxford and Cambridge scholars and university professors, the housewives, attended side by side.[49]

Bill wrote many books during his life, one of the most popular being *Thief in the Night*. As he walked across the park, a young man fell into step beside him, glancing at him frequently as though wanting to confirm that he recognized Bill. Suddenly, the fellow blurted out. 'Aren't you the *Thief in the Night* man?' He had obviously recognized Bill from his picture on the back of the book.[50]

The final talk of the World Congress, on 2 May, was given by Rúḥíyyih Khánum and she spoke of Shoghi Effendi, the Guardian, of his life and sacrifice. Many of her stories were very personal. She said that he gave himself a budget to live on and anyone who accompanied him on his trips had to live on that budget, as well. The Guardian, she noted, was 'impervious to love, to hate, to everything. I remember an instance when Shoghi Effendi was displeased with a Bahá'í, so he refused to accept his contribution to the Fund.' She said:

> He loved beautiful things. He had an extraordinary sense of proportion (proportion is beauty). When the maids and I cleaned his room, we always tried to put everything back precisely as it was before. Invariably, the Guardian would know when something was out of place. He would move the articles on his desk a fraction of an inch either way until they were exactly as he had placed them previously.[51]

At one point, she was overcome by emotion and stopped speaking. After a short silence, some of the African believers began softly singing 'Alláh'u'Abhá' while she recovered. Rúḥíyyih Khánum finished her address by saying:

> Friends, do not fail Shoghi Effendi. You have not finished with him and he has not finished with you. It is the time to put your step on new trails, to make new vows . . . to go out and please Shoghi Effendi and make him happier than he ever was in this world . . . Let us all carry on the work of our beloved Lord, Bahá'u'lláh, every day of our lives, because we are His people and we are blessed far beyond our deserts.[52]

Hand of the Cause Faizí closed the Congress with stories. He told about a little boy and his father who were standing on the edge of a crowd watching a juggler. Neither the father nor the son could see through the crowd so the father lifted the boy up on his shoulders and soon the child was laughing and clapping and asked his father why he did not join in the merriment. The kind father did not answer the boy's question but a man standing nearby said to the child, 'My dear boy, you can see all these things because you are up on the shoulders of your father. Do not be ungrateful to your father!' Mr Faizí added, 'So let us not forget the early believers, because we are standing on their shoulders when we see all these glorious victories of Bahá'u'lláh's Faith today. . . Please have patience. God will work through you and, even if it is not in your lifetime, in the lifetime of generations after you, all services will be rewarded.'[53]

When it was all over, stories about the Congress had appeared in at least 22 British newspapers. One article proclaimed the injustice of the persecution of the Bahá'ís in Morocco while another celebrated the visit to Cardiff of the sister of the famous boxer, Joe Lewis, who was herself a Bahá'í. Anything Bahá'í seemed worthy of attention, including Bahá'í weddings in London and Burnley. The *London Evening News* carried a special two-page spread of Congress photographs.[54]

The tenth stage of Shoghi Effendi's majestic process

In their first message to the Bahá'í world, the newly elected Universal House of Justice wrote that the successful conclusion of the Ten Year Plan marked

> at one and the same time the fulfilment of Daniel's prophecy, the Hundredth Anniversary of the Declaration of the Promised One of all ages, the termination of the first epoch of the Divine Plan of 'Abdu'l-Bahá designed to establish the Faith of God in all the world, and the successful conclusion of our beloved Guardian's world-encircling Crusade . . .[55]

In looking back at the tumultuous and exciting time just concluded, the House of Justice paid tribute to those who, unexpectedly and without notice, were thrust into the position of Custodians of the Cause of God:

> Historians will unhesitatingly accord credit for mobilizing the effort that had made this moment possible to the Hands of the Cause, who provided the coordination of which the loss of the Guardian's leadership had deprived the Bahá'í world. Tirelessly coursing the earth in promotion of Shoghi Effendi's Plan, coming together in annual conclaves to provide encouragement and information, inspiring the endeavours of their newly created deputies, and fending off the efforts of a new band of Covenant-breakers to undermine the unity of the Faith, this small company of grief-stricken men and women succeeded in ensuring that the Crusade's ambitious objectives were attained in the time required and that the necessary foundation was in place for the erection of the Administrative Order's crowning unit.[56]

In its first Riḍván message in 1964, the Universal House of Justice wrote of what had been accomplished during the momentous Ten Year Plan and what those accomplishments had set in motion:

> The divinely propelled process, described in such awe-inspiring words by our beloved Guardian, which began six thousand years ago at the dawn of the Adamic cycle . . . is now entering its tenth and last part.

The Ten Year Crusade, so recently consummated in a blaze of victory and rejoicing, constituted the entire ninth part of this process. It saw the Cause of God leap forward in one mighty decade-long effort to the point at which the foundations of its Administrative Order were laid throughout the world, thus preparing the way for that awakening of the masses which must characterize the future progress of the Faith.

From the beginning of this Dispensation the most urgent summons of the Word of God, voiced successively by the Báb and Bahá'u'lláh, has been to teach the Cause. 'Abdu'l-Bahá, in His own words, 'spent His days and nights in promoting the Cause and urging the peoples to service'. Shoghi Effendi, discharging the sacred mission laid upon him, raised the Administrative Order of the Faith, already enshrined within the Sacred Writings, and forged it into a teaching instrument to accomplish through a succession of plans, national, international, and global, the entire Divine Plan of 'Abdu'l-Bahá, and he clearly foresaw in the 'tremendously long' tenth part of the process already referred to, a series of plans to be launched by the Universal House of Justice, extending over 'successive epochs of both the Formative and Golden Ages of the Faith'.[57]

For thirty-one years, Shoghi Effendi had prepared the Bahá'í world for the climactic event of the First Epoch of the Formative Age, the Ten Year Crusade. For four and a half years, he had himself directed the multifarious activities of that Crusade then, with his passing, the Hands of the Cause guided it to its successful conclusion. With the election of the Universal House of Justice, the Bahá'í world entered the Second Epoch of the Formative Age and the tenth stage of Shoghi Effendi's majestic process in which the light of Bahá'u'lláh would 'penetrate',

in the course of numerous crusades and of successive epochs of both the Formative and Golden Ages of the Faith, into all the remaining territories of the globe through the erection of the entire machinery of Bahá'u'lláh's Administrative Order in all territories, both East and West, the stage at which the light of God's triumphant Faith shining in all its power and glory will have suffused and enveloped the entire planet.[58]

During the previous stages of this majestic process, the Light of Bahá'u'lláh had been projected into the West by 'Abdu'l-Bahá and then diffused throughout the world by Shoghi Effendi. In this next stage, the task of causing the Faith of Bahá'u'lláh to 'penetrate' and then 'suffuse and envelope the entire planet' had now been placed into the divinely-guided hands of the Universal House of Justice.

Appendix I

KNIGHTS OF BAHÁ'U'LLÁH BY GOAL AREA

Names in parentheses are the modern names or the nationality of the goal areas.

Admiralty Islands
(Papua New Guinea)
Violet Hoehnke

Aleutian Islands
(Alaska)
Elaine Caldwell
Jenabe Caldwell
Elinore Putney

Andaman Islands
(Indonesia)
Khodadad Fozdar

Andorra
William Danjon

Anticosti Island
(Quebec, Canada)
Mary Zabolotny

Ashanti Protectorate
(Ghana)
Benedict Eballa

Azores
Richard Lois
Richard Nolen

The Bahamas
Gail Curwin
Gerald Curwin
Ethel Holmes
Maurice Holmes
Andrew Matthisen
Nina Matthisen

Balearic Islands
(Mallorca)
Tove Deleuran
Jean Deleuran
Charles Ioas
Virginia Orbison

Baranof Island
(Alaska)
Gail Avery
Grace Bahovec
Helen Robinson

Basutoland
(Lesotho)
Elizabeth Laws
Frederick Laws

Bechuanaland
(Botswana)
Audrey Robarts
John Robarts
Patrick Robarts

Bhutan
Shápúr Aspandiar
Ardishír Furúdí

British Cameroon
(Cameroon)
Enoch Olinga

British Guiana
(Guyana)
Malcolm King

British Honduras
(Belize)
Cora Oliver
Shirley Warde

British Togoland
(Ghana)
Albert Buapiah
Edward Tabe

Brunei
Harry Clark
Charles Duncan
John Fozdar

Canary Islands
Gertrude Eisenberg
Riaz Rouhani
George True
Margaret (Peggy) True

Cape Breton Island
(Nova Scotia, Canada)
Jeanne Allen
Frederick Allen
Grace Geary
Irving Geary

Cape Verde Islands
Howard Menking
JoAnne Menking

Caroline Islands
(Papua New Guinea)
Virginia Breaks

Chagos Archipelago
Pouva Murday

Channel Islands
(United Kingdom)
Ḍiá'u'lláh Asgharzádih
Evelyn Baxter

Chiloe Island
(Chile)
Zunilda de Palacios
Louise Groger

Cocos Island
(Australia)
Frank Wyss

Comoro Islands
Mehraban Sohaili

Cook Islands
Edith Danielson
Dulcie Dive

Crete
Rolf Haug

Cyprus
Hugh McKinley
Violet McKinley
Abbás Vakíl
Samíra Vakíl

Daman
(India)
Ghulám Karlawala

Diu Island
(India)
Gulnar Aftábí
Kaykhusraw Dahamobedi
Bahíyyih Rawhání

Dutch Guiana
(Surinam)
Elinor Wolff
Robert Wolff

Dutch New Guinea
(Indonesia)
Elly Becking
Lex Meerburg

Dutch West Indies
Matthew Bullock
John Kellberg
Marjorie Kellberg

Falkland Islands
John Leonard

Faroe Islands
(Denmark)
Ljungberg, Eskil

Franklin
(Canada)
Jameson Bond
Kathleen Bond

French Cameroon
(Cameroon)
Mehrangiz Munsiff
Samuel Njiki Njenji

French Equatorial Africa
(Congo)
Max Kanyerezi

French Guiana
Eberhart Friedland

French Somaliland
(Djibouti)
Fahima Elias
Sabri Elias
Fred Schechter

French Togoland
(Togo)
Mavis Nymon
David Tanyi
Vivian Wesson

French West Africa
(Senegal)
Habíb Esfáhaní
Labíb Esfáhaní

Frisian Islands
(Germany)
Ursula von Brunn

Frisian Islands
(Germany, Netherlands, Denmark)
Geertrui Ankersmit
Elsa Maria Grossmann

Galapagos Islands
Haig Kevorkian
Gayle Woolson

Gambia
(The Gambia)
Fariburz Rúzbihyán

Gilbert & Ellice Islands
(Kiribati)
Elena Fernie
Roy Fernie

Goa
(India)
Roushan Aftábí
Firúzih Yigánigi

Grand Manan
(New Brunswick, Canada)
Doris Richardson

Greece
Carole Allen
Dwight Allen
Amín Banani
Sheila Banani

Gulf Islands
(British Columbia, Canada)
Catherine Huxtable
Cliff Huxtable

Hadhramaut
(Yemen)
Adíb Radí Baghdádí
Mahída Baghdádí
Ḥusayn Ḥalabi

Hainan Island
(China)
John Chang

Hebrides Islands
(United Kingdom)
Geraldine Craney

Italian Somaliland
(Somalia)
Mihdí Samandari
Suhayl Samandari
Ursula Samandari

Juan Fernandez Islands
(Chile)
Adela Tormo
Salvador Tormo

Karikal
(India)
Salisa Kirmání
Shírín Núrání

Keewatin
(Ontario, Canada)
Dick Stanton

Key West
(Florida)
Arthur Crane
Ethel Crane
Howard Snider

Kodiak Island
(Alaska)
Ben Guhrke
Jack Huffman
Rose Perkal

Kuria Muria
(Oman)
Munír Vakíl

Labrador
(Canada)
Howard Gilliland
Bruce Matthew

Leeward Islands
(Caribbean)
Charles Dayton
Mary Dayton
Earle Render
David Schreiber
Benjamin Weeden
Gladys Weeden

Liechtenstein
Amir Hushmand Manúchihrí

Lofoten Island
(Norway)
Mildred Clark
Loyce Lawrence

Loyalty Islands
Daniel Haumont

Macao
(China)
Frances Heller
Carl Scherer
Loretta Scherer

Madeira
Ella Duffield
Elizabeth Hopper
Sara Kenny
Ada Schott

Magdalen Islands
(New Brunswick, Canada)
Kathleen Weston
Kay Zinky

Mahé
(India)
Khudárahm Muzhgání
Lionel Peraji
Qudratu'lláh Rawhání

Malta
Mary Olga Mills
John Mitchell
Una Townshend

Margarita Island
(Venezuela)
Katharine Meyer

Mariana Islands
Cynthia Olson
Robert Powers

Marquesas Islands
Gretta Jankko

Marshall Islands
Marcia Steward

Mauritius
Ottilie Rhein

Mentawai Islands
(Indonesia)
Iran Muhájir
Rahmatu'lláh Muhájir

Miquelon Island and St Pierre
Ola Pawlowska

Moldavia
Annemarie Krüger

Monaco
Nellie French
Olivia Kelsey
'Azízu'lláh Navídí
Shamsí Navídí
Florence Ullrich

Mongolia
Sean Hinton

Morocco (International Zone)
(Morocco)
Hussein Ardekani
Nosrat Ardekani
Elsie Austin
Manúchihr Hezárí
Muhammad-'Alí Jalálí
'Abbás Rafí'í
'Álí-Akbar Rafí'í
Sháyistih Rafí'í
Richard Suhm
Mary Suhm
Richard Walters
Evelyn Walters
Hormoz Zendeh

New Hebrides
(Vanuatu)
Bertha Dobbins

Nicobar Islands
(India)
Jeanne Frankel
Margaret Bates

Northern Territories Protect.
(Ghana)
Julius Edwards
Martin Manga

Orkney Islands
(United Kingdom)
Charles Dunning

Pondicherry
(India)
Shyam Bhargava
Saʻíd Naḥví
Shawkat Naḥví

Portuguese Guinea
(Guinea-Bissau)
José Rodrigues
Hilda Rodrigues (Summers)

Portuguese Timor
(East Timor)
Harold Fitzner
Florence Fitzner
José Marques

Queen Charlotte Island
(British Columbia, Canada)
Edythe MacArthur

Reunión Island
Leland Jensen
Opal Jensen

Rhodes
(Greece)
Elizabeth Bevan

Río de Oro
(Spanish Sahara)
Amín Battáh

Romania
Fereydoun Khazrai

Ruanda Urundi
(Ruanda, Burundi)
Dunduzu Chisiza
Mary Collison
Rex Collison

Sakhalin island
(Russia)
ʻAbbás Katirai
Rezvanieh Katirai

Samoa Islands
Lilian Wyss

San Marino
Suhráb Paymán
Tábandih Paymán

Sardinia
Marie Ciocca Holmlund

Seychelles
Kámil ʻAbbás
ʻAbdu'l Raḥmán Zarqání

Shetland Islands
(United Kingdom)
Brigitte Hasselblatt Lundblade

Sicily
Carol Bagley
Florence Bagley
Gerrold Bagley
Stanley Bagley
Susan Bagley
Emma Rice

Sikkim
(India)
Udai Narain Singh

Society Islands
(Tahiti)
Gladys Parke
Gretta Lamprill

Socotra
Kamálí Sarvístání

Solomon Islands
Alvin Blum
Gertrude Blum

Southern Rhodesia
(Zimbabwe)
Aynu'd-Dín ʻAláʼí
Ṭáhirih ʻAláʼí
Kenneth Christian

Roberta Christian
Claire Gung
Ezzat Zahrai

South West Africa
(Namibia)
Edward (Ted) Cardell

Spanish Guinea
(Equatorial Guinea)
Elise Schreiber

Spanish Morocco
(Morocco)
Erleta Fleming
John Fleming
Alyce Barbara May Janssen
Luella McKay
Bahíyyih Zaynu'l-Ábidín,
Fawzí Zaynu'l-Ábidín

Spanish Sahara
Muḥammad Mustafá

St Thomas Island
(São Tomé and Príncipe)
Elise Schreiber

St Helena
Elizabeth Stamp

Spitsbergen
Paul Adams

Swaziland
John Allen
Valera Allen
Bula Mott Stewart

Tibet
Udai Narain Singh

Tonga Islands
Dudley Blakely
Elsa Blakely
Stanley Bolton

Tuamotu Archipelago
Jean Sevin

White Russia
(Belarus)
Helmut Winkelbach

Windward Islands
(Caribbean)
Esther Evans
Lillian Middlemast

Yukon
(Canada)
Ted Anderson
Joan Anderson

Appendix II

KNIGHTS OF BAHÁ'U'LLÁH BY NAME

Names in parentheses are the modern names or the nationality of the goal areas.

A
'Alá'í, Aynu'd-Dín – Southern Rhodesia (Zimbabwe)
'Alá'í, Ṭáhirih – Southern Rhodesia (Zimbabwe)
'Abbás, Kámil – Seychelles
Adams, Paul – Spitsbergen
Aftábí, Gulnar – Diu Island, India
Aftábí, Roushan – Goa, India
Allen, Carole – Greece
Allen, Dwight – Greece
Allen, Frederick – Cape Breton Island, Nova Scotia, Canada
Allen, Jeanne – Cape Breton Island, Nova Scotia, Canada
Allen, John – Swaziland
Allen, Valera – Swaziland
Anderson, Joan – Yukon, Canada
Anderson, Ted – Yukon, Canada
Ankersmit, Geertrui – Frisian Islands
Ardekani, Hussein – Morocco, International Zone
Ardekani, Nosrat – Morocco, International Zone
Asgharzádih, Ḍiá'u'lláh – Channel Islands, United Kingdom
Aspandiar, Shápúr – Bhutan
Austin, Elsie – Morocco, International Zone
Avery, Gail – Baranof Island, Alaska

B
Baghdádí, Adíb Radí – Hadhramaut, Yemen
Baghdádí, Mahída – Hadhramaut, Yemen
Bagley, Carol – Sicily
Bagley, Florence – Sicily
Bagley, Gerrold – Sicily

Bagley, Stanley – Sicily
Bagley, Susan – Sicily
Bahovec, Grace – Baranof Island, Alaska
Banani, Amín – Greece
Banani, Sheila – Greece
Bates, Margaret – Nicobar Islands, India
Battáh, Amín – Río de Oro, Spanish Sahara
Baxter, Evelyn – Channel Islands, United Kingdom
Becking, Elly – Dutch New Guinea (Indonesia)
Bhargava, Shyam – Pondicherry, India
Bevan, Elizabeth – Rhodes, Greece
Blakely, Dudley – Tonga Islands
Blakely, Elsa – Tonga Island
Blum, Alvin – Solomon Islands
Blum, Gertrude – Solomon Islands
Bolton, Stanley – Tonga Islands
Bond, Jameson – Franklin, Canada
Bond, Kathleen – Franklin, Canada
Breaks, Virginia – Caroline Islands (Papua New Guinea)
Buapiah, Albert – British Togoland (Ghana)
Bullock, Matthew – Dutch West Indies

C

Caldwell, Elaine – Aleutian Islands, Alaska
Caldwell, Jenabi – Aleutian Islands, Alaska
Cardell, Edward (Ted) – South West Africa (Namibia)
Chang, John – Hainan Island, China
Chisiza, Dunduzu – Rwanda Urundi (Rwanda and Burundi)
Christian, Kenneth – Southern Rhodesia (Zimbabwe)
Christian, Roberta – Southern Rhodesia (Zimbabwe)
Ciocca Holmlund, Marie – Sardinia
Clark, Harry – Brunei
Clark, Mildred – Lofoten Island, Norway
Collison, Mary – Ruanda Urundi (Rwanda and Burundi)
Collison, Rex – Ruanda Urundi (Rwanda and Burundi)
Crane, Arthur – Key West, Florida
Crane, Ethel – Key West, Florida
Craney, Geraldine – Hebrides Islands, United Kingdom
Curwin, Gail – The Bahamas
Curwin, Gerald – The Bahamas

D

Dahamobedi, Kaykhusraw – Diu Island, India
Danielson, Edith – Cook Islands
Danjon, William – Andorra
Dayton, Charles – Leeward Islands, Caribbean
Dayton, Mary – Leeward Islands, Caribbean

de Palacios, Zunilda – Chiloe Island, Chile
Deleuran, Jean – Balearic Islands
Deleuran, Tove – Balearic Islands
Dive, Dulcie – Cook Islands
Dobbins, Bertha – New Hebrides (Vanuatu)
Duffield, Ella – Madeira
Duncan, Charles – Brunei
Dunning, Charles – Orkney Islands, United Kingdom

E

Eballa, Benedict – Ashanti Protectorate (Ghana)
Edwards, Julius – Northern Territories Protectorate (Ghana)
Eisenberg, Gertrude – Canary Islands
Elias, Fahíma – French Somaliland (Djibouti)
Elias, Sabrí – French Somaliland (Djibouti)
Esfáhaní, Habíb – French West Africa (Senegal)
Esfáhaní, Labíb – French West Africa (Senegal)
Evans, Esther – Windward Islands, Caribbean

F

Fernie, Elena – Gilbert & Ellise Islands (Kiribati)
Fernie, Roy – Gilbert & Ellise Islands (Kiribati)
Fitzner, Florence – Portuguese Timor (East Timor)
Fitzner, Harold – Portuguese Timor (East Timor)
Fleming, Erleta – Spanish Morocco (Morocco)
Fleming, John – Spanish Morocco (Morocco)
Fozdar, John – Brunei
Fozdar, Khodadad – Andaman Islands, India
Frankel, Jeanne – Nicobar Islands, India
French, Nellie – Monaco
Friedland, Eberhart – French Guiana

G

Geary, Grace – Cape Breton Island, Canada
Geary, Irving – Cape Breton Island, Canada
Gilliland, Howard – Labrador, Canada
Groger, Louise – Chiloe Island, Chile
Grossmann, Elsa Maria – Frisian Islands, Germany
Guhrke, Ben – Kodiak Island, Alaska
Gung, Claire – Southern Rhodesia (Zimbabwe)

H

Ḥalabi, Ḥusayn – Hadhramaut, Yemen
Hasselblatt Lundblade, Brigitte – Shetland Islands, United Kingdom
Haug, Rolf – Crete
Haumont, Daniel – Loyalty Islands
Ḥázarí, Manúchihr – Morocco, International Zone

Heller, Frances – Macao
Hinton, Sean – Mongolia
Hoehnke, Violet – Admiralty Islands (Papua New Guinea)
Holmes, Ethel – Bahamas Islands
Holmes, Maurice – Bahamas Islands
Hopper, Elizabeth – Madeira
Huffman, Jack – Kodiak Island, Alaska
Huxtable, Catherine – Gulf Islands, Canada
Huxtable, Cliff – Gulf Islands, Canada

I
Ioas, Charles – Balearic Islands

J
Jalálí, Muḥammad-'Alí – Morocco, International Zone
Jankko, Gretta – Marquesas Islands
Janssen, Alyce Barbara May – Spanish Morocco
Jensen, Leland – Reunion Island
Jensen, Opal – Reunion Island

K
Kanyerezi, Max – French Equatorial Africa (Congo)
Karlawala, Ghulám – Daman, India
Katirai, Abbás – Sakhalin island, Russia
Katirai, Rezvanieh – Sakhalin Island, Russia
Kellberg, John – Dutch West Indies
Kellberg, Marjorie – Dutch West Indies
Kelsey, Olivia – Monaco
Kenny, Sara – Monaco
Kevorkian, Haig – Galapagos Islands
Khazrai, Fereydoun – Romania
King, Malcolm – British Guiana (Guyana)
Kirmání, Salisa – Karikal, India
Krüger, Annemarie – Moldavia

L
Lamprill, Gretta – Society Islands
Lawrence, Loyce – Lofoten Island, Norway
Laws, Elizabeth – Basutoland (Lesotho)
Laws, Frederick – Basutoland (Lesotho)
Leonard, John – Falkland Islands
Ljungberg, Eskil – Faroe Islands

M
MacArthur, Edythe – Queen Charlotte Island, Canada
Manga, Martin – Northern Territories Protectorate (Ghana)
Manúchihrí, Amír Hushmand – Liechtenstein

Marques, José – Portuguese Timor (East Timor)
Matthew, Bruce – Labrador, Canada
Matthisen, Andrew – Bahamas Islands
Matthisen, Nina – Bahamas Islands
McKay, Luella – Spanish Morocco (Morocco)
McKinley, Hugh – Cyprus
McKinley, Violet – Cyprus
Meerburg, Lex – Dutch New Guinea (Indonesia)
Mehraban Sohail – Comoro Islands
Menking, Howard   Cape Verde Islands
Menking, JoAnne – Cape Verde Islands
Meyer, Katharine – Margarita Island, Venezuela
Middlemast, Lillian – Windward Islands
Mills, Mary Olga – Malta
Mitchell, John – Malta
Muhájir, Iran – Mentawai Islands, Indonesia
Muhájir, Raḥmatu'lláh – Mentawai Islands, Indonesia
Munsiff, Mehrangiz – French Cameroon (Cameroon)
Murday, Pouva – Chagos Archipelago
Mustafá, Muḥammad – Spanish Sahara
Muzhgání, Khudárahm – Mahé, India

N
Naḥví, Sa'íd – Pondicherry, India
Naḥví, Shawkat – Pondicherry, India
Navídí, 'Azízu'lláh – Monaco
Navídí, Shamsi – Monaco
Njiki Njenji, Samuel – French Cameroon (Cameroon)
Nolen, Lois – Azores
Nolen, Richard – Azores
Núrání, Shírín – Karikal, India
Nymon, Mavis – French Togoland (Togo)

O
Olinga, Enoch – British Cameroon (Cameroon)
Oliver, Cora – British Honduras (Belize)
Olson, Cynthia – Mariana Islands
Orbison, Virginia – Balearic Islands

P
Parke, Gladys – Society Islands
Pawlowska, Ola – Miquelon Island and St Pierre (off Canada)
Paymán, Suhráb – San Marino
Paymán, Tábandih – San Marino
Peraji, Lionel – Mahé, India
Perkal, Rose – Kodiak Island, Alaska
Powers, Robert – Mariana Islands

Putney, Elinore – Aleutian Islands, Alaska

R
Rafí'í, 'Abbás – Morocco, International Zone
Rafí'í, 'Álí-Akbar – Morocco, International Zone
Rafí 'í, Sháyistih – Morocco, International Zone
Rawhání, Qudratu'lláh – Mahé, India
Rawhání, Bahiyyih – Diu Island, India
Render, Earle – Leeward Islands, Caribbean
Rhein, Ottilie – Mauritius
Rice, Emma – Sicily
Richardson, Doris – Grand Manan, Canada
Robarts, Audrey – Bechuanaland (Botswana)
Robarts, John – Bechuanaland (Botswana)
Robarts, Patrick – Bechuanaland (Botswana)
Robinson, Helen – Baranof Island, Alaska
Rodrigues, José – Portuguese Guinea (Guinea-Bissau)
Rouhani, Riaz – Canary Islands
Rurúdí, Ardishír – Bhutan
Rúzbihyán, Fariburz – Gambia

S
Samandarí, Midhi – Italian Somaliland (Somalia)
Samandarí, Suhayl – Italian Somaliland (Somalia)
Samandarí, Ursula – Italian Somaliland (Somalia)
Sarvístání, Kamálí – Socotra
Schechter, Fred – French Somaliland (Djibouti)
Scherer, Carl – Macao
Scherer, Loretta – Macao
Schott, Ada – Madeira
Schreiber, David – Leeward Islands, Caribbean
Schreiber, Elise – Spanish Guinea (Equatorial Guinea), and St Thomas Island (São
    Tomé and Príncipe)
Sevin, Jean – Tuamotu Archipelago
Singh, Udai Narain – Sikkim, India, and Tibet
Snider, Howard – Key West, Florida
Stamp, Elizabeth – St Helena
Stanton, Dick – Keewatin, Canada
Steward, Marcia – Marshall Islands
Stewart, Bula Mott – Swaziland
Suhm, Mary – Morocco, International Zone
Suhm, Richard – Morocco, International Zone
Summers, Hilda – Portuguese Guinea (Guinea-Bissau)

T
Tabe, Edward – British Togoland (Ghana)
Tanyi, David – French Togoland (Togo)
Tormo, Adela – Juan Fernandez Islands, Chile

Tormo, Salvador – Juan Fernandez Islands, Chile
Townshend, Una – Malta
True, George – Canary Islands
True, Peggy – Canary Islands

U
Ullrich, Florence – Monaco

V
Vakíl, 'Abbás – Cyprus
Vakíl, Munír – Kuria Muria, Oman
Vakíl, Samíra – Cyprus
von Brunn, Ursula – Frisian Islands, Germany

W
Walters, Evelyn – Morocco, International Zone
Walters, Richard – Morocco, International Zone
Warde, Shirley – British Honduras (Belize)
Weeden, Ben – Leeward Islands, Caribbean
Weeden, Gladys – Leeward Islands, Caribbean
Wesson, Vivian – French Togoland (Togo)
Weston, Kathleen – Magdalen Islands, Canada
Winkelbach, Helmut – White Russia (Belarus)
Wolff, Elinor – Dutch Guiana (Surinam)
Wolff, Robert – Dutch Guiana (Surinam)
Woolson, Gayle – Galapagos Islands
Wyss, Frank – Cocos Islands (Australia)
Wyss, Lilian – Samoa Island

Y
Yigánigi, Fírúzih – Goa, India

Z
Zabolotny, Mary – Anticosti Island, Quebec
Zahrai, Ezzat – Southern Rhodesia (Zimbabwe)
Zarqání, Abdu'l Rahmán – Seychelles
Zaynu'l-Ábidín, Bahíyyih – Spanish Morocco
Zaynu'l-Ábidín, Fawzí – Spanish Morocco
Zendeh, Hormoz – Morocco, International Zone
Zinky, Kay – Magdalen Islands, Canada

BIBLIOGRAPHY

'Abdu'l-Bahá. *The Will and Testament of 'Abdu'l-Bahá*. Wilmette, IL: Bahá'í Publishing Trust, 1990.

Alaska Bahá'í News. Periodical. National Spiritual Assembly of Alaska.

Allen, Valera. *Haifa Impressions*. Available at: http://bahai-library.com/pilgrims/allen.html, 1954.

Allison, Bill. *Pilgrim Notes*. United States Bahá'í National Archives, Sam & Mildred McClellan Papers, 1957.

Allison, Thelma. *Haifa Notes*. United States Bahá'í National Archives, Evelyn & Floyd Hardin Papers, 1957.

— *Pilgrimage to Haifa*. United States Bahá'í National Archives, Sam & Mildred McClellan Papers, 1957.

Amatu'l-Bahá Rúḥíyyih K͟hánum. 'The Completion of the International Archives', in *The Bahá'í World*, vol. XIII, pp. 403–34.

— *Eagle and Pillar over Shoghi Effendi's Resting Place*. Available at: http://bahai-library.com/shoghieffendi_scotland_ruhiyyihkhanum_edinburgh, n.d.

— Audio recording of a talk to the Bahá'ís of New York, 5 June 1960.

— Letter to the National Spiritual Assembly of Central and East Africa, 11 February 1961. United States Bahá'í National Archives, Amelia Collins Papers.

— Letter to the National Spiritual Assemblies of the United States and Canada, 9 March 1961, Amelia Collins Papers.

— and John Ferraby. *The Passing of Shoghi Effendi*. London: Bahá'í Publishing Trust, 1958.

(see also Rabbani, Rúḥíyyih).

Appa, Margaret. Account in *UK Bahá'í Histories*, 2013. Available at: http://bahaihistoryuk.wordpress.com/2013/04/05/margaret-appa/.

Archibald, E. S. United States Bahá'í National Archives, Doris Ballard Papers, 1955.

Austin, Elsie. Audio recording, 23 November 1973. The Heritage Project of the National Spiritual Assembly of the United States.

Bach, Marcus. *The Circle of Faith*. New York: Hawthorn Books, 1956.

Bahá'í International Community. *Freedom of Religion on Trial in Morocco: The Nador Case*, 1963. Available at: http://www.h-net.org/~bahai/diglib/books/A-E/B/BIC/Morocco_Case_1963.pdf.

— Bahá'í World News Service. Haifa, Israel. Available at: news.bahai.org.

Bahá'í Journal UK. Periodical. National Spiritual Assembly of the United Kingdom.

Bahá'í News. Periodical. National Spiritual Assembly of the Bahá'ís of the United States.

The Bahá'í World: An International Record. Vol. XII (1950–1954). RP Wilmette, IL: Bahá'í Publishing Trust, 1980, 1981; vol. XIII (1954–1963), Haifa: The Universal House of Justice, 1970; vol. XIV (1963–1968), Haifa: The Universal House of Justice, 1974; vol. XV (1968–1973), Haifa: Bahá'í World Centre, 1976; vol. XVIII (1979–1983), Haifa: Bahá'í World Centre, 1986; vol. XIX (1983–1986), Haifa: Bahá'í World Centre, 1994; vol. XX (1986–1992). Haifa: Bahá'í World Centre, 1998; *In Memoriam*, 1992–1997, Haifa: World Centre Publications, 2010.

Balyuzi, H. M. *'Abdu'l-Bahá: The Centre of the Covenant of Bahá'u'lláh*. Oxford: George Ronald, 1971.

Banani, Amín and Sheila. *Pilgrim Notes of Sheila and Amin Banani*. The Heritage Project of the National Spiritual Assembly of the United States, 2 September 1975.

Bates, Geertrui Ankersmit. *Bahá'í Story, Geertrui (Ankersmit) Bates, Knight of Bahá'u'lláh*. Transcription of a video interview in New Zealand, 2005.

Beales, Brigitte. Account in *UK Bahá'í Histories*, 2013. Available at: http://bahaihistoryuk.wordpress.com/2013/10/21/brigitte-beales-ferraby/.

Beasley, Elmer and Gladys. *Our Pilgrimage to Haifa*. Available at: http://bahai-library.com/beasley_pilgrimage_haifa, 1957.

Bennett, Irene. *My First Pilgrimage to Haifa – 1954*, in *UK Bahá'í Histories*. Available at: http://bahaihistoryuk.wordpress.com/2013/04/01/irene-bennett-pilgrimage-1954/, 2013.

Blum, Gertrude. United States Bahá'í National Archives, Charlotte Linfoot Papers, 1953.

Brown, Ramona. United States Bahá'í National Archives, Alice Dudley Papers, 1954.

Cameron, Earl. Account in *UK Bahá'í Histories*, 2015. Available at: https://bahaihistoryuk.wordpress.com/2015/03/23/earl-cameron/.

Cameron, Glenn. *A Basic Bahá'í Chronology*. Oxford: George Ronald, 1996.

Cardin, Heather. *The Bright Glass of the Heart*. Oxford: George Ronald, 2013.

Chapman, Anita. *Leroy Ioas: Hand of the Cause of God*. Oxford: George Ronald, 1998.

Christian, W. Kenneth. United States Bahá'í National Archives, Hattie Chamberlain Papers, 1955.

Collins, Amelia. *A Tribute to Shoghi Effendi*. Wilmette, IL: Bahá'í Publishing Trust, n.d.

Cruver, Harriet. United States Bahá'í National Archives, Harriet Cruver Papers, 1963.

Davis, Laura. *Notes of Laura R. Davis. Pilgrimage.* Document no. 057-017-66. Bahá'í National Archives, Canada, Laura Davis Papers.

— United States Bahá'í National Archives, Document 156.019.

Dudley, Alice. *Pilgrimage to Haifa, April 15–23, 1957.* United States Bahá'í National Archives, Alice Dudley Papers, 1957.

Edge, Clara. *Haifa Notes.* United States Bahá'í National Archives. Available at: bahai-library.com/edge_haifa_notes.

Emerson, Elizabeth. *My Bahá'í Journey,* in *UK Bahá'í Histories,* 2012. Available at: http://bahaihistoryuk.wordpress.com/2012/11/30/liz-emerson/.

Enayat, Mohsen. *A Little Story from Fezzan,* email to the author, 11 December 2014.

Faizí, 'Abu'l-Qásim. *Milly: A Tribute to Amelia E. Collins.* Oxford: George Ronald, 1977.

Faizi-Moore, May. *Faizi.* Oxford: George Ronald, 2013.

Ferraby, Dorothy. Account in *UK Bahá'í Histories,* 2012. Available at: http://bahaihistoryuk.wordpress.com/2012/11/20/dorothy-ferraby-1904-1994/.

Fox, Jeremy. Account in *UK Bahá'í Histories,* 2012. Available at: http://bahaihistoryuk.wordpress.com/2012/03/02/jeremy-fox/.

Freeman, Dorothy. *From Copper to Gold.* Oxford: George Ronald, 1984.

Furútan, 'Alí-Akbar. *The Story of My Heart.* Oxford: George Ronald, 1984.

Giachery, Ugo. *Shoghi Effendi: Recollections.* Oxford: George Ronald, 1973.

Guhrke, Ben. Letter written five months after arriving at his goal on Kodiak Island, June 1954.

— *Ben's Story.* Manuscript, 2015.

Hainsworth, Philip. *Looking Back in Wonder.* Stroud, Skyset Ltd, 2004.

Harper, Barron. *Lights of Fortitude.* Oxford: George Ronald, 1997.

Hassan, Gamal. *Moths Turned Eagles: The Spiritual Conquests of Sabri and Raissa Elias.* National Spiritual Assembly of Ethiopia, 2008.

Hellaby, Madeline. 'Some thoughts on the Guardian's death', letter to Marion Hofman, 13 November 1957. Marion Hofman Papers, private collection.

Hofman, David. *George Townshend.* Oxford: George Ronald, rev. ed. 2002.

Hofman, Marion. *The World Crusade* (1959), Marion Hofman Papers, private collection.

— *Notes taken in Haifa, Feb. 9-17, 1954 at Dinner with Shoghi Effendi.* Marion Hofman Papers, private collection.

— Letter to 'the beloved Pioneers of the Islands', 20 November, 1957. Marion Hofman Papers, private collection.

Hornby, Helen (comp.). *Lights of Guidance*. New Delhi: Bahá'í Publishing Trust, 1997.

Ioas, Leroy. Letter to D̲h̲ikru'lláh K̲h̲ádem, 1 November 1959. United States Bahá'í National Archives, Leroy Ioas Papers, 1959.

Kelsey, Olivia. United States Bahá'í National Archives, Olivia Kelsey Papers.

Kent, Eric and Beatrice. Account in *UK Bahá'í Histories*, 2014. Available at: http://bahaihistoryuk.wordpress.com/2014/03/27/eric-and-beatrice-kent/.

Khadem, Javidukht. *Zikrullah Khadem: The Itinerant Hand of the Cause of God*. Wilmette: Bahá'í Publishing Trust, 1990.

K̲h̲ázeh, Jalál. *After the Passing of the Beloved Guardian*. Audio recording of a talk given at Monkstown, Ireland, 1969.

— Letter to Sylvia and Leroy Ioas, 12 June 1960. United States Bahá'í National Archives, Leroy Ioas Papers, 1900-1952, 1960.

Knox, Dermod. Audio recording, 3 September 2013. Account in *UK Bahá'í Histories*, 2013. Available at: http://bahaihistoryuk.wordpress.com/2013/08/29/dermod-knox/.

Kolstoe, John. *Crazy Lovers of Bahá'u'lláh*. Manuscript, 2015.

Lamb, Artemus. *The Beginnings of the Bahá'í Faith in Latin America: Some Remembrances*. San Salvador: VanOrman Enterprises, 1995.

Leach, Bernard. *Excerpts from a letter from Bernard Leach after his visit to Haifa*, December 1954. From Lucy Marshall's notes. Available at: http://bahai-library.com/leach_letter_visit_haifa, 1954.

Lee, Anthony Asa. *The Establishment of the Baha'i Faith in West Africa: The First Decade, 1952-1962*. Los Angeles: University of California, 2007.

Levy, Ben and Marguerite Sears. United States Bahá'í National Archives, Bertha Hyde Kirkpatrick Papers, 1953.

Locke-Nyrenda, Suzanne. 'Hand of the Cause, Knight of Bahá'u'lláh, Enoch Olinga, Visit to Malawi 1972', email report, 25 Nov 2014.

Logsdon-Dubois, Judith Kaye. *Knight with a Briefcase*. Oxford: George Ronald, 2013.

Macdonald, Iain. Account in *UK Bahá'í Histories*, 2011. Available at: http://bahaihistoryuk.wordpress.com/2012/05/01/iain-macdonald/.

Macke, Marlene. *Take My Love to the Friends: The Story of Laura R. Davis*. St Mary's, Ont: Chestnut Park Press, 2009.

Maxwell, May and Mary Maxwell. *Haifa Notes of Shoghi Effendi's Words: Taken at Pilgrim House during the Pilgrimage of Mrs May Maxwell and Miss Mary Maxwell, January, February, March 1937*. 2 vols. Available at: http://bahai-library.com/maxwell_haifa_notes, 1937.

Maxwell, William. *Pilgrimage Notes of Haifa*. United States Baháʼí National Archives, Asian Teaching Committee, Box 8: William Maxwell, 1959.

Mayberry, Florence. *The Great Adventure*. Manotick, Ont.: Nine Pines Publishing, 1994.

— *Pilgrim Notes*. The Heritage Project of the National Spiritual Assembly of the United States, 1957 and 1969.

McCormick, Alan. United States Baháʼí National Archives, Nancy Bowditch Papers, 1953.

McKinley, Deborah. *Violet and Hugh McKinley: Knights of Baháʼuʼlláh for Cyprus 1953–1963*. Manuscript 2015.

McLaren, Edith. *Notes of the Pilgrimage of Edith McLaren, May 2–10, 1954*. Available at: http://bahai-library.com/mclaren_pilgrims_notes, 1954.

The Ministry of the Custodians, 1957–1963. Haifa: Baháʼí World Centre, 1992.

Moffett, Ruth. *Pilgrim's Notes of Ruth Moffett*. United States Baháʼí National Archives, Laurence & Ruth Laroque Papers, 1954.

Mohtadi. *Haifa Notes of Mohtadi*, United States Baháʼí National Archives, Charlotte Linfoot Papers, 1956.

Momtazi, N. United States Baháʼí National Archives, Viola Tuttle Papers, 1956.

Morgan, Adrienne. *Claire Gung*. Johannesburg: National Spiritual Assembly of the Baháʼís of South Africa, 1997.

Morgan, Adrienne and Dempsey. *The Most Great Jubilee*. United States Baháʼí National Archives, Zylpha Mapp-Robinson Bapers Papers, 1963.

— *Servants of the Glory*. Manuscript, 2014.

Mottahedeh, Roy. United States Baháʼí National Archives, Mildred Mottahedeh Papers, undated.

Muhájir, Írán Furútan. *Dr Muhajir: Hand of the Cause of God, Knight of Baháʼuʼlláh*. New Delhi, Baháʼí Publishing Trust, 2nd rev. ed, 2005.

Nakhjavání, ʼAlí. 'The Ten Year Crusade', 22nd Hasan M. Balyuzu Memorial Lecture, presented at the 28th Annual Conference of the Association for Baháʼí Studies–North America, Calgary, Alberta, Canada, 5 September 2004, in *The Journal of Baháʼí Studies,* vol. 14, no. 3 /4, 2004. Available at: http://www.bahai-studies.ca/journal/files/jbs/14.3-4.Nakhjavani.pdf.

— 'Glimpse of the life of Enoch Olinga', interview in July 2012. Available at: http://www.youtube.com/channel/UCfEMbaU1tuUAzLWsw_4ZB-g/videos.

Nakhjavani, Violette. *Notes from the Archives Building, in Haifa*. United States Baháʼí National Archives, 1965.

— *Pioneering in The Time of Guardian*, audio recording, 20 January 1981.The Heritage Project of the National Spiritual Assembly of the United States.

— *A Tribute to Amatu'l-Bahá Rúḥíyyih Khánum*. Ottawa, Ont.: Bahá'í Canada Publications, 2000.

Pfaff-Grossmann, Susanne. *The Life of a Pioneer*. San Diego, CA: Island Resort Publishing, 2008.

— *Hermann Grossmann, Hand of the Cause of God: A Life for the Faith*. Oxford: George Ronald, 2009.

Rabbani, Rúḥíyyih. *The Priceless Pearl*. London: Bahá'í Publishing Trust, 2000.

— *Enoch Olinga, Hand of the Cause of God*. Kenya: Bahá'í Publishing Agency, 2001.

Reimholz, Maud and Albert. *Pilgrimage to Haifa*. United States Bahá'í National Archives, Albert L and Maud S. Reimholz Personal Recollections, 1954.

Robarts, Audrey. 'Reminiscences about Shoghi Effendi' in *The Vision of Shoghi Effendi*, pp. 165–70.

Robarts, John A. 'A Few Reminiscences about Shoghi Effendi Taken from Pilgrim Notes of January 1955, from the Canadian National Spiritual Assembly Film *Retrospective*, and from Some Other Words of the Beloved Guardian', in *The Vision of Shoghi Effendi*, pp. 171–7.

Roe, Vivian. Account in *UK Bahá'í Histories*, 2012. Available at: http://bahaihistoryuk.wordpress.com/2012/05/22/vivian-isenthal-roe-1909-1997.

Rohani, Aziz. *Sweet and Enchanting Stories*. Hong Kong: Juxta Publishing Co., 2005.

Rowlands, Latifeh. Account in *UK Bahá'í Histories*, 2012. Available at: http://bahaihistoryuk.wordpress.com/2012/07/31/latifeh-rowlands/.

Ruhe, David. *Door of Hope*. Oxford: George Ronald, 1983.

Rutstein, Nathan. *He Loved and Served*. Oxford: George Ronald, 1982.

— *From a Gnat into an Eagle*. Wilmette: Bahá'í Publishing Trust, 2008.

Sabri, Isobel. *Pilgrim Notes Recorded after the Nightly Dinner-table Talks of the Beloved Guardian, Shoghi Effendi 19-28 April 1957*. Available at: http://www.h-net.org/~bahai/diglib/MSS/P-T/S/i_sabri.htm, 1957.

Samandarí, Ursula. *Notes of My Pilgrimage*. Marion Hofman Papers, private collection, 1957.

Saunders, Keithie. *Of Wars and Worship*. Oxford: George Ronald, 2012.

Sears, William. *Pilgrimage to Haifa*, parts 1 and 3. United States Bahá'í National Archives, Edith Segen Johnson Papers, 1954.

— *Pilgrimage to Haifa* [part 2], 1954. Available online at: bahai-library.com/sears_pilgrimage_haifa.

— Letter to Sylvia and Leroy Ioas, 20 Sept 1962. United States Bahá'í National Archives, Leroy Ioas Papers, 1962.

Sears, Marguerite. *Bill*. Eloy, AZ: Desert Rose Publishing, 2003.

Semple, Ian. 'The Guardianship and the Universal House of Justice', talk given in London, 28 Jan 2006.

— Account in *UK Baháʼí Histories*, 2012. Available at: http://bahaihistoryuk.wordpress.com/2012/03/21/ian-semple-1928-2011.

Shoghi Effendi. *Citadel of Faith: Messages to America /1947-1957*. Wilmette, IL: Baháʼí Publishing Trust, 1965.

— *Dawn of a New Day: Messages to India 1923-1957*. New Delhi: Baháʼí Publishing Trust, 1970

— *Directives from the Guardian*. New Delhi: Baháʼí Publishing Trust, 1973.

— *God Passes By* (1944). Wilmette, IL: Baháʼí Publishing Trust, rev. ed. 2004.

— *Letters from the Guardian to Australia and New Zealand, 1923-1957*. Sydney: National Spiritual Assembly of the Baháʼís of Australia, 1970.

— *The Light of Divine Guidance: The Messages from the Guardian of the Baháʼí Faith to the Baháʼís of Germany and Austria*. 2 vols. Hofheim Langenhain: Baháʼí-Verlag, 2006.

— *Messages to Alaska*. National Spiritual Assembly of the Baháʼís of Alaska, 1976.

— *Messages to America, 1932-1946*. Wilmette, IL: Baháʼí Publishing Trust, 1947. Published online by the Project Gutenberg.

— *Messages to the Antipodes*. Mona Vale: Baháʼí Publications Australia, 1997.

— *Messages to the Baháʼí World, 1950-1957*. Wilmette, IL: Baháʼí Publishing Trust, 2nd ed. 1971.

— *Messages to Canada*. Toronto: Baháʼí Canada Publications, 1998.

— *This Decisive Hour*. Wilmette, IL: Baháʼí Publishing Trust, 2002.

— *Unfolding Destiny: The Messages from the Guardian of the Baháʼí Faith to the Baháʼí Community of the British Isles*. London: Baháʼí Publishing Trust, 1981.

— *The World Order of Baháʼuʼlláh: Selected Letters by Shoghi Effendi* (1938). Wilmette, IL: Baháʼí Publishing Trust, 2nd rev. ed. 1991.

Schreibman, Ben. United States Baháʼí National Archives, Anna Mikuriya Papers, 1956.

Smith, Peter. *A Concise Encyclopedia of the Baháʼí Faith*. Oxford: Oneworld, 2000.

Sohrab, Ahmad. *Ahmad Sohrab's Diary*. The Heritage Project of the National Spiritual Assembly of the United States, 1914.

Stee, Marjorie. *Haifa Notes*. Baháʼí Archives Canada, Laura Davis Papers (15-24 January 1956).

Stirratt, Charlotte. *Pilgrim Notes of Charlotte Stirratt - written to the Lisbon friends, April 30 1956*. Baháʼí World Centre.

Taherzadeh, Adib, *The Child of the Covenant*. Oxford: George Ronald, 2000.

— *The Covenant of Bahá'u'lláh*. Oxford: George Ronald, 1992.

— *The Revelation of Bahá'u'lláh*, vol. 3. Oxford: George Ronald, 1983.

Takano, Hiroyasu. 'Words of the beloved Guardian to Mr. Hiroyasu Takano in Haifa, March 1954'. Translated from the Japanese in *Asia Teaching Committee Report, 1959*, in United States Bahá'í National Archives.

Thorne, Adam. *'This glorious harvest of victory' – the 1963 World Congress*. Unpublished, 2013.

Universal House of Justice. *Century of Light*. Haifa: Bahá'í World Centre, 2001.

— *Mason Remey and Those Who Followed Him*, 1997. Available at: http://bahai-library.com/uhj_mason_remey_followers.

— *Messages from the Universal House of Justice, 1963–1968*. Wilmette: Bahá'í Publishing Trust, 1996.

Vickers, Patrick (Paddy). Account in *UK Bahá'í Histories*, 2011.Available at: http://bahaihistoryuk.wordpress.com/2011/12/16/paddy-vickers/.

The Vision of Shoghi Effendi, Proceedings of the Association for Bahá'í Studies Ninth Annual Conference, November 2–4, 1984, Ottawa, Canada. Ottawa: Association for Bahá'í Studies, 1993.

Vreeland, Claire. *And the Trees Clapped Their Hands*. Oxford: George Ronald, 1994.

Wade, John, Account in *UK Bahá'í Histories*, 2015. Available at: http://bahaihistoryuk.wordpress.com/2015/03/16/john-wade-1910-1998.

Washington, Bill. United States Bahá'í National Archives, Beatrice Ashton Papers, 1957.

Wiebers, Jennifer. Personal communication, 2012.

Wilkin, Mary Magdalene. *Notes, June 3rd, 1957*. United States Bahá'í National Archives, Charlotte Linfoot Papers, Item 148, 1957.

Whitehead, O. Z. . *Shoghi Effendi*, audio recording at the Irish Summer School, Waterford, 1990.

Woolson, Gayle. *Pilgrim Notes*. United States Bahá'í National Archives, Albert Windust Papers, 1956. Available at: bahai-library.com/woolson_haifa_notes.

Woodward, Michael. *The Unforgettable Hands of the Cause*. New Delhi: Bahá'í Publishing Trust, 2008.

REFERENCES

Preface

1. *Ministry of the Custodians*, p. 113.
2. Letter from Shoghi Effendi to the National Spiritual Assembly of the United States and Canada, 28 July 1936, in Shoghi Effendi, *Messages to America, 1932-1946*, p. 7.
3. Letter from Shoghi Effendi to the National Spiritual Assembly of the United States and Canada, 14 November 1936, ibid. p. 8.
4. Shoghi Effendi, 'The Challenging Requirements of the Present Hour', letter to the National Spiritual Assembly of the United States and Canada, 5 June 1947, in Shoghi Effendi, *Citadel of Faith*, p. 12.
5. 'Abdu'l-Bahá, quoted by Shoghi Effendi, ibid. p. 28.
6. Letter from Shoghi Effendi to the National Spiritual Assembly of the United States, 18 July 1953, ibid. pp. 120–21.
7. Letter from Shoghi Effendi to the National Spiritual Assembly of the United States, 21 September 1957, ibid. p. 157.
8. May and Mary Maxwell, *Haifa Talks*, pp. 12–13.
9. Ben Guhrke, letter written in June 1954.
10. Marion Hofman, *The World Crusade*, pp. 60–61.
11. Shoghi Effendi, *Directives from the Guardian*, no. 147, p. 54.

Introduction

1. 'Abdu'l-Bahá, *Will and Testament*, para. 17.
2. ibid. para. 25.
3. ibid.
4. ibid. para. 36.
5. The Universal House of Justice, *Century of Light*, pp. 77–8.
6. Jessie Revell, letter dated 9 July 1952 'to the friends in America'. Available at: http:/www.bahai-library.com/revell_letters.

The Significance and Launching of the Ten Year Crusade

1. Shoghi Effendi, *God Passes By*, p. 329.
2. Letter from Shoghi Effendi, 4 May 1953, in Shoghi Effendi, *Messages to the Bahá'í World, 1950-1957*, pp. 153–6.
3. The Universal House of Justice, *Century of Light*, pp. 90–91.
4. Shoghi Effendi, *World Order of Bahá'u'lláh*, p. 35.

5. ibid. p. 98.
6. Letter from Shoghi Effendi, 4 May 1953, in Shoghi Effendi, *Messages to the Bahá'í World*, pp. 154-5.
7. The Universal House of Justice, *Century of Light*, p. 79.
8. Shoghi Effendi, *Unfolding Destiny*, p. 261.
9. *The Bahá'í World*, vol. XX, p. 95.
10. ibid. p. 96.
11. Letter from Shoghi Effendi, 30 June 1952, in Shoghi Effendi, *Messages to the Bahá'í World, 1950-1957*, pp. 38-9.
12. 'Alí Nakhjavání, *The Ten Year Crusade*, p. 8.
13. *The Bahá'í World*, vol. XX, p. 97.
14. Cablegram from Shoghi Effendi, 8 October 1952, in Shoghi Effendi, *Messages to the Bahá'í World, 1950-1957*, p. 40.
15. Cablegram from Shoghi Effendi, 30 November 1951, ibid. p. 17.
16. Cablegram from Shoghi Effendi, 8 October 1952, ibid. pp. 40-41.
17. ibid. p. 41.
18. ibid. p. 42.
19. ibid. pp. 152-3.
20. Chapman, *Leroy Ioas*, p. 254.
21. ibid. p. 167.
22. ibid. p. 249.
23. *The Bahá'í World*, vol. XII, pp. 256-7.
24. Cablegram from Shoghi Effendi, 28 May 1953, in Shoghi Effendi, *Messages to the Bahá'í World, 1950-1957*, p. 49.
25. ibid. p. 49.
26. Shoghi Effendi, *Dawn of a New Day*, p. 164-5.
27. Logsdon-Dubois, *Knight with a Briefcase*, p. 144.

1953: Projects at the World Centre

1. Marion Hofman, *The World Crusade*, p. 27.
2. Giachery, 'An Account of the Preparatory Work in Italy', in *The Bahá'í World*, vol. XII, p. 243.
3. Rabbaní, *The Priceless Pearl*, pp. 174-5.
4. Giachery, 'An Account of the Preparatory Work in Italy', in *The Bahá'í World*, vol. XII, p. 243.
5. ibid.
6. Ben Weeden,'Reports on the Construction of the Arcade', ibid. p. 251.
7. Giachery, 'An Account of the Preparatory Work in Italy', in *The Bahá'í World*, vol. XII, p. 244.
8. Giachery, *Shoghi Effendi*, p. 97.
9. Giachery, 'An Account of the Preparatory Work in Italy', in *The Bahá'í World*, vol. XII, p. 246.
10. Giachery, *Shoghi Effendi*, pp. 98, 100.
11. ibid. pp. 98, 101.
12. ibid. pp. 104-06.
13. ibid. p. 106; see also Chapman, *Leroy Ioas*, pp. 224-5.
14. ibid. pp. 106-07.

15. Chapman, *Leroy Ioas*, pp. 226-7.
16. ibid. pp. 231-2.
17. Smith, *A Concise Encyclopedia of the Bahá'í Faith*, pp. 319-20.
18. Chapman, *Leroy Ioas*, p. 224.
19. Letter from Shoghi Effendi, October 1953, in *Messages to the Bahá'í World*, p. 170.
20. Marion Hofman, *The World Crusade*, pp. 14-15.
21. Rohani, *Sweet and Enchanting Stories*, pp. 18-19.
22. Chapman, *Leroy Ioas*, p. 213; Giachery, *Shoghi Effendi*, p. 210.
23. Chapman, *Leroy Ioas*, pp. 213-14.
24. ibid. p. 214.
25. ibid. pp. 214-15.
26. ibid. pp. 215-16.
27. Giachery, *Shoghi Effendi*, p. 170.
28. *The Bahá'í World*, vol. XII, p. 550.
29. Giachery, *Shoghi Effendi*, p. 170.
30. ibid. p. 173.
31. ibid.
32. Rohani, *Sweet and Enchanting Stories*, pp. 19-20.
33. Reimholz, *Pilgrimage to Haifa*, p. 6.
34. Chapman, *Leroy Ioas*, pp. 211-12.

1953: Four Intercontinental Teaching Conferences

1. *The Bahá'í World*, vol. XII, pp. 124-5; Chapman, *Leroy Ioas*, p. 200.
2. Chapman, *Leroy Ioas*, p. 201; *The Bahá'í World*, vol. XII, p. 120.
3. ibid. pp. 130-31.
4. Freeman, *From Copper to Gold*, pp. 270-71.
5. 'Alí Nakhjavání, "Glimpse of the life of Enoch Olinga", interview in July 2012.
6. Khadem, *Zikrullah Khadem*, p. 72.
7. ibid. p. 73.
8. Marguerite Sears, *Bill*, p. 16.
9. Hainsworth, *Looking Back in Wonder*, p. 167.
10. Chapman, *Leroy Ioas*, pp. 203-04.
11. ibid. p. 258.
12. *The Bahá'í World*, vol. XII, pp. 152-3.
13. ibid. p. 147.
14. Chapman, *Leroy Ioas*, pp. 250-51.
15. Shoghi Effendi, *Messages to the Bahá'í World*, p. 147.
16. Chapman, *Leroy Ioas*, p. 250.
17. Freeman, *From Copper to Gold*, p. 269.
18. ibid. p. 270.
19. Ramona Brown, in USBNA, Alice Dudley Papers, p. 2.
20. Chapman, *Leroy Ioas*, p. 258; see also Freeman, *From Copper to Gold*.
21. Ben Guhrke, *Ben's Story*, p. 6.
22. *The Bahá'í World*, vol. XII, p. 666; Shoghi Effendi, *Messages to the Bahá'í World*, p. 55.
23. Kolstoe, *Crazy Lovers of Bahá'u'lláh*.

24. *The Bahá'í World*, vol. XII, p. 171.
25. Pfaff-Grossman, *Hermann Grossmann*, p. 138.
26. Furutan, The Story of My Heart, p. 95.
27. Pfaff-Grossman, *Hermann Grossmann*, p. 138.
28. Chapman, *Leroy Ioas*, p. 223
29. *The Bahá'í World*, vol. XII, pp. 173, 177.
30. Furútan, *The Story of My Heart*, p. 96.
31. Freeman, *From Copper to Gold*, p. 276.
32. *The Bahá'í World*, pp. 181, 188.
33. Saunders, *Of Wars and Worship*, p. 150; Faizi-Moore, *Faizi*, p. 206.
34. Shoghi Effendi, *Dawn of a New Day*, p. 152.
35. Faizi-Moore, *Faizi*, p. 205.
36. ibid. pp. 205–6.
37. Freeman, *From Copper to Gold*, p. 283.
38. *The Bahá'í World*, vol. XII, p. 182.
39. ibid. p. 183.
40. Bahá'í World News Service, 'Royal Welcome at Jubilee in Samoa', 30 November 2004.
41. Furútan, *The Story of My Heart*, pp. 98, 100.
42. ibid. p. 101.
43. Shoghi Effendi, *Messages to the Bahá'í World*, p. 172.

1953: Pilgrims, Visitors and Pioneers

1. Freeman, *From Copper to Gold*, p. 263.
2. ibid. p. 264.
3. ibid. p. 278.
4. *The Bahá'í World*, vol. XII, p. 187.
5. Freeman, *From Copper to Gold*, p. 283.
6. ibid. p. 286.
7. ibid. pp. 298, 300.
8. ibid. p. 301.
9. ibid. p. 311.
10. Elsie Austin, audio recording, 23 Nov 1973.
11. *The Bahá'í World*, vol. XV, p. 538.
12. Elsie Austin, audio recording, 23 Nov 1973.
13. Bach, *The Circle of Faith*, p. 13.
14. ibid. p. 58.
15. ibid. p. 59.
16. ibid. pp. 61–2.
17. ibid. pp. 62–5.
18. ibid. pp. 69–70.
19. ibid. pp. 76–7.
20. ibid. p. 79.
21. Marguerite Sears, *Bill*, p. 16.
22. Ben Levy and Marguerite Sears, USBNA, Bertha Hyde Kirkpatrick Papers, pp. 1–4.
23. ibid. p. 12.
24. ibid. p. 14.

25. ibid. pp. 15–16.
26. ibid. p. 17.
27. The Universal House of Justice, *Century of Light*, p. 45.
28. Marguerite Sears, *Bill*, pp. 17–18.
29. ibid.
30. ibid. p. 20.
31. ibid. pp. 20–22.
32. ibid. pp. 23–5.
33. ibid. p. 32.
34. *The Bahá'í World*, vol. XII, p. 687; Khadem, *Zikrullah Khadem*, p. 98.
35. Shoghi Effendi, *Messages to the Bahá'í World*, p. 170.
36. Faizí, *Milly*, pp. 23–4.
37. ibid. p. 24.
38. *The Bahá'í World: In Memoriam, 1992–1997*, p. 227.
39. Lee, *The Establishment of the Baha'i Faith in West Africa: The First Decade, 1952–1962*, pp. 97–100.
40. *The Bahá'í World: In Memoriam, 1992–1997*, pp. 225–7.
41. Philip Hainsworth, in *Bahá'í Journal UK*, May 2001, p. 1.
42. *Bahá'í News*, No. 259 (Sept. 1952), p. 4.
43. *Bahá'í News*, No. 277 (March 1954), p. 8.
44. *The Bahá'í World*, vol. XIX, p. 595.
45. Lamb, *The Beginnings of the Bahá'í Faith in Latin America*, p. 29.
46. Saunders, *Of Wars and Worship*, pp. 152–4.
47. Gertrude Blum, USBNA, Charlotte Linfoot Papers, p. 3.
48. Saunders, *Of Wars and Worship*, pp. 154–5.
49. Gertrude Blum, USBNA, Charlotte Linfoot Papers, p. 2.
50. Saunders, *Of Wars and Worship*, pp. 151, 155–6.
51. Rutstein, *He Loved and Served*, p. 50.
52. ibid. pp. 170–72.
53. *The Bahá'í World: In Memoriam, 1992–1997*, p. 352.
54. Rutstein, *He Loved and Served*, pp. 171–2.
55. Alan McCormick, USBNA, Nancy Bowditch Papers, p. 1.
56. ibid. pp. 1–2.
57. ibid. p. 2.
58. ibid. pp. 2–3.
59. ibid. p. 3.
60. Muhájír, *Dr Muhajir*, pp. 22–4.
61. Violette Nakhjavani, *Pioneering in the Time of Guardian,* audio recording, 20 January 1981.
62. Sohrab, *Ahmad Sohrab's Diary*, 14 Mar. 1914, p. 791.
63. Maud and Albert Reimholz, *Pilgrimage to Haifa*, USBNA, Albert L. and Maud S. Reimholz Personal Recollections, 1954, pp. 6, 9.
64. Mohsen Enayat, *A Little Story from Fezzan*, letter report, 11 December 2014.
65. ibid.
66. Rowshan Mustafa, email to the author, 1 July 2014; Mohsen Enayat, email 3 July 2014; Mohsen Enayat, *A Little Story from Fezzan*, letter report, 11 December 2014.

1954: Helping Pilgrims Understand the Goals of the Ten Year Crusade

1. Letter on behalf of Shoghi Effendi to the Treasurer of the National Spiritual Assembly of the Bahá'ís of Canada, 2 January 1954, in Shoghi Effendi, *Messages to Canada*, pp. 167–8.
2. Chapman, *Leroy Ioas*, pp. 210.
3. Valera Allen, *Haifa Impressions*, p. 3.
4. Chapman, *Leroy Ioas*, pp. 211.
5. Marion Hofman, *Notes Taken in Haifa*, p. 1.
6. ibid. p. 2.
7. ibid. pp. 3, 5.
8. ibid. pp. 6–7.
9. ibid. pp. 10–11.
10. ibid. p. 19.
11. ibid. p. 16.
12. ibid. p. 14.
13. Maud and Albert Reimholz, *Pilgrimage to Haifa*, pp. 1–2.
14. ibid. p. 4.
15. ibid. p. 4.
16. Irene Bennett, *My First Pilgrimage to Haifa*, p. 2.
17. ibid. pp. 1–2.
18. ibid. pp. 2–3.
19. ibid. p. 3.
20. ibid. p. 5.
21. ibid. p. 6.
22. Reimholz, *Pilgrimage to Haifa*, pp. 6–7.
23. Bennett, *My First Pilgrimage to Haifa*, p. 7.
24. ibid. pp. 8–9.
25. Hiroyasu Takano, 'Words of the beloved Guardian to Mr. Hiroyasu Takano in Haifa, March 1954', p. 1.
26. Bennett, *My First Pilgrimage to Haifa*, p. 10.
27. ibid. p. 12.
28. William Sears, *Pilgrimage to Haifa*, part 2, pp. 2–3.
29. ibid. p. 4.
30. ibid. part 1, pp. 2–3.
31. ibid. p. 4.
32. ibid. part 2, p. 6.
33. ibid. part 1, pp. 7–8.
34. ibid. part 3, p. 2.
35. Chapman, *Leroy Ioas*, pp. 185–6.
36. ibid.
37. Shoghi Effendi, *Messages to the Bahá'í World*, p. 59.
38. Glenn Cameron, *A Basic Bahá'í Chronology*, p. 316.
39. Shoghi Effendi, *Messages to the Bahá'í World*, p. 62.
40. ibid. p. 66.
41. ibid. pp. 61–2, 68.

1954: Pilgrims and Pilgrim Knights

1. Giachery, *Shoghi Effendi*, p. 113.
2. Ramona Brown, in USBNA, Alice Dudley Papers, p. 2.
3. Marion Hofman, *The World Crusade*, p. 188a.
4. Clara Edge, *Haifa Notes*, p. 1.
5. ibid. pp. 4–5.
6. Roy Mottahedeh, in USBNA, Mildred Mottahedeh Papers, p. 27.
7. Edith McLaren, *Notes of the Pilgrimage of Edith McLaren*, May 2–10, 1954, p. 1.
8. ibid. p. 2.
9. Shoghi Effendi, *Messages to the Bahá'í World*, p. 64.
10. 'Alí Nakhjavání, 'The Ten Year Crusade', p. 18.
11. Ruth Moffett, 'A Word Picture of Shoghi Effendi', in *Pilgrim's Notes of Ruth Moffett*, p. 10.
12. ibid. p. 15.
13. Shoghi Effendi, *Citadel of Faith*, pp. 127–8.
14. Deborah McKinley, *Violet and Hugh McKinley: Knights of Bahá'u'lláh for Cyprus 1953–1963*, pp. 9–10.
15. Giachery, *Shoghi Effendi*, pp. 153–4.
16. Valera Allen, *Haifa Impressions*, pp. 2–3.
17. ibid. p. 5.
18. ibid. p. 6.
19. ibid.
20. Olivia Kelsey, in USBNA, Olivia Kelsey Papers, p. 12.
21. Wikipedia, https://en.wikipedia.org/wiki/Josephine_Baker
22. Allen, *Haifa Impressions*, pp. 2, 7–8.
23. ibid. p. 8.
24. Alice Dudley, in USBNA, Alice Dudley Papers-3, *Notes on Pilgrimage to Haifa*, p. 1. See Giachery, *Shoghi Effendi*, pp. 127–9; also Redman, *Shoghi Effendi Through the Pilgrim's Eye*, vol. 1, pp. 376–9.
25. Allen, *Haifa Impressions*, pp. 8–12.
26. ibid. pp. 12–13.
27. ibid. p. 14.
28. ibid. p. 6.
29. Bernard Leach, *Excerpts from a letter . . .*
30. Olivia Kelsey, in USBNA, Olivia Kelsey Papers, pp. 9–10.
31. ibid. p. 12.
32. ibid. p. 13.
33. ibid. p. 15.
34. Laura Davis, *Pilgrim Notes,* document no. 156.019, no. 12, in USBNA.
35. Laura Davis, *Pilgrim Notes*, document no. 057-017-6, in Bahá'í National Archives, Canada, Laura Davis Papers.
36. ibid.
37. ibid.
38. ibid.
39. Balyuzi, *'Abdu'l-Bahá*, p. 54.
40. Laura Davis, *Pilgrim Notes*, document no. 057-017-6, in Bahá'í National Archives, Canada, Laura Davis Papers.

41. ibid.
42. Taherzadeh, *The Covenant of Bahá'u'lláh*, pp. 345–6.
43. Gayle Woolson, *Haifa Notes*, p. 5.
44. Shoghi Effendi, *Messages to the Bahá'í World*, p. 69.

1955

1. Giachery, *Shoghi Effendi*, pp. 149–50.
2. Chapman, *Leroy Ioas*, p. 239.
3. *The Bahá'í World*, vol. XIII, p. 424.
4. ibid. p. 417.
5. Shoghi Effendi, *Messages to the Bahá'í World*, p. 64.
6. Giachery, *Shoghi Effendi*, pp. 157–9.
7. ibid. pp. 167–8.
8. ibid. pp. 161–3; *The Bahá'í World*, vol. XIII, p. 422.
9. ibid. p. 164.
10. Sheila Banani, *Pilgrim Notes of Sheila and Amin Banani*, p. 3.
11. Giachery, *Shoghi Effendi*, pp. 165–6.
12. Marion Hofman, *The World Crusade*, p. 386.
13. *The Bahá'í World*, vol. XVIII, pp. 390–91.
14. *The Bahá'í World*, vol. XIII, pp. 789–90.
15. Marion Hofman, *The World Crusade*, p. 394.
16. *The Bahá'í World*, vol. XIII, pp. 789–90.
17. *Bahá'í News*, no. 294 (August 1955), pp. 6–7. See also Elias, *Moths into Eagles*.
18. Marion Hofman, *The World Crusade*, pp. 395–6, 400.
19. Whitehead, *Shoghi Effendi*, audio.
20. ibid.
21. ibid.
22. ibid.
23. Audrey Robarts, 'Reminiscences about Shoghi Effendi', in *The Vision of Shoghi Effendi*, p. 166.
24. Tom Roberts, email to the author, 8 March 2014.
25. John A. Robarts, 'A Few Reminiscences about Shoghi Effendi . . .', in *The Vision of Shoghi Effendi*, p. 172.
26. Tom Roberts, email to the author, 8 March 2014.
27. John A. Robarts, 'A Few Reminiscences about Shoghi Effendi . . .', in *The Vision of Shoghi Effendi*, p. 175.
28. ibid. pp. 175–6.
29. Adrienne Morgan, *Claire Gung*, pp. 23–4.
30. ibid. pp. 24–5.
31. ibid. p. 26.
32. ibid.
33. ibid. pp. 26–7.
34. ibid. pp. 27–8.
35. ibid. pp. 29–30.
36. E. S. Archibald, USBNA, Doris Ballard Papers, p. 1.
37. ibid. p. 2.
38. ibid. pp. 2–3.

39. ibid. p. 3.
40. ibid. p. 4.
41. ibid.
42. Dorothy Ferraby, *UK Baháʼí Histories*.
43. Shoghi Effendi, *Messages to the Baháʼí World*, pp. 76–8.
44. Kenneth Christian, USBNA, Hattie Chamberlain Papers, p. 2.
45. ibid. p. 3.
46. Nureddin Momtazi, USBNA, Viola Tuttle Papers, p. 2.
47. Christian, USBNA, Hattie Chamberlain Papers, p. 5.
48. Momtazi, USBNA, Viola Tuttle Papers, p. 18.
49. ibid. pp. 7, 9, 11.
50. Christian, USBNA, Hattie Chamberlain Papers, p. 6.
51. ibid. pp. 6, 8.
52. ibid. p. 10.
53. ibid.

1956

1. Kenneth Christian, USBNA, Hattie Chamberlain Papers, pp. 12–14.
2. ibid. p. 15.
3. Marjorie Stee, *Haifa Notes*, Baháʼí Archives Canada, Laura Davis Papers, p. 4.
4. ibid. p. 5.
5. Gayle Woolson, USBNA, Albert Windust Papers, p. 4.
6. ibid. pp. 8–9.
7. Ben Schreibman, USBNA, Anna Mikuriya Papers, p. 3.
8. Pfaff-Grossmann, *Hermann Grossmann*, pp. 166–7.
9. Ehsan Reyhani, personal communication, 28 June 2015.
10. Pfaff-Grossmann, *The Life of a Pioneer*, pp. 46–47.
11. ibid. pp. 48, 54.
12. Sheila Banani, *Pilgrim Notes of Sheila and Amin Banani*, 2 September 1975, The Heritage Project of the National Spiritual Assembly of the United States.
13. ibid.
14. *The Baháʼí World*, vol. XIII, pp. 284–5.
15. Marion Hofman, *The World Crusade*, p. 354.
16. ibid. pp. 335–6.
17. Rowshan Mustapha, email 19 November 2014.
18. Elsie Austin, audio recording, The Heritage Project of the National Spiritual Assembly of the United States.
19. *The Baháʼí World*, vol. XII, pp. 721–7, 744–8, 753–7, 760–61, 763–5, 767–9, 771–4.
20. Shoghi Effendi, *Messages to the Baháʼí World*, pp. 92–3.
21. Charlotte Stirratt, *Pilgrim Notes*, p. 1.
22. Mohtadi, USBNA, Charlotte Linfoot Papers, pp. 1, 6.
23. *The Baháʼí World*, vol. XIV, pp. 386–7.
24. Chapman, *Leroy Ioas*, pp. 286–7.

1957: The Crusade Surges Ahead

1. Bill Washington, USBNA, Beatrice Ashton Papers, p. 2.
2. ibid. p. 3.
3. ibid. p. 4.
4. *Bahá'í News*, no. 334 (December 1958), p. 4.
5. Chapman, *Leroy Ioas*, p. 263.
6. Pfaff-Grossmann, *The Life of a Pioneer*, pp. 40–41.
7. 'Enoch Olinga: The pioneering years', in *Bahá'í News*, no. 638 (May 1984), p. 8.
8. Ursula Samandari, *Notes of My Pilgrimage*, Marion Hofman Papers.
9. Rabbani, *Enoch Olinga, Hand of the Cause of God*, pp. 20–21.
10. Harper, *Lights of Fortitude*, pp. 466–7.
11. Rabbani, *Enoch Olinga*, pp. 22–3.
12. Samandari, *Notes of My Pilgrimage*, Marion Hofman Papers.
13. Rabbani, *Enoch Olinga*, p. 66.
14. Suzanne Locke-Nyrenda, email report, p. 3.
15. Rabbani, *Enoch Olinga*, p. 23.
16. ibid. pp. 62–3.
17. 'Alí Nakhjavání, 'Glimpse of the life of Enoch Olinga'.
18. Rabbani, *Enoch Olinga*, pp. 26–7.
19. Aileen Beale, letter dated 27 February 1957, Marion Hofman Papers.
20. Cardin, *The Bright Glass of the Heart*, pp. 326–7.
21. David Hofman, *George Townshend*, p. 365.
22. Shoghi Effendi, *Messages to the Bahá'í World*, p. 174.
23. Shoghi Effendi, *The World Order of Bahá'u'lláh*, pp. 3–4.
24. Rabbani, *Priceless Pearl*, p. 445.
25. Alice Dudley, USBNA, Alice Dudley Papers-6, *Pilgrimage to Haifa*, p. 1.
26. ibid. p. 4.
27. ibid. pp. 4–5.
28. ibid. p. 6.
29. ibid. pp. 7–8.
30. ibid. pp. 10–11.
31. ibid. pp. 8–9.
32. ibid. pp. 9–10, 13.
33. ibid. pp. 12–13.
34. ibid. p. 13.
35. ibid. p. 15.
36. Alice Dudley, USBNA, Alice Dudley Papers-3, p. 1.
37. Isobel Sabri, *Pilgrim Notes*, p. 2.
38. Alice Dudley, USBNA, Alice Dudley Papers-6, *Pilgrimage to Haifa*, pp. 15–16.
39. Taherzadeh, *The Revelation of Bahá'u'lláh*, vol. 3, pp. 68–9.
40. Alice Dudley, USBNA, Alice Dudley Papers-6, *Pilgrimage to Haifa*, p. 17.
41. ibid. pp. 18–20.
42. ibid. p. 21.
43. ibid. pp. 21–2.
44. ibid. p. 18.
45. Isobel Sabri, *Pilgrim Notes*, pp. 3–5.
46. Alice Dudley, USBNA, Alice Dudley Papers-3, pp. 1–2.

47. Isobel Sabri, *Pilgrim Notes*, p. 10.
48. Alice Dudley, USBNA, Alice Dudley Papers-6, *Pilgrimage to Haifa*, p. 11.
49. ibid. p. 13.
50. Mayberry, *The Great Adventure*, p. 139.
51. ibid. p. 140.
52. ibid. p. 141.
53. ibid. p. 142.
54. ibid. p. 143.
55. ibid. p. 144.
56. Florence Mayberry, letter to Hand of the Cause 'Alí-Akbar Furútan, 30 September 1969, addendum to *Pilgrim Notes*, The Heritage Project of the National Spiritual Assembly of the United States.
57. Jennifer Wiebers, story told to Jennifer by her parents.
58. Mayberry, *The Great Adventure*, pp. 144–45.
59. *The Bahá'í World*, vol. XIII, p. 270.
60. Shoghi Effendi, *Messages to Alaska*, p. 17.
61. *Bahá'í News*, No. 329, July 1958, p. 9.
62. Marion Hofman, *The World Crusade*, p. 101.
63. Shoghi Effendi, *Messages to the Bahá'í World*, pp. 105–6.
64. *The Bahá'í World*, vol. XIII, pp. 409, 411.
65. ibid. p. 419.
66. ibid. p. 422.
67. Chapman, *Leroy Ioas*, p. 245.
68. *The Bahá'í World*, vol. XIII, p. 422; Giachery, *Shoghi Effendi*, p. 166.
69. Nakhjavani, Violette, *Notes from the Archives Building in Haifa*, p. 1.
70. *The Bahá'í World*, vol. XIII, pp. 429–33.

1957: Shoghi Effendi's Last Visitors

1. Ian Semple, in *UK Bahá'í Histories*.
2. Ian Semple, 'The Guardianship and the Universal House of Justice', p. 10.
3. Pfaff-Grossmann, *Hermann Grossmann*, p. 166.
4. ibid. pp. 167–8.
5. ibid. p. 165.
6. Logsdon-Dubois, *Knight with a Briefcase*, pp. 194–5.
7. ibid. p. 201.
8. ibid. pp. 202–5.
9. ibid. p. 206.
10. ibid. p. 198.
11. ibid. pp. 208–11.
12. ibid. pp. 217–19.
13. Elmer and Gladys Beasley, *Our Pilgrimage to Haifa*, pp. 1–2.
14. ibid. pp. 3–4.
15. ibid. pp. 4–5, 7.
16. ibid. p. 9.
17. ibid. pp. 16–17.
18. Mary Magdalene Wilkin, USBNA, Charlotte Linfoot Papers, pp. 1, 3.
19. Shoghi Effendi, *Unfolding Destiny*, pp. 364–5.

20. Thelma Allison, *Pilgrimage to Haifa,* USBNA, Sam & Mildred McClellan Papers, p. 1.
21. ibid.
22. ibid. p. 2.
23. ibid. pp. 2–3.
24. ibid. p. 4.
25. ibid.
26. ibid. p. 6.
27. ibid. p. 2.
28. Roger Dahl and Lewis Walker, archivists, USBNA, email 20 Dec. 2014.
29. Bill Allison, *Pilgrim Notes,* USBNA, Sam & Mildred McClellan Papers, pp. 2–3; Thelma Allison, *Haifa Notes,* USBNA, Evelyn & Floyd Hardin Papers, p. 3.
30. Thelma Allison, *Haifa Notes,* USBNA, Evelyn & Floyd Hardin Papers, p. 8.
31. Thelma Allison, *Pilgrimage to Haifa,* USBNA, Sam & Mildred McClellan Papers, pp. 5–6.
32. ibid. p. 7.
33. ibid. p. 5.
34. Beasley, *Our Pilgrimage to Haifa,* p. 8.
35. Cablegram from Shoghi Effendi, 3 June, in *Messages to the Bahá'í World,* pp. 120–21.
36. ibid. p. 122.
37. ibid. p. 124.
38. Rabbani, *The Priceless Pearl,* p. 234.
39. Ruhe, *Door of Hope,* p. 118.
40. Hornby, *Lights of Guidance,* no. 454, p. 136.
41. Marion Hofman, *The World Crusade,* p. 54.
42. Shoghi Effendi, *Messages to the Bahá'í World,* p. 127.
43. Marguerite Sears, *Bill,* pp. 45–6.
44. ibid. p. 47.
45. John Robarts, 'Reminiscences about Shoghi Effendi', in *The Vision of Shoghi Effendi,* p. 176.
46. Rabbani, *Enoch Olinga, Hand of the Cause of God,* p. 24.

1957: The Passing of the Guardian

1. Rabbani, *The Priceless Pearl,* p. 445.
2. Shoghi Effendi, *Messages to the Bahá'í World,* p. 175.
3. Amatu'l-Bahá Rúḥíyyih Khánum and John Ferraby, *The Passing of Shoghi Effendi,* pp. 3–4.
4. ibid. pp. 6–7.
5. ibid. p. 7.
6. ibid. p. 8.
7. ibid. p. 10.
8. Rabbani, *The Priceless Pearl,* pp. 444–7.
9. Amatu'l-Bahá Rúḥíyyih Khánum and John Ferraby, *The Passing of Shoghi Effendi,* pp. 11–13.
10. Dorothy Ferraby, in *UK Bahá'í Histories.*
11. Amatu'l-Bahá Rúḥíyyih Khánum and John Ferraby, *The Passing of Shoghi Effendi,* pp. 11–13.

12. ibid. pp. 13–15.
13. ibid. pp. 16–17.
14. ibid. p. 17.
15. ibid. pp. 18–19.
16. ibid. pp. 19–21.
17. Marion Hofman, letter to 'the beloved Pioneers of the Islands', 20 November 1957, in Marion Hofman Papers.
18. Giachery, *Shoghi Effendi*, p. 181.
19. Marion Hofman, letter to 'the beloved Pioneers of the Islands', 20 November 1957, in Marion Hofman Papers.
20. Cardin, *The Bright Glass of the Heart*, p. 176.
21. Amatu'l-Bahá Rúḥíyyih Khánum and John Ferraby *The Passing of Shoghi Effendi*, pp. 20, 23; Giachery, *Shoghi Effendi*, p. 182.
22. Marion Hofman, letter to 'the beloved Pioneers of the Islands', 20 November, 1957, in Marion Hofman Papers.
23. ibid.
24. Madeline Hellaby, 'Some thoughts on the Guardian's death', letter to Marion Hofman, 13 November 1957.
25. John Wade, *UK Baháʼí Histories*.
26. Ian Semple, *UK Baháʼí Histories*.
27. *Ministry of the Custodians*, p. xix.
28. Shoghi Effendi, *Messages to the Baháʼí World*, p. 123.
29. ibid. pp. 127–8.
30. *Ministry of the Custodians*, p. 9.
31. Violette Nakhjavani, *A Tribute to Amatu'l-Bahá Rúḥíyyih Khánum*, pp. 61–2.
32. Jalál Kházeh, *After the Passing of the Beloved Guardian*, audio, p. 2.
33. *The Baháʼí World*, vol. XIII, p. 341.
34. Jalál Kházeh, *After the Passing of the Beloved Guardian*, p. 2.
35. ibid. pp. 2–3.
36. ibid. pp. 3–4.
37. Chapman, *Leroy Ioas*, pp. 292–3.
38. Jalál Kházeh, *After the Passing of the Beloved Guardian*, pp. 4–5.
39. ibid. p. 5.
40. ibid.
41. ibid. pp. 5–6.
42. ibid. p. 6.
43. ibid.
44. *Ministry of the Custodians*, pp. 27–35. See also *The Baháʼí World*, vol. XIII, pp. 341–7.
45. *Ministry of the Custodians*, pp. 35–8.
46. Ian Semple, *UK Baháʼí Histories*.
47. Speaking in 1985. Available at: http://web.archive.org/web/20090213152355/http://www.bahaistudy.org/audio-talks.html.
48. Amatu'l-Bahá Rúḥíyyih Khánum, *Eagle and Pillar over Shoghi Effendi's Resting Place*.
49. ibid.
50. ibid.

1958

1. Pfaff-Grossmann, *Hermann Grossmann*, pp. 174–7.
2. *Ministry of the Custodians*, p. 61.
3. ibid. p. 65.
4. ibid. p. 67.
5. ibid. p. 101.
6. Violette Nakhjavani, *A Tribute to Amatu'l-Bahá Rúḥíyyih Khánum*, pp. 62–3.
7. *Bahá'í News*, no. 327 (May 1958), pp. 4, 6.
8. *The Bahá'í World*, vol. XIII, p. 710; Hainsworth, *Looking Back in Wonder*, p. 230.
9. *Bahá'í News*, no. 327 (May 1958), p. 12.
10. *The Bahá'í World*, vol. XIII, pp. 319–20.
11. *Bahá'í News*, no. 328 (June 1958), p. 4.
12. ibid.
13. ibid. pp. 4–5.
14. ibid. p. 5.
15. *The Bahá'í World*, vol. XIII, pp. 323–4.
16. *Bahá'í News*, no. 329 (July 1958), p. 6.
17. ibid. p. 7.
18. *The Bahá'í World*, vol. XIII, p. 325.
19. Collins, *A Tribute to Shoghi Effendi*, quoted in Taherzadeh, *Child of the Covenant*, pp. 315–19.
20. Muhájír, *Dr Muhajir*, pp. 72–4.
21. *The Bahá'í World*, vol. XIX, p. 41.
22. Chapman, *Leroy Ioas*, p. 300.
23. Muhájír, *Dr Muhajir*, pp. 72–4; Chapman, *Leroy Ioas*, p. 300.
24. *The Bahá'í World*, vol. XII, p. 331.
25. Chapman, *Leroy Ioas*, p. 302.
26. Quoted in Cardin, *The Bright Glass of the Heart*, p. 51.
27. *Ministry of the Custodians*, p. 114.
28. ibid. pp. 81–2.
29. Dempsey and Adrienne Morgan, *Servants of the Glory*, p. 1.
30. pp. 2–6.
31. ibid. pp. 9, 14–15.
32. ibid. pp. 18–19.
33. ibid. p. 22.
34. ibid. pp. 29, 36–7, 42.
35. *Ministry of the Custodians*, p. 110.
36. Faizi-Moore, *Faizi*, pp. 245–6.
37. *Ministry of the Custodians*, p. 133.
38. ibid. pp. 117, 135–6.
39. Amatu'l-Bahá Rúḥíyyih Khánum, audio recording of a talk to the Bahá'ís of New York, 5 June 1960.
40. Marion Hofman, *The World Crusade*, pp. 60–61.
41. ibid. p. 87.

1959

1. Letter from the Hands of the Cause in the Holy Land, 14 September 1961, in *Ministry of the Custodians*, pp. 307–8.
2. Marion Hofman, *The World Crusade*, p. 349.
3. Hands of the Cause in the Holy Land, Riḍván Message 1959, in *Ministry of the Custodians*, pp. 137-38.
4. Cardin, *The Bright Glass of the Heart*, p. 143.
5. William Maxwell, USBNA, Asia Teaching Committee, William Maxwell Papers, p. 1.
6. ibid. pp. 2-3.
7. ibid. pp. 15-16.
8. ibid. pp. 16-17.
9. ibid. p. 17.
10. ibid. p. 18.
11. ibid. pp. 18-19.
12. ibid. p. 19.
13. ibid. p. 10.
14. ibid. pp. 11-12.
15. ibid. p. 20.
16. Jalál Kházeh, *After the Passing of the Beloved Guardian*, pp. 6-7.
17. Hands of the Cause, Conclave Message, 4 November 1959, in *Ministry of the Custodians*, pp. 166-68.
18. Personal notes.
19. Amatu'l-Bahá Rúhíyyih Khánum, audio recording of a talk to the Bahá'ís of New York, 5 June 1960.
20. ibid.
21. Leroy Ioas, letter to Dhikru'lláh Khádem, 1 November 1959, USBNA, Leroy Ioas Papers, 1900-1952 Papers.
22. Hainsworth, *Looking Back in Wonder*, p. 238.
23. John Wade, *UK Bahá'í Histories*.
24. ibid.
25. Letter from the Hands of the Cause in the Holy Land to all National Spiritual Assemblies, 4 November 1959, in *Ministry of the Custodians*, p. 171.

1960

1. 'News from the World Centre of the Faith', in *Ministry of the Custodians*, pp. 179, 181.
2. Geertrui Bates Ankersmit, *Bahá'í Story*, p. 10.
3. ibid. pp. 10–11.
4. ibid. p. 11.
5. Suzy Cardell, email to the author, 9 October 2013.
6. Bates Ankersmit, *Bahá'í Story*, pp. 10-13, 15.
7. Richard Mereness, email to the author, February 2015.
8. Riḍván Message, 1960, in *Ministry of the Custodians*, pp. 185-7.
9. ibid. pp. 184-5.
10. Letter from the Hands of the Cause in the Holy Land to the Hands of the Cause of God throughout the World, 8 January 1960, ibid. p. 177.

11. Ian Semple, *UK Bahá'í Histories.*
12. Amatu'l-Bahá Rúḥíyyih Khánum, audio recording of a talk to the Bahá'ís of New York, 5 June 1960.
13. Ian Semple, *UK Bahá'í Histories.*
14. Faizi-Moore, *Faizi*, pp. 248–9.
15. Marguerite Sears, *Bill*, p. 76.
16. Quoted in a letter from the Hands of the Cause in the Holy Land to all National Spiritual Assemblies, 15 October 1960, in *Ministry of the Custodians*, p. 232.
17. First Conclave of the Hands of the Cause, Proclamation to the Bahá'ís of East and West, ibid. pp. 35–6.
18. Letter from the Hands of the Cause in the Holy Land to the Hands of the Cause of God and the National Spiritual Assemblies throughout the Bahá'í World, 10 May 1960, ibid. p. 198.
19. Letter from the Hands of the Cause in the Holy Land to the Hands of the Cause of God throughout the World, 7 July 1960, ibid. p. 211.
20. Letter from the Hands of the Cause in the Holy Land to the Hands of the Cause of God, 15 June 1960, ibid. p. 208.
21. Jalál Kházeh, letter to Silvia and Leroy Ioas, 12 June 1960, p. 3.
22. Quoted in *Ministry of the Custodians*, pp. 213, 215, 217.
23. ibid. pp. 213–14.
24. ibid.
25. Jalál Kházeh, letter to Silvia and Leroy Ioas, 12 June 1960, p. 3.
26. Quoted in *Ministry of the Custodians*, p. 217.
27. Jalál Kházeh, letter to Silvia and Leroy Ioas, p. 3.
28. Cablegram from the Hands of the Cause to all National Spiritual Assemblies, 3 August 1960, in *Ministry of the Custodians*, p. 223.
29. Letter from the Hands of the Cause in the Holy Land to the Hands of the Cause of God, 9 August 1960, ibid. p. 224.
30. Letter from the Hands of the Cause in the Holy Land to the Hands of the Cause of God, 14 June 1963, ibid. p. 432.
31. Letter from the Hands of the Cause in the Holy Land to the Hands of the Cause of God, 16 July 1961, ibid. p. 295.
32. Chapman, *Leroy Ioas*, pp. 310–11.
33. Jennifer Wiebers, personal communication, 2012.
34. Agnes Alexander, letter to Marion Hofman, 24 October 1960, Marion Hofman Papers.
35. The Universal House of Justice, *Mason Remey and Those Who Followed Him*, pp. 4–5.
36. The Universal House of Justice, letter to an individual believer, 4 June 1997.
37. Harper, *Lights of Fortitude*, pp. 305–6.
38. Chapman, *Leroy Ioas*, p. 309.
39. Jalál Kházeh, *After the Passing of the Guardian*, p. 1.
40. *Bahá'í News*, no. 420 (March 1966), p. 2, in *Lights of Guidance*, no. 1080, p. 322.
41. *Ministry of the Custodians*, p. 219.
42. Letter from the Hands of the Cause in the Holy Land to all National Spiritual Assemblies, 27 August 1960, ibid. p. 228.

43. Conclave Message from the Hands of the Cause to the Bahá'ís of East and West, 2 November 1960, ibid. pp. 238-9.
44. ibid. pp. 239, 245.
45. Kolstoe, *Crazy Lovers of Bahá'u'lláh*.
46. ibid.
47. ibid.
48. ibid.
49. ibid.
50. ibid.

1961

1. Dermod Knox, transcript of an audio recording, 3 September 2013.
2. Dermod Knox, *UK Bahá'í Histories*.
3. ibid.
4. Dermod Knox, transcript of an audio recording, 3 September 2013.
5. ibid.
6. Dermod Knox, *UK Bahá'í Histories*.
7. *The Bahá'í World*, vol. XIII, pp. 705-9; Hainsworth, *Looking Back in Wonder*, pp. 217-18.
8. *The Bahá'í World*, vol. XIII, p. 705.
9. Hainsworth, *Looking Back in Wonder*, p. 241.
10. *The Bahá'í World*, vol. XIII, pp. 713-14.
11. ibid. pp. 715-17.
12. Amatu'l-Bahá Rúḥíyyih Khánum, letter to the National Spiritual Assembly of Central and East Africa, 11 February 1961, USBNA, Amelia Collins Papers.
13. Amatu'l-Bahá Rúḥíyyih Khánum, letter to the National Spiritual Assemblies of the United States and Canada, 9 March 1961, USBNA, Amelia Collins Papers.
14. *Ministry of the Custodians*, pp. 259-62.
15. ibid. pp. 263-4.
16. *The Bahá'í World*, vol. XIII, pp. 395-7.
17. Conclave Message 1960, from the Hands of the Cause to the Bahá'ís of East and West, 2 November 1960, in *Ministry of the Custodians*, p. 242.
18. 'Introduction', ibid. p. 10.
19. *Ministry of the Custodians*, p. 282.
20. Ian Semple, in *UK Bahá'í Histories*.
21. *Ministry of the Custodians*, p. 286.
22. Brigitte Beales, in *UK Bahá'í Histories*.
23. ibid.
24. *The Bahá'í World*, vol. XIII, p. 727.
25. ibid; see pp. 721-32 for a full account of these events.
26. Violette Nakhjavani, *Notes from the Archives Building, in Haifa*, in USBNA, p. 1.
27. *The Bahá'í World*, vol. XIII, pp. 425-6.
28. Violette Nakhjavani, *Notes from the Archives Building, in Haifa*, in USBNA, p. 3.
29. ibid. p. 4.
30. ibid. p. 1.
31. *The Bahá'í World*, vol. XIII, p. 430.

32. Violette Nakhjavani, *Notes from the Archives Building, in Haifa*, in USBNA, pp. 4–5.
33. ibid. p. 2.
34. ibid. p. 3.
35. *The Bahá'í World*, vol. XIII, p. 430.
36. ibid. pp. 429–33.
37. ibid. p. 433.
38. Violette Nakhjavani, *Notes from the Archives Building, in Haifa*, in USBNA, p. 4.
39. Woodward, *The Unforgettable Hands of the Cause*, p. 47.
40. Chapman, *Leroy Ioas*, pp. 319–20.
41. Conclave Message 1961, from the Hands of the Cause to the Bahá'ís of East and West, 5 November 1961, in *Ministry of the Custodians*, p. 315.
42. The Universal House of Justice, *Century of Light*, p. 82.

1962

1. Faizí, 'Abu'l-Qasím, *Milly*, pp. 37–40.
2. Iain Macdonald, in *UK Bahá'í Histories*.
3. ibid.
4. Jeremy Fox, in *UK Bahá'í Histories*.
5. Riḍván Message 1962, in *Ministry of the Custodians*, pp. 341–4.
6. ibid. pp. 342–5.
7. USBNA, emails to the author, 20 and 29 December 2014.
8. Letter from the Hands of the Cause in the Holy Land to all National Spiritual Assemblies, 27 July 1962, in *Ministry of the Custodians*, pp. 363–4.
9. ibid. p. 364.
10. Ian Semple, talk given in London, 28 January 2006.
11. Bahá'í International Community, *Freedom of Religion on Trial in Morocco*, p. 1.
12. ibid. pp. 2–3.
13. *Ministry of the Custodians*, pp. 368, 373, 395.
14. Bahá'í International Community, *Freedom of Religion on Trial in Morocco*, p. 4.
15. ibid. pp. 4–5.
16. ibid. pp. 5–7.
17. ibid. pp. 9–10.
18. *Ministry of the Custodians*, p. 397.
19. Letter from Hands of the Cause in the Holy Land to National Spiritual Assemblies of the United States and Europe, 4 April 1963, *Ministry of the Custodians*, pp. 415–16.
20. ibid. p. 415.
21. Bahá'í International Community, *Freedom of Religion on Trial in Morocco*, p. 12.
22. ibid. pp. 14–15.
23. ibid. p. 15.
24. Rutstein, *From a Gnat into an Eagle*, p. 119.
25. ibid. pp. 119–20.
26. Letter from Hands of the Cause in the Holy Land to National Spiritual Assemblies of the United States and Europe, 4 April 1963, *Ministry of the Custodians*, pp. 417–18.

27. ibid. p. 418.
28. 'Introduction', *Ministry of the Custodians*, p. 19.
29. Letters from the Hands of the Cause in the Holy Land to the Hands of the Cause of God, 7 September, 26 September and 10 October 1961, ibid. pp. 371, 374-6.
30. William Sears, letter to Sylvia and Leroy Ioas, 20 September 1962, pp. 1-2.
31. Message to the Bahá'ís of East and West, 31 October 1962, in *Ministry of the Custodians*, pp. 387-8.
32. ibid. p. 388.
33. ibid. p. 390.

1963

1. Rabbani, *The Priceless Pearl*, p. 433.
2. Letter from Shoghi Effendi to Dr Mühlschlegel, 16 May 1933, in *The Light of Divine Guidance*, vol. 1, pp. 47-8.
3. Cablegram from Shoghi Effendi to the National Spiritual Assembly of the United States and Canada, 31 December 1945, in *Messages to America, 1932-1946*, p. 85; also in *This Decisive Hour*, no. 150.1, p. 110.
4. Letter from Shoghi Effendi to an individual believer, 29 December 1946, in *The Light of Divine Guidance*, vol. 2, pp. 54-5.
5. Rabbani, *The Priceless Pearl*, p. 433.
6. ibid.
7. Letter from Shoghi Effendi to the National Spiritual Assembly of the Bahá'ís of Australia and New Zealand, 30 October 1955, in *Messages to the Antipodes*, p. 396; also in *Letters from the Guardian to Australia and New Zealand, 1923-1957*, p. 128.
8. 'The Mother Temple of Europe', in *The Bahá'í World*, vol. XIII, pp. 733-4.
9. ibid. p. 735.
10. ibid. pp. 733-7.
11. ibid. p. 739.
12. ibid. pp. 737, 741; vol. XIV, p. 483.
13. Marguerite Sears, *Bill*, p. 76.
14. Ian Semple, talk given in London, 28 January 2006.
15. ibid.
16. ibid.
17. Violette Nakhjavani, *Amatu'l-Bahá Rúḥíyyih Khánum*, pp. 65-6.
18. *The Bahá'í World*, vol. XIV, p. 427.
19. Mayberry, *The Great Adventure*, p. 185.
20. *Alaska Bahá'í News*, no. 55 (May-June 1963), pp. 1-2.
21. Letter from the Hands of the Cause in the Holy Land to the International Bahá'í Council, 12 April 1963, in *Ministry of the Custodians*, p. 423.
22. Hainsworth, *Looking Back in Wonder*, p. 247.
23. Vreeland, *And the Trees Clapped Their Hands*, pp. 225-6.
24. John Wade, in *UK Bahá'í Histories*.
25. *Alaska Bahá'í News*, no. 55 (May-June 1963), p. 2.
26. Mayberry, *The Great Adventure*, p. 186.

27. Hainsworth, *Looking Back in Wonder*, p. 247.
28. *Alaska Bahá'í News*, no. 55 (May-June 1963), p. 2; Adrienne and Dempsey Morgan, *The Most Great Jubilee*, p. 3.
29. *Alaska Bahá'í News*, no. 55 (May-June 1963), p. 2.
30. Chapman, *Leroy Ioas*, p. 331; Hainsworth, *Looking Back in Wonder*, pp. 247-8.
31. Harriet Cruver, USBNA, Harriet Cruver Papers.
32. Jalál Kházeh, *After the Passing of the Beloved Guardian*, pp. 7-8.
33. 'Alí Nakhjavání, 'The Ten Year Crusade', p. 17.
34. ibid. p. 18.
35. ibid.
36. ibid. pp. 19-20.
37. ibid. p. 18; Marion Hofman, *The World Crusade*, p. 385.
38. *The Bahá'í World*, vol. XIII, pp. 459-60.
39. ibid. vol. XX, p. 105.
40. ibid. vol. XII, pp. 721-7, 744-8, 753-7, 760-61, 763-5, 767-9, 771-4.
41. Shoghi Effendi, *Messages to the Bahá'í World, 1950-1957*, p. 147.
42. ibid. p. 149.
43. ibid. p. 147.
44. ibid. p. 61.
45. ibid. p. 68.
46. ibid. p. 62.
47. ibid. p. 76.
48. ibid. p. 77.
49. ibid. p. 78.
50. ibid. p. 92.
51. ibid. p. 92.
52. ibid. p. 92.
53. ibid. p. 93.
54. ibid. p. 105.
55. ibid. p. 106.
56. ibid. p. 106.
57. *Ministry of the Custodians*, p. 82.
58. ibid. p. 81.
59. ibid.
60. ibid. p. 82.
61. ibid. p. 138.
62. ibid. p. 137.
63. ibid.
64. ibid. p. 138.
65. ibid. p. 186.
66. ibid. p. 185.
67. ibid.
68. ibid. p. 187.
69. ibid. p. 264.
70. ibid. p. 263.
71. ibid.
72. ibid. p. 265.

73. ibid. p. 345.
74. ibid. p. 342.
75. ibid. p. 343.
76. ibid. p. 345.
77. *The Bahá'í World*, vol. XIII, pp. 953–1060.
78. ibid. pp. 460–61.
79. ibid. p. 462.
80. ibid. pp. 462–4.
81. ibid. pp. 461–4, 953–1060.
82. ibid. vol. XII, pp. 721–7.
83. ibid. vol. XIII, pp. 1036–41.
84. ibid. vol. XII, pp. 753–4.
85. ibid. vol. XIII, p. 299.
86. ibid. pp. 283, 287.

The Most Great Jubilee

1. Chapman, *Leroy Ioas*, p. 280.
2. Dorothy Ferraby, in *UK Bahá'í Histories*.
3. May Hofman, email to the author, December 2015.
4. Brigitte Beales, in *UK Bahá'í Histories*.
5. John Wade, in *UK Bahá'í Histories*.
6. Dorothy Ferraby, in *UK Bahá'í Histories*.
7. Latifeh Rowlands, in *UK Bahá'í Histories*.
8. Harriet Cruver, USBNA, Harriet Cruver Papers.
9. Margaret Appa, in *UK Bahá'í Histories*.
10. May Hofman, email to the author, December 2015.
11. Mayberry, *The Great Adventure*, p. 186.
12. Brigitte Beales, in *UK Bahá'í Histories*.
13. Harriet Cruver, USBNA, Harriet Cruver Papers.
14. Eric and Beatrice Kent, in *UK Bahá'í Histories*.
15. Corinne Hainsworth, email to the author, 29 March 2014.
16. Adam Thorne, 'Sally Tempest', in *'This glorious harvest of victory' – World Congress 1963*, personal communication. 22 July 2014.
17. ibid.
18. Quoted in *Bahá'í News*, no. 387 (June 1963), p. 8.
19. Vivian Roe, in *UK Bahá'í Histories*.
20. Adam Thorne, *'This glorious harvest of victory' – the 1963 World Congress*.
21. Liz Emerson, in *UK Bahá'í Histories*.
22. Paddy Vickers, email to the author, 23 May 2013.
23. *Bahá'í News*, no. 387 (June 1963), pp. 8–9.
24. Iain MacDonald, in *UK Bahá'í Histories*.
25. John Wade, in *UK Bahá'í Histories*.
26. Paddy Vickers, email to the author, 23 May 2013.
27. Dorothy Ferraby, in *UK Bahá'í Histories*.
28. Jeremy Fox, in *UK Bahá'í Histories*.
29. *The Bahá'í World*, vol. XIV, pp. 60–61.
30. Adrienne and Dempsey Morgan, *The Most Great Jubilee*, p. 2.

31. Hainsworth, *Looking Back in Wonder*, p. 246.
32. Jeremy Fox, in *UK Bahá'í Histories*.
33. Iain MacDonald, in *UK Bahá'í Histories*.
34. *The Bahá'í World*, vol. XIV, p. 64.
35. Qudrat Jamshidi, personal comment to the author, Northern Irish Bahá'í Summer School, July 2013.
36. *Bahá'í News*, no. 387 (June 1963), p. 9.
37. ibid. no. 389 (August 1963), p. 6.
38. *The Bahá'í World*, vol. XIV, p. 66.
39. Mayberry, *The Great Adventure*, p. 186.
40. The Universal House of Justice, in *The Bahá'í World*, vol. XIV, p. 431.
41. *Messages from the Universal House of Justice, 1963–1986*, p. 51.
42. Adam Thorne, 'Nabil Mustapha', in *'This glorious harvest of victory' – the 1963 World Congress*.
43. *The Bahá'í World*, vol. XIV, p. 71.
44. Saunders, *Of Wars and Worship*, pp. 258–9.
45. *The Bahá'í World*, vol. XIV, pp. 71–2.
46. Paddy Vickers, in *UK Bahá'í Histories*.
47. Earl Cameron, in *UK Bahá'í Histories*.
48. Adam Thorne, 'Steve Jenkerson', in *'This glorious harvest of victory' – the 1963 World Congress*.
49. Marguerite Sears, *Bill*, pp. 137–8.
50. ibid.
51. Adrienne and Dempsey Morgan, *The Most Great Jubilee*, pp. 9–10.
52. *Bahá'í News*, no. 389 (August 1963), p. 6.
53. *The Bahá'í World*, vol. XIV, p. 78.
54. Adam Thorne, *'This glorious harvest of victory' – the 1963 World Congress*.
55. The Universal House of Justice, *Messages from the Universal House of Justice, 1963–1986*, p. 5.
56. The Universal House of Justice, *Century of Light*, p. 82.
57. The Universal House of Justice, *Messages from the Universal House of Justice, 1963–1986*, p. 31.
58. Shoghi Effendi, *Messages to the Bahá'í World 1950–1957*, p. 155.

INDEX

Individual Knights of Bahá'u'lláh mentioned in the text are listed in the Index; if not mentioned they are listed in Appendixes 1 and 2.

Wolcott, Charles 260-61, 293
Woolson, Gayle 128-9, 321, 332
Wyss, Frank 126, 320, 332
Wyss, Lilian 43, 324, 332

Yahyá, Mírzá 63
Yazd, Iran 109
Yazdi, 'Abdu'l-Rahim 132
Yazdi, Aziz 116, 132, 178, 301

Zabolotny, Mary 135, 319, 332
Zaire 218
Zambia *see* Rhodesia, Northern
Zarqani, Abdu'l-Rahman 43, 324, 332
Zahrai, Ezzat 164-7, 325, 332
Zaynu'l-Ábidin, Fawzi 274
Zimbabwe *see* Rhodesia, Southern
Zomba, Nyasaland 57
Zurich, Switzerland 71

ABOUT THE AUTHOR

Earl Redman is a geologist who worked for two decades for the US Bureau of Mines, studying mineral deposits in more than 220 abandoned mine workings in the Juneau Gold Belt, Alaska. In 1999 he moved with his wife Sharon to Ireland, where he has researched and written five books, exploring the gold mines of the stories included in *'Abdu'l-Bahá in Their Midst*, the two volumes of *Shoghi Effendi Through the Pilgrim's Eye*, and forthcoming volumes on the Knights of Bahá'u'lláh and on pilgrims who visited 'Abdu'l-Bahá in the Holy Land. He now travels widely and for long periods of the year and is much in demand as a speaker and storyteller.

SHOGHI EFFENDI THROUGH THE PILGRIM'S EYE

VOLUME 1:
BUILDING THE ADMINISTRATIVE ORDER, 1922-1952

Shoghi Effendi Through the Pilgrim's Eye tells the story of the Guardian's ministry from 1922 when the young Shoghi Effendi, just 24 years old, was charged with guiding the affairs of a worldwide Faith. Rather than a biography, it draws on the diary entries and letters (many now published for the first time) of the many pilgrims and visitors to the Bahá'í Holy Places in Haifa and 'Akká, as well as the accounts of those who worked to assist the Guardian in his many extraordinary achievements.

Volume I (1922-1952) covers the years when the Guardian was laying the foundations of the Bahá'í Administrative Order destined to culminate in the World Order of Bahá'u'lláh, while at the same time planning and carrying out the extension and development of the Shrines of the Báb and Bahá'u'lláh, translating the Writings of Bahá'u'lláh as well as *The Dawn-Breakers* and writing his own major works, as well as facing challenges to his authority and responding to the confiscation of the House of Bahá'u'lláh in Baghdad and the persecution of Bahá'ís in Iran and Egypt. The volume ends just before the dramatic decade that was to begin in 1953.

ISBN: 978-0-85398-588-4
Soft Cover, 480 pages, 23.4 x 15.6 cms (9.75 x 6.25 ins)

'ABDU'L-BAHÁ IN THEIR MIDST

If the believers . . . establish, in a befitting manner, union and
harmony with spirit, tongue, heart and body, suddenly they shall
find 'Abdu'l-Bahá in their midst.
'Abdu'l-Bahá

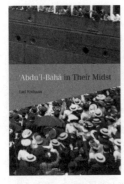

'Abdu'l-Bahá in Their Midst is the story of the journey of 'Abdul-Bahá to Europe and North America over the period 1911 to 1913. Rather than focusing on the public talks he gave, inspiring though these were, it narrates how 'Abdu'l-Bahá affected and transformed the lives of those he met, described in their own words.

Time after time, 'Abdu'l-Bahá would delay his departure to catch a train, meet 'important people' or attend a meeting, to the consternation and frustration of those around him, because he 'knew' someone who needed to see him was coming to visit him. Many times the 'someone' was unknown and poor or roughly dressed, but 'Abdu'l-Bahá would wait for them, then surround them with his love. There were also stories of those who thought themselves important, but who were reduced to wordlessness in his presence. 'How gentle and wise he was, hundreds could testify from personal knowledge,' wrote one notable Christian cleric. And 'Abdu'l-Bahá himself wrote: 'If the believers . . . establish, in a befitting manner, union and harmony with spirit, tongue, heart and body, suddenly they shall find 'Abdu'l-Bahá in their midst.'

ISBN: 978-0-85398-557-0

Soft Cover, 384 pages, 23.4 x 15.6 cm (9.75 x 6.25 in)

Soon to be published:

THE KNIGHTS OF BAHÁ'U'LLÁH

Why would a legal counsel with the rank of brigadier general in the Department of Defence go to a desolate island with just a few score inhabitants? Where it was so hot that he cooked his eggs on rocks on the beach and so isolated that the arrival of an eggplant on the tide was the cause of celebration?

Why would a young doctor give up a potential job that included a nice house, servants, car and driver and a good salary, for a job paying just $25 a month in a place where the toilet was two boards placed over a stream full of water snakes?

These and other stories of indomitable spirit, courage, steadfastness and self-abnegation are the subject of this forthcoming book on the Knights of Bahá'u'lláh, those Bahá'ís who left their homes to bring the message to Bahá'u'lláh to countries and territories where it was unknown, and whose names are inscribed on Shoghi Effendi's Roll of Honour. They came from over two dozen countries scattered over the earth representing every continent; 131 of them were men and 126 women. The oldest left home at the age of 85, while the youngest was a youth no older than 14. They endured loneliness and made sacrifices, and in so doing experienced the greatest adventure of their lives.